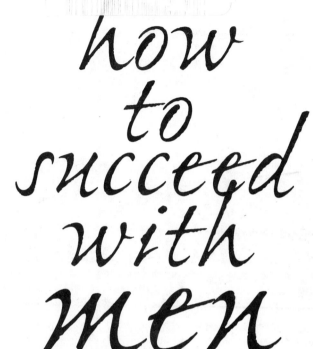

how to succeed with men

David Copeland
Ron Louis

REWARD BOOKS

Library of Congress Cataloging in Publication Data
Copeland, David.
    How to succeed with men / by David Copeland & Ron Louis.
        p. cm.
    ISBN 0-13-014509-2 (case)—ISBN 0-7352-0140-4 (paper)
        1. Dating (Social customs) 2. Men—Psychology.
    3. Man-woman relationships. I. Louis, Ron. II. Title.

HQ801 .C719 2000
646.7'7—dc21

                                                        99-051498

© 2000 by Reward Books

Printed in the United States of America

10 9 8 7 6 5 4 3 2 1   10 9 8 7 6 5 4 3

0-13-014509-2 (ppc)   0-7352-0140-4 (p)

ATTENTION: CORPORATIONS AND SCHOOLS

Reward Books are available at quantity discounts with bulk purchase
for educational, business, or sales promotional use. For information,
please write to: Prentice Hall Special Sales, 240 Frisch Court, Paramus,
New Jersey 07652. Please supply: title of book, ISBN, quantity, how
the book will be used, date needed.

REWARD BOOKS
Paramus, NJ 07652

http://www.phdirect.com

Contents

3

Making Yourself Worth Winning   54

4

Prepare to Meet Your Mate   87

14

The Commitment Deal: Preparing for the Commitment Conversation   367

15

The Commitment Conversation   391

16

Loving a Man for the Long Term   414

17

Conclusion   440

Introduction

"When are you going to write a book for women?"

This was the question we heard most often after we wrote our first book, *How To Succeed with Women*. In that book we gave men the inside scoop on meeting and romancing women. More than just a collection of tips, it was a cohesive program about how any man could attract and date the women he desired. The reception for the book was wonderful, and it has sold well. Along with the success came the question from women: "When are you going to write a book for us?" The time is now.

How To Succeed with Women was a success because it tapped into the underlying dynamics of what is left of the old dating rituals. It gave men the ability to get down to the psychological bedrock upon which those rituals were originally founded. By following our techniques, thousands of men have been able to successfully meet and date the women of their choice. It seems only fair to complete the picture, and to give women the ability to dance their part of the dating dance as well.

In *How to Succeed with Men* you'll learn how to do the dating dance in a way that works for you. You'll learn the key steps and moves you must make to meet the right man and develop a successful long-term relationship. You'll learn the ten-step Master Plan for developing a long-term relationship of your dreams. You'll learn how to make a man feel like a winner and a provider, and the importance of doing both. You'll learn how to meet a *lot* of men—without wasting a lot of time. You'll learn the importance of testing men, and how to do it properly so you can separate the men who are interested in long-term relationships from the scammers who are simply using the techniques from our first book for casual sex. You'll learn how to be approachable, and how to keep conversation alive when a man does approach you. You'll learn the one phrase to avoid when going for a commitment ("We need to talk about our relationship") and the one phrase you should always use when doing so ("I need some advice"). You'll learn how to handle problems and difficulties as they arise, and how to keep a long-term relationship alive.

So what makes us think we have the know-how to write this book? For one thing, we know a *lot* about men. We know the moves they'll make to seduce you (having taught those moves to them) and are in a unique position to teach you how to counter those moves, if you so desire. We understand the deeper psychology that is at work when a man is seducing you. We know what he thinks he wants—an unending procession of desirable women in his bed. We know what he *really* wants—to feel like a winner with women. We'll show you how to make him feel like that winner, so he'll desire you.

To get the most out of this book, we suggest you adopt the following practices:

• *Be coachable*. It won't do you a bit of good to read this book if you go through the entire thing rejecting everything we say before you have even tried it out. Of course, you will inevitably disagree with some of the things we tell you to do. Don't worry about it.

Think of us as your personal dating coaches. Part of a coach's job is to push you into trying something new. Imagine a professional basketball player arguing with his coach every time the coach tried to teach him a new move or critiqued his performance. The player would fight a lot and get nowhere. As a woman being coached about dating, you have to be willing to set aside what you know to be true and to try out something different once in a while. So, if you want to get the most out of this book, don't run mental arguments with us as you read it. Pretend what we are saying is true and try it out, at least for a while, and see how something new works for you.

• *Have a "study partner."* Do you know why, on the average, Asian students get better grades than non-Asian students? According to the experts who study this kind of thing, it's not because they are inherently smarter. It's because they are much more likely to study together than they are to study alone. Students who study with other students master the material faster, have more fun, and get better grades than students who study alone. You would do well to take advantage of this principle.

If you know another woman you can study this method with, then by all means study with her. You can discuss chapters and ideas together and egg each other on to try out the techniques we will teach you. A study partner can pump you up before an interaction with a man, and debrief you afterwards. She will be able to give you feedback and coaching, and you will be able to give the same to her. She will be able to celebrate your successes with you and help you quickly get over your disappointments.

• *Write in the book!* We know that you were probably taught never to write in a book. To this we say fiddlesticks! Feel free to customize this book to make it work best for you. Underline things you think are important and take notes in the margins about ideas or questions you might have. This will substantially help your retention of the material and make it easier to find parts of the book you may want to refer back to later.

We believe that having good intentions and being a good woman are not enough to get you the relationship of your dreams. These qualities are important, but by themselves they will almost never generate romance with a man. If you are going to have success with men, you must be able to create the romantic structures that work on them. You must be able to intentionally create interactions, conversations, events, dates and moments that, by their very nature, make men feel romantic feelings and think romantic thoughts about you. Sometimes these structures just happen, but with a little know-how you can ensure that they happen consistently. Teaching you how to create these structures is what this book is about.

Remember, dating is like a dance. It's an important dance, but it is a dance, nonetheless. All dancing is frustrating when you are first learning the proper steps. But, like all other dances, dating becomes fun once you master it. Stick with it through the first few numbers and hang in there through the possible confusion. Keep at it, and it will become fun. Eventually dating will take you dancing into the relationship you desire.

We'd like to thank our editor, Doug Corcoran, and all the wonderful people at Prentice Hall who have helped make this book a reality. We'd also like to thank Dmitri Bilgere and Roan Kaufman for all they did to help turn this project into a reality.

Much of the material in this book comes from questions and comments we have received from our students, both during courses we've taught on dating and during individual coaching sessions. If you have questions or comments for the authors, please feel free to contact us at succeed@pobox.com, or by regular mail at P.O. Box 55094, Madison, WI 53705. You can also find us on the Web at www.howtosucceedwithmen.com.

CHAPTER 1

So You Want Success with Men

MEN ARE TROUBLE. YOU KNOW IT. WE KNOW IT. MEN ARE DIFFICULTY and trouble and strife and bother. Let's not pretend that it's any other way. They are obsessed with sex, have a bizarre love of sports and toys, can't share their feelings, are helpless bumblers on the first date and all throughout a romance. The fact is, having a man in your life can be one of the most annoying experiences you'll ever have.

And at the same time, men are necessary. Men are compelling. Men are fun. Men are romantic. Men are exciting. Men are fascinating. Men are sexy. Men will protect you and provide for you, feel joy when you are happy and try—however naively—to fix things when you are not. Having a man in your life can be one of the most fulfilling experiences you'll ever have.

The simple truth is, having a man in your life is at once frustrating and enlivening, aggravating and fulfilling. A man can lift you to new heights of intimacy, connection, and passion for life, while at the same time leaving his dirty socks on the floor and neglecting to change his underwear until they threaten to develop a life of their own. A man can make you feel more special than you've ever felt—loved, appreciated, cherished, worshipped, idolized, and tenderly taken care of—and then say some stupid, boneheaded thing that makes it all seem like a waste of your time.

Yet you go back for more, again and again, and who can blame you? Despite discouragement, despite difficulty, you think that having men in your life is worth it. If you didn't, you wouldn't have bothered to pick up this book—a book by two yahoos who wrote a best-selling book for men on dating women, and who might just know something that would be incredibly useful for women wanting to understand relationships with men.

We think you are right, and promise that you are in for a thrilling ride—a ride that will be bumpy and exciting, confronting and ecstatic. We believe, and our experience shows, that it is possible to have relationships with men that work once you understand the nature of the beast. The way we do this, however, will be different from any way you've seen before, so we want to spend a little time, right now, warning you—er, telling you, that is—what you can expect from this book.

∞ How We'll Speak to You in This Book

Be prepared! *We'll talk to you the way men talk.* Unlike most books you may have read about relationships, this one cuts to the chase and doesn't use flowery speech to conceal the harsh realities of male/female relationships. While we are sensitive, intelligent, educated men, we want you not only to understand the material we are presenting, but also to begin to understand the way men think and the way men approach relationships. One way to do this is to teach you to have some familiarity with the way men talk. Men are, after all, the ones you are going to be dealing with in the dating world, right? We want to teach you to "see through" the way men talk, into what they truly mean. You may not know it now, but you are probably in the habit of rejecting information from a man if he doesn't present it in the way you might. That is to say, you expect men to talk and present information the way women do. This is terribly destructive to your relationships. We want you to get used to listening to men—when they're talking like men—and to see the value in what they have to say. To this end we'll talk like men, and translate for women. You can expect that this book will teach you to be a fluent listener, at least, to the language of men.

We won't oversimplify. Lots of books about relationships are built around ridiculously oversimplified ideas, which are useful now and then, but don't hold up if you build an entire life-philosophy around them. Ideas such as "Men are linear and women are random," "Women are right-brained and men are left-brained," "Women operate on sixteen tracks, while men operate on one," and "Men are from Mars and women are from Venus" are insulting and oversimplify the interactions between men and women. You can count on us to discuss men and women as individuals first, and to present material that will help keep your relationships with men on track.

We won't give you unrealistic advice. Have you ever noticed that people like to give you unrealistic advice about your relationships? People love giving advice that is so idyllic and so all-encompassing that it denies individual experience and real-world applicability: "You shouldn't date for a year after ending a long-term relationship." So, does that mean you are a bad person when you inevitably do? "If a man doesn't meet all of your criteria, get rid of him right away." So, what are you supposed to do, feel badly when you *don't* ditch that otherwise wonderful man who doesn't exactly fit your ideal? We will give you real-world advice that will make a verifiable difference in creating relationships and making them thrive. We won't shame you for not following impossible rules. We won't make blanket statements that deny the confusing nature of relationships. We won't give you advice that presents a moral platform, nor will we pretend to know what is best for you.

We won't sell you short. Many relationship books attempt to be diplomatic and sweet, almost as though they could protect the reader from the harsh truths about romantic relationships with men. We'll be sensitive, but we won't withhold important information that we believe you *must* know. Look: we are on your side. We want you to have terrific relationships with the men of your choice. Most people who write relationship books for women leave out important information that they are afraid you might find "too harsh," because they are afraid you won't buy the book. They fear offending you or coming across as too bold, too intense, too blunt. We will leave it all in, and ask you to bear with it, keeping in mind your ultimate goal—the relationship of your dreams. We will be honest about male/female relationships from our experience and our observations. We will present information so that you can see the potential pitfalls and potential traps, and learn how you have caused them and how to avoid them.

We may offend you. We apologize in advance for offending you with something we say. As men, we will likely put our feet in our mouths, be too crude, too obnoxious, or too much. You will have to put up with our humor, our grandiosity, and our cocky attitudes. We are men, and, as a result, cause trouble. The book is designed to teach you to understand the minds of men and to understand how we approach relationships. We are dealing with difficult topics that are hard to handle, and chances are high that you will be confronted or upset by some of the things we talk about. Bear with us.

To some extent, interacting with men means learning how to handle being inevitably offended. You need to know how to handle the occasional affront without letting it get in the way of your long-term goal of having a happy relationship. We'll talk later about how women disqualify men they could have good relationships with by not knowing how to handle the simple fact that men will, from time to time, insult or slight them. This book will teach you how to successfully handle offensive male behavior, in part by giving you some chances to practice handling being offended by us.

This is not to say that we will intentionally go out of our way to offend you; we would prefer not to. When we say something that insults you, we suggest that you just keep moving forward in the book. Let it go, and focus on what's most important—learning all you can about creating working relationships with men. At the same time, take note whenever you are offended by things we say, and be willing to observe all the ways in which men in your life also offend you in a similar manner. If you read this book with that filter in mind, you'll get past anything that you don't like, and get to the heart of the book.

∞ You've Got What It Takes

If you've ever learned any skill, then you can learn how to create the relationship you want with a man you desire. You've simply never been taught how. Like any other skill, once you've learned the basics, the rest comes easily.

We like to say that many women are just "one skill away" from having the kind of relationships they want. Donna was an example of this. She was a 36-year-old, moderately attractive insurance adjuster. She had read all the books about developing relationships with men, she had been in therapy, and was a sweet and vivacious woman. Donna simply could not understand what was wrong with her. No matter what she did, she wasn't able to get a relationship to last with a man she desired. She kept dating men who were really romantic at first, but then, after having sex with her, seemed to disappear. After experiencing this over and over again, she became depressed, and convinced herself that she was fundamentally flawed in relationships with men. Donna became hopelessly unromantic, resigned to the "fact" that she would never have a loving man by her side in a committed relationship.

It turned out that Donna's problem was much smaller than she thought. She *was* a good woman. There *were* many men who would have been happy to have had a relationship with her. But she was missing the skill of *testing* men. She kept choosing men she should have rejected because she didn't know how to decide which ones to keep. Once she learned how to *test* men early on, she found she could weed out the ones who were trouble, and develop a relationship that allowed all of her great qualities to be expressed. She eventually attracted a man who could truly appreciate all of her; the good, bad, and the ugly.

You may have a similar problem. Secretly, like Donna, you may have wondered if there was something wrong with you. You may have thought that there was something about you that you couldn't see, but that men could, that drove them away. Or, like Donna, you may fear that you have some basic flaw that attracts all the bums to your door and continually sets you up in relationships that don't work.

Nothing could be further from the truth. Sure, you've got problems. Everybody does. But, as you've no doubt seen, plenty of women with more problems than you have relationships with men that they enjoy. The good news is, there's no basic flaw inside of you that keeps you from having the relationship you desire. If you can communicate at all, even if it is by typing out messages with a pencil between your teeth, you can create a relationship that brings you happiness.

When you are "one skill away" from a good relationship, you are like a car that has one flat tire. A car with one flat tire drives as though it has something seriously wrong with it. It's impossible to control, the ride is rough, and it will never take you where you want to go. Driving it is unsafe at any speed, and you'd be likely to conclude that it has serious, serious problems.

Once you realize that the problem is a flat tire, though, you see that, just because the problem was *noticeable* didn't necessarily mean that it was *serious*. By fixing the flat—a simple, ten-minute procedure once you know how to do it—you transform the entire car, and can get where you wanted to go easily and safely.

When Donna learned that the "flat tire" in her dating system was around *testing* men, she was able to correct the problem, and her relationships with men improved instantly. You may be like Donna, but your main problem might not involve testing men. It might be not knowing what you want from a relationship, poor skills for interviewing "applicants," not giving men "wins," or a variety of other problems.

More good news: You probably have fewer of these "flat tire" problems than you think. And even better news: There are a finite number of ways you might be consistently screwing up with men, and this book will cover *all* of them. If you have a consistent problem with men, or don't have the relationship you desire, then you have a breakdown in one or more of the ten distinct areas we will cover in this book. Take the simple steps we will teach you, correct your specific problem areas, and you will be on your way to having a relationship you love.

The Ten Step "Master Plan" To Get a Relationship You Love

That's right: There are only ten areas in which you can screw up with a man, and each area is an essential step in creating a healthy relationship. This book will take you through each step. Here are the ten steps to succeeding with men:

1. Figure out exactly what you want in a man and in a relationship.
2. Make yourself worth winning.
3. Interview a *lot* of applicants.
4. Test the applicants.
5. Give men emotional wins and losses.
6. Spend time with a man.

7. Handle problems.

8. Present him with a "commitment deal."

9. Close the "commitment deal."

10. Keep the "commitment deal" closed.

The steps are simple, but they act like links in a chain. Women we know who have failed with men have usually done so because they left out one or more of the "Master Steps." They knew what they wanted, but haven't interviewed enough applicants. They made themselves worth winning, but didn't let the man feel like he had won their hearts. They presented a "commitment deal" to a man, and closed the deal, but didn't keep the deal closed, so the relationship fell apart. They removed links from the chain, so of course, the chain did not hold together and everything fell apart.

The ten Master steps are as simple as we can make them. Don't bother trying to create a shortcut—these ten steps *are* the shortcut. Follow them, and you will create a healthy long-term relationship.

The Results You Can Expect

If you read this book and use the material it presents, you can expect to understand how relationships with men work. You can expect to be able to have relationships with men who act like men. You won't be stuck trying to get men to act like women, *but will still be able to get what you want from your relationship.* You'll understand the major errors you've been making in your relationships with men, and how to correct them. Better yet, you'll have a clear understanding of the boneheaded errors that men make in romance and dating, and you'll be able to compensate for them. You'll be able to get things back on track in any dating, romantic, or committed relationship, no matter what stupid thing he does. You'll be able to prevent and fix the "flat tires" that keep driving your relationships off the road. What we teach you won't fix all problems imaginable—some relationships are just unworkable. It is wise to accept that, but most of the time, what we are going to teach you will get you where you want to go.

∞ Eight Myths About Dating You Can't Afford to Believe

You probably have trouble with men because the truths about dating men don't jibe with the myths about dating that you subconsciously believe. The constant clash between myth and reality grinds your relationships with men to a halt. You must know about these myths or they will discourage you and trash any possible relationships you may create.

On some level, you probably already know that most of these myths are not true. But on a deeper level, you may still believe in them. You may find that you *act* as though the myths are true, even while you know, in your mind, that they are not.

We'll ask you to look at your life, and see if you are sometimes operating as though the myths are true, even when you know that they are not. If you see your beliefs in any of these myths, just recognize it. Don't worry about changing it. This book is about breaking up the myths, and creating in their place a congruent, effective ability to generate the relationships that you desire. Be happy that you noticed, and get ready for a whole new way of being with men.

The exercise of getting to know the dating myths is not academic. The testing field is there in your life. We don't tell you about the myths from a "men's rights" desire to make life better for men. We are interested in making life better for *you*. Some of the myths may seem unfair to men, but the reason to give them up has nothing to do with fairness. If we could think of "unfair" ways for you to get a great relationship in your life, we'd teach them to you without a moment's hesitation. It's not about fairness. It's about what works—and believing the relationship myths simply doesn't work.

And now, the dating myths for women . . .

Dating Myth Number One: Men Can't Handle a Powerful Woman

We've heard many women use this as an excuse for not pursuing men, or as an excuse to give up on pursuing the relationships they want. We can't let you sell yourself out like that. You must be proactive in creating the relationship of your dreams. Don't worry. Once you get started it really will be fun. But if you believe that men can't handle a powerful woman, you will sabotage yourself every time.

It works like this: Susie was very interested in her co-worker Dean, and went out of her way to make herself available to him. She was always friendly and smiled, and flirted with him when she saw him. Eventually Susie mustered up her courage to ask him out. "After all," she told herself, "I'm a powerful woman. I should be able to stand up and ask for what I want." So she asked him out to dinner. Dean hemmed and hawed, then said no. He didn't want to go out with her.

Susie was crushed by his rejection. In her pain, she retreated to the myth. "I knew I shouldn't have asked him out," she told herself. "Men want to be the pursuers, I should have remembered that. Damn it—men just can't handle a powerful woman."

Now, it might be true that Dean was put off by Susie's pursuit of him. But Susie, like many women we know, forgot an alternate, and much more likely explanation. It wasn't that Dean couldn't handle a powerful woman who went after what she wanted. Dean simply didn't want to go out with Susie. He simply was not romantically interested in her. He didn't reject "powerful women" as a class, the way Susie explained it to herself. He rejected Susie, individually and personally. Susie then ran to the myth that men can't handle a powerful woman as a way of feeling better about herself. It was a way to place the blame on Dean, rather than looking at herself for answers about why he rejected her.

We are not against feeling better after a rejection—in fact, we'll show you empowering ways to turn rejection into your best friend. We would not even object to Susie thinking men can't handle powerful women, if that belief helped her get a better relationship. But it does not. As long as Susie believes the myth that men can't handle a powerful woman, she'll be less likely to ask a man out again, or to pursue a man in any way. After all, she'll tell herself, she's too powerful, and men can't handle it. *That* attitude is suicide to your relationships, and you cannot allow yourself to have it. It will stop you in your tracks and leave you angry and helpless with men. The truth is, while some men will adore you, other men will reject you. When you get rejected it usually isn't because you are too "powerful." It's usually because the guy doesn't like you or you simply are not his "type." It probably isn't even personal. It seems harsh, but you can't use it as an excuse to get out of the game.

Other women use "men can't handle a powerful woman" as an explanation every time they are pushy, rude, or domineering to a man, and the man lets her know that he doesn't like it. The truth is, men can handle a powerful woman. They just don't like rude and pushy people, male or female, any more than you do. If you are rude and pushy, and explain men's lack of responsiveness by telling yourself they can't handle your "power," this attitude is not helping you. We'll show you how to be the kind of powerful woman who has a life she wants, who is turned on by the men she is dating as well as how she lives her life. That is the kind of powerful woman every man desires.

Another spin on this myth is the belief that men want passive and stupid women. This idea is usually another excuse that women run to when they are rejected by a man. After all, it's a lot easier to say "He must want a passive and stupid woman, and I'm not like that," than it is to say "He didn't like me because of *me*." It's basically the same excuse, and causes the same problems as believing that men can't handle a powerful woman. It makes you angry and helpless, and makes it harder for you to get along with men.

Dating Myth Number Two: All the Good Ones Are Married or Gay

This is another myth which, if you believe it, will keep you out of the dating game. But if all the good ones *aren't* married or gay, then how do we explain that so many self-assured, self-possessed, relaxed and seemingly wonderful men are married or gay? It certainly does *seem* to be true, at least according to our female friends and students, but it is an excuse and a myth.

As you no doubt know, having a relationship gives you a certain amount of confidence. When you know that you have someone in your life—someone to come home to, someone to have sex with, someone who adores you—you naturally have more confidence. And this shows up in men who are married or otherwise "taken." They appear more confident and self-assured than men who are "on the market."

Another way to say this is that your nervousness with men is mediated by the amount of risk that you perceive in the interaction. If you feel there is a lot of risk—that this person you are meeting might be your soulmate, so you'd better not blow it, and so forth—you are adding a lot of significance to the interaction, and you will be very nervous.

Men who are already married, in committed relationships, or who are gay, have none of this "significance risk" in their interactions with you. They are free to make mistakes, to screw up, try new things, and to generally just be themselves. They are relaxed, so naturally you like them, and they seem like "good ones."

Now compare these married or gay men to the men who are trying to date you. Some of these men haven't had a date in months or had sex in years. For these men—who will, by default, be the ones you date—most interactions with you are filled with some level of tension. They need to make a good impression. To them, you might be their one chance for a great relationship and a happy life. They fear that you might crush their hopes with a rejection at any moment. They are scared, and that comes through in their interactions with you.

We'll show you how to compensate for men's fears, and how you can help them be the wonderful, worthwhile men that they can be when they aren't feeling tongue-tied and terrified. Once you are able to identify the permeability of this myth in your own life, you'll then see that all the good ones aren't married or gay. The good ones are all around you, ready to be found.

Dating Myth Number Three: Men Have Fragile Egos

There's been a lot of talk about the "fragile male ego." Many of our female students can be heard gossiping to one another about this apparent weakness in men. The idea that men have a fragile ego is a variation on the idea that men are basically babies, and can't take care of themselves. It's the idea that men are not able to hear the truth from you, or that they are incapable of admitting when they are wrong, acting with humility, or even asking for directions when they are lost.

This is a dangerous myth for you to believe, and it will wreck your dating if you let it. Believing that men have fragile egos, and that they have to be treated like babies because of it, will make you seem both resentful and condescending to them. You'll be angry because men seem like such babies, and condescending when you treat them as if they aren't able to take care of themselves emotionally. You will be completely oblivious to the significant ego-risks that men take in every step of pursuing you, and treat them brutally because you think they aren't putting in as much effort as you are.

There's no reason for a man to want to be with a woman who thinks he has a "fragile male ego." Would you want to be with someone who judges you so harshly? One of the main complaints that our male students have about the women they date is that women rarely understand the level of ego-risk men take at every stage of a seduction. Men risk rejection when they say "hi" to you, when they strike up a conversation, when they flirt, when they ask you out, when they go for the first kiss, and in just about every step of a dating interaction. Men put their egos on the line again and again and again, and each inevitable rejection is a blow to their egos from which they must recover. To endure this, a man's ego has to be exceptionally strong.

In the face of this, men don't like to hear about the "fragile male ego." You can be building a great interaction with a man, and trash it all with one comment about the weak male ego. He'll move on to someone who appreciates the risks he's taken, and you'll be alone again. We don't want that to happen to you.

Of course it is true that some men do have weak egos. There are always variations in abilities and skills in any group of any gender. The point is that it will serve you in the long run to cease interacting with men like they are weak-ego'd babies. Treating them like they have a handicap will only make things worse for both of you. You will have better relationships with men if you respect their ego-strength, rather than tear it down. We'll get very specific about how you do that, without selling yourself short, in upcoming chapters.

Dating Myth Number Four: All Men Are Jerks

Want a great way to trash any potential relationships with men? Allow yourself to indulge in the idea that all men are jerks. Even after we mention this a thousand times, you may refuse to give up this perspective, no matter what the costs.

Can you find men who are jerks? Of course. We're not here to argue the point with you. We don't even care if the myth is true or not, because we know that simply believing it is destructive to your relationships with men. It's okay to believe it from time to time; it's soothing to get together with your girlfriends and gripe about what jerks men are.

We are simply telling you that when you are done griping about what jerks men are, *be done*. Don't bring those gripes into your interactions with men.

Giving up the idea that all men are jerks is one of the hardest things we'll ask you to do in this book. But if you go into an interaction with a guy expecting him to be a jerk "just like all the others," you'll draw that behavior out of him.

When Barbara first went out with Jeff, they met for coffee at a local restaurant. One of the first things Jeff did was take a good look at the waitress's cleavage while they were being seated. Obviously, he thought he was being slick, but to Barbara, he just came across as a jerk. Immediately, she made a decision. "This guy is a jerk like all the rest. *Next!*"

For the rest of the date, she saw him through the filter of his being a jerk. Everything he did, she asked herself if he was being a jerk again. Naturally, she found that he was. Eventually, this left her feeling totally soured toward him, and gave him no reason to pursue her further. In that moment Barbara conceded to herself that Jeff was a jerk and only a jerk. From then on she was simply gathering evidence to prove her point.

By believing the myth that all men are jerks, Barbara effectively trashed her chances with Jeff. We can't let you do this. Don't worry—we'll show you how to handle the dumb things men do on dates. But you have to be willing to let go of the myth that all men are jerks, or the myth itself will wreck your relationships.

Dating Myth Number Five: All Men Want Is Sex

Okay, so, this one has a strong grain of truth in it. Most any man you meet—and probably any man you'd want to be in a relationship with—will want sex. That's a good thing, because you probably want a long-term relationship that is sexual, as well as romantic and committed.

While men clearly have a huge sex drive and will focus on sexual fulfillment at the beginning of a relationship, the truth is that they don't just want sex. A great many want everything that goes along with a committed relationship; the love, the romance, and the work. Most men we have worked with admit that at the start, sex is what they focus on, but that they want a committed relationship that includes elements other than sex.

If you believe that all men want is sex, it leaves you resentful, suspicious, and difficult to be with. You can't afford to approach your relationships with men with obvious resentment and suspicion. The men you are interested in will think you are too angry and too much work to date, and they will be right. If you seem sex-phobic to boot, and think that all men want is sex, it will make matters even worse.

Let's look at men's experience with sex, because understanding that will help you let go of the "all men want is sex" myth. Most men grow up in a desperate struggle to get sex. Though it sounds funny, the truth about men is that they've been intensely horny for more years than they can count, and lack of sexual fulfillment has made getting sex a top priority. This isn't to say that you haven't had a similar experience, but for women, the lack is usually different. While men usually grow up with a profound lack of sexual attention and satisfaction, women usually feel a lack of romance, caring, and gentle touching. As a result, men want sex as much as, or more than, you want romance. The intensity of the need actually hurts them, and *certainly* causes them to do stupid things. You'll get more mileage out of believing that men have an unfortunate deficit of sex than you will out of believing that all men want is sex. You'll be more compassionate and less resentful of men's sex drive, whether you decide to be sexual with him or not. And that will make it much easier to get what you want in a relationship.

Dating Myth Number Six: Only Women Suffer

This myth is a variation of the idea that "it's a man's world." While this certainly is true in some areas, it is not true across the board in life. If you live your life believing that men lead some wonderful, easy existence while you are suffering and struggling, you will be angry with men. This anger will make you want to punish the men you are dating, and you will drive them away. Men will avoid you because they don't need the trouble.

Jane had this problem. Deep in her heart of hearts, she really believed that men's lives were basically easy, when compared to women's. She was fond of mentioning how men, having never been women, could never know what it was like to be a woman in our society. True though this was, she also never seemed to grasp the idea that, as a woman, she had no idea what it was like to be a man. On the contrary, she seemed to think she had a pretty good idea of what it was like to be a man. She Knew, with a capital K, that men had it much easier than women.

The only problem with this line of reasoning was that men didn't like to be around her. They knew that life wasn't particularly easy for anyone, male or female. They were put off by her constant insinuations that only women suffer limitations and difficulty in life. Even when she tried to be nice, her belief that only women suffer came through loud and clear to the men she was dating.

If you believe this myth, you need to practice putting yourself in men's shoes. You need to start to get that men's lives are rough, too. Once again, we don't tell you to do this for the good of men. We tell you to do this for your own good, for the good of your relationships. If you go through life dismissing the difficulty and pain that men experience because it could never equal the suffering women experience, few men will want to date you.

To make matters worse, men do everything they can to keep you *believing* this myth. After all, they are taught from birth to make everything look easy, never to complain, and never to show weakness or ask for help. So there's no help there. Left to their own devices, men would stupidly reinforce this myth, even though it damages their relationships with women. It's up to you to give this myth up. But if you believe that men's lives are, by and large, as hard as women's, men will sense that in your behavior and want to date you. When you are able to understand both men's and women's experience simultaneously, you will attract more men and those more interested in being around you.

Dating Myth Number Seven: Men Understand What You Want and Are Just Being Difficult by Not Giving It to You

As Madonna sang, "You've got to make him express how he feels, and then you'll know your love is real." Worse advice has rarely been given. Men aren't holding back their feelings—or anything else, for that matter—just to torment you. The more you pressure men to deliver, in any area, the more distant they will naturally become. When you think about it, you probably already know that this is the case. But even though you know that the myth isn't true, you may still be living as though men are just being difficult when they don't give you what you want.

Later in the book we will examine the differences in men's and women's experience in dating and the different styles of flirting and communication which cause confusion. For now, it will be helpful to know that men probably do not understand 80 percent of the signals you give them. If you think men are being difficult by not providing what you want, it will be useful to look at how you can make your requests more apparent and more obvious.

When a woman wants something from a man, and he doesn't deliver, she tends to think that the demand is reasonable, and the man is unreasonable. We aren't saying the women are wrong about this—for all we know, every demand you've ever made of a man has been completely reasonable in every way. We are saying that believing the myth that men are holding back just to be difficult will have a corrosive effect on all of your relationships with men.

If you want to be successful with men, you are much better off thinking of men as generous than you are thinking of them as stingy and withholding. You can do this by noticing all the things that men do for you, and for women, that they don't actually have to do. You can notice when a man holds a door open for you, and say to yourself, "Ah—there's a man being generous." You can appreciate it when a man takes you out for dinner, rather than wondering what he wants from you in return. You can notice how many men are willing to take risks for women, to sacrifice themselves to protect women, and all the things that men do to try to make life easier for women. You can appreciate men's generosity. It will do a lot more for your relationship than believing that men are holding back on you.

Dating Myth Number Eight: Men Can't Commit

The men we work with often complain that they do not feel acknowledged by the women in their lives. The women they know, it seems to them, don't praise them. They seem more interested in tearing men down than in building them up. One of the major skills you will learn in this book is how to make a man into a winner. You'll learn to do this honestly and from your heart, without lying or deceit, without putting yourself in a supplicant position. The ability to make men winners— most importantly, winners of your heart—is a skill that will serve you in every interaction with men that you have. But as long as you believe the myth that men can't commit, you will be making the men around you into losers, rather than winners. Your relationships will suffer as a result.

It's worth taking a few moments to consider that men may, in fact, be excellent at committing. What do men commit to? Well, men commit to their careers in an almost fanatical fashion. Men give up their relationships, their family, even their health because of their commitment to their careers.

Every man is committed to something. You just have to look for it. A man may be fanatical in his commitment to his car, for instance. You may not approve of his commitment, but he is committed, none the less. He may be committed to recording every episode of *Star Trek* on videotape, or knowing every word of every *Monty Python* skit ever produced. He may be committed to his family. He may be committed to making a lot of money. He may be committed to proving that he's a loser. But he's committed to something, and if you look for it, you can find out what it is. You'll find that men certainly are able to commit.

In a relationship, a woman may complain that her man *can't* commit when the truth is that he simply doesn't want to commit to her at the level she wants. Often this isn't because he has an "issue with commitment." His commitment muscle works just fine; the problem is that he doesn't want to commit to that particular woman in the exact way that she wants. It looks like a losing proposition to him, and it may well be.

In this book we'll teach you how to create a "commitment deal" for a man that he won't be able to resist. But you'll never be able to create that deal if you still believe that the "real" problem is that he's basically unable to commit. You need to see how committed he can be in his life, to appreciate it, and to create a "commitment deal" that he can love as much as he loves the other parts of his life that he's committed to. You'll learn how to step into his shoes, learn how he sees commitment inside relationships and from there, you will be able to speak commitment so he can hear it.

We aren't kidding about the danger of believing these myths. Each myth seems small, but any one of them can trash any relationship you are trying to build. Each and every one of them creates resentment in you, distance in your relationships, and trouble in your interactions. Simply put, most women we've met and worked with tend to buy into several of these myths, and this keeps them alone and without a relationship.

If you have been operating as if the dating myths were facts, it's amazing you've had any relationships at all. Imagine trying to develop loving, supportive, romantic relationships against a backdrop of believing that men are such losers that they can't handle a powerful woman; that the good ones are married or gay; that women suffer while men don't; that male egos are fragile and that men are basically babies; that all men are jerks anyway; that they only want sex; and that they don't give you what you want because they are basically being difficult. And add to that the idea that it doesn't matter anyway, because men simply can't commit. It's hard to see a good relationship coming out of that, isn't it? Yet that is precisely what many women try to create.

The good news is that you can stop believing these myths, and when you do, many of your problems with men will disappear immediately. Every one of the steps in the "Master Plan" will help break up these myths, and free you to be with men in a happy, positive, successful way. Simply understanding and noticing how these myths play out in your life will provide you with access to new freedom with men, and increase your ability to attract Mr. Right.

➣ *Conclusion*

Welcome to the journey called *How to Succeed With Men*. Please put all your carry-on baggage in the overhead compartments. Fasten your seat belts and put your seatbacks and tray tables in their full, upright position. You're on a ride which will sometimes be bumpy, sometimes be smooth, and may even do an occasional loop-the-loop. But all the twists and turns will eventually take you to your final destination—knowing what you need to know to create, build and maintain successful long-term relationships with men.

Enjoy the trip.

CHAPTER 2

Assess Yourself: What Do You Want?

IT HAS BEEN SAID THAT IF YOU HAVE NO DESTINATION IN MIND, ANY road can take you there. You can wander randomly your whole life, seeing what turns up and living the life that the world gives you. If, however, you've always fantasized about a certain kind of life, or desire a certain kind of relationship, living your life randomly will not give you the outcome you want. In fact, it will lead to disappointment and frustration. If you only have a vague picture of what you want, you also won't be clear when you get it. You may even get what you want and not recognize it, because in your own mind, what you wanted was never well thought out.

Being clear about the qualities of the relationship you want to produce is step one of the ten-step Master Plan: "Figure out exactly what you want in a man and in a relationship." Knowing what you want gives you a target to go for and a frame of reference that lets you know when you are getting closer or farther away from your ultimate goal. If you don't have a specific outcome in mind, our system won't work well. Without a goal, our system is like a four-legged table with one leg missing: It might stand up, but it will never work efficiently or effectively and it will eventually fall apart. When you have a clear idea about what you want and what you are creating, every step of the process is easier.

If you don't get clear about what you want in a relationship, the world will provide you with whatever it will, and you will be stuck with what life hands you rather than be in control of your own destiny. If you do not have a clear picture of what is most important to you, you won't know what qualities to test men for. You won't know which men to walk away from (except for the most obvious cases), and you will eventually end up in a de facto relationship of convenience. You will date a guy because he is around and seems "not too bad." If you'd had a list of must-have criteria, you would have known to move on. Being in a relationship with the wrong man will keep you from meeting the right one, because the guy you are with will fill up all of your time and psychic space. Knowing what you want and being absolutely crystal clear about it will help you tremendously in your quest for a great long-term relationship. It will also keep you out of relationships that make you unhappy.

It is also easier to "settle" if you do not have a specific list of requirements. Often the self-doubts that make a woman fail to create a list in the first place are the same doubts that make her settle for less than she really wants in every area of her life. Kelly had this problem. She was afraid to create a list of what she wanted because she was afraid that, basically, she was such a loser with men that she would have to take whatever man wanted her or spend her life alone. She was afraid that her list would just end up accentuating her humiliation when she couldn't find what she wanted, and ultimately she would have to settle for a guy she didn't want, anyway. So why bother? Through working with us she learned that her list of criteria was a crucial first step.

Kelly learned that when she combined making a list of relationship criteria with making herself worth winning (step two of the Master Plan), she was charged up and ready to interview a lot of male applicants for the job of winning her heart (step three). As she took what she learned from us and "interviewed"—that is, flirted with and tested—a lot of men, she realized that she could be pickier than she thought. Kelly didn't have to settle, because she had learned how to get so many men moving through her dating system that she knew if one didn't meet her criteria, there were always more where he came from. Her list of criteria, her assessment of what she really wanted, was her guide in using the other steps of our program successfully.

"What If I Know I Want Him, And He Doesn't Want Me?"

Sometimes you will want a man who doesn't want you, even using our system. No one thing works a hundred percent of the time. We would be liars if we didn't tell you that. But wanting a man who does not want you will happen less than you think because, unlike you, most of the men you will be interviewing, flirting with, and dating will have almost no clue about what they really want. They'll think they know, but because they never sat down and thought about it, they will be more vague in their thinking than they realize.

If you don't think men are vague and confused about what they want in a relationship, consider this: A recent Auburn University study of what men wanted found that men wanted ridiculously contradictory and nebulous qualities in the woman they claimed to desire. They wanted women who were sexually inexperienced, yet who really loved sex. They wanted women who were slim and petite, yet who had large breasts. They wanted women who were innocent to the ways of the world, yet who were well versed in responsibility. They wanted women who were virtuous and reserved, yet flirtatious and adventuresome. If a woman took this as a serious list of criteria, it would be enough to drive her crazy.

Fortunately, the findings from Auburn University are not a serious list of men's criteria for women. They are simply a measure of how confused and uncertain men are about what they really want. Men want to feel happy, and they strike out blindly for what they think will bring them happiness: tiny, big-breasted reserved and virtuous flirters who are sexually innocent little nymphomaniacs. Don't worry about it. If you can make a man feel happy—and we'll show you ways to do that which will bring him happiness like no other woman has—he'll almost certainly desire you. His vague fantasy woman will fall to the wayside as he realizes how much he likes *you.*

⌒ *You Get to Say, and You Get to See*

In goal-setting, you get to say what you want. "I want to date a man who is at least six feet tall, who likes classical music and has a solid career," you might write on your list of criteria for the ideal man. You have said what you wanted. End of story.

Or is it? After you say what you want, a little thing called "life" intervenes. You follow our program and meet a lot of guys. As you are testing them against your criteria, you are also testing your criteria to see if it is really accurate. When you are faced with real life you will learn which of your criteria are accurate representations of what you absolutely *must* have, and which of your criteria do not really have much to do with your requirements, after all. For instance, you may meet a man who is not six feet tall; he may be five feet seven inches. Yet he may fulfill all of your other criteria so wonderfully that being with him helps you see that height isn't so important to you. You can then change your criteria about your potential partner's height.

We have a saying: "You get to say, and you get to see." After you have said what you want in a man and in a relationship, you get to go out into the world and see how well what you have said works for you. First you say what you want, then you see if you really want it. You say what's most important, and then see if it really is.

Saying and then seeing is different from bending your criteria because you are giving up. You aren't saying, "Well, I guess there are no guys who meet my criteria, so I'd better lower them." Women who say this usually say it because they aren't following every step of our system. In step three, you will learn to interview a *lot* of applicants. When your "throughput" is high, you are encountering so many men that you are not desperate for applicants. You aren't changing your criteria because you don't think you'll be able to find a man. You are changing your criteria because you have learned that something you thought was important wasn't so important after all.

∽ *Your Ideal Relationship*

Now we would like to take you on a mental journey. It is time to look into the future, and see what your life would be like if you had that ideal relationship and if it lasted all the way into your old age.

Business consultant Stephen Covey, author of *The Seven Habits of Highly Effective People*, teaches the importance of looking at your current life as if you were looking back on it from the end of your life. If you pretend that you are looking back on your life from your rocking chair, it will help you considerably in deciding what kind of a life you want to live, today. It will make what's actually important to you more clear, while helping the less important things disappear.

Most people realize that the quality of their relationships is, in the final analysis, more important than the kind of car they drive or how big a house they live in. When you look at your life from your current perspective, it is very easy to get caught up in the material aspects of it—after all, we spend a lot of almost every day dealing with financial and economic survival issues. When you look back on your life as if you are already in the future, survival issues fall away, and what you really want in your relationships becomes clearer. With this in mind, we are going to take you into your future. From there, you will learn about what is really important to you in your relationships in the present.

Having said that, let's begin. Get out your notebook and pen or pencil. This list will be something you will want to refine over the course of this chapter, and over the course of working our program. Here's what we'd like you to do:

Imagine that you met and married your dream man, and that you've grown old together. You have celebrated your ten-year anniversary, your twenty-year anniversary, your thirty-year anniversary, and so on. It has all been wonderful. You are an elderly woman, sitting in your rocking chair. Your husband and life-partner is in his rocking chair and is sitting next to you. Look at him and smile to yourself as you feel what it's like to have had a wonderful, fulfilling, long-term relationship.

Thinking back over all these years—over the joys and triumphs, over the difficulties and challenges—what was it that made you able to stay together and be (more or less) happy through all of it? What were his qualities that made it work out, and ultimately made you a happy woman with him? Take a few moments to write about those qualities, now.

What did you find out was important? Many women are surprised by the lists they create. They find that qualities that would be essential to them, if you asked them to make a list from "today," sometimes disappear when they are looking back from their rocking chairs. Height requirements, some elements of looks or other physical features, or some economic fantasies may drop away. What did you learn from your list?

It may help to look at someone else's list, in refining and formulating your own. Here are some of the things Maggie wrote when she did this exercise. She said that her long-term relationship man made everything work between them because:

- He was an inherently supportive person.
- I always felt like he was "on my team."
- He could give criticism without making me feel defensive.

- I never worried he would have sex with another woman.
- There were always things about him I admired tremendously.
- I admired his mastery of his field, his skill and ability.
- He always made me laugh, and could always make me laugh when I was feeling down. More than anybody else in the world, he seemed to cheer me up.
- He always seemed to say the right thing.
- He was highly ethical and put a tremendous amount of value in honesty and integrity.
- He was always generous and supportive.
- He had friends I really loved being around.
- He was smart and interesting.
- He loved and still loves animals and gardening, just like I do.
- He loved to take long walks with me.
- He was always very sensual and physical.
- He was always cuddly and loved sex.
- He made sex fun, uninhibited, joyful, and passionate.
- He was intellectually stimulating—we've never run out of things to talk about.

You may want to take some time to refine your list now. Creating this list, and really feeling good about it, is an important step in designing what you want.

Refining Your List

According to dating expert Juli Vinik (www.matemagic.com), it is crucial for you to create your list and examine it often. Vinik claims that women must find the essential qualities they require in a man and in a relationship and find ways to test men against this list (we'll show you how to do that all through this book). Her research shows that selection is best done by identifying the key characteristics you are looking for and the key characteristics you aren't looking for, then using this information when interviewing male applicants. Any applicant who does not fit the criteria are quickly disqualified. Now that you have your list, it is time to reevaluate what is important to you and put it into a format that you can use to assess the men you meet.

REQUIREMENTS

Put your list in front of you. Circle five or ten "key-words" that jump out at you. On a fresh page write down the words from your list that stand out. Feel free to summarize the qualities into broad categories if you find it easier. The words you circle and write down will become the essence of your criteria list. As Trisha did the exercise and imagined sitting in a rocking chair looking over her life, these are the top qualities that summarize the man she could imagine spending her life with. Trisha's man must be:

- Supportive
- Loyal
- Have a good sense of humor and be fun to be around
- Ethical
- Intellectually stimulating
- Admirable
- Sexual

Bottom-line Qualities

The requirements you are looking for will be primarily behavioral and emotional qualities, but you might also be looking for a man who looks a particular way, or is interested in particular topics, or has a certain income. After you look at your list, also look inside yourself to determine if there are other qualities you absolutely must have in your ideal relationship. Then write down the top one to four things you must have in a man that you feel are non-negotiable.

Trisha found that when she focused on her long term vision of a relationship, she discovered that a man must love animals if she was to have the life with him she imagined. When Bonnie did the exercise she realized that she could not imagine being in a long-term relationship with a man who wasn't taller than she is. Because Bonnie is a tall woman, she considered height to be a non-negotiable item on her list. "I know it sounds silly, but in all of my visions of an ideal man I always imagine us holding each other, dancing, holding hands, and all the time I always look up at him. I couldn't do that with a shorter man." By being honest with herself and writing down her requirements truthfully, she will eventually get the man she wants.

Molly is thirty-one and has always dreamed of being a mother. When she did the exercise it became clear that she was unwilling to date any men who were not interested in having kids within the next five years. She determined that she wanted to have her first child within the next five years and any man she dated or married must also want kids in the same time-frame.

Rachael was a wild woman. She was an artist and lived the bohemian lifestyle. She sold jewelry on the street and at rock concerts all over the country. Rachael had always pretended that she wanted a stable home and a stable man. After doing this exercise, she realized that her ideal relationship was with a man who would travel with her throughout the world. She discovered that what she most valued was a long-term mate who wanted to see the world and was up for constant adventures.

We want you to look deep inside yourself and come up with a rigorous list of exactly what you want. We want you to get crystal clear about what you honestly would accept in a man and what you honestly would not. This is your opportunity to finally map out the relationship of your dreams. Keep digging deeper into what will make *you* happy in the long term. Keep imagining you are on your rocking chair looking back on your life, at all the magical things you accomplished and experienced, and keep noticing what traits were essential for your man to have for all those good experiences to happen.

Nice Features, but Not Required

As you go through your list you may find qualities and characteristics that seem important but do not seem like requirements. These qualities might be great additions to a relationship or a man, but seem like items you could honestly be happy without.

After going through her list, Trisha discovered that it would be wonderful for her man to love gardening. She loved gardening, and enjoyed gardening with her mate. After a few moments, she realized that gardening would be fun and fulfilling, but wasn't important enough to be a requirement in a man. Trisha also realized that she would love to have a mate who would enjoy spending time with her and her friends, but she also realized that, although it would be a nice addition, it was not required.

Bonnie was a huge opera fan and had always hoped to be with a man who loved opera, too. However, after going through this exercise, she realized that opera could be her passion, yet not have to be a passion for the man she would marry. Bonnie also loved men with muscular bodies and hairy chests. She loved to look at muscular men and it drove her crazy when she hugged a hunky man. While doing the exercise she realized that it would be a great addition to any relationship, and it would be fun to show off a hunky man to her friends, but she realized that a relationship could be just as fulfilling with a man who had a normal body. In the end, there were other qualities that were much more important.

Chrissy loved rock music. She went to concerts and danced all night long. She had always dated musicians and been around the music scene. After considering what an ideal relationship would look like from her rocking chair, however, she realized that she could be satisfied going to rock concerts with her girlfriends. If a man wasn't interested in doing those sorts of things, they could still have a wonderful relationship. It wouldn't have to be a problem or take away from the other qualities which seemed much more important. "25 years from now," she reasoned, "who cares if a guy likes rock music or not? Other qualities are much more important."

Molly says, "All of my images of marriage have always had to do with being utterly swept off my feet, having a husband who supported me financially, and having a life where I was a special, cherished princess." After going through the exercise, Molly realized that she had gone through her life with the desire for a rich man, but it wasn't the money she wanted—it was the security. In fact, Molly had a very high-paying job and was doing well for herself in the corporate world. "What I want more than anything is a real partner. Someone who will support me through the ups and downs of life. Having lots of money would be great, but what is more important to me is that a man be compassionate and supportive."

Take time right now to list a few features in a man that you would appreciate, but do not see as requirements in a long-term relationship. It is important for you to write these down so that you can use your list to test a man once you begin dating.

∽ The Test

So how the heck do you evaluate a man and determine if he has these qualities? In the flirting chapters (chapters 6 and 7) and the qualifying date chapters (chapters 8 and 9) we will walk you through the process of testing men against your list. In later chapters we will continue to explore the testing process. For now, you should understand the basic skills required for testing men.

To properly test a man, you must consider several factors: his demonstratable behaviors, his observable behaviors, and your response to him. These factors will help you construct your assessment of a man and determine how closely he fits your criteria.

Observable qualities are those you can see. For instance, if you want a man who has a certain body type, you can test him easily by looking at him. No questions asked. If you want a man who is patient, for example, you can see how a man responds when you are late, and notice his level of patience (more on this in chapter 7). You can also have in mind what your ideal response would be, and see if he comes through with it. Once you are clear about your bottom-line requirements and optional features, it is important that you use these criteria as you test potential men.

You can also judge a man on your own response to him. Trisha places "intellectually stimulating" as one of her requirements in a man. She determines a man's ability to be intellectually stimulating based on whether or not he holds her interest, and whether or not he brings up interesting subjects during their conversations. "If he can't hold my interest for an evening, how the heck will he be able to keep me interested for a lifetime?" she aptly notes.

Testing a man is essential, and we will go into much greater detail on how to do so in later chapters. For now it will be very helpful to begin looking at how a man would display the required qualities, so you can begin to recognize them.

⊚ *Evaluation*

You should now have a list of the criteria for the man of your dreams, along with your long-term goals, visions, and desires. Now that you've put in the required time to create these lists and dug deep into your soul for what you really want, guess what? Trouble happens! The man actually shows up in your life, and blows the whole darn thing apart.

The paradox of goal-setting is that the qualities and behaviors you always thought were required may change when you are actually dating a man. Your preferences about dating a man who is a certain weight and height or who has specific hobbies might seem less significant when you are in the flow of romance.

This is natural. In the process of going after what you want it is important to keep re-evaluating your list. As you continue to struggle for clarity you will make your list a living and breathing document, rather than a static memory or a set of rules carved in stone you never look at anymore. We encouraged you to use your list as a way of testing for non-negotiable qualities. At the same time, there may be qualities you currently value that may turn out to be unimportant after you start dating a man. We want you to become clear about your values and criteria in choosing the man you date, so when he eventually shows up and radically turns your life upside-down, you will not be completely unprepared.

As you date, keep examining your list from a long-term perspective. One of the qualities on Jane's list was that her ideal man be very muscular. When we took her through the process of examining her relationship goals from twenty and fifty years in the future, she found that having a muscular man was not the most important thing to her (though it would be a wonderful bonus). Some women have commented that over the next twenty years what is really important to them is that a man be a good father, funny, stable, a good listener, have a good relationship with his family, and be emotionally available. What seemed less significant over time were items like sharing favorite foods, music, or types of movies, body type, or income. We recommend that you stay with this process long enough to come up with a realistic and romantic picture of the essential qualities. The clearer you become about what you want in a man, the easier it will be for you to notice him when he inevitably steps into your life.

Also, you may find that you date a man who changes what you thought was important. Jane might think that her ideal man must be muscular, only to start dating a fascinating man who rarely works out. She can then decide to change her list or get rid of the guy. Either way she makes a conscious choice about her own future.

∞ Creating Your Timeline

Now that you have created and re-evaluated your list, it's time to create your "business plan of love"—your action plan. We've found that having visions and goals without a plan for how they will be carried out leads to failure and frustration. You must have a plan.

Imagine if you were a pilot flying a plane to Norway and had no idea where you were going nor any idea how to fly the plane you were in. If you took off at all it would likely be a short flight, ending in tragedy. Having an action plan is like having an understanding of the guiding instruments in your airplane. The process of learning how to execute a take-off is like understanding how to motivate yourself to get out and meet men. Learning how to fly the plane once it is off the ground is like understanding how to keep a man interested in you and to test men. Learning how to land the plane at the end of the flight is like understanding how to move the relationship into a commitment. Your action plan is a concrete document that will guide you in your project, and help you understand how to arrive at your goal in the most expeditious manner.

The Essential Components of an Action Plan

The most significant element in your action plan is the specific and measurable actions that you can take to move you closer to your goals with men. Start this process by reviewing your long-term relationship goal. Your long-term goal probably is to be married, to be in a committed relationship, or at least to have a boyfriend. For the sake of this example, let's use the goal of being married. At the top of your action plan you would write, "My long-term goal is to be married."

Your next step is to pick a date by when your goal will be accomplished. Be outrageous and bold in setting your goals, while also avoiding the temptation of setting your goals too high. Assume that it is fine to achieve goals more quickly than you planned. One woman decided that she would be married within a six-month time frame. "It could happen," she told us. "Anything is possible and I say it will happen." To us, it was possible, but highly improbable. We suggested that she make her time frame a little longer. We want you to be open to magic, while remaining realistic.

We've had students set goals that were so conservative and so safe that they became non-inspirational and useless. One woman set her goal as having a committed relationship with a man within the next five years. We told her that even in the worst case scenario, finding a relationship should take substantially less time. Setting goals so far into the future makes it hard to see how today's actions will lead to accomplishing them. Have some optimism, as well.

For the sake of this example, we will make up an approximate timeline for this project. You must create a timeline that inspires you, yet seems realistic. You must examine your own situation and create goals that reflect your past experience, yet inspire you to live outside of your past constraints. After you pick your timeline, you will then write down a date; for instance, "my goal is to be married within the next twenty-two to twenty-five months, by _____ (specific date).

After you have come up with a date by when your long term goal will be accomplished, the next step is to break the process down into increments. If you know you want to be married within the next twenty-two months, you can then decide when you want to be engaged. The engagement is the next smallest increment. Factor in time to plan a wedding; you will likely want nine to twelve months to plan it. Let's say you give yourself nine months: If you set the wedding date twenty-two months from this moment, and then subtract nine months to plan the wedding, that puts your engagement date around thirteen months from today. Using our formula on paper you would write, "I will be engaged within the next thirteen to sixteen months, or by _____ (specific date). If you find this difficult to visualize, it will help to create a timeline on paper, and fill in all of the tasks that will have to be accomplished to fulfill your goal, starting with the marriage and working backwards. When you list what must be accomplished there might be twenty increments on your list, or there might be only five or six. Either way, give them all dates by when they will be accomplished.

You are now ready for the next step. You now know you will have to be engaged in the next thirteen months if you want to be married within twenty-two months. You can then make "get engaged" your goal, and break it down into step-by-step increments. Perhaps the next step might be to decide by what date you want to have your first conversation about marriage with your future fiancé. It is unlikely that a man will purchase an engagement ring and propose without a lot of prior planning on his part. We think you would probably start talking about being engaged approximately six months before he decided to purchase a ring. Return to your plan and write, "I will be having marriage conversations with my potential mate within the next seven to ten months, or by _____ (specific date).

Let's continue working backwards with your love plan. The next increment is to be in a committed relationship which is so solid that you could even discuss marriage. To have a man considering marriage you probably have dated him for *at least* three or four months. Following our format, you would then write down, "I will be in a committed relationship within the next three months, or by_____ (specific date).

Let's continue to move backwards. There is one thing missing from this picture; a man. If you want to be in a committed relationship within the next three months you need to have a boyfriend. As you know, most guys are sheepish about commitment. A guy will need at least ten or twelve weeks before he is willing to consider dating you exclusively. Following our format you would then write down, "I will have a boyfriend within the next three months, or by _____ (specific date).

You will probably have to date at least ten to twenty men, probably more, to find one you might be interested in dating for the long term. Tell yourself how many men you will date over the next three months.

"I will date at least eighteen different men over the next ten weeks, or by _____ (specific date)."

You can now see how you can use this process to create things you can do today which will impact the entire chain of events and eventually get you to your goal. When you create a timeline, the required tasks become obvious. When you lie in bed dreaming of marriage, the required actions you must take become confusing, seem unobtainable, and are much less clear. Your plan, your timeline, can always tell you the action you need to take next.

Once you create a plan with a timeline, you can determine how achievable your overall goal seems. When you look over your action plan, some increments may even seem impossible. If this is the case, go back to the drawing board and change the timeline until it seems achievable to you. Many times our students go through several revisions before their timeline makes sense. Give yourself approximately an hour or two to complete this exercise.

We have found that the more specifically you write your goals, the higher the probability is that they will be accomplished. Most people avoid specificity, especially when it pertains to goals they have been avoiding for years. Creating your action plan with specific "to do's" is one of the keys to reaching your goal. You will gain power and velocity by being able to take baby steps today which will move your overall plan forward. The actions you need to take one day might be flirting with a certain number of men, smiling at a certain number, asking out a certain number, attending a singles event, placing a certain number of personal ads, or talking with a certain number of people on the Internet. Each action you take is on your plan, and moves you toward your goal.

We recommend you now spend the time it takes to construct your action plan and refer back to it often (we'll give you more specifics on your action plan for meeting men in chapters 4 and 5). The whole point of an action plan is for you to see your progress toward creating the relationship of your dreams.

Keeping It Alive

Most people set themselves up to fail because they fail to create the necessary structures to keep a plan in place. Most people create a wonderfully inspired goal, become excited and charged up to complete their goal, and then proceed to forget about the whole thing. Other people give up on their steps along the way the moment they seem hard or challenging. We always look for concrete ways to support people in keeping their goals alive and keeping them up with their dating "to do" lists. Write down your goals and "to do's" in a journal or some place where you will see them on a regular basis (like the bathroom mirror, the refrigerator door, the steering wheel of your car, or in any other place you frequently look). The easier you make it to keep up with your "to do" list, the more likely it is that your long-term goal will be accomplished.

Everyone thought Andrea was a space cadet. She would forget appointments with friends and would frequently fail to send birthday cards and call people on important holidays. Andrea came to us because she could not keep a man. She was able to get men to ask her out, but she could never hold on to a man once they started dating. We helped Andrea create her action plan and quickly learned that she had no system in place to keep track of her appointments and her promises. By simply purchasing a daily planner she began to change her whole life. She began to write down all of her appointments and planned ahead when she had to send cards to friends and family members. Her dating with men changed in the process. Andrea began to do what was on her to-do list, because her planner kept it in front of her. She began showing up on time for dates, and even began to plan dates with men weeks in advance—something she never would have been able to do previously. When Andrea put a system in place to keep track of her "to do" list and her goals, she became more successful in every area of her life.

We recommend you break each goal down into smaller and smaller pieces until you are left with something that you can do today. For example, Barbara had a goal of going on ten dates over a three-month period. She decided that she would go on three dates the first month, three dates the second, and four the last month. Barbara then calculated that she would have to go on a date approximately every ten days for the first two months and a date every seven days during the last month. From there, she created a game plan to accomplish this task. In the past, Barbara found that out of every twelve guys she flirted with, one guy would ask her out. From there, one of every four guys who asked her out actually turned out to be a date. Barbara figured out that she had to flirt with forty-eight guys to get one date. Don't panic, we are not the math patrol, and we'll show you how to do all this. Barbara simply began to keep a rough tally of how many flirting interactions equaled one date, and how many dates equaled a boyfriend. It may sound daunting at first, but when you are able to track your dates and determine the numbers, you begin to get a much clearer picture of what it takes to get what you want. You can then alter your course, depending on where you want to go and what you want to achieve, taking into consideration the problems along the way.

Charting Your Men

Another important tool for keeping a project alive is a chart of your progress. The most important aspect of a charting system is that you be able to see, move, and manage a project quickly and easily. The Red Cross is masterful at creating charts which call people to action. Their blood drive thermometer is now seen everywhere. At any time members of a community can see their progress in relation to their goal—how full is the picture of the thermometer? We recommend you create a way to chart your progress toward your goal. Here are a few things that you will likely be measuring over the next few months, and will want to keep track of on a chart:

- The number of dates you plan to go on in a certain amount of time
- The number of men you flirt with

- The number of personal ads you write or respond to
- The number of social events you attend
- The number of friends you ask for leads on single men
- The number of Internet ads you place

The point of developing a measurement system is that it allows you to see your target goals and where you are in relation to them. Part of the chart should include a column to mark if you accomplished what you set out to accomplish, and a space to keep track of what prevented you from being successful. You may even want to bring out the gold stars from childhood school assignments and give yourself a star or a sparkle sticker each time you do something from your "to do" list.

An Inspirational Picture

We also recommend that you create some type of inspirational picture. The goal of an inspirational picture is to inspire you and to keep the possibility of fulfilling your goals in the forefront of your mind. It keeps you motivated. We have found that an inspirational picture—be it a collage of lovers kissing with the words, "Married in June" handwritten on the bottom, or a more elaborate piece of art complete with photos and slogans—will help to keep you inspired and focused on accomplishing your goals.

One of our students created a collage that inspired her greatly. She cut pictures of successful, attractive men out of magazines, taped them on a big piece of poster board, and typed out a list of all the qualities she wanted in a man. She also left sections of the display blank so she could list all the men she dated and whether or not they fit her criteria for a long-term mate. She posted this on her bedroom wall and looked at it daily. She found this collage kept her motivated in her search for a man, and also helped her stay positive when a man was rejected.

The best inspirational picture for you will be something extremely personal to you. It will be something that makes sense to you and touches a nerve inside of you. It will call you forward. It may be something as small as an index card with a slogan scrawled across the top that you put on your desk or in your wallet, a note on your bathroom mirror, a poster on your wall, or even a necklace that has a special meaning to you; it is your choice. The only stipulation with your inspiration is that it be something that will help you stay focused on your goal, and that you look at on a daily basis.

Creating Support Structures

Another critical flaw that most singles make is that they tend to go at this process alone. They let their feelings of embarrassment, sadness, or other emotional issues become a wedge between themselves and others. In the process, they fail to let others support them in their search. We greatly encourage women to seek out a female friend, or even a group, to help support one another in finding men. You can also act as sounding boards for each other and provide the necessary support and friendship throughout this process.

We recommend that you create a team of as many friends, family members, co-workers, associates, friends of friends, distant cousins, politicians, sports figures, and loved ones as you can think of. Gather a few female friends to support you and talk to them on a regular basis about your new project to find a man. Talking about your dating game will increase the chances of you keeping your word and continuing to play.

If you want quick and efficient results, we recommend that you get yourself a coach. A coach or a mentor is someone who can help guide you and keep you moving forward. A coach can show you the areas where you get stuck. If you are stuck, the coach will encourage you and show you how to get back on the playing field. Great athletes like Michael Jordan always have a coach. A coach will see things you cannot see and help you improve your game. In our dating coaching business we help our clients stay in the dating game longer. We help our students become more successful than they ever thought possible because we are able to help them improve their game and to help them create a plan for themselves in the process. If you cannot work directly with us you can find a friend to be your dating coach, or someone whom you have respect for and who seems successful with men.

If you ever learned how to put on your makeup, you had a coach who showed you how to do it. A good coach is able to examine areas of your life and shed light on aspects of your life that you have not previously thought about. A good coach helps you see your problem areas, as well as your strengths. Get a coach.

⬡ *Lights . . . Camera . . . Action Plan: The Seven Steps of Creating Your Relationship Action Plan*

We recommend that you complete the process of designing your strategy by creating a complete action plan. Our process will produce the best results if you follow it exactly as we have outlined. Here is the process presented in a step-by-step manner.

1. What Is Your Specific Goal and by What Date Will This Goal Be Accomplished?

As we mentioned earlier, it is crucial that you make your goal as specific as possible. Make sure it has a time limit by when it will be completed.

2. What Are the Increments Along the Way?

If your goal is to be married within twenty-two months, these are the steps you might have to take to get to your goal:

    a. Go on twenty-five dates.

    b. Decide on a man to be with in a committed relationship.

    c. Mutually and formally decide to be in a committed relationship.

    d. Go through the courting process and spend lots of time together.

    e. Live together.

    f. Be engaged.

    g. Make marriage arrangements.

Give each component a date by which it will be accomplished.

3. Create a Measurement System to Chart Your Progress

You must have:

    a. A chart which has a space to list out the number of dates you go on, and also the number of dates you are committed to going on.

    b. A chart that measures how many men you flirt with on a particular day.

    c. A chart which measures the number of social events you attend each week or month.

4. Create an Inspirational Picture as a Way to Keep the Project Alive and to Keep You Motivated

    a. A display like a poster with pictures of lovers kissing or wedding dresses.

    b. A special piece of jewelry you can wear every day to remind you of the project.

    c. A page in your daily planner with slogans about marriage that inspire you.

5. Create a Support Team to Motivate and Keep You Inspired

a. Pick at least four people to be on your support team.

6. Create a List of Resources

These resources include groups you belong to, groups you want to join, places where you want to go to meet men, dating services, and personal ads. Don't worry too much about this list now; you'll work on it extensively in chapters 4 and 5.

7. List the Issues and Problems that Might Prevent You from Keeping Your Word and Accomplishing Your Goals

Take time to get honest about what will probably get in the way of your successfully keeping up with your "to do's." When you have your blocks in front of you from the start, you can then handle them when they come up during the program. Tina, for example, knew that she would likely want to quit the process because of her fear of men. "I knew that at some point, my fear of being hurt and my fear of men would prevent me from following through on my to-do list. When I listed out what would block me, I was able to recognize and get support from friends whenever those issues came up. Being honest with myself ahead of time about these potential problems gave me room to have problems, but not be stopped by them."

What will stop you? Will it be problems with your time-management system? Will you want to resist success? What are you scared of? Will you get so upset at rejection that you will quit? Will you get bored in the process? Whatever you imagine getting in your way, write it down on your action plan as a way to prevent it from stopping you. By writing down your potential blocks, you can also make plans to get support whenever you feel your resistance coming into the picture.

Theresa's Action Plan

TODAY'S DATE:
November 2, 1999

SPECIFIC GOAL AND SPECIFIC DATE BY WHEN IT WILL BE ACCOMPLISHED:
To be married by June 2, 2001

METHOD TO KEEP TRACK OF "TO DO'S":
Writing everything down in a special journal, and keeping notes in a daily planner. Each Sunday night, plan the week for dating goals and actions.

INSPIRATIONAL PICTURE TO KEEP THE PROJECT ALIVE:
Creating a series of collages to put around the house. Creating a picture collage for my daily planner. Purchasing an ankle-bracelet to represent a committed relationship.

RESOURCES:
Personal ad, local singles club, swing dance class, my friend Maureen's parties, my friend Joe who keeps telling me he'd set me up with his friends, my coed volleyball club.
(This list will be expanded in chapters 4 and 5.)

MY SUPPORT TEAM:
My best friend Wanda, Sally, my hairdresser Barb, my mom, my cousin Stephanie, Mike and his buddies.

An incremental listing of the project phases:

End goal: Be married by June, 2, 2001

Increment #1 Be engaged by October, 2000

Increment #2 Move in with a man and live with him for at least six months by April, 2000.

Increment #3 Be in a committed relationship by March, 2000.

Increment #4 By February 12, 2000, I have a met a minimum of one man that I am interested in creating a commitment with and he is also interested in a committed relationship.

Increment #5 Go on fifteen dates by November 25, 1999.

Now that you have seen an action plan created, when will you have yours complete? We recommend you spend the time to create a comprehensive plan as soon as possible. We also recommend you make commitments to date at least a few men each week and each month. Take action each week and your goals will be fulfilled. So what actions are you going to take this week?

The Nine Most Common Reasons Why Women Stop Pursuing the Right Guy

Are you excited? Does the idea of having tons of dates and being desired by many eligible bachelors seem wonderful to you? If you are like most of our students, you see the potential for success and can also imagine yourself reaching your goals. At the same time, you probably feel sort of sick to your stomach, nervous, confronted, and scared that this wonderful relationship might be unobtainable; that all this dreaming is going to lead to more failure, and that there is no hope. Yes, both the excitement and the concern occur in the same moment. It's normal.

Here are the most common reasons why women stop playing the dating game. Keep an eye on these yourself as you date and see where you tend to slip and fall into a state of resignation and inaction. Remember, the authors are here to support you. We are committed to seeing that you reach your goals and exist to support you in dreaming, acting, and achieving your dating desires. You can trust us and this process as a road map for you.

1. Lack of Support

Without the necessary support in your dating game, you will probably fail. Throughout this chapter we have stressed the necessity of having support from other people in the fulfillment of your goals. Support can take the form of a study partner, confidant, best friend, friends, and your family. All of these people can give you emotional support, assist you in setting up dates and provide you with dating leads. There will be times when dating sucks; without a shoulder to cry on or a friend to talk to, you might give up. You must make an effort to get the love and support you need to carry this project through.

2. Lack of Resources

By resources we mean both financial resources and qualified leads for male applicants. Many women stress themselves out financially when they go after men. Don't do this.

In our experience, it is customary to let the man spend money and energy on *you*, not the other way around. If you find that money stops you from meeting men, then find lower-cost options for meeting them. There are always other options for meeting men, as you will learn in the upcoming chapters.

The other form of resource which tends to become a problem for women is a lack of dating options, or places and ways to meet men. We'll clear this up once and for all in chapters 4 and 5. We'll describe different "markets" and teach you how to tap into them to meet your mate. If you follow our instructions in chapters 4 and 5, you will meet as many men as you need to.

3. Inability to Handle Rejection

Your ability to thrive even when you are rejected is the key to being able to stay in the dating game long enough to build your ideal long-term relationship. In chapter 3 we will give you specific tools for overcoming rejection fear, and we'll show you how to handle rejection easily when it comes your way.

4. Unwillingness to Take Initiative

Some women have been raised to believe that they are above asking men out. They learned early on that men are the ones who initiate dates, and that it is women's job to accept or reject those invitations. We agree that this would be a wonderful way for male/female relationships to develop, but since all of the rules have changed this is no longer the case. We encourage men to pursue women, and even tell them that it is solely their jobs to do so. Sadly, however, most men in the world haven't read our book, *How to Succeed with Women* and have not followed our advice. If you feel upset and stopped in the dating game because you feel that you shouldn't have to initiate with men, you will have to change your tune. Given that you are currently alone and that if your approach to dating worked you would have a man already, you must consider trying something new. Besides, the more you follow our advice, the more men *will* be asking you out, because you will be the type of woman men are attracted to. The first step is to begin flirting with men, and make yourself more available to men. You must be willing to approach men, whether you like it or not.

5. Lack of Ability to Follow Through on the Plan

One of the most common problems women have with our system is they find that they are unable to manage it over time. They get bursts of inspiration and insight followed by long periods of inactivity. To combat this problem we recommend you take small and consistent steps each week, rather than depending on huge steps to move you forward. You can create this project any way you want, and you can fit it into any schedule you have. If you can't make five calls a week, make two. If you can't take several evenings per week to look for men, take one. You get to create this project so that it supports you, and part of support is that you have a balanced life while pursuing men. If your life is completely turned upside down and every other project in your life suffers, that won't help you in the long run. Pacing is required in the dating game. Keep taking consistent steps, no matter how small.

Another solution is to have a friend who is also playing the game. When you are playing the dating game with a girlfriend, you can support each other when times get tough. You can attend social events together and even double-date. If you are the type of person who tends to not carry through with your plans, making specific promises on a weekly basis to a friend will help you keep your "to do" list alive.

If you find yourself not being able to follow through on your plan, you may also be having a problem with your planning system. You might need to spend more time with you daily planner and put in more "to do's" to accomplish each week. Then follow your social schedule as though it were a work meeting. Keep making small and achievable progress every week no matter what. When you are able to keep the project alive by creating promises in your calendar, it will increase your effectiveness.

6. A History of Being Hurt By Men

There are many ways you may have been hurt. Men have probably been jerks to you in the past. You have probably been through at least a few failed relationships, maybe a marriage or two, and had your heart broken at least once in your lifetime. Those are reasons enough to be hesitant to open your heart once again to a man. We are on your side and understand the world in which most singles find themselves. The hurt can be so bad that you don't want to leave the house. It can make trusting any man seem impossible.

There is no easy solution to this problem. We would never tell you to stop being cautious. We can speak from experience when we recommend you move forward even when you feel hurt. Time and time again we've seen female students date and flirt even when they feel hurt. These students make choices about how they are going to live the rest of their lives and get in touch with the goals that will make them happy in the long run. While they go after their dream relationship, they don't deny their pain, but they also don't let it completely interfere with the process. Later in the book we will offer an exercise to help you let go of pain and release the constraints of the past.

For now, it is important for you to just be aware of your resistance and be clear about what it is saying to you. Decide what you really want to do. Do you want to stay alone while you heal? Do you want to go into therapy and work these issues out for yourself? Do you want to go to a personal growth workshop? Or, do you want to just go for it and get dating? The decision is up to you. More than anything, we want you to have many options along the way and begin dating when you feel comfortable doing so.

7. Standards So High that No Man Can Ever Meet Them

We have met many women who keep their sights on "the perfect man." They are looking for their personal version of Superman who is perfect in every way. They create a picture that no man can ever match.

The first part of the solution is to realize that the perfect man is a myth; he does not exist. The cost of having impossible standards is that no man can measure up and you end up alone again. Realizing this cost is part of the solution. Once you realize that you are constantly setting up barriers between you and every man in the world, you can then begin making changes to your strategy and how you interact with men. Until that time, you will likely keep men at bay.

The second part of the solution is to keep updating your list of what behaviors are most important to you in a man. Armed with this information, you can measure men against your list, not your ideals.

8. Lack of Faith that You Can Get What You Want

Part of being a powerful woman is to balance your past rejections and failed relationships with your visions for future ones. You do this by holding your idyllic vision for your relationship in front of you, while also being aware of the things that could block you.

One reason we have you create an inspirational picture and create specific goals is because they help you stay positive and focused. They keep you from being sidelined by doubt. We have found that students tend to lose faith that they can accomplish their goals when they lack support. Students lose faith when they don't have anyone in their lives to help them figure out how to overcome blocks, someone to encourage them to continue dating when it seems hard and scary.

Whenever you find yourself losing faith, the key to overcoming this problem is to talk to friends, talk to co-workers, and be with people, until you feel hopeful again. Talk to friends and family until you can remember your goals and the most precious dreams you desire. Keep yourself engaged with others and you will move through your feelings of desperation, and return to a state of grace.

9. No Personal Style or Confidence

A woman who has no confidence or personal style isn't attractive to men. You can be the most wonderful woman in the world, but if you lack personal style and confidence you'll still have a hard time getting a man. This is so important that the entire next chapter is about "Making Yourself Worth Winning" by developing your style and confidence.

∞ Conclusion

This chapter has given you a ton of information and many tools which will push you toward your goals. We've given you an opportunity to dream about what you *really* want, looking twenty years, thirty years, even fifty years into the future, and then brought that vision back to this moment. We've helped you clarify the qualities, characteristics, desired behaviors, and non-required behaviors you want in the man you will meet and spend the rest of your life with.

It may take time to integrate this information and put it all into action in your life, but it will be worth it. Take one step at a time, and the process will work wonders.

CHAPTER 3

Making Yourself Worth Winning

Now you know what kind of a man you want, and what sort of a relationship you want to be in. How does it feel?

Many women find themselves empowered and inspired after a process like the one you just completed. It makes them feel like they have focus and direction. They feel ready to get out there and make something happen. They feel like they have a game plan at last, and are ready to use it.

Other women aren't quite so inspired. They look at their list, and instead of feeling charged up, they feel doomed. "Of course, every woman would want a relationship with a tall, attractive, fit and successful man, who loves animals and has a great sense of humor," such a woman might say. "So who cares if I want a guy like that, too? The only thing this list has done is show me how useless and naively hopeful I am! I'll never get what I want!"

Now, now; none of that talk. Remember who's talking to you, here—two of the most outcome-oriented relationship experts on the planet.

And no, we are not going to tell you to just have a good attitude, or write affirmations, or to sit back and watch while all your relationship goals are mysteriously fulfilled, just because you wrote them down. Life doesn't work that way. You usually do have to do *something* if you want to end up with what you are after. That "something" is what this book is about, and believe us: We wouldn't be wasting your time teaching you this information if it didn't work. So cheer up. If the previous chapter made you feel any feelings you didn't like, don't worry about it. In this chapter we are going to tell you the basics of *making yourself worth winning*. We are going to cover the keys to the style and confidence that will open a man's heart.

"But wait a minute!" you may say. "Aren't I worth winning the way I am already?" Our answer is, of course—but you may not be advertising that fact in a way that will motivate a man to pursue you. Making yourself worth winning is step two of your Master Plan for getting the relationship of your dreams.

First, we must look again at that man you desire. Many women, when given the opportunity to chose the kind of man they want, go into a sort of kid-in-a-candy-store trance. "I want a guy who is rich, well-spoken, and who wears really great suits," they'll say. "He needs to be a veterinarian, play concert piano in his free time, and be a great lover who never thinks about anything but me. He takes care of me financially, we have a fleet of servants, we summer in the south of France, and travel the world on his private jet!"

When these women really look at their desires from a future perspective (as you did in chapter 2), most of them find that they don't really need all these trappings to have a great relationship with a great guy. Once again, we are *not* telling you to settle for less than you want. We are telling you that your fantasies probably outstrip your actual desires. Fantasies are usually larger than life, and tend to take our inner impulses to extremes. Most women we've worked with really don't desire those extremes in any real way. Most women we've worked with want men who are attractive, though not models; intelligent, though not Nobel-prize winners; successful, though not so much so that they have to spend all their time working, and who have style, but aren't vain.

You will probably discover that this same truth holds for you. You probably want a man who is "out of your league," but not so much so that he is intimidating or fantastical. Let intimidating, fantastical men be material for your bodice-ripping daydreams and fantasies, not your serious relationship goals.

Once you've toned your dream man down from fantastical proportions—if, indeed, you feel that is the right thing to do—here's the next step: Think about this man, his "feel," his style. Now ask yourself: "What kind of a woman would I have to be to have a man like this in my life?" This question is critical because it will guide you in making yourself worth winning.

The first mistake women make in answering this question is that they think they would have to be more than they could ever possibly be. They doom themselves with impossible limitations like, "To have the man I really desire, I'd have to be Cindy Crawford," or, "To have the man I really desire, I'd have to be twenty years younger, with larger breasts," or, "To have the man I really desire, I'd have to be thirty pounds thinner, taller, and with a more beautiful face." Or they may doom themselves by thinking they need to change their situation: "To have the man I desire, I'd have to have a much better job," or, "To have the man I desire, I'd have to not have these children," or, "To have the man I desire, I'd have to not have all this debt."

That is all nonsense. You don't have to be fundamentally different from what you are to get a man you desire. You don't have to be thinner, or richer, or better looking in some fundamental way. Look: The truth about men is very simple. You can have the man you desire if you can make him feel that, by winning you, he has won something precious and wonderful. While it is true that men *believe* they know what a precious and wonderful woman is—a woman who is cute and hot and twenty-six years old—men can be re-educated.

You cannot re-educate him; that's too big of a job. When you have the style and confidence of a woman who is worth winning, however, that will speak to him, touch him, and draw him to you. How you make him feel will re-educate him. That's all you'll need.

You may be saying that all of this is a bunch of garbage. The kind of man you'd desire wants a woman who is a cheerleader in bobby-socks, and no matter how "winnable" you make yourself, he's still going to find you to be too old and too fat. We won't lie to you—that *is* true about some men. It is even true about some successful, attractive, possibly even wonderful men. But it is *not* true of all of men, or even of the majority.

The bottom line is that men want to feel loved, acknowledged, and touched on a deep level. Men want to feel that *their* woman is a prize. If you make yourself into a prize by being the kind of woman who has her own style and confidence, he'll find himself saying to his buddies, "She has a few extra pounds on her [or whatever], but you know, I'm thinking I kind of *like* women like that!" Men like women who make themselves worth winning. You need to find a way to do that which doesn't require you to be fundamentally different from what you are now. We'll show you how to do that in this chapter.

The second mistake women make in answering the question, "What would I have to be like to have the man I desire?" is that they decide that they have to become somebody they are not: fake women or pseudo-supermodel women. They think that in order to get men, they'll have to betray themselves, and put themselves through ridiculous and ultimately unsuccessful contortions to wear exactly the latest fad styles and follow exactly the latest fad diets. They decide that they have to put on fake "perky" attitudes and somehow become new, "kicky" younger women. It's not true. As you'll see in this chapter, you'll need to stretch yourself, but not betray yourself, to be worth winning by a man.

Just as we wanted to take away the fantastical extremes of the "ideal man," we also want to strip away the fantastical extremes of "what you'd need to be." When we do this, most of the women we work with revise what they think they'd have to be to have the man they desire. They say something like Patti said: "Well, I'd have to be more confident and talkative with men, I think. I think I'd need to be more fired up, more excited about my life if I was going to hold the attention of the kind of guy I'm interested in. I'd have to not hide in the corner so much. I'd need to go out more, say yes more, and not spend so much time at home alone playing on the Internet."

Most women discover, while they don't need to be fundamentally different from who they really are, they do need to develop and value the positive, unique, interesting qualities of who they are more thoroughly. They find that they need to develop their *personal style*. Personal style has two parts: *style*, which is how you dress, move, and look, and *confidence*, which is how you behave. While you don't have to change who you are as a person, you will probably find that you have to change how you express who you are—your personal style—if you want to get the man of your dreams.

∞ Why Have Personal Style?

Renee doesn't want to change anything about herself to get a man. She's sure that if she changes her looks or her behavior in any way, she'll be a "big faker." "I want a man to accept me the way I am!" she asserts. Many women tell us things like this: "If only men could know me, I'm sure they'd want to be with me." But, for some reason, the men they want to know never seem to want to get to know them. When we examine how these women dress and their level of confidence, we find again and again that they dress and behave in ways that put men off.

Renee was one of these women. Very proud of the fact that she always did things her own way, she called herself a "maverick" and a "rebel." She liked to wear torn-up clothes that looked terrible. She didn't care about how she looked, and was surprised that men who *did* care about how *they* looked were never interested in her. Day after day she looked bad, and day after day she wasn't attractive to the men she desired. Day after day she held out for that special someone who would love her "just the way she was."

She fared little better in her confidence—that is, in her behaviors with men. She worried her way through every interaction with attractive men. She was always asking herself, "What am I doing wrong? Am I offending him? What if he doesn't like me? Did I laugh too loud?" She never had any idea what to say to men. Her confidence was low, and she never varied her approach. Day after day she behaved in exactly the same manner, and day after day she wasn't attractive to the men she desired. Again, day after day, she was surprised and angered by that fact.

The funny thing was, Renee was obviously a wonderful woman. She was well-read and well-educated. She even liked sports! She was a marathon runner, in great shape, and was full of interesting ideas. She'd obviously make a wonderful companion, and any man who was with her would be lucky. But Renee had a fatal flaw that left her helpless with men: she was unwilling to change anything about her dress or approach. You may have heard this definition of insanity: to be insane is to do the same thing over and over, and to expect different results. This is exactly what Renee was doing. It is what many women, quite possibly you included, do as well.

Think about it. Most women have a set pattern that they go through to become attractive to men, and they rarely vary it. They go on a diet to lose weight. They swear they will go to the gym more. They spend more time with fashion magazines or buying make-up. They try harder to look like models. Ultimately, most of them end up more depressed and helpless around men than they were before.

We claim that this unvarying approach doesn't work because it takes *you* out of the picture. It is just about *style*, while not being at all about *person*. Losing weight might be part of expressing your personal style. It might not be. That depends on you. Dressing like a model might be part of your personal style. It might not be. That depends on you, as well. If you try to take a cookie-cutter approach to style and confidence, it will leave you in the dust, because a cookie-cutter, "look like a model" approach may have very little to do with you. With our approach, you want to express your *self* though your style and confidence. This is about discovering yourself, not about covering yourself up. This simple shift can make all the difference in making yourself worth winning.

∞ *What You Say with How You Dress*

A wise person once said, "I've never met a person who wasn't carefully costumed." We agree. No matter how you are dressed right now, on some level you have chosen your outfit because it makes a statement that some part of you wants to make. Renee, in our example above, wore torn up clothes as a way of saying that she was a rebel and a maverick. On a subconscious level, it was more important to Renee to show what a rebel she was than it was for her to have a relationship with a man.

When men look at how you dress, it makes a statement to them. To men, Renee's way of dressing said, "I don't care about what you think about how I look." Not surprisingly, men were not very attracted to her. Other women make other statements with how they dress that also prevent men from being attracted to them.

One of the most common messages that women send to men through how they dress is, "I dress to please fashion designers and other women, not to look good to men." As you are no doubt deeply aware, many styles that look pretty good on models don't always look so good on a woman who isn't thirty pounds underweight, or on a woman who is overweight. Yet some women, on whom these styles look wildly inappropriate, go out of their way to dress in them anyway, in a mistaken notion that they will be more attractive to men than if they didn't.

Often, this simply isn't true. If a new style doesn't look good on you, you shouldn't wear it. Remember, you want to be clarifying and refining the message you send to men through how you dress, and *men don't care about the latest fashion*. They are not going to say, "Wow, I'd date her, but she's wearing last year's styles." They simply don't care. When you care about being up-to-date in style more than you care about how that style looks on you, you are sending the message, "I dress to please fashion designers and other women, not to look good to men." You can't afford to do this.

How do you dress to please men, then, if wearing the latest styles might not do it? The best message you could possibly send a man is that you are turned on by your life, by who you are, and by what you are up to. A woman like that would wear clothes that look good on *her*, whether or not they met the stringent requirements of the latest fashions. She'd wear the latest fashions if she liked how she looked in them, and if she liked how they made her feel. But she wouldn't be a fashion lemming, because she'd know that being a fashion lemming wouldn't necessarily make her look and feel her best, or send the best message she could to men.

The other common message women send to men through what they wear is, "I've given up." Monica was this way. She had been trying to lose the same thirty pounds for years, and kept putting off pursuing a relationship until the pounds were finally off, which they might never be. As a result, she had grown used to being alone, and her routines for making herself look attractive became perfunctory. She ran an office, so she wore appropriate office clothing, but there was no flair about her. She did nothing to personalize the "business clone" way she dressed. She didn't wear interesting pins or jewelry, or go to any lengths to find out what hairstyle would look best with her face—she kept things simple, plain, and boring.

This underlying discouragement came through to men, and they treated her, at best, like a sister. This discouragement also came through in her confidence: she didn't have any confidence with men, so couldn't pursue any romantic connections with them. Worse, she became used to being platonic friends with men she was attracted to, which put her in the habit of becoming friends, rather than lovers. This reinforced her discouragement even more, made her dress even more blandly, and continued to send the message, "I've given up," to men.

Other women, even women who aren't more physically attractive than Monica, make more constructive statements to men through the way they dress. Think about women you know, or whom you have seen, whose style of dress sends a positive message to men. Don't just think of supermodels; think of women who perhaps are overweight, "too tall," or who share whatever bodily complaint you have. These women probably have a way of dressing that says, "I'm an attractive woman on my own terms, and I know what I'm about. I'm not stuck in making some statement to other women or proving myself to the fashion industry. I haven't given up on myself, or on relationships. I'm not a model, but I do well with what I've got, and that's the kind of woman you want in your life." This is what you want to say, too.

As we worked with Renee, she changed her style and thereby changed what she was saying to men. She realized that saying she was a rebel was not as important as being attractive to the men she desired. She decided that, in order to be the kind of woman that got the kind of man she desired, she'd have to have a style of dress that said "I'm an attractive, mature woman." She made the changes, as you'll learn to do in this chapter, and immediately noticed improvements in her relationships with the opposite sex.

What does your way of dressing say to men?

∽ The Four Keys to Creating the Message You Send to Men

No matter what your way of dressing currently says to men, there are some simple steps you can take to improve the message you are sending.

While we aren't fashion experts, following these tips will make a difference, no matter what kind of fashion you discover works for you.

1. Do Well with What You've Been Given

So many people, both men and women, are never able to improve their lot in life because they are basically unwilling to work with what they've got. They want to somehow get rid of the hand they were dealt, and replace it with something better, rather than take the steps necessary to do as well as they can with what they already have.

This is a huge error, but an easy one to overcome. If you are overweight, for instance, stop exclusively focusing on weight loss. That exclusive focus leaves you spending too much of your time thinking about and working on what's "wrong" with you. Instead, look at yourself the way you actually are, and do as well as you can with yourself, the way you are now. This will put your focus on enhancing what's "right" about you. Yes, you can be attractive to men, even if you have a few extra pounds. You know it's true, because you have seen overweight women in good relationships and overweight women with wonderful men. Are you fully making use of your most attractive features, or are you waiting to somehow have a different body before you do so? Concentrating on doing the best you can with what you've been given will bring out the best in *you*. You'll be loving and appreciating the best parts of what you have now. This will make you happier with yourself, which will make you more attractive to men, as well as make you look even better to them.

2. Get a Coach

When you ask other women for advice about how to dress and present yourself to men, who do you ask? Do you ask women who you feel intimidated by, women who have naturally perfect bodies, skin, hair, or some other feature that you feel you do not have? Or do you ask women whose features are more like yours, only who do exceptionally well with them? This second group are the women you want to have coaching you. A naturally perfect beauty may not be able to give you good guidance about your situation, while a woman who looks like you, but who has done exceptionally well with her looks, can.

We suggest you go looking for these women. Make them your role-models and coaches.

3. Think About the Woman You Are Committed to Becoming

There is the woman you are now, and there is the woman you are committed to becoming. The woman you are committed to becoming might have the qualities you thought about when we asked you what kind of a woman you would have to be to get the man you desire. If you don't have a clear picture of what this woman might be like, you probably have a feeling. This feeling or picture can help guide you in developing your personal style.

Let your picture of the woman you are committed to becoming guide you in the decisions you make about how you dress and behave. At any time you can ask yourself, "What would the woman I'm committed to becoming do in this situation?" Because you are drawn to becoming that kind of woman, your mind will give you some sort of answer.

How would you dress if you were the woman you're committed to being, with exactly the body you've got?

4. Think in Terms of Health and Vitality Rather than Beauty

While beauty may be ephemeral, health and vitality shine out from the core of who you are. A woman who is healthy and vital tends to have an enthusiasm for her life that draws men, no matter how she looks. You've known people who seemed so charged up that, afer spending time with them, you felt like you left with more energy than you had before you saw them. These people have a deep vitality that is enhanced by good health.

You may want to get a massage or find a workout program you enjoy. You may want to do deeper bodywork to increase your sense of vitality and energy; some women get a great deal out of a massage program called "Rolfing," or another called "neuro-muscular therapy." These kinds of bodywork can fundamentally improve how you carry your body, your level of vitality, and how you look to men.

In the meantime, you can remind yourself, from time to time, to walk, sit, gesture and move like a woman who has excellent health and vitality. This will help bring out your innate vitality, and make you more attractive to men.

∞ *Confidence*

The Fear of Rejection

If there's one fear that both men and women have in common, it's the fear of rejection. You can be in love with your life, committed to becoming the kind of woman you fantasize about being, and doing incredibly well with what you are given, but still be paralyzed by the fear of rejection. Admittedly, the fear will be easier to handle if you have those other factors in place, but until you tackle the fear of rejection head-on and make it into your friend, it will slow you down or stop you on your quest for a man.

One of the myths of dating and seduction is that it should be easy; that there are perfect people out there who never get turned down, never hear the word "no," and never have to deal with rejection. That's the way things should be, this myth tells us. If you get rejected, it's because you weren't being one of these wonderful people. You did something wrong. You should feel ashamed.

Nothing could be further from the truth. Rejection is the most fundamental part of dating. It's everywhere. It's omnipresent. Even the most masterful, perfect and wonderful people experience it. You must learn to deal with it, and to make it into a friend.

Imagine you are on a third date. You know it's time to take things to "the next level," but he hasn't even tried to kiss you yet. He seems to like you, but who can tell? Maybe he's thinking about sports scores, or still wondering if it is a good idea to go out with you at all. You are thinking about kissing him. But what if he says "no"?

Or imagine you aren't even out on the date yet. Maybe you are looking across the room at him, that possibly perfect man, who you only wish you could bring yourself to talk to. But what if he rejects you? What if he walks away from you? What if he says "no"?

Physical safety issues aside, you are scared of a man for one reason only: you are afraid of the pain and humiliation you'll feel if he rejects you. If he says "no," you'll interpret it to mean all sorts of things: that you'll never get a man, that you are not good enough, and that there is something basically wrong with you. You'll feel humiliation and pain for days, perhaps longer. Each rejection makes you even less likely to initiate anything with a man again.

For Sandra, doing something as simple as flirting with a man at a party takes a significant effort. "If he doesn't like me," she muses, "I'll look like a fool. I can just see that horrified look on his face already. I wonder what excuse he'll make for 'slipping away.' Then he'll tell all of our mutual friends that I, of all people, tried to flirt with him. They'll all laugh at me and make fun of me behind my back. My reputation will be ruined."

Sandra causes herself pain by picturing the worst possible outcomes. She paralyzes herself with fear. She's picturing all these worst possible outcomes whenever she interacts with a man, and her sheer level of fear alone, if nothing else, makes men want to avoid her. She acts so strangely and so hesitantly that she's always at her worst around men.

There's nothing light, playful, or easy about her. Men sense this, and rejection is practically assured.

Like many people, Sandra thinks it is good to imagine the worst that could happen in a risky situation, so she can "steel herself against it." She thinks that looking realistically at the "downside" of being rejected is the best way to do this. She is wrong. Drawing unpleasant mental pictures of being rejected, along with getting completely absorbed in previews of how you'll feel when you are rejected, doesn't help you—it makes your rejection almost inevitable.

The confident woman has learned to see things completely differently. Rather than seeing rejection as a reflection of her value as a woman, the confident woman has taught herself one simple rule about it: "Rejection is the key to the relationship of my dreams." A confident woman thinks about rejection differently than an unsure, scared, and doubtful woman does. She makes better decisions about what a man's rejection means to her.

For instance, imagine you have taken a "basics of investing" mini-course at the local university as part of your program for meeting men (we discuss this program in a later chapter). You approach one of the men in the class, a strikingly handsome, tall man, with deep blue eyes and a short beard. You want to start a flirting interaction, so you ask him for help on one of the problems the teacher has assigned as a way of getting a conversation started.

Immediately, it seems like a mistake. He keeps looking around, as if he hopes no one sees you with him. He thrusts his answer-sheet to you wordlessly, for you to copy down his answer. He responds to your flirty little questions with mono-syllabic grunts. In every way he can, short of walking away while you are talking to him, he rejects you.

Let's look into the mind of an unconfident woman after this interaction. She might be thinking, "Wow, I really blew it with him. I can't believe I talked to him like that. I must have been really out of line. Once again, the men I desire don't desire me. Won't I ever be able to talk to a man without him rejecting me? What's wrong with me? Why do I try?" The unconfident woman explains the interaction to herself in a way that causes her humiliation and shame.

To the confident woman, rejection is a stepping stone to an ideal relationship because she sees it as one more "no" she doesn't have to hear on the way to the inevitable "yes," with some other man, who is waiting for her. After that same interaction, a confident woman might say to herself, "Wow, he sure didn't have much to say for himself. I wonder if he's not feeling well. Perhaps he just got some really bad news. Who knows?" If she thought he didn't like her, her only thought would be, "Well, it's a good thing I found out now, before wasting more time and energy on him. Now I can concentrate on the men who will want to be with me! Who should I talk to next?" The confident woman explains the interaction in such a way that she feels good about herself. She's gotten one more "no" out of the way, and can move on to a "yes" with some other man.

When taking the plunge and asking a man out, the confident and unconfident woman think differently, as well. Imagine you are at an outdoor music event, and you've struck up a conversation with a man who looks to be pretty interesting. You say "Hey, you seem pretty cool. Would you like to go out for coffee sometime?" He awkwardly responds, "Uh, no. I gotta go!" and disappears.

Here's how the unconfident woman might think about the interaction: "Oh, how humiliating. I'm crushed. I can't believe I did that. That's what I get for thinking a guy that cute and interesting would want to go out with me. I must look terrible today. I'll never do that again."

Meanwhile, here's how the confident woman thinks about it: "Wow, that's weird. How 'bout that. He must have a girlfriend or something, or he's gotten hurt somewhere along the line. Perhaps he's gay, or confused about his sexual identity. That kind of thing happens. Perhaps he's just caught up in his own little world. Or perhaps I'm just not his type. Oh well. That's one more 'no' I don't have to hear on my way to the relationship of my dreams. I wonder who else can I go talk to right now?" The confident woman explains the rejection in a way that's not personal for her; it doesn't mean anything about her, except that it's one more "no" that she won't have to hear again.

Ultimately, there are two steps you must follow when faced with a rejection. Whether or not you follow these two steps will make all the difference in your life. If you follow these two steps, you will make rejection into your friend (or, at least, into your ally). You will become a confident woman, and inevitably get the relationship you want, because you will keep at it, keep trying new things, and never give up. If you don't follow these two steps you will be stopped by rejection, and only get a relationship with a man through sheer luck, if at all. Because rejection is an inevitable part of finding the relationship of your dreams, your ability to carry out these two steps is crucial.

After you experience a rejection, take these two important steps:

1. COME UP WITH AN EXPLANATION OF THE REJECTION THAT
   EMPOWERS YOU TO FURTHER ACTION.

Your first order of business when you get rejected is to find a way to explain the rejection to yourself without deciding that there is something wrong with you. In this instance, it is permissible, and even desirable, to come up with explanations that make the rejection his problem, not yours.

You could tell yourself:

- "He's really wrapped up in his own world right now."
- "He must have a girlfriend."
- "He must be married."
- "Perhaps he's not feeling well."
- "He may have just gotten some bad news."
- "He may be gay."
- "He may be confused about his sexual orientation."

It's worth noting that most any of these explanations could be true. *You don't know.* But because you don't know—and often cannot know—which explanation is true, you are free to choose the explanation that is least humiliating to you. It might *not* be that you are a loser no man will ever want. Any one of these explanations could be the proper one. So choose one, don't make the rejection personal, and move on.

At this point we must take you back to chapter 1, in which we talked about the dating myth, "Men can't handle a powerful woman." As you may recall, we advised you to avoid using this myth to explain rejection from a man. It may seem like we are now telling you the opposite, so some explanation is in order.

There is a big difference between saying "That guy can't handle a powerful woman," and saying "*Men* can't handle a powerful woman." The difference is in what these two explanations do to your attitude. When you tell yourself that *men* can't handle a powerful woman, you are dooming your future interactions with men, and setting up the expectation for yourself that men won't be able to handle you, and will thus reject you. You want to make sure that your explanation only applies to that man, in that interaction.

The most confident women believe that men, as a whole, are great; It's just that certain men, for reasons all their own, occasionally reject women. It's not personal, and it's also not global. It's not about you, and it's not about men in general. It's about that guy, at this time. That's all there is to it.

2. CHANGE YOUR FOCUS AND THINK ABOUT (OR DO) SOMETHING ELSE.

An unconfident women will dwell on her rejection. She will replay it over and over for herself, looking for what she did wrong and deepening the feelings of humiliation and pain. A confident woman redirects her attention immediately. "Who else can I talk to right now?" she may ask herself. Almost any question will do here. "What's on TV?" "Which friend can I call and talk about something else?" "Where can I go right now that will engage my attention in something other than this rejection?"

You have most likely done this at some time or other. You've probably had the experience of having something upsetting happen, then gotten so involved in thinking about something else that you totally forgot to feel badly about the incident. By the time you returned to thinking about it, it may have appeared much smaller and less significant.

When you meet rejection with the knowledge that moving past it is the key to a successful long-term relationship, and follow this simple two-step process, your eventual success with men is pretty much guaranteed.

∞ *The Numbers Game*

Confident women constantly remember that finding the right man, like so many other pursuits in life, is a numbers game. Crass as it may seem, dating men is like selling a product. Instead of selling a vacuum cleaner or some other product, however, you are selling *you*—and, eventually, the idea of a committed, long-term relationship with you. Salespeople know that they rarely make a sale on the first call they make. They know that if they do, it was luck, and they don't count on it again.

Let's watch a top saleswoman at work. Mary sells insurance, and has for four years. She's 29, and has stunned her company by again and again meeting and beating her sales goals. She's made herself the best salesperson in the company by following a simple philosophy. She's learned, by keeping track of her efforts, that for every seventy-five people she calls, she makes four appointments, and out of those four appointments she makes one sale.

Unlike her associates, who don't sell as much as she does, Mary has accepted these facts of life. She understands that it is not personal when people hang up, or aren't home, or yell at her. It's all part of the numbers game she's playing, a game which she knows will eventually, inevitably, make the sale. All she has to do is keep dialing the phone, and sooner or later she will sell some insurance. So she keeps dialing, with that end in mind.

Her associates who fail don't see it as a numbers game. They take the rejections and difficulties personally. Instead of knowing that they are working their way through inevitable rejection to get to inevitable success, they get caught up in bad feelings and lose sight of their goal. They eventually give up, while Mary goes on to succeed. Mary is like the infamous Energizer Bunny. She keeps going and going, unwilling to be stopped by pitfalls along the way. Sure, Mary gets flustered, upset, and angry when things don't go her way. But she is always, eventually, able to bring it back to the numbers game she is playing.

Confident women see dating as a numbers game, as well. Even the most successful, confident women know that they won't have a wonderful interaction with every man they approach—far from it. They know that most of their "cold calling"—that is, their flirting with men—will not lead to anything more than one interaction.

A confident woman expects that eight out of ten men won't make it past the flirting stage with her. She knows that she'll disqualify them for some reason, or that they won't ask her out. She also knows that, for every five guys she goes out with on *"Qualifying Dates"* (chapters 8–9), only two or three of them will qualify for *"Middle Dates"* (chapters 10–12). Further, she knows that for every four middle dates she has, only one man will stand a chance of being good relationship material. She accepts these facts of life. She thinks about dating like baseball— knowing that those who have the most home runs often have the most strike-outs, too. She understands that it's not personal when men say "no" to her, don't show up for dates, or reject her. It's all part of the game she's playing, a game she knows will eventually get her the relationship she desires. All she has to do is to keep following the ten step plan, and she *will* find men for relationships. So she keeps on, through all the rejection, keeping her attention firmly on the goal she has in mind.

An unconfident woman doesn't see dating as a numbers game—in fact, she is very, very offended by the whole concept. She takes rejections and difficulties personally. Instead of knowing that she is working her way through inevitable rejection to inevitable success, she gets caught up in her momentary bad feelings. As a result, she loses sight of the inevitability of her goal. She eventually gives up, while the confident woman goes on to succeed.

At the beginning, when you are first developing your dating skills, your numbers may be discouraging. Unlike more practiced women, you may have to flirt with twenty-five or thirty men before three ask you out, and of those three only one may qualify. You may have to look harder for the available men, while you are developing your skills at spotting them. No matter; as long as you remember that it is a numbers game, you will have success with men.

Some women object to the idea that a man's rejection could just roll off their backs. They don't want to desensitize themselves to men—after all, they want to open up to men, not close down to them!

We think you should be sensitive to what the men you date say and do, but *not* in the early stages of dating. When you are first getting to know one another, too much sensitivity will only cause problems. Too many dates go nowhere, or end in rejection, for you to flay your heart and ask the world to do to you what it will. Later, that may be appropriate. At the beginning, you simply must be more circumspect. In the atmosphere of early dating, you must be insensitive in the face of rejection if you want to develop a relationship of your dreams with a man. Once a man has won the right to your heart, you can open up. Until then, don't let rejection get you down.

The Thirty-Day Program for Getting Over Fear of Rejection

You must get yourself so accustomed to rejection from men that it no longer has any negative meaning to you. A simple way to do this is to start small, with our easy-to-follow, thirty-day, rejection-stomping, confidence-building program.

If you are scared to talk to men and scared of rejection from men, this simple program will get you talking to them daily, and laughing in the face of rejection. It's straightforward, painless, and easy to do. It's based on a simple two-letter word that, when you use it with men, will build your confidence, start you talking, and be the first step toward getting men into your life.

Are you ready for the word? The word is "Hi!"

To build your confidence with men and to overcome your fear of rejection, for the next thirty days, say "Hi" to men in public at least six times a day. That's all there is to it. You are walking down the street, you see an attractive man, you say "Hi" to him, and walk on. You see the next attractive man, and you say "Hi" to him, too. And so on.

Don't be deceived by the simplicity of this program. If you are willing to actually do it, and to actually say "Hi" to a number of men out in public every day, you're confidence will rise, your fear of rejection will diminish, and your success with men will improve. Here's why:

First, your confidence will improve because you actually will be talking to men. Saying "Hi" is wonderful because the interaction ends quickly. The "Hi" interaction doesn't put your ego on the line, and doesn't give him much chance to reject you. What's the worst he'll do? Glare at you as you walk by? Who cares? It's not like you've put your whole ego on the line by asking him to father your children. You're getting into the habit of seeing men who attract you, and talking to them. And that's good.

Second, men's responses to you will become less important. You'll find that you are being the kind of woman you want to be, the kind of woman who says hello to whatever kind of man appeals to her, no matter what his response might be. You'll become less scared of rejection as you notice that some men smile and say "Hi" back; that some men are in their own world and don't even seem to notice you spoke; and that some men just glare at you darkly. You'll start to see that it doesn't matter; all that matters is that you are making life work for you by starting to approach the men who attract you. You are doing this, not so much to turn one of these men into the relationship of your dreams, but to turn yourself into the woman of your dreams. It's not about his response; it's about who you are becoming as a woman.

Third, you actually will get into more conversations with men if you set a precedent of talking to them right away. Have you ever been in a situation in which you would have spoken to a man, but the fact that you've initially ignored him makes it hard to start? This happened to our friend Laura just the other day. "I was in a line waiting to buy tickets to a movie," she reports. "There was a gorgeous guy in line in front of me, but when I first saw him, I went back into my old fear mode, and didn't look at him or say 'Hi.' After about five minutes of waiting, I really wanted to start talking to him, but it seemed a lot more awkward because I hadn't said 'Hi' at first." After you've practiced saying "Hi" for a few weeks, it'll be second nature for you to see that man in line, look him in the face, smile, and say "Hi." You'll be relaxed and not concerned with his response, because you already will have "seen it all." It will then be natural for the two of you to talk more, and for you to be able to use the tools from the rest of this book to flirt with him, test him, and possibly even build a relationship with him.

The Four Excuses that Keep You from Feeling Confident

There are four main excuses that hold women back, keep them from becoming the confident women they want to become, and stop them from having the relationships they desire.

Confidence Excuse Number One: "I'm not attractive enough."

Very few women think that they have the right body for attracting men. We heard this story about a women's group, in which the women were talking about being attractive to men: Each woman had some other woman in the group who she thought the men were attracted to. Eventually they all ended up pointing to the same woman: "All the men are attracted to you!" they told her. "Are you kidding?" she responded. Then, pointing to some other woman in the room, she said "They want you, not me!" Almost no woman thinks she is "attractive enough." The most beautiful women in the world have a body part they complain about; everybody's got the wrong body.

You may try to live up to the beauty standards placed on women in our society, but it cannot be done. The more you try, the more unfulfilling the whole process is. If even the most beautiful woman still feels like she isn't beautiful enough, what's the point of even trying to look perfect?

The key is to stop trying to live up to an impossible cultural standard of beauty, and to start really appreciating the beauty that you've got. Admittedly, this is easier to say than it is to do. Easy to say or not, however, it should be said because it is true. There are some things you can do to start bringing the *feeling* of being beautiful "home."

There's an excellent book called *Beyond the Blame Game: Creating Compassion and Ending the Sex War in Your Life*, that we recommend you get. In it, author Dmitri Bilgere describes an "attractiveness exercise" that is worth learning. Here it is, paraphrased from Bilgere's words:

It's natural to think that other women are attractive, and to feel helpless and unattractive when that thought occurs. You think, "She's so beautiful. I'm ugly. She's hot. I'm worthless." Psychologists call this *projection*. Somehow, seeing that attractive woman seems to suck all feelings of beauty and worthiness out of you. It's as if she has a claim on all of your feelings of attractiveness. You've projected them onto her, and are left feeling jealous and unworthy. Fortunately, there is a visualization technique you can use to begin to get those feelings back, and even enhance them in yourself. If you can intercept your thoughts as they occur, "She's beautiful, I'm not. She's gorgeous, I'm nothing," you can put the visualization into action.

Bringing the feeling of attractiveness back from her to you takes a little imagination, but anyone can do it. First, imagine what you think it feels like to look like she does. Imagine yourself in her body, walking down the street. Hold your body the way you imagine she holds hers. Let yourself think what you imagine she may be thinking. (These thoughts may be wildly inaccurate, but let yourself think them anyway.) For example, you may imagine that she is thinking, "I'm so attractive. I'm so beautiful. Everybody desires me." Let yourself have those thoughts, and notice how she feels when she is thinking this. If you are really pretending to be her, holding your body the way you think she is holding hers and thinking the thoughts you imagine she is thinking, you will start to have a feeling of attractiveness somewhere in your body.

Look for that feeling. Is it a lightness in your chest? A relaxation in your shoulders? Everyone is different, so you may have to look around inside before you recognize the feeling. It will be a good feeling; that much is certain.

Bilgere says that this feeling is actually *your* feeling of attractiveness, which you have projected onto other women. It's a sense of attractiveness you could feel for yourself, no matter how you look. Think of what it might be like if you spent a lot of time feeling this way. There might be an energy in this feeling that would motivate you to talk to men, to dress in a way that accents your best features, or to work out on a regular basis.

Now, focus on your body, while still recognizing this feeling in your body. If you have difficulty doing this, it may help to go back to imagining the attractiveness while pretending to be this other woman, and ask yourself, "where is this feeling in my body?" Once you have it localized, ask yourself, "What's this feeling's shape? If I were to give it a color, what color might I say it is? What is it like?"

Different women come up with different metaphors for the feeling. It might be a bright sun shining in your chest. It might be lines of fire going down your arms and out your fingers. It might be like a tiger in your hips; whatever your imagination says.

When you have a concrete idea of what the energy is like, then you can slowly let yourself return to your own body, *keeping the metaphor and the sense of attractiveness in your consciousness*, bringing it back into yourself and feeling how it feels to have it as your own. You will probably find that your posture has improved after such a visualization, and you can enjoy, at least for a while, the feeling of being attractive *as you*. You have that sun, or that fire, or that tiger in you. And you'll see how good it feels.

If you do this visualization a lot, you will find that you start to project your feelings of attractiveness onto other women less frequently. Is this a cure-all? No. Will there still be women who are more attractive than you? Certainly. But you can start to learn to feel the attractiveness that is rightfully yours, instead of giving that feeling away. It is a certainty that there is something attractive about you, and you can use that if you let yourself feel this energy.

Confidence Excuse Number Two: "I'm Too Old"

You aren't too old. It's a myth. How could you be too old to be in a relationship? Are the women who've been married fifty or sixty years "too old" to be in their relationships? Of course not. So how could you be too old to be in one yourself?

Perhaps you think you are too old to get a relationship started. Perhaps you think that starting relationships is a young person's game, and that, once you've reached whatever age you are now, it's basically too late. You are old and worn out, and no man would ever want you.

If you want, you can make yourself feel even worse by wryly noting that older men often go out with younger women, but that older women rarely go out with younger men. You can then comment about how, because men drop dead at a younger age than women do, the pool of possible partners for you is getting smaller by the minute. And if you manage to have all of these thoughts at once, you can have yourself fully believing in the myth, and as a bonus, get yourself totally depressed.

But it's all unnecessary. You don't need to kick yourself out of the relationship game just because you aren't as young as you once were. Who cares if there are fewer available guys? A woman who is committed to building a relationship realizes that she doesn't need hundreds of guys, she just needs the *one* she is looking for.

It is true that there are challenges in dating. It is true that if you are older, it may be more difficult. But it is not true that you are too old to do it. Read the next two chapters on where to meet men, put into action as many of those suggestions as you can, and you will move your project forward. You'll begin meeting men.

Don't let dating challenges stop you. Don't use your age as an excuse. Don't deny a wonderful man a chance to have a relationship with you by giving up. Do the confidence exercises, develop your personal style, and get going.

Confidence Excuse Number Three: "No Man Will Want a Woman Who Has Kids"

Many women effectively keep themselves from even starting to develop their confidence by reminding all who will listen that they have kids. But this excuse doesn't hold up either, and it shouldn't keep you out of the dating game.

As dating gurus for men, we get to hear all the male excuses, and, "I have kids" is a common one for guys, too. In fact, there are a lot of divorced men out there who have kids, who are looking to date a woman like you.

The upside of dating a man who has kids, when you have kids yourself, is the bonding that can take place when you all do things together as a unit. As a man sees you with your kids, and also interacting with his, he gets a chance to evaluate your possibilities as a step-mother, as well as your possibilities as a girlfriend. This can work in your favor. Interacting with each other's kids can also help integrate you into each other's lives.

This doesn't mean you can only date men with kids if you have children. We know a surprising number of men who have taken on a fathering role for kids who aren't genetically theirs. It does happen. As the guy falls in love with the woman, he also commits himself to the child or children. The kind of men you are going to be finding through our program—men who are deeper then they look at first glance, much of the time—are prime candidates for this role.

Of course, if you use the "kids" excuse to keep you out of the game, you'll never find one of these wonderful men. So don't buy it. Clear whatever time in your schedule that you can, and get out there and date.

Confidence Excuse Number Four: "I'm Afraid of Getting Hurt"

The fear of getting hurt actually is a pretty good excuse. You are less likely to get your heart broken if you stay home all the time than you are if you reach for something more in your life. If you demand more from yourself, and commit yourself to becoming the confident woman you know you can be, you risk failing in that task. That failure can hurt. Not trying doesn't present that risk. If you follow the ten-step Master Plan in this book, and begin having more relationships with men, you risk getting hurt more than you risk if you stay home, too.

Interacting with life as a powerful woman is full of risks. It's true. But when you are thinking of taking a risk and doing what it takes to become a confident woman, who lives out of her own personal style, ask yourself this: How is it working for you *not* to take that risk? How is it working for you to hide behind excuses, and not to do what it takes to become the kind of woman you can be, the kind of woman you are committed to becoming? Is it giving you the life you want? Is it giving you the relationship you want?

Going for the relationship of your dreams is emotionally risky. Interacting with men is emotionally risky. You could get hurt. But it's likely that you are feeling some of that hurt already, in the form of loneliness and discouragement. And if you are feeling those feelings anyway, perhaps it makes sense to go ahead and take the risks. At least then you have a chance of getting the rewards.

∞ Other Confidence Builders

Being in "The Zone"

Peak performers talk about being in "the zone" or in "the flow." You are in the zone when you are at your best, when all your inner resources are available to you, and when you seem to automatically handle everything well.

We've all had these moments. Sometimes they take place while engaged in sports. When a rock-climber, for instance, becomes engaged in the climb, she forgets about everything else in the world but the rock wall in front of her. Surgeons report that when they are doing surgery, they are so involved in what they are doing it's like they are in perfect harmony with the world around them. If you can remember a time when you effortlessly and peacefully performed beyond what you usually were able to do, you have been in the zone.

People who are falling in love are in the zone. You probably have felt it. When you were with him, it was like time stood still. You could do no wrong, and life, when you were with him, seemed effortless. When you were together you were creative, happy, and not worried about yourself or about your life. This is the zone, as well.

Kay had this experience when she first met Nick. "I'd seen him at a couple of parties and been very attracted to him, but from the start I never felt tense or nervous around him, like I usually do when I meet a man I'm interested in. It was like I knew in my heart that we'd get along fine, and I wasn't worried about it. I felt like, if it was meant to be, then it would happen. I really didn't worry about it.

"I remember running into him at a park, and we talked a bit and sat together on the grass. I didn't feel like I had to say anything, and there were these long periods where neither of us said anything at all, but I knew it was just fine. I felt present and happy and didn't need to fill the silences.

"After one of those silences, he said to me 'I just want to find out everything about you.' It was the start of our relationship. I was in the zone that day, that's for sure."

How did Kay do this? What made her so irresistible to Nick that he couldn't help but want to open up to her, even though she said very little? Kay accidentally did what all peak performers do, and what you can do with men, too. She pursued her outcome (being romantic with Nick) and, *simultaneously,* let go of having to make that outcome happen (having faith that if it was meant to be, it would happen). She stopped worrying about whether he would like her or not. Any outcome would have been fine with her. If Nick had not wanted to be with her she might have been disappointed, but she wouldn't have been upset. Similarly, she wasn't overly obsessed about Nick's interest, even though she was pursuing him.

Let's look at the opposite example. Donna was very interested in Randy. She thought he was cute and mysterious and very much wanted to explore a romantic relationship with him. It was terribly important to her that all of her interactions with him went well, so that he'd like her and want to go out with her. She was so focused on this goal, and on how bad it would be if he didn't like her, that she was weird and distracted when she was with him. "I was such a ninny," she says now. "I so wanted to impress him that I talked a mile-a-minute, made jokes that weren't funny, and was all-around a tense, jumpy girl." Because she couldn't stop thinking about her desired outcome—having him like her—she could never be relaxed and unconcerned with him. "I scared him off," she says. "I was so wrapped up in my fantasies about what I wanted to have happen with him, I was never able to really be present with him when we were together." Her inability to pursue her goal with Randy without worrying about that goal at the same time, took her out of the zone, made her interactions seem forced, and made her appear unattractive.

When you have chemistry with a man, you are, by definition, pursuing him without worrying about the outcome. For some reason, with certain men, it's easy for you to not worry, and to get into the zone. You can, however, train yourself to worry less and less in your interactions with men by simply setting your intention on not worrying. You can remind yourself, when you go into interactions with men, that the outcome isn't important. When you do this, you'll find you are more relaxed, and have better chemistry with men. When Donna learns to not be worried about how it goes with Randy, and has some faith that everything will be okay, she will relax, and make it easier for Randy to get to know her and to find her attractive. Getting into the zone by letting go of worry about the outcome of your interactions with men is crucial. All the rest of the tools you learn in this book—where and how to meet men, flirting, testing men, and so on—will be much easier to practice and have success with if you train yourself to pursue the relationship of your dreams, and to give up worrying about the outcome at the same time.

Not Looking to Him for Validation that Everything Is Okay

This is a key concept that we will return to again and again. People, both men and women, are looking to you to see if the interaction they are having with you is going well, or going badly. They look for the signs: does she seem nervous, afraid, or worried that she might do something wrong at any moment? Does she seem terrified that something bad will happen? Is she hesitant about her thoughts, feelings, and opinions? If you do seem nervous and hesitant, the odds of people relaxing in your presence drop considerably.

On the other hand, people are also looking for indicators in your behavior that everything is going well. They are asking: Does she seem unapologetic about herself and her preferences? Does she seem to believe that everything is going just fine? Does she stay upbeat, even when there are problems? If you do seem to believe that everything is fine, the people around you will begin to relax and believe that, too.

When you are interacting with a man, it is doubly important that you keep this principle in mind. One of the main seduction principles that we teach men is that they must stop looking to women for validation that any given interaction is going okay, and start getting that validation from themselves. However, the men you flirt with may not know this, and may look to you for validation. They will be utterly useless if you are looking to them for validation as well. Don't even bother.

Eileen made this mistake when she first met Harry. She flirted with him in the ways we will teach you, but she lost her sense of confidence by feeling hesitant about the interaction until she got some clear signal from Harry that he was enjoying it. "I couldn't tell if he was having fun talking to me or not," she said later. "I kept hoping he'd be confident and relaxed, so I could relax too. It wasn't 'til afterwards that I realized that he was waiting for *me* to relax before he did. I ended up leaving the interaction feeling like there was something wrong with me. If I had just let myself believe everything was okay instead of looking to him for that information, he probably would have ended up asking me out."

∞ *Conclusion*

A woman who has personal style is worth winning, because she's won herself. She expresses herself, and her love of her life, in how she dresses and behaves. She sends a mature and "together" message to men, rather than a message of being immature, dressing for other women, or of having given up. She does well with what she's got, and, while she doesn't like or enjoy rejection, she endures it well and uses it to empower her to move on, from one more "no" she never has to hear again to the inevitable "yes" that is waiting for her. By having a personal style that sends a message she likes through how she dresses, by sending a message of confidence through how she behaves, she values herself. As she values her own heart, it becomes more valuable to men. She also becomes happier in the process.

A deeply unconfident woman who has no personal style is simply not worth winning in most men's view. She makes no effort to make the most of what she has, or to learn to handle rejection. Instead she believes the worst about herself, indulging in the harshest explanations about herself when men reject her, and sending messages with how she dresses that she doesn't value herself as a possible relationship partner. The unconfident woman has a personal style that continuously keeps her unhappy and tells men that her heart is not worth winning. Sadly, such a personal style is self-reinforcing: the more she believes, dresses and behaves like she isn't worth winning, the more men will reject her, and the more the belief of her low self-worth will grow.

Such a woman can change, however. If you sometimes feel like you are such a woman, you can stop worrying about it. The most common mistake women make about changing is that they wait to "feel like" changing before they do so. They think of changing as a big, global, life-shaking *event*. It's not. You can change without feeling like changing—in fact, when you don't feel like changing is the best time to do so. Just take one of the actions that we recommend in this chapter—any action. It doesn't have to be big and dramatic. Make a simple change, just for today. Ask a woman you trust, someone who sends a great message to men, to give you a suggestion or two about your look. Don't make it a big deal; take her suggestion.

Ask yourself, "How can I do well with what I've been given, right now, today, and even have fun in the process?" Enroll yourself in our thirty-day "Hi" program for overcoming your fear of rejection, and say "hi" to six men today, without worrying about their reaction. See how it feels.

These little actions all add up. Rome wasn't built in a day, and habits don't change in an instant, so you can stop worrying that they ought to. Take some small action, then notice how it feels. If it feels good, let yourself enjoy it. Let yourself enjoy the fact that you are saying hi to men. Let yourself enjoy making one little change, whatever it is, in the messages you send to the men you desire. Let yourself enjoy the feeling of being the kind of woman you are committed to being. Don't go making lots of resolutions at this moment, about how, from now on, everything will be different. Personal style comes and goes as you are building it, and it will come and go for you, too. But as you feel good about it, and as you develop it, you will notice that you have the personal style of the kind of woman you are committed to being on a more and more consistent basis. You are becoming worth winning.

And, as that happens, you are also winning yourself.

CHAPTER 4

Prepare to Meet Your Mate

"WHERE CAN I GO TO MEET A MAN?" WE GET ASKED THIS QUESTION all the time by our students, on the radio or television, via the Internet, or on the street. It seems that women all over America want to know where they can go to meet qualified men.

By the end of these next two chapters we want you to fully understand that you, yes you, have spheres of influence, hobbies, resources, and networks of people in your life right now, and all of them can assist you in meeting men. So stop acting confused and let's get to work.

A common misconception among women is that there is a lack of single men to choose from. We call this the "myth of scarcity." Our experience and research shows that there is no lack of men to choose from, even in your town. Many single women simply fail to notice all of the men they come into contact with throughout their typical day. In fact, most women are surrounded by men throughout their daily routines, but are too blinded by the "myth of scarcity" to notice. Single women can become so caught up with their routines that they don't realize that one of these men who become the wallpaper of their lives could actually be one of the finest and most romantic men they have ever met. Instead, most men fade into the background and go unnoticed, and single women stay alone.

Every indicator we know shows that the "myth of scarcity" is not true. There is a man out there for you, no matter what you look like, what your background, what your skin color, your age, your height, or the size of your breasts. Where are these men that we so arrogantly insist are everywhere? They are in bookstores, restaurants, on trains, boats, airplanes, and even riding hovercrafts. At this moment, there are qualified men walking down your street, spending time in nature, hanging out in shopping centers, going to bars, attending sports events, concerts and fairs, taking elevators, flirting on the Internet, answering personal ads, going to church, and even attending your favorite self-help seminar.

To find qualified men you will have to change your perspective. You will begin by starting to notice all of the men around you, and looking for ways to flirt with them. Then you will find ways to turn the flirting interactions into dates. From there you can move the flirting to more intimate matters. We know the dating world can be harsh and confusing. That is why the authors are here to save you. Luckily, Copeland and Louis are so chivalrous that we will save you from the otherwise cold and harsh world. Yes, we are your knights in shining armor, here to rescue you, the fair damsel in distress; and we will assist you in finding the road that leads to your castle built for two.

The majority of our female students have failed because of useless advice like, "just play hard to get" or, "never accept a date after Thursday night," or, "just be approachable," or, "the man will appear when you are spiritually ready," or, "be more outgoing." Dating advice for women is usually full of outrageous claims guaranteeing meeting a man in twenty-four hours or less, cosmic babble from psychic hot-line failures, thoroughly manipulative and coercive claims, and little practical information and guidance.

There is no shortage of charlatans who will tell you an impractical theory without even telling you how to apply it. Learning principles and theory alone without explanation of practical application, will leave most people feeling frustrated, empty, and worse off than when they started.

Theory alone won't get you a man. One of the fundamental skills in dating is the ability to understand where and how to meet men. Meeting men is step two in our ten-step program. This chapter will prove to you once and for all that there are places for you to meet men in every economic, social, psychological, recreational or intellectual bracket you could ever wish for. This chapter will show you the exact steps to take to find a man. We will also offer insight into how you can use any of your hobbies or interests to find the man of your dreams. How's that for cool?

∞ The Six Excuses that Keep You From Meeting Men

Before we step into the action phase, we must examine what stops you from meeting men. It has been our experience, in running seminars and two-on-one coaching, that until a person is aware of what stops them in dating, they have a difficult time moving forward. The first step in this process is understanding.

So we ask you, what are your excuses? What keeps you from talking to men and interacting with them? What keeps you home on a Saturday night rather than out with your friends, flirting with men? In the next section we will examine the common excuses and possible solutions to each.

Excuse Number One: It Takes Too Much Time

Sara looks at her schedule and complains that she does not have enough time. Sara claims that she could not possibly spend time meeting men because she is too busy with work, friends, hobbies, reading, and daily chores. We, the experts, know that Sara's excuses are just not real. Meeting men is not as time-consuming as you think, and much of the "dead time" you spend in life, waiting in lines and shopping, for instance, is actually prime time, filled with opportunities to meet men. We could follow Sara around for a day and point out dozens of these opportunities, chances Sara has to meet men with very little extra effort.

At the same time, we will not pretend that meeting men is not time-consuming at all. When taking on any new project there is no way around having to spend some time to produce the end result. At this stage of your life, you have to decide how badly you want a man. Are you willing to take time from your schedule and make dating one of your top priorities for the next three to nine months? If you aren't, then this book is probably not for you. If you take the time and put in the hard work up front, the rewards will be wonderful, spectacular, and will even make your heart sing. You are the only one who can judge how much time you would put in to have a steady boyfriend, mate, or boy toy. If you feel that you can take on this project for the next several months and make it one of your top priorities, we can then move on.

If you want to become a great artist, you have to buy the right paints and brushes, a sketch pad and an easel, and put in the time to learn the basic skills and strategies. As your ability to paint simple objects increases, the process seems easier. At a certain point, you can get away with simply maintaining your skills. The same is true of success with men. Once you have the basic skills and action plan in place you won't have to spend nearly as much time on it. Belinda is one of our success stories. On a daily basis she continues to pursue her goals with men. Each day she stays in "practice" by flirting with men, smiling, striking up innocent conversations, and charming all the men she interacts with. These little things don't take much time on their own, but the cumulative effect is tremendous. Belinda was able to overcome this excuse by starting with small actions each day, and in the process she noticed them adding up to big results.

Excuse Number Two: It Will Hurt My Reputation

Some of our students worry about, or are totally preoccupied with, their reputations. These students fear being "found out," and being seen as desperate or sleazy. They worry that their friends will judge them harshly or tease them. If you are stopped by this excuse, we recommend that you work on your dating project with a hand-picked team of people you really trust, and examine those you trust in terms of the likelihood of their spreading harmful gossip about you. If someone seems to have a propensity for gossip and you fear that they will hurt you, don't share your project with them. Instead of being worried about your reputation, be cautious and protect yourself from potential gossip, *and* continue to pursue men.

Excuse Number Three: There Are No Good Men

We constantly hear women say that there are no good men left in the world. It seems as though there once were an abundant population of good men and then they somehow disappeared off the face of the earth only to be replaced by total jerks.

In our experience working with men, we have noticed that most men are good guys deep down, but they have learned to hide this fact. Men have a shell of jerk energy surrounding them, but it is thin and can often be quickly removed. After years of bad experiences with women, men tend to be cautious and suspicious, and then seem less than wonderful. When men try to meet and impress women, they are unclear how to do so, and end up messing things up in the process; probably coming off as jerks or morons. Next, women (probably you included), misinterpret men's signals and intentions. Women, reacting to men's dumb advances or flirtacious interactions, once again think all men are jerks. Men then become upset because in their mind they were attempting to be sweet and romantic. They then react, and become even more cynical, doubting that they could ever have wonderful relationships with women. The signals between the sexes keep getting messed up, and the communication breaks down into a self-perpetuating circle of doom. We are here to break this vicious circle by explaining how this phenomenon occurs, and showing how you can react positively, or how you can react negatively, to the situation. When you understand what is happening, you can do your part to break the cycle.

Remember that men are a combination of rude and graceful, sweet and insensitive, fun and obnoxious. Now that you know that men are a mixed bag of pain and pleasure, let's turn the focus back on you. Blaming men for your problems, and being upset that they are annoying and sweet at the same time, won't help you get a man. Blaming men will only accomplish one thing: keeping you stuck in the same place you are now—alone.

We are now going to tell you more crushing and horrible news. Your "ideal man" does not exist. The "ideal man" is a figment of your imagination, a mythical character, an unreachable goal. While there are thousands of good men available, they are always a combination of sweet and stupid, obnoxious and caring. No man, no matter how rich, gorgeous, or sweet will ever match your ideal. Until you rid yourself of your desire for this ultimate man, no man you meet will ever be good enough. All men will fail in comparison to the ideal.

Prepare now to kill off your vision of the idealized male. You can use a knife, gun, jar of poison, or any other weapon, and kill the idea of an "ideal man." Cremate him before moving on.

From now on, your new task is to examine a man's essence when you meet him. Examine how he acts overall, knowing full well that all men will make dumb mistakes (see chapter 6 for more on this). You've probably disqualified many high-quality single men out in the world because they didn't act exactly as you wanted at all times. We have often seen men approach women in a thoughtless and clumsy manner. When this happens, women tend to look at the man, listen to his stupid pickup line

or approach, and immediately disqualify him, without knowing anything more about him. For the most part, we see women making judgments about men based on how they look, and whether or not they have
a bunch of smooth moves and romantic pickup lines. Women fail to
base their judgments on their own criteria, or on their long-term goals.
Chapter 2 focused on developing a plan for meeting Mr. Right and the
qualities he must possess. We want you to begin assessing the men you
meet based on the criteria on your list, not on his tactful approach. It is
predictable that a man with the smoothest moves won't have the qualities you want, anyway. That said, let's move on.

Excuse Number Four: I Just Can't Do It

Learning a new skill or taking on a new project can be intimidating. The
learning curve is steep. The project seems like hard work. The end result
appears to be an unreachable fantasy. To make matters worse, the beginning of the project is likely to be full of mistakes and miscalculations.

At some point, most of our students have felt as though they were
fundamentally inadequate when it came to the opposite sex. Some students want to quit in the middle of our courses and throw their arms in
the air because dating simply seems too hard. For other students, the
failures along the way are too painful; they take a few steps backward
and resist starting over again. Whatever the reason, at some point in
this process you will feel as though you can't do it, and you will want to
give up.

When you feel upset and want to quit the dating game, the best solution is to get support from other women. Your girlfriends, or even your
mom, will be able to relate to your problems, comfort you, offer advice,
and bring you up from the depths of the darkness in a way no one else
can. It is crucial that you get the support you need whenever you feel
upset or want to quit. If you have female friends who are also reading
this book, go to them and discuss how you are doing with our program.

Have your friends remind you of the long- term benefits of this program and how good it will feel when you eventually have the man of your dreams. Talk to friends who can see the progress you have already made, and have them frequently remind you of your progress.

Here is the good news: Feeling like a failure can actually be a good thing. The pain can act as a springboard and get you back into action. When things seem too hard and you do not seem to be making any forward movement in dating, you will probably continue to feel bad until you get your butt back into gear and start over. Many of our students use the moments when they want to quit as opportunities to make stronger commitments to achieve their goals. You've probably had the experience of feeling stuck in an area of your life for so long that you finally couldn't stand feeling stuck any longer, and you took the actions necessary to change. It is sometimes said that it is best to kick a person when they are down; that way, the person will get up faster. When you feel like a failure and rejection feels too painful, get back on the playing field to improve your mood, and get the ball rolling again.

Excuse Number Five: I Don't Know How to Get a Man

We have never met a woman who was so repellent to men that she could be categorized as undatable. The ability to get a man is not based on your genetic disposition or your psychic abilities. The ability to get a man can be learned, taught, and replicated. While some women seem to be "naturals," most women have to work at it. In the past, you may have relied on luck, hoping, and even praying for things to work out with men. In the end, none of these work very well. So what is the solution?

The solution is the bible you hold in your hands. Yes, we are the solution to all of your troubles, woes, tears, and lonely nights. All your life you have waited for men like Ron Louis and David Copeland to arrive and save the day. This book contains the answers to your questions and offers a step-by-step program to securing the man of your dreams. This means you can no longer let your excuses stop you. Once you finish the book, and continue to practice, study, get support from your friends, and practice some more, you will succeed.

Excuse Number Six: I Shouldn't Have to Work to Get a Man

Some women feel as though they are above initiating dates with men. They have been raised to believe that the entire responsibility should fall on men's shoulders. We agree that in the best of all worlds, men would be asking you out in droves. Requiring all men to read *How to Succeed With Women* would be a good start. If men aren't asking you out, however, who is to blame? We call a woman who uses this excuse a prima donna, for she must have everything perfect and on her own terms. When things do not go her way, the prima donna blames the world for not meeting her needs. She complains and complains, but refuses to do anything to correct her situation.

The best way to overcome being a prima donna, no matter how bad your case is, is to start taking responsibility for your dating satisfaction. How is that done? By placing yourself in situations where men can approach you. You can also ask yourself if you put out a "mean vibe," or are unapproachable. Most women who use this excuse confess to feeling scared of men. In fact, they secretly like to keep men at a distance so they do not have to deal with them.

If you are a prima donna, you should know that most prima donnas end up alone, or go through a long string of failed marriages. The typical prima donna wants love and comfort from a man more than anything else in the world, yet she will not let men into her life. As a result, men feel that they can never win, and move on, searching for a woman who will let them win her heart.

THE FIVE-STEP CURE FOR THE PRIMA DONNA

Since there are no twelve-step groups for the recovering prima donna, we will provide you with the cure-all solution. To begin recovering, you must first explore the ways in which you put distance between yourself and men. Second, you must explore the ways in which you do not let men win when they are around you, and begin finding ways to let them win. Your third step is to then look at how you criticize and belittle men when they do not match up to the ideal male figure in your imagination. By becoming clear that you often judge men harshly when they inevitably do not act in the most ideal ways, you can begin letting men be the combination of wonderful and terrible traits that they are. Your fourth step is to learn to be more approachable. You do this by examining the vibe you put out, and by visiting places where men can approach you. The fifth and last step is to begin taking responsibility for your own dating satisfaction and make a commitment to stop blaming men. Eventually, you may even want to take on the dreadful habit of flirting with men and asking *them* out.

What Are Your Excuses?

We empathize with the painful emotions you might feel when you are in dating situations. Sometimes it hurts to look at the ways we've been rejected. Sometimes we just want to hide and let ourselves dwell on our excuses for a while. We recommend that you give yourself a little bit of time to resist the dating process. Finding a man is a long-term project and pacing yourself can be helpful.

After reading the above list of excuses, which ones do you use to avoid meeting men? What excuses not listed above do you use to justify being alone? What are the fatal flaws you attribute to yourself that keep you from living your dream life? Take time to write these down as a way to become conscious of your internal process. We now declare war on these excuses, along with any other self-deprecating internal conversations you may have. By being crystal clear about what they are and how they work, the battle can be won. Let's start right now!

The Goddess List of the Top Eight Routines for Meeting Men

We will continue to encourage you to examine the excuses that stop you while at the same time encouraging you to take small steps toward your specific goals. Our approach is a double-edged sword that alternates between taking specific actions in the world and examining the excuses that stop you from being successful. We will now explain eight routines for you to put into practice that will assist you in easily meeting qualified men.

Routine Number One: Flirt With Every Man Who Seems Interesting

Janet knows how to approach men in such a way that they are aware of her flirting signals. She knows that each man she comes into contact with is a potential date, and another possibility for love. Janet flirts and talks to men, knowing that eventually she will meet the man of her dreams. She is unrelenting in her search. Janet learned a long time ago that passivity leads to loneliness. As a result, she has dedicated herself to doing the work she needs to do to create a long-term relationship. Janet knows that every relationship is predicated on a thousand interactions; from first glance to first kiss; from first conversation to marriage proposal. Janet is successful with men because she is aware that she may have to go through a thousand interactions to achieve her long-term goals. Taking this approach gives her power to date, flirt, and have long- and short-term relationships with men. Ultimately, this approach will make all her dreams come true.

Flirting with men can often become one big mess. Men are often clueless when it comes to reading your signals, and worse when they attempt to flirt with you. You probably don't realize it, but men don't understand your signals, even when *you* think they are blatant. Men are usually so programmed to fail with women that the slightest sign of rejection usually has them fleeing. We have all seen a man approach a woman, attempt to flirt, and then give up after a brief conversation, or after receiving even the subtlest sign that she might not be totally thrilled to talk to him. Women often fail to realize that smiling at a man or flipping their hair is not enough to get a man's attention, or to convey interest. At every step along the way, there is work to do and information to communicate, so that a man will know what you are trying to tell him (we'll explore this in depth in chapter 6).

If you are interested in a man, it will be useful for you to keep looking for ways to keep him interested in you, especially if you have received signals that there is some degree of mutual attraction between the two of you. Janet is able to keep a man focused on her over the duration of an evening, and well beyond. She makes requests of him, asks him questions, gets his phone number, calls him, leaves him seductive messages, and keeps him focused on her throughout his day. More than anything, Janet is bold, strong, and persistent in her pursuit of a man and a potential relationship. Small consistent steps add up to a big seduction and big relationship success. Always remember that it takes dozens, if not hundreds, of initiations to get a man and keep him.

Routine Number Two: Get Encouragement From Friends

We've said it before and we'll say it again, so you get it: It is absolutely crucial to your success with men that you get support from your female friends to counsel, confide, discuss, strategize, and recharge yourself after letting yourself become vulnerable in the dating game. Allow your friends to encourage you. It will keep you in the game much longer than going at it alone. Our research shows that the most successful women have abundant support from other women in their lives.

The authors of this book have used this principle frequently to push each other to ask women for dates. We have encouraged each other to call a woman when we were scared to do so. We used our natural propensity for obnoxious antics to make bets on who could meet and flirt with the most women, and have even dared each other to approach beautiful women and talk to them. By supporting each other, we were able to stay in the game much longer than we would have if we were doing it all alone.

We know how nerve-racking it can be to face rejection and go through the trials and tribulations of single life. The support of friends will get you through dating troubles and successes every time. If you don't have close female friends, and mostly hang out with men, this must change immediately. Having female friends to encourage you will produce results that will far exceed any advice a man can give you (not including the authors' advice, of course). Besides, having too many male friends will make it much more difficult to meet men to date. Potential dates will likely be jealous or intimidated by your motley crew of male friends. In the process, your male friends will likely mess things up; many of them probably have a secret crush on you anyway.

Routine Number Three: Relentlessly Follow Up Leads about Men You Are Interested In

The most successful women stay focused on their goals. They follow up leads with men, focus on being approachable, and find ways to have fun in the process. The most successful women have several men to choose from at any given time. Having options with men gives these women freedom to choose which men to date and pursue. Consequently, they tend to have men competing for their attention. When a woman follows the program outlined in this book, and is out in the world flirting with men and seducing them she eventually won't care if one or many of them doesn't work out. Instead, she is focused on her long-term goals: having a special man, a male harem, or a love slave.

Our most successful female students are constantly meeting men at singles events, in restaurants, bars, on the street, everywhere. Like successful saleswomen, they do whatever it takes to get what they want. On the way to the end result, they relentlessly follow up leads and pursue the men they are interested in.

Routine Number Four: Prospect Many Men

Dating is a numbers game. The most successful women have learned to avoid placing all their eggs in one basket. They pursue lots of men. These women understand that dating can be an unpredictable ride. The game is not over until he has proposed, ring in hand, flowers in his teeth, and money in hand. And his bonus assignment is to take you on the most glamorous honeymoon of all time. You have to go through a lot of guys to find this one man.

Dating is also a numbers game in that you will have to flirt with a certain number of men to have a certain number ask you out: Of those, a certain number will meet your criteria. Of those, a certain number will want to explore a relationship with you. Of those, there may be one or maybe more that you will want to marry. Get it?

We also suggest you begin to view this process as a numbers game as a way to take away the serious edge. Dealing with numbers is not personal, it is just a made-up system of counting. It takes the focus off of whether an individual guy likes you, dislikes you, or even if your bad-hair day is affecting your desirability. When you view things as a numbers game, you can mathematically figure out how long it will take to get what you want, then view each task as a hoop to jump through on the way to fulfilling your goal.

By flirting with large numbers of men, your confidence and vitality will expand. When you are dating several men at any given time, your successes build on one another, and your expanded confidence helps you get more dates. This will cause more vitality and confidence in other areas of your life, as well. One definition of vitality is that it is a reflection of how bold you are in life. It can be measured by how much of a public personality you are willing to be, how willing you are to be outrageous, whether or not you are afraid of your sexual power, and whether or not you seem to apologize for who you are. When you flirt, date, and interact with large numbers of men, you will be more confident, vital, and bold.

Another aspect of going through many applicants (i.e., seeing it as a numbers game) is that it will lead to big results. Small and consistent actions eventually lead to successes. We all know the story of the tortoise who was successful because he was slow and steady, unlike the hare, who was quick, but lazy and sloppy. The same is true with the pursuit of men; consistent flirting will add up, eventually leading to success.

Routine Number Five: Pretend You Are a World-Class Goddess

We highly recommend that you model the clothes, look, approach, lines, thoughts, and general demeanor of successful women. One of our top male students, Dmitri, constantly acts as if he is "the man" whenever he is around women. He acts confident and playful. Dmitri secretly models himself after a character John Travolta played in the movie *Get Shorty*. He also uses his friend Roan as a role model. Dmitri has learned that if he does what Roan does, he tends to be more successful with women than if he doesn't. Modeling successful men has helped Dmitri become a success.

Karen models herself after a character in one of her favorite books. Before a date, Karen gets into the confident mood by pretending she is a bold and sexy woman in her favorite romance novel. She even purchased a skirt that she thought the character would wear. Karen knows that she tends to be a secretive and very private person, bordering on the reclusive. Karen has found ways to avoid dealing with men, not because she is not interested, but because she is afraid.

Karen began to model herself after a character in a novel as a way to break out of her habitual patterns and fear. She knew that if she approached the situation as she had in the past it would lead to more lonely nights and more failure. Taking on a different persona helped her get over her shyness. Like most things in this book, we are not suggesting using modeling as a one-time cure-all. Karen has used this tool to become more confident by modeling her behaviors after this character over several months of steady work. Karen progressed slowly and steadily until she met her goal. By having a role model, she was able to overcome her fears and be successful.

Routine Number Six: Leave the House Ready to Party

Looking good, no matter what situation you are in, is an important part of succeeding with men. Some women fail to prepare mentally and physically to meet that special someone. Women often ignore the possibility of meeting a man at an odd moment, or through a series of unusual circumstances. Yet there are thousands of couples for whom this was the case. From now on, prepare to meet the man of your dreams each time you leave the house. We are not suggesting that you always leave home in a business suit or in lingerie, though it might not be a bad idea. We are suggesting, however, that you always consider what you are wearing and whether or not it is appropriate for meeting men. Guys can be attracted to any style: ripped jeans, lingerie, sweat pants, or western-wear. What is most important is the attitude you convey through your dress. Part of your attitude is putting yourself together in an attractive style in which you feel comfortable and confident. Cupid may be looking down on you at the most unsuspecting moments. Keep this in mind at all times.

Routine Number Seven: Evaluate Men Quickly and Move on Quickly

You will have to improve your confidence and your self-concept if you want to be the hot and sexy babe who gets any man she wants. Eventually, you will no longer have time to waste on men who do not fit your criteria. Even though you don't yet realize it, you are a hot and sexy babe who is in demand and who is on a mission. You do not need the heartache of dating and becoming attached to a man who doesn't fit your long-term profile. When you settle for less than you really want, it pulls you off track from your long-term goals and will delay the meeting of the man of your dreams.

You must learn to quickly discern the gems from the pebbles; the men who might work for you from those that just do not fit. The purpose of having a list of criteria is to use it to evaluate so you do not base your decisions on looks, opening lines, or other superficial qualities. If you go to a party to meet men and there are none that meet your criteria, leave immediately. Why waste your time? You are there for one reason only— to find a man for the long-term!

Learning to evaluate men quickly and move on is probably a new skill for you. In fact, moving through men quickly may be the opposite of how you've done things in the past. Like many other skills we teach in this book, moving through men quickly will probably require practice and awareness. It may seem uncomfortable and unnatural the first few times you eliminate a man quickly because he lacks the qualities you are looking for. Eventually, it will become easier. We must continue to remind you that you are a hot commodity and do not have time to waste on losers. This awareness will greatly assist you in achieving your long-term goal.

Routine Number Eight: Make Dating a Game and Know the Rules

When we say "game" what do you think of? Many of us associate games with competition, complications, losing, and being upset. We want to shape your view of games into something that can be useful in dating. We want you to go back to a time in your life when games were still fun and joyful. Spend a moment going back in your memory banks, perhaps to age four or five. Go back to an age when you played with Barbies, cards, dolls, hide and seek, board games, or with any toy or game where you had fun and felt excited. Can you recall the imaginary worlds you created where there were no consequences? Who were your friends then? What were your favorite games at that age? What is one of the most crazy and fun experiences you remember from those days? For most of us there were times, even if they were few and far between, that were filled with fun, freedom, and play. We want you to use that sense of innocence, fun, creative expression, spontaneity, freedom, and wonder while you're dating.

For the remainder of this book, "game" means something that is fun, and has no negative consequence if you make mistakes while playing it. Use your memories of playing games or playing with dolls as your new model for the dating game. Use the same sense of freedom throughout the next few months as we take you through the process of finding a man.

YOUR OFFICIAL DATING GAME RULE BOOK

With all games there are rules. This is your very own dating game rule book. These rules are the most important set of guidelines and rules pertaining to dating that you have ever read, anywhere. Follow these rules and your life will improve overnight.

Rule One: Nothing Is Personal. Have you ever been playing a game when it suddenly stops being a game and somehow starts being personal?

Alenya was one of our students who played on a women's volleyball team and explained to us in great detail how easily and quickly games can change from fun to unpleasant. "The game was going great," she said, "when suddenly one of the players on the other team purposefully pounded the ball into one of my teammates and hurt her. Suddenly, it wasn't a game anymore. We were all shocked that another team would allow such aggression. It was a friend of mine who got hurt. Suddenly it wasn't a game anymore, it was real." Before the incident Alenya was having fun, feeling relaxed and "in the flow." Afterwards, it was hard to make it into a game anymore, because, suddenly it had became a fight.

Let's examine the notion that dating can become a game again. The first rule of the game is no matter what a man says or does, don't take it personally. If you approach a man at a bar and he ignores you, don't take it personally. If you are out with a hunk and he does not kiss you at the end of the date, even when you put out your best sexy signals, don't take it personally. Whatever the case may be, nothing men do or say is personal to you, and you must never make it personal. When you make things personal to you, it only leads to suffering and self-criticism, and delays winning the game.

As we mentioned in chapter 3, one of the best ways to handle any form of rejection is to find a way to creatively interpret it. When a man does something that you do not like, you find a way to interpret his actions that leaves the problem in his lap, not yours. If a man ignores you when you say "Hi" to him on the street, you might interpret this to mean that he just found out bad news about his mother being ill. Another creative interpretation might be that he has a hearing problem and didn't even hear you say hello. If a man wanders off when you meet him in a bar, you might creatively interpret his behavior to mean that he has a stomach ache from drinking too much beer. The point is that you do not really know the reasons why he rejected you anyway, so you might as well create an interpretation that empowers you, rather than one that makes you feel rotten about yourself. If you take men's behaviors personally, things will quickly shift from a game to a war. Your process will cease being fun and definitely become hard work.

When to take things personally: On the other hand, if a man does respond favorably to your flirtations, looks, or any other initiation on your part, you sure as hell *better* take it personally. In fact, you should try to savor it as long as possible. Remember, he is attracted to you. And the one who caused him to give you positive attention was none other than you. When things go well, it is a time to celebrate your power. The rule is that you feel acknowledged when things go well, and do not take it personally when things do not work out. You can't argue with the rules; they work.

Rule Two: Be Playful. We recently watched a forty-five-year old woman meet a muscular twenty-eight year-old guy. The woman came in to pick up a food order and she commented to the guy about one of the felt paintings of Elvis on the wall. He smiled, and joked with her about how silly the art looked. They joked back and forth about it for several minutes, both having a good time. Before she left he said, "It has been a pleasure meeting such a beautiful and lovely woman." She blushed and fanned herself with a menu, pretending that he had made her hot and bothered. By being spontaneous and playful, she created an opening for him to talk to her. She learned how to be playful and approachable, and consequently, probably has men wanting to date and flirt with her regularly. When you are playful, you can develop the same skills, and have similar results.

Rule Three: Don't Give Up. As with any game or skill, persistence makes all the difference. Even if you don't think you will win the game, you'll enjoy it much more if you don't give up, and play to win anyway. Besides, by reading this book, you are getting the inside secrets, the information that most women will never understand. You have the upper hand!

When you are persistent and playing to win, men will be more attracted to you. They will be attracted both by your tenacity and your determination. When you never cease going after what you want, success will come your way.

Rule Four: Use Probabilities. In the dating game we always recommend that our students use probabilities. Yes, math is fun for all of us (smile). Using probabilities will make things more fun and shift the focus of interacting with men into a game of numbers rather than a huge ego risk. One night you may see a wonderful man in a bookstore and use probabilities to create a percentage chance that you might exchange phone numbers. You might give yourself a fifty percent chance that he will talk to you. You might decide that there is a sixteen percent chance that you will exchange phone numbers, and an eight percent chance that you will sit and have coffee at a nearby restaurant that night. Probabilities are fun, and they take the serious edge off of the dating game.

These are the rules for dating and we expect you to follow them from now on. These rules provide you with a framework to make flirting and dating fun and painless. Do not let the simplicity and lightness fool you. These rules are very powerful and useful when you apply them to your life. When you follow these rules, dating becomes more of a game, less scary, and less intimidating. As in all games, you will have ups and downs, wins and losses. You cannot go into a game, putting yourself on the line and playing full out, and not expect to lose sometimes. Wins and losses are all part of the game, but staying strong and keeping the faith will help you every step along the way.

∞ *Conclusion*

This chapter has laid out for you the Copeland and Louis time-tested secrets for finding the man of your dreams. We began by smashing the "myth of scarcity," the myth that there are no single men out there. We then examined the excuses that stop you from meeting Mr. Right. Here are the excuses again, in case you have forgotten them already:

Excuse number one: It takes too much time. Now you know this is not true.

Excuse number two: It will hurt my reputation. Now you know how to handle this excuse without being paranoid.

Excuse number three: There are no good men. You can now see how this is ridiculous.

Excuse number four: I just can't do it. Now you know that you can do anything you set your mind to.

Excuse number five: I don't know how to get a man. This one may still be true, but the solution is contained in this book.

Excuse number six: I shouldn't have to work to get a man. Now you have the five-step cure for the prima donna, and see how you can make a relationship happen for you.

From the excuses we explored the solutions, in the form of the eight routines. The routines have been proven successful by a wide variety of women in a variety of situations. To recap:

Routine number one: Flirt with every man who seems interesting.
Routine number two: Get encouragement from friends.
Routine number three: Relentlessly follow up leads.
Routine number four: Prospect many men.
Routine number five: Pretend that you are a world-class goddess.
Routine number six: Leave the house ready to party.
Routine number seven: Evaluate men quickly and move on quickly.
Routine number eight: Make dating a game, and know the rules.

In the next chapter we will put these routines to work and create an action plan for getting out there and meeting men. Prepare for victory!

CHAPTER 5

Where the Boys Are

WE BEGAN THE PREVIOUS CHAPTER BY CLARIFYING WHAT HAS stopped you from meeting men. We then presented solutions to these problems that will bring you closer to meeting your ideal man. We will now explore your natural "markets," including the groups and organizations you already belong to, which can help you to find your mate.

Single men and women everywhere believe that if they do only one thing it will work and lead to the perfect relationship. Singles believe that if they place one ad or talk to one person at a coffee shop, it should lead to a relationship. In this chapter, we train you to increase your chances of creating the relationship you desire by placing you in situations where the likelihood of meeting someone is greatly increased. There is hope; don't worry.

∞ Men Are Everywhere

Men are everywhere. They are in grocery stores, on street corners, in dance clubs, on the bus, in museums, in airports, working out in health clubs, and buying books in your favorite book store. Men take courses and attend wine tasting parties, go to church and run in the park. The most important thing we want you to understand from is that men are everywhere. There is no shortage. You must begin noticing the men that are around you all the time. The perfect man is out there right now. You just haven't found him yet.

The Six Best Daily Routine Places to Meet Men

Our research shows that there are easy places to meet men. The problem? You probably ignore them. Begin by looking at your daily life and the places in which you see men. You can then determine what has stopped you from meeting them in the past, or if you have been automatically disqualifying them when you noticed them.

Once you begin to notice men in your life, we want you to create daily routines around seeing and interacting with men. Developing a routine means going to the same places at the same times, on the same days, each week. You will then become a "regular" wherever you go. Being a regular has many advantages. It opens you up to meeting and getting to know the other regulars, kind of like a membership in a special club. When you see men on a regular basis you have time to plot and plan how to approach a particular man, or even a group of men. To make matters even better, studies show that the more frequently two people see each other, the more attractive they appear to each other. That means that if you go to a coffee shop at the same time every day and see the same 33-year-old man drinking coffee and reading the paper, he will likely seem more attractive to you, and you to him, over time. We call this the "law of familiarity." Understanding this law will help you develop rapport with the men you see on a regular basis. The more they see you, the more they will desire you. Take our advice and become a "regular" at places like these:

BOOKSTORES

Are you looking for a smart, sexy, and imaginative man? By regularly visiting bookstores you can meet some very interesting men. In fact, many bookstores encourage singles to meet at their stores. They even feature singles events. On any weekend night, many large chain bookstores are packed full of singles hoping to meet each other. They are looking for something, and it isn't another John Grisham novel. They are looking for you!

Pauline met an attractive single man who was reading a business journal in the magazine section of a large chain bookstore. She smiled at him and commented on the cover story. The conversation went well, and Pauline found herself sitting and talking to him for the next hour in the store's coffee shop. They laughed, smiled, and set up another date for the following week. Pauline ended up dating this man for a few months and had a great time. She created an entire relationship solely because she had the courage to make a comment to a cute guy in the magazine section. When you show up at bookstores on a regular basis, this sort of thing can happen to you, too.

CHURCHES, SYNAGOGUES, AND MOSQUES

We have known dozens of women who have met men at church. One student claimed that church was the ultimate place to meet men. Her name was Diane and she was the poster girl for nerds everywhere. She wore big, thick glasses, dressed frumpy, and had absolutely no sense of style. Diane, however, was always active in her church and a devout follower of her faith. She decided to use this setting to meet men and eventually get married.

Diane was smart to take this approach. Church is a good place to meet someone because you have at least one thing in common, and you can meet in an environment which encourages discussion and community spirit. Church provided many opportunities for Diane. She attended singles events on weekends. She even told several members that she was interested in meeting a man of faith. Since many church communities promote dating and relationships from within the church, several members of her congregation began setting her up on dates. In the end, Diane ended up dating Mike. After a few months they became engaged, and eventually married.

A church or synagogue is a perfect place to meet your mate because of the large number of social connections and outlets it provides for all of its members. No matter what your faith is, we recommend church as an excellent way to meet your mate.

COFFEE SHOPS

Ready for simplicity? Coffee shops are rapidly becoming the hottest new place to meet qualified men. Singles all over the country are using them as potential meeting spots. Time and time again we have seen how useful it is to become a regular at a coffee shop. Coffee shops are perfect places to meet people because they tend to attract customers who come alone, and spend long periods of time chugging down their coffee or tea. When you spot a man in a coffee shop, it is easy to start a conversation with him about a current news item or any other topic that comes to mind—even the weather. After you have a man's attention, you can then move in for a date (don't worry, we'll show you how to do this later). Go out to your favorite coffee shop today; drink coffee, get excited, and raise hell.

THE GYM

Many of our students have had good luck making contacts with men at the gym. Our students claim that gyms are full of hunky macho men wanting to flirt. Our students, especially those in larger cities, meet fit and friendly singles at the gym.

We recommend the gym to you because working out improves your body, and frankly, your net worth to men. By working out a few times per week, you can lose weight, tighten your butt, and increase your stamina. It may even emit pheromones to men; a certain bonus.

The other advantage is that a lot of men go to the gym solely to meet women. When you find a man you like, you can become familiar with his workout schedule, start conversations with him, and melt his heart over time. You can get to know one another in a safe environment and allow yourself weeks or even months to slowly accelerate the flirting process.

RESTAURANTS

How do you handle a hungry man? Become the man handler. Restaurants are another great place to find dates. Men love to eat. You know that by now. Even if you get rejected, it is good for your self-confidence to be interacting with men who are out for the night and dressed attractively. The best restaurants for meeting men are the ones with a big bar area or patio seating.

By becoming familiar with a restaurant and a waiter or other staff member, you can easily turn food service into love service: From the young bus boy with his shy look and bangs hanging down, on through management staff, bartenders, waiters, and of course, customers.

∞ *Places to Meet Men Based on Your Hobbies and Interests*

Think about your hobbies and interests. If you are a party girl, look at our listing of party girl events to attend. If you are more athletic, look at places to meet men where you can work out in the process. There are a multitude of things you can do today to meet men.

We are about to give you some lists of places to meet men. Use these lists to spark your imagination, to try out a new approach, or to do something completely out of the ordinary for you. Circle anything on these lists that seems interesting to you, and consider attending several events each week that sound fun and exciting. Most importantly, use the lists to get into gear, to go out and experiment with new ideas and new places to meet men.

Keep track of your success at each type of event you attend. Track your feelings and your results. Look back at your journal to see which events were the most fun, and which were the least; which events produced the best results, which the worst. You can then visit the successful places more often and the least successful places less.

Here we go:

The Top Eight Cultural Events to Attend to Meet Men

1. Art openings
2. Fundraising parties and events
3. Art fairs
4. Classical music events
5. Museums
6. Concerts
7. Wine tasting parties
8. Film festivals

The Top Five Organized Singles Events For Meeting Men

1. Singles parties
2. Cruises
3. Church events
4. Pool parties
5. Museum singles nights

Eight Ways to Improve Your Health while Meeting Men

1. Yoga classes
2. The gym
3. Golfing
4. Co-ed sports leagues
5. Ice skating
6. Roller blading
7. Biking
8. Martial arts courses

Eight Things Men Volunteer for—and So Should You

1. Habitat for Humanity
2. The singles volunteer network
3. Political campaigns
4. The Red Cross
5. Nonprofit community organizations (e.g., hospitals or publicly funded radio stations)
6. Literacy programs
7. PTA's
8. Artists' organizations

Thirteen Ways to Learn While Meeting Men: Classes Men Will Likely Attend

1. Auto mechanics
2. Business fundamentals
3. Investment management
4. How to pick up women

5. Nature walks
6. Bird identification
7. Wine tasting
8. History or current events
9. Firearms safety and use
10. Body piercing
11. Alternative health
12. Toastmasters
13. Acting

Thirteen of the Freakiest Places to Meet Men

1. Adult sex clubs
2. The Society for Creative Anachronisms
3. Renaissance fairs
4. Rainbow gatherings
5. The "Burning Man Festival"
6. "Channeling" sessions and other way-out new age stuff
7. Psychic fairs
8. Sci-fi conventions
9. Performance art gigs
10. Weird nightclubs
11. Nudist clubs, associations, and organizations
12. An S&M night club (Caution! Don't go alone.)
13. Motorcycle conventions

Eight Stupid, Strange, and Silly Ways to Meet Men

This list is intended to open up your mind to the unlimited possibilities available to you.

1. Call a phone sex line
2. Go to a strip club's amateur night

3. Become a porn model
4. Write to prisoners (not recommended)
5. Go to Antarctica (ratio: 1 woman to 250 men)
6. Dress as a man and go to a men's only club
7. Go to a Militia group meeting
8. Join a multi-level-marketing group and hit on the guy who makes the most money

Six Places to Get Spiritual and Find a Mate

1. Personal growth seminars
   For example: the Forum, MORE University, Miracle of Love
2. New Age spiritual communities
3. Meditation class
4. Spas
5. "The Artist's Way" courses
6. Support groups for any addiction or health problem

Six Things Your Friends and Family Can do to Help

1. Set you up with their exes
2. Set you up with their relatives
3. Set you up with their co-workers
4. Set you up with their friends
5. Set you up on blind dates
6. Help you create a singles party at your home

Ten Places to Meet a Certifiable Macho Man

1. Adventure travel groups
2. Cigar nights
3. Rugby games

4. Auto shows
5. Boxing matches
6. Roller derby matches
7. Professional wrestling events
8. Strip clubs
9. Deer hunting clubs
10. Target shooting ranges

Eight Places to Find the Intellectual Man of Your Dreams

1. Libraries
2. Book discussions
3. Historical society presentations
4. Political debates
5. Book conventions
6. Computer conventions
7. Graduate school parties
8. MENSA meetings

Thirteen Places to Meet Rich Men

1. Medical conventions
2. Club Med
3. Expensive cruises
4. Law conferences
5. Support groups for auto racers
6. Country clubs
7. Golf courses
8. Tax court
9. The stock exchange
10. Banking conventions

11. The homes of Louis and Copeland
12. The Sundance Film Festival
13. Support Groups for Hollywood actors

Twelve Places for Party Girls to Meet Men

1. Bars
2. Punk rock concerts
3. Crashing house parties
4. Attending DEA sting operations
5. Backstage at a rock concert
6. Raves
7. Outdoor music events
8. Tattoo conventions
9. Heroin needle exchange programs
10. Drug rehab programs
11. Prisons
12. The Jerry Springer Show

The Seven Clubs to Join or Attend to Meet Men

1. Film discussion groups
2. Book clubs and salons
3. Dancing
   a. Swing
   b. Folk
   c. Punk
   d. Latin
   e. Ballroom
4. Outdoor adventure clubs
5. Singles travel clubs

6. Hunting and fishing clubs

7. NRA events

Five Unusual Circumstances in which to Meet Men

1. Waiting in a line

2. On the scene of a car accident

3. At a service station

4. On the train or bus

5. In a laundromat

Three Ways for the Shy Woman to Meet Men

1. PERSONAL ADS

Meeting men through personal ads in newspapers or magazines is another good, low-risk way to practice your flirting skills. You can interact with men and get to know them safely through in-depth conversations, before actually meeting them in person.

Most men who place ads will be pretty honest about what they are looking for in a woman. They may lie a bit about what they look like—for instance, about their weight—but otherwise it is a good way to meet them. As in any interaction with men, you must be cautious. We consider safety issues to be crucial for women and you must always protect yourself. Follow your instincts when it comes to safety. Never agree to meet a man if you don't feel safe.

Tips on Writing Effective Personal Ads. The ad should be short. Many people think that longer ads will work better, but our experience shows that this is simply not true. Short messages are intriguing; they leave male readers wondering and dreaming of the divine creature who wrote the ad.

Long ads often put men off. If you've ever looked at personal ads you have seen the ones that go on and on for twenty or thirty lines about everything she ever wanted from a man—down to the type of fabric he enjoys wearing and the color of his favorite belt buckle. By being overly specific, you make men feel uncomfortable that they can't measure up. Most men will just consider you to be stuck up. That is not to say that you should be overly vague either. A solid personal ad offers some specific details about yourself that are honest, yet leaves room for mystery.

The cardinal sin in writing a personal ad is to be too demanding. To get a man's attention from an ad you must first step into his shoes, and try to understand what he considers attractive. A long list of demands including marriage and kids within the next four weeks will scare off most guys, as will ads about staying home to play with the children. These are female fantasies, not male fantasies. Remember the difference and you will be miles ahead of the competition.

A man is interested in what you will provide for him and what he will gain from the relationship, not in the problems and neuroses you might suffer from or the insecurities you might have. The time to be demanding is when you sort through all the ads and figure out who to respond to. You will likely toss out over sixty percent of the responses. These will probably be from horny guys looking for sex. The other responses will probably be worth considering. Placing and responding to personal ads is a good way to practice interacting with men and will bring you at least one step closer to meeting that magic man.

Words and Facts about Yourself to Avoid in Your Ad. There are several phrases it's good to avoid in your ad:

Marriage minded. As mentioned earlier, this will likely turn off men who would otherwise be potential candidates. Even men who are looking to be married will likely avoid you. They probably do not want to hurry the marriage process and would rather get to know someone over time before considering marriage.

Lonely. This is a code word for loser. Telling a man that you are lonely and that your life sucks is not attractive at all. It puts you into a category with the losers and the desperate, and will keep you there, too.

Personal ads are filled with clichéd drivel. It is important that your ad stand out so that a man will circle your ad and be intrigued with the idea of meeting you. Most newspapers and magazines feature pages and pages of ads. Using clichés will turn off men and put you into the boring category.

Some women make the error of telling the world that they are in the process of mending from past hurts. These women tell everyone who reads their ad that they are recovering from the aftershocks of breaking up after a six-year relationship. They make a point to tell the world that they are now on the rebound and are vulnerable. Any man who has half a brain will avoid women who describe themselves this way. We know you are vulnerable, but mentioning this fact in an ad makes you *more* vulnerable. It is not a selling point. In fact, it makes you sound like a high-maintenance woman who will be trouble from the get-go. Any man who dates you even once will be worried that he will hurt you or that you will be too needy. Keep this information to yourself and everything will turn out much better.

Words and Facts about Yourself to Use in Your Ad. *Energetic/fun/loves life.* "Energetic" means you are happy with your life and do not need a man to entertain or take care of you. "Loving life" implies that you are a good companion and someone who is low-maintenance. By using these code words you convey that you are a woman who is exciting and has a life she enjoys.

Sexy. Men love sex and seek out women who want sex as frequently and as intensely as they do. So by using sex in your ad, you will get every horny jerk who reads the ad to respond. This may not be good, because you will have to sort through the huge number of ads and pull out the few normal guys in the pack to consider dating. It's good to use, however, if you need to get your numbers up.

We recommend you only use the word *sexy* when it is combined with other adjectives to balance out the sexual implications. For example, you might write, "highly successful CEO-type, enjoys the outdoors, loves life, is attractive and sexy, and seeks romance." Using the ad just mentioned will get positive attention, without attracting sleazy men. In this case, mentioning you are sexy shows that you are comfortable and confident with yourself.

Romantic. This is a good word because it implies both sexual interactions as well as chivalrous acts on the part of the man. Romantic women are gentle souls who love being swept off their feet by a loving man. Romantic women appreciate what men bring to a relationship.

Easy going. An easy going woman is someone who will let the guy be himself around her. An easy going woman is accepting, sweet, and nonjudgmental.

Low Maintenance. Men believe that women are constant trouble. If you think you are low-maintenance, you can say so. It will attract men. Who knows? If it's not exactly true, they won't find out until it's too late, anyway.

2. THE INTERNET

Are you really shy? Scared of talking to men? Scared of being vulnerable or getting hurt? Of course you are. No problem: there is a place where you can practice flirting with men and refine your style, where any rejection seems minimal, and successes are easy. This place is the Internet.

If you are lonely, shy, or even horny, you must take a spin on the international dating superhighway called the Internet. The parts of the Internet we are concerned with here are the World Wide Web, personal ads newsgroups, pay sites, Internet chat rooms and America Online.

The World Wide Web. The Web is, by and large, a dumb place to look for mates. The Web is also where most women go right away. Men love to search Web pages because of the pornography options. Finding attractive pictures is not the same, however, as interacting with men. To actually find men to interact with romantically, you need to leave the Web alone and concentrate on personal ads newsgroups, chat rooms, and pay sites for singles.

Usenet. With a Newsreader application you can explore "Usenet," a selection of thousands and thousands of special interest "newsgroups." Anyone can post to most of these groups, putting up letters that anyone can read and respond to, either in the group or personally directed to their email addresses. There is a large section of groups that consist mostly of personal ads, and that is where you want to start placing your own. Use the same model as mentioned above in the "personal ad" section.

Pay Sites. There are many singles-only sites available online that offer opportunities for singles to list personal ads and view ads by category. You can search, for instance, by location, interest, etc. We have found that these are mostly a waste of time and too expensive. The men that frequent these sites are usually only wanting sex and nothing else. While there will be an occasional man who may fit your criteria, we recommend you skip them and utilize AOL instead.

Chat Room. Most easily accessed if you are on a large service like America Online, chat rooms are places where everybody types at once, and what they write shows up on each other's screens. Most of what goes on in chat rooms is infantile ("Hey, who's here?" or "Are there any women here?") But with some looking you can find eligible bachelors and men to flirt with.

AOL. No, we're not representatives from America Online. No, this is not a commercial. We do, however, recommend using America Online. We've even nicknamed it America's online dating network. We recommend AOL because they offer numerous opportunities for singles to meet. You can create several different ads and screen names, which will attract different types of men. You might place one ad that discusses your love of spirituality, one that mentions that you are looking for a professional man, one ad about another of your hobbies, and one just for sex. You can use as many different profiles as you want. You can also keep track of the type of men who respond to each one and see which group or groups you most want to pursue.

Another avenue available on AOL is instant messaging. This system allows you to send private messages to men who are conversing in the chat room areas. You will likely get lots of horny guys hitting on you (and this will quickly become irritating), but you can also meet men with whom you have a lot in common. One of our female students met her husband on AOL while discussing Ireland in a chat room. Such connections happen all the time.

Can you find men you will end up dating on the Internet? Possibly, but bear in mind several things. First, you are there to practice. Second, he may be a jerk. Third, he may live far away, be married, or be holding back some other unpleasant surprise. If you keep these three caveats in mind, you can definitely have success flirting with men on the Internet.

The Top Four Reasons to Meet Men Online

1. You get to practice. We advise all our students to hone their flirting skills on the Internet.

2. You get successes. Many very good and honest men are online. These are men who really do want a deep connection with a woman and don't like the bar scene or have the time to be out in the world looking for women. We have known many people who have met online and ended up marrying. It does happen.

3. Casual sex. If you want casual sex, this is one of the easiest places to get it. You can also meet men for phone sex. We're just giving you this information in case that is your secret desire.

4. You can achieve unexpected results. People do find the partner of

their dreams on the Internet. It happens every day. You simply must be persistent and willing to put the time in.

3. USING A DATING SERVICE

Dating services continue to be a popular method for setting up dates for singles. You can usually watch a video of potential men first before selecting anyone to go out with. The question lies in the number of members. Services in larger cities tend to be better because there is a wider selection. These services are good for shy women because much of the work is in waiting for men to contact you. If you have the extra money and are willing to be patient, you might pursue this option.

∞ How to Think about Finding Places to Meet Men

The big mistake singles make is to pursue just one or two candidates at a time. This reduces their probability of success because they simply don't meet and flirt with enough men.

Janet was a failure with men, and came to us for help. She came to us nearly in tears, complaining that she couldn't find any single men. Upon further diagnosis, we learned that Janet only searched for men in two places: singles events at her church and at her favorite lunch spot. While neither of these places are particularly bad, the problem for Janet was that she simply didn't visit enough places on a consistent basis. Janet continued on this losing path for years, even though she didn't come any closer to her goal of being married.

Many women who contact us are in Janet's situation. They only pursue a few avenues in their search for a man, and are surprised when they fail to achieve their long-term goals. Remember that this is a numbers game and the trick is to be in contact with the maximum number of men possible.

We teach the "scatter shot" approach. In this approach you aim at many "targets" at once in the hope that the bullet (or in this case,

Cupid's arrow) will land in the heart of one eligible bachelor. In practical terms, you draw on many groups of friends, organizations, hobbies, and other social networks during your search. One of the problems with Janet's approach was that she simply did not give herself enough opportunities to meet men. By listing your "natural markets" and creating a game plan to tap each one, you are more likely to be successful. Taking the "scatter shot" approach can expand your field of vision to see available men you were not aware of before.

Making Your Lists

We recommend that you spend a few minutes making the following lists. We will work with them throughout the remainder of this chapter.

1. *List all of the formal groups you belong to.* This can include groups like the PTA, AA, Lion's Club, AARP, the Association of Beer Lovers, religious groups, fraternal groups, or any other group you belong to.

2. *List any work-related organizations you belong to.* This can include trade organizations, professional organizations, and even business networking groups associated with your business. For instance: the State Bar Association, Women's Entrepreneur's Association, National Jewelers' Association, the Alliance of Hearing Professionals, Realtors associations, the International Professional Secretary's Organization, and so on.

3. *List the organizations you belong to.* This can include groups like a neighborhood homeowners association, Greenpeace, YWCA, World Mustard Association, March of Dimes, Women's Philanthropy Institute, or a political group of any persuasion.

4. *List the places you go to on a regular basis.* Include the train you take to work in the morning, coffee shop, grocery store, book store, gym, or anywhere else that you visit at least once every nine days or so.

5. *List the friends and family you most frequently communicate with.* List them in order of frequency.

6. *List the friends you talk to infrequently.* List them regardless of their geographical location.

7. *List the dating networks in your area that you could join.* This includes any singles groups, singles social societies, personal ad opportunities, dating services, professional Yentas, and so on.

8. *List the hobbies you enjoy in which you could potentially meet men.* Include hobbies like horseback riding, hiking, wine tasting, art, movie production, bowling, dancing, Jello eating contests; any hobby in which men are likely to join and attend.

9. *List the resources in your area which support singles in meeting one another.* Include any potential resources you could use if you decided to. Remember, the operative word here is *could*. We are looking for possible groups, not those you definitely will pursue. Having this list in front of you will assist you down the road in creating your specific action plan.

Later in this chapter we will create an action plan in which you identify goals, along with specific dates and times at which you will pursue each network and each organization. You will then use this list to help you get into action and draw upon resources that will help you find a man. This list can become a gold mine of ideas for you. When we go through this exercise with our students, we are often surprised that a woman who claims to have very few opportunities to find dates suddenly sees that there are dozens of areas in her life where she can find men.

◌ *Where to Meet Men*

You are now armed and ready to go to war. You are now ready to capture the heart of Mr. Right. The next section will help you in creating your game plan. Your game plan will help you open up new options and new opportunities to meet and date men. Your game plan will also highlight key friends and groups you will begin to tap for assistance in your game.

Most of us go through life oblivious to the groups and social networks we belong to. We go through life feeling basically alone. As a result, we focus on feeling disconnected from other people. When you create your initial game plan, begin by focusing on the areas of your life in which you are connected to people. Go through your daily life and look at all the different people you contact, be it at work, the bank, the laundromat, the bus, wherever you contact other people. What if you saw each person whom you contact in your daily and social life as someone who could assist you in meeting your mate? Your close friends and even family members can be very useful resources in meeting men.

Let's look at Dina's lists. By listing out all of her potential groups, Dina constructed a plan to utilize this information for the maximum results. She created a plan to visit the groups on her list. The groups that produced the best results—by which we mean introduced her to the most men—she visited again. The groups which seemed barren of potential men she visited less often, or not at all. Dina also used her connections to start spreading the news that she was in the market for a man. She told all of her girlfriends about her plans and asked them all for leads and to set her up on blind dates. Let's look at Dina's lists, and see how she used them:

WORK RELATIONSHIPS

These are relationships with co-workers in which Dina feels comfortable and safe sharing her goals. These co-workers can all help set Dina up on blind dates and give her leads for potential men.

1. Dan/co-worker
2. Jean/co-worker
3. Barbara/co-worker
4. Jim/client who is a friend
5. Lucy/co-worker

6. Donna/boss who is also a friend
7. Darlene/co-worker
8. Pam/client who has become a friend

CLOSE FRIENDS

For the sake of this exercise, we define a close friend as someone you talk to at least once every nine days. All of the friends on Dina's list know she is in the market for a man and have agreed to support her.

1. Paula
2. Carole
3. Sara
4. Ginny
5. Ron
6. Louis
7. Nancy

MEDIUM CLOSE FRIENDS

We define medium close friends as the people Dina talks to at least a few times per month. Dina likes the people on the list, and even feels close to them. She has asked each of them to help her meet men.

1. Pat
2. Rick
3. Robin
4. Tom
5. Erica
6. Jill
7. Marcy
8. Jennifer

DISTANT FRIENDS

We define distant friends as those she is glad to see when they run into each other.

1. Myrna
2. Jill

3. Chris
4. Tony
5. Claire
6. Steve
7. Molly
8. Carlita
9. Larry
10. Dale
11. Maureen
12. Cathy
13. Melinda
14. Jack
15. Frank
16. Loren

FAMILY MEMBERS

These are family members who are close enough to Dina that she asked them to be on her dating team.

1. Mom
2. Dad
3. Theresa/sister
4. Jim/brother in law (married to Theresa)
5. Bonnie/sister
6. Conrad/brother in law (married to Bonnie)
7. Roy/brother
8. Vince/uncle

COUPLES

Dina also made a list of friends who are already married or in committed relationships. She has contacted each couple and asked them to help her succeed in her dating game.

1. Pat and Mark
2. Heather and Ray

3. Tracy and Seamus

4. Barbara and Don

5. John and Exene

7. Rich and Charlene

8. Cliff and Mary Ellen

9. Lisa and Mic

10. Lilly and Jonathan

FORMAL GROUPS

1. Toastmasters

2. State Historical Society

INFORMAL GROUPS

1. Women's Book Club

2. Film Society

3. Bird Watchers Association

ORGANIZATIONS

1. League of women voters

2. Republican party

3. Audobon Society

4. Save the Children

5. The Special Olympics

6. National Rifle Association

WORK ORGANIZATIONS

1. National Association of Writers and Editors

2. Writer's Club

3. Technical Writers Association

HOBBIES

1. Rollerblading

2. Internet

3. Nature hiking

4. Meditation group

5. Dog-related events
6. Garden Group

DINA'S LIST OF PLACES SHE GOES ON A REGULAR BASIS

1. Starbuck's coffee shop
2. The bookstore
3. Laundromat
4. The gym
5. The dog park

DATING NETWORKS

1. Local weekly newspaper personal ad
2. Dating services
3. Singles groups
4. Church singles group

Putting the Plan into Action

After creating her extensive list of affiliations and support people in her dating game, the next step for Dina was to create her social calendar for the next few months. By setting up her social calendar, Dina made commitments to attend meetings, to go out on dates with girlfriends where she might meet men, to call friends for support in her dating game, and to schedule time to place and respond to personal ads.

DINA'S CALENDAR

GOAL:
Go out on 20 dates over the next two months

INCREMENTAL MEASUREMENTS:
Weekly target goals

Goals for Week One

- Ask Paula and Carole to support her in her project and to work through this book with her as a way to support her dating.

- Flirt with two men at the gym.
- Attend lecture series at local university and talk to at least four men.
- Call John and Exene and ask them for potential leads for dates. Follow up on those leads.
- Place a personal ad on the Internet.
- Call Ron and Nancy for leads on dates. Follow up on those leads.

Goals for Week Two

- Place a personal ad in a local paper.
- Call Myrna, Jill, Chris, and Tony for dating leads. Follow up on those leads.
- Flirt with at least two men at the dog park.
- Attend meditation group and flirt with Frank, an attractive man in the group.
- Attend Toastmasters meeting and get at least one date.
- Go on *qualifying dates* (see chapters 8 and 9) with any men with whom she's made dates.

Goals for Week Three

- Attend church singles group to see if there are any qualified men who seem interesting.
- Flirt with at least three men while rollerblading.
- Call Rich and Charlene for leads on dates. Follow up on those leads.
- Attend wine tasting course and look for suave men to date.
- Call Scott for leads on dates. Follow up on those leads.
- Go on qualifying dates with any men with whom she's made dates.

Goals for Week Four

- Attend a singles dance.
- Attend writers group and look for men.
- Call Claire, Steve, Molly, and Carlita for leads on dates. Follow up on those leads.

- Call up the DJ on favorite radio station and ask him out on a date.
- Call Cliff and Mary Ellen for leads on dates. Follow up on those leads.
- Get information about the singles volunteer network.
- Go on qualifying dates with any men with whom she's made dates.

Goals for Week Five
- Go out to a dance club with co-workers Jean, Barbara, and Lucy.
- Call Larry, Dale, and Maureen for leads on dates. Follow up on those leads.
- Attend Bird Watcher's Association meeting.
- Call Lisa and Mic for leads on dates. Follow up on those leads.
- Set up party and invite at least fifteen people. Ask all of them to bring single friends.
- Go on qualifying dates with any men with whom she's made dates.

Goals for Week Six
- Result: Personal ad came out and there are responses from 22 men. Dina promises to call back three men a day and screen them.
- Flirt with at least four men on the Internet.
- Go on a singles camping trip sponsored by the state park system.
- Call Lilly and Jonathan for dating leads. Follow up on those leads.
- Sign up for a personal growth seminar.
- Call Steve and Earl about dating their friends. Follow up on those leads.
- Go on qualifying dates with any men with whom she's made dates.

Week Seven
- Call back eight men who responded to personal ad.
- Flirt with three men at the bookstore.
- Call Cathy, Melinda, Jack, Frank, and Loren for leads on dates. Follow up on those leads.
- Attend an opening at a local art gallery.

- Attend a Toastmasters meeting.
- Go on qualifying dates with any men with whom she's made dates.

Week Eight
- Attend party with Ginny.
- Call back four men who responded to the personal ad.
- Attend the Film Society new film series opening night.
- Attend a political debate on a hot new topic.
- Call Rick, Robin, and Tom for leads on dates. Follow up on those leads.
- Go on qualifying dates with any men with whom she's made dates.

Creating Your Own List

Now it's your turn to start listing the organizations, hobbies, and friendship circles you are part of. At this stage of the game it is important that you concentrate on creating the most comprehensive list you can. Don't worry whether or not certain people seem applicable or relevant; just write down everyone that comes to mind. Later you can determine if they are applicable. By making your list you will be able to see the areas and groups in which you could ask for dating leads. Copy the structure from this book as a model for your own plan. Utilize this list as a way to make requests of friends and family members, and use the other areas as places to meet men. After you make the lists, the game will become easier.

Now you must find ways to turn your list of possibilities into a specific to-do list. The easiest way to create specific plans is to create a goal and then reduce its parts to the smallest increments. Create weekly goals, monthly goals, and even two-month goals. Make this process your own. Create it in any way that you feel supports you in fulfilling your goals. We are not creating random busy-work. Our students have consistently had positive results by using this system. We want you to create a game plan in which all of your dreams are realized. This is an important step.

⌒ *Conclusion*

The point of this chapter is to get you into *action* and meeting men. We've shown you how to create an action plan and offered concrete and specific examples of successful plans. We have revealed the limitations of "one-thing thinking" ("I'll do one thing, and meet a man!") and dispelled the myth of scarcity. We encourage you to replace these naive and overly simplistic ideas with a concrete plan for meeting men and achieving your relationship goals. When you follow the structure we've outlined, you will be truly dangerous and powerful in the dating game. Congratulations. You have done wonderfully so far. Now it's time for the next step.

CHAPTER 6

Flirting Without Disaster

WAKE UP, GIRLS! IN THIS CHAPTER YOU'RE GOING TO LEARN THINGS that will change your dating life forever. You've learned where the men are, and that there are *lots* of them. Now you are going to find out that there are far, far more *good* applicants than you ever dreamed of before. You are going to annihilate the myth that "there are no good men." You're going to learn how to find them, how to keep them around, how to talk to them, flirt with them, and to get them on a date. You're going to learn how to handle the inevitable problems that men cause in flirting. You'll learn how to keep the "good man" who doesn't know how to flirt, instead of kicking him out of your life prematurely. You're going to learn the essential, important tests you must run on men during the flirting interactions, to separate the keepers from the losers. And to make matters that much better, it will even be fun!

Get ready for *flirting without disaster*.

∞ So You've Found Men to Talk to: Now, How Do You Do It?

Many women are smart and analytical in their approach to life, but surprisingly vague and prone to "magical thinking" in their interactions with men. They think that *real* romance should "just happen." They are offended by the idea that they might have to put thought into creating a seduction that leads to a great relationship. They want it to unfold naturally, and will disqualify any relationship that seems to require "scheming," or learning techniques. This approach disqualifies good applicants before they're even given a chance.

Meanwhile, men make matters worse by approaching romance the same way they would a business deal. Believe it or not, a man might tell himself, "Women say they like men who are direct and honest. What could be more honest than telling them about my sexual attraction to them?" He'll then try to seduce a woman by explaining to her how logical it would be for them to have a relationship, or to have a one-night stand. This practical, logical approach drives women away.

While men tend to be too logical in their approach to relationships, women tend not to be logical enough. While a man might expect to create a business plan of love and have you logically agree to it (and then hop in the sack with him), women tend to get upset if it looks like the seduction isn't "just happening" all by itself. Women get upset when the romance is anything other than spontaneous fireworks and hearts fluttering, or the deep stares and slow advances of a romance novel.

Neither of these approaches will work. You must have spontaneous, warm feelings in order to build a relationship, but such feelings rarely happen on their own. You must intentionally create interactions in which those feelings can arise. You have to create interactions in which feelings of romance and attraction can start to "just happen." The first step of creating that "space for romance" is in your flirting.

∞ *What Is Flirting?*

Flirting comprises steps three and four of the Master Plan. It is a key part of interviewing and testing numerous applicants. In chapters 4 and 5 we taught you where to meet applicants. In this chapter you will start the interviewing process.

To date men successfully, you must know something about flirting. Flirting is not practical or direct, but it does follow basic principles, and once you understand them, you'll be miles ahead of other women in talking to and being successful with men. As we told you early on in this book, we will not give you overly simplistic or trite advice on dating. We also avoid this approach in terms of flirting. Flirting is a paradoxical dance; but we can teach you the basic steps.

Flirting is also a game. Think about kids playing together. They don't try to accomplish anything in their play; all they are interested in is having fun with whatever game they are playing. They take on roles with each other effortlessly. If they play cops, one kid is the police officer, another is the criminal. If they play house, one kid is the mother, while the other is the father. If they play doctor, one kid is the doctor and the other is the patient. They may dress up to get into the roles better. They let their imaginations run free. It's all ultimately meaningless, but they don't care; they just want to play the game.

Most of the time kids at play aren't overly concerned about winning. Just being together playing is enough to make them happy. Kids relate by playing, and if they can play, they feel related.

Play is just as important to adults as it is to children, but adults play differently. First, let's look at how men play with men. Men usually don't think of it as play, but watching sports together, or talking about sports, is a way men play with each other. After all—as you are well aware— sports are ultimately meaningless. Which team wins the NBA title this year really isn't going to make that big a difference in the grand scheme of things, no matter what your male friends might think. By caring about the games together, by watching them, yelling and screaming at the players, and keeping track of the player's statistics, men play together. This play leaves them feeling the togetherness and unselfconscious love for each other that kids feel, even if they would never put it that way.

The other way men play together is through joking with each other: shooting the bull, exchanging obnoxious banter, and playing jokes on each other. The little jokes that men make about each other, the loving insults traded back and forth, are how men bond with one another.

Men and women, on the other hand, play together differently. While *horseplay* is the way men play together, *flirting* is the way men and women play together. Most men don't know this, so they often try to flirt with women the way they would *play* with other men. That won't work. Women, on the other hand, often attempt to flirt by taking emotional risks and playing with emotional availability. This is not play from men's perspective, and so this also doesn't work. Most women don't know how to flirt, so they also don't know how to handle men's flirting mistakes. This can lead to misunderstandings that make women disqualify men for the wrong reasons. Then the game is over.

The challenge you face in flirting is men's lack of skill at it, combined with your own. In this chapter, we'll correct all that. We'll show you all the possible problems his lack of flirting skill can cause, and how you can get the flirting interaction back on track. We'll show you how to control the speed of the seduction by giving him emotional "wins" and "losses." And we'll teach you the key tests you must perform during flirting, to find out accurately if he's your prince charming, or simply more trouble than you need. We'll show you how to be approachable for flirting interactions, how to approach a man, and how to close the deal and set up a date with a man, even with a man who's too shy to ask you out properly. By the end of this chapter you'll be able to flirt with those men, be able to emerge from the game knowing what the man is like, and get a date if you want it.

∞ What Flirting Does

Flirting is a key to building a successful relationship. It is a way you can initially make contact with a man and find out if he is even remotely close to what you ideally want in a man. If you do not flirt, you will have trouble finding enough male "applicants" to test. If you master flirting, you will always be able to find men to date and to have relationships with.

Here's what flirting does:

Flirting Builds Rapport

Having "rapport" simply means that he likes talking to you, and that he feels good doing it. There is a spark, a connection between the two of you. When you are flirting, you usually aren't talking about anything heavy or deep. You are probably talking about something fun, or silly. You are like children playing. He feels pleasure out of it, and so do you. This creates rapport. Having rapport creates a bond. The bond creates the opening for a date, and a date can become the foundation for your relationship.

Flirting Makes You Both Feel Safe By Returning To the Same Topics Over and Over

As you'll learn in this chapter, in flirting you'll often have a "running joke" with a man. For example, Molly, a 44-year-old college instructor, had been flirting at her gym with a man who worked out at the same time she did for several weeks. The joke began because Ted always seemed to be using the same exercise machines and weight machines that Molly wanted. She finally made a sarcastic comment that he was trying to foul up her routine. This became a running joke between them and an opening for many conversations. Molly would see him using a machine and would pretend to be an impatient and angry exercise queen demanding that he speed up his routine and get out of her way. They would tease each other frequently. It became an opening for more serious conversations and built trust in the process. Molly started going to the club at the same times as Ted, and their connection continued to expand and deepen.

Since then, almost every time she's seen him, one of them has built on this comic scene. He's always happy to see her, and they've built a special little world together. Now, Molly always has something to talk about when she sees him.

Flirting Lets You Test the Man

A woman who dates succesfully determines whether a man fits within the realm of what she is looking for or if he's what she is looking to avoid. We'll go over the nine flirting tests in the next chapter.

Flirting Helps You Feel Safe with Each Other

We stress the importance and seriousness of safety with all of our female students; of not being naive and overly trusting of strangers. We know that a woman's number one fear when she first meets a man is that he might be a dangerous psycho. When you play with a man through flirting, you are both able to relax. The time you take flirting lets you see if you feel safe with him, without having to reveal too much about yourself.

Flirting Makes You Happy

When you flirt, you are spontaneously and creatively making up new ways to have fun. It is an easy way to "get in the flow." You can't do this if you're depressed, needy, resentful, moody, and shut down. Flirting creates a state of being energetic and creative, which is quite simply not compatible with feeling down. Practicing flirting as we describe in this chapter will actually take you out of your moodiness and make you into the alive, vital kind of woman that men want to be with. It will have you be the woman you have always wanted to be and access the most romantic and perspicacious parts of yourself.

Flirting Gets You The Guy!

There's not much more to say. The more you flirt successfully with a man, the more natural it will be for him to want to have a relationship with you. The more men you flirt with, the more applicants you go through, the shorter the time it will take to find the right one—or ones, in the case of those wishing to create a harem of hunks.

Making a Man into a Flirting "Winner"

During flirting interactions, the man is looking for some positive feedback from you that he is winning you and/or winning with you. If you think you might like the guy, you need to give him this feedback, even if his every word and movement is not absolutely perfect. Giving men "wins" is extremely simple at this stage. Smile at him. Laugh at his jokes. Look into his eyes. Be forgiving of the boneheaded blunders he'll inevitably make during flirting (much more on that later). Listen to him brag and find something about him to admire. Or tell him about what you admire in him. Bingo: you're flirting! That's really all you need to do.

As you get to know him better, of course, giving him "wins" will become more personal and complicated; at this stage, as long as you aren't a scowling demon, he'll be back for more.

Being able to give a man emotional wins—and emotional losses, which we'll cover later—is an absolutely core and crucial part of creating flirting interactions that get you the date.

∞ Flirting Your Way to the Date

The main problem you face is that men, like everybody else, resist change—even changes they would probably like. It's entirely possible that dating you would be the best thing that ever happened to the man you desire. In spite of the truth that you may be the best thing that ever happened to him, he'll resist you because he resists change. You represent the *potential* for pain, discomfort, nagging, commitment, even—gasp!—*monogamy*. At the very least, you represent unfamiliarity. You are a monkey wrench of disorder in his otherwise free and easy life. While you are dreaming of a wonderful long-term relationship, a white house with a picket fence and a flock of children, he's thinking of rarely being able to see his buddies again and having to work all the time to support a family. He's also thinking about never having sex with any woman except for you for *the rest of his entire life* (hint: for most men, that's a bad thought). So even in the best of times, when you meet a man, you'll encounter resistance.

It's really no different from any other sales situation (which, fundamentally, all dating is). If you've ever been in sales, you know: People resist most products and services on principle, even if the products and services you offer would improve their lives. They let their skepticism run their decision making and as a result often deny themselves what they most want. While you are thinking about selling them a great product, they are wondering just how badly you are going to rip them off. It's exactly the same with men. Men will be resistant to any concept of commitment until you sell them on the benefits and features. You need to learn to become the best flirter you can, to overcome this natural resistance. In the process, you will get what you want.

∞ The Three Steps of a Flirting Interaction

Step One: Meeting Him and First Talking to Him

There's your quarry, across the room. He's looking this way! What should you do? There can be a lot of space between the acts of meeting eyes with the man you are interested in and an actual flirting interaction. Pick yourself up from under the table. Quit hiding! In those moments leading up to the first flirting interaction, you have plenty to do.

First off, the guy is probably scared (unless he is one of our students. Alas, that may not be the case). He'd love to have an excuse to come over and say "Hi," but he's been burned as often as you have, so enticing him is a step-by-step process. You have to take steps to get him talking to you.

Meet eyes with his, and hold them for a moment "too long." Give him a smile. Holding eye contact "too long" is a basic seduction skill for both women and men. When you do it, you create a small, intimate moment for just the two of you. You look past the fact that he is a stranger, and directly into the fact that he is a *man*. Holding his eyes from across the room is step one. Your smile should also be bigger than you think. Most people estimate that their smiles are bigger than they really are. Give him a *big* smile, and the odds are it will come across as a moderate smile he will notice.

But doing this once might not be enough to embolden your prey. Look at him, then return your eyes to your own business. A few minutes later, do it again, once again with a smile. This will help him know that he is, if not exactly welcome, at least moderately desired as a conversation partner.

Now that you've made it obvious that you won't chase him away, he'll come right up to you to talk, won't he? Wrong! He might think you are interested, but he's still scared. And more men than you realize wouldn't recognize a sign of interest from a woman if she tore her clothes off and waved her breasts in his face. (We are only slightly exaggerating here. Before we became Master Seducers, we both spent a lot of time in varying degrees of failure with women. One of the authors has since had several women tell him that, many years ago, they were coming on to him as hard as they could, to no avail. He was so deep in his own world of rejection-fear that he couldn't even see these women's advances, no matter how brazen they thought they were being.) Sometimes men don't notice signals, and it could happen to you.

THE SEVEN THINGS YOU MUST DO TO MAKE A MAN APPROACH YOU

Making eye contact is not enough to get him to come to you. You must also have *already* taken actions to make yourself more approachable. Here they are. You don't have to do all of these things, but if you want to be approachable, you should at least do some of them.

He knows you are interested. You've given him "the look," and a smile. Now he needs an excuse to approach you. He's across the room, thinking, "She seems interested. But what would I say to her? I could go up and say hello, but then what?" Then what, indeed? That's why you must provide your soon-to-be-flirting partner with an excuse to talk to you.

1. Wear a Button with a Message on It. We got this one from Helen Gurley Brown, former editor of *Cosmopolitan* magazine and author of the classic, early sixties dating book for women, *Sex and the Single Girl*. If you haven't read it, you should check it out.

A button with something written on it gives a man a reason to talk to you. After all, you do have something written on you, for the world to see. It's not rude to mention it, or to read it.

Buttons can be purchased at gift or card shops. You want to get one that invites conversation without being too insulting or too overtly sexual. One woman we know has gotten a lot of good mileage out of a button that says "I'm like this because I didn't have a pony as a child."

Men read it, and ask her about it. She then tells them that she's so tired of people who complain all the time about what other people did to them. The men get to see that she's not a whiner, and she gets a conversation started.

Buttons to avoid are ones that say things like "I support Lorena Bobbit" or "A man's place is in the stove." Anything hostile will likely put men off, or in the case of the above buttons, it will have men running for shelter. You also probably want to avoid the ones that say things like "Honk if you are horny" or "Former Playboy Bunny." These, too, will attract the wrong sort of attention and attract men who are likely to be the *exact* type you should avoid. So go to a store that sells buttons and pick out a few that look interesting. Try them out and see which ones have the best luck in making you more approachable. Experiment with different social, political, humorous, lyrical, and cultural ideas presented in this easy to understand package: the button.

2. Wear Something He Can Talk About. Something out-of-the-ordinary about your person will give your man something to ask you about. We know women who get great mileage from vintage clothing, exotic hats, bracelets from India, or necklaces from Japan. It should look good on you, but be unusual enough that he feels safe asking you about it. Of course, you'll want to be forthcoming and interesting when he *does* ask. Nothing is worse than asking a woman about some detail of her appearance, only to have her barely respond. Make his life easy. Once he's asked, do your part to keep the conversation alive.

3. Carry a Controversial Book. Don't worry, you don't have to read it. You can simply say "I'm just starting it," if the man asks more than the most rudimentary question about it. We suggest that you carry the book that is currently in your hands as the perfect conversation starter. It will have men ask you about your preferences in a man, and they will be dying to know you due to the fame of the authors.

You do want to carry a book that is odd enough to start a conversation, but not so odd that it puts the man off or gives him the wrong idea. While *Lady Chatterley's Lover* or *Fear of Flying* might be an appropriately racy title, *The Story of O* or *Our Bodies, Our Selves* is taking things too far. We also recommend romantic poetry books, or whatever seems both racy and controversial at the time. We know one woman who has gotten great results carrying around a copy of a book entitled, *The Alchemy of Love and Lust,* which gets men talking to her about romance and love right away. She's even read it, but, like we said, that part isn't required.

4. Show Your Hobbies to the World. Having obvious hobbies gives men something to talk to you about, as well. It gives them a reason to approach you. If you are in full biking gear in the coffee shop, for instance, you make it easier for men to approach you and talk about biking. If you have your computer, it makes it easier for them to talk to you about computers. If you knit, it makes it easier for them to talk to you about knitting. You can also bring a book or magazine about your hobby which they could comment on. If you are into sailboarding, bring a sailboarding magazine. It almost doesn't matter what it is, as long as it gives men something with which to open a conversation with you.

5. Have A Newspaper and Mention The News To People Around You. If you mention noteworthy news to the people around you, men see you as a social person, and as such you are more approachable. When you are a person other people can talk to, you become a person *he* can talk to. You provide an opening for men around you to engage in discussions with you, and this can lead to much more. We have seen this to be an effective way for women to initiate conversations with men and to present themselves as approachable.

6. Frequent the Same Places at the Same Times on a Regular Basis. Once again, all this is made a lot easier if you go to the same places at the same time on a regular basis. Your quarry may be too scared to talk to you the first time he sees you, but once you've seen each other over and over, you become familiar. The more frequently you see each other, the higher the probability you will have of conversing and feeling comfortable together. This may start by one of you saying "Hello." Eventually, this will lead to a conversation, which will then lead to flirting!

7. Be Nice Once He Starts Talking To You. When he asks you a question about yourself, be nice! Talk to him. Answer his question. Give him wins.

In a way, the cultural climate of suspicion and hostility toward men works to your advantage once a man actually starts talking to you. You probably don't realize it, but most men think women are mean, especially during the first flirting interactions. If you are nice to him, he is likely to be so shocked and happy that he will want to talk to you, and to talk to you again. Remember, these guys are used to being snubbed, blown off by women, and are living in terror of rejection. When you give him a win early on by being nice, it gives you a big advantage over women who make men work too hard to prove themselves in the first moments of the first interaction. He'll have to work to prove himself to you later, if you use our method, but he doesn't have to know that now. For now, you just want to keep him talking to you.

HANDLING HIS LAME PICK-UP LINES

Do guys use lame pick-up lines? You bet they do! If a man says to you, "Can I borrow your cell phone? I wanna call Heaven and tell them I found the missing angel," should you instantly get rid of him? Believe it or not, the answer is, not necessarily. As a point of clarification here, we see two distinct categories of pick-up lines: the sweet, but stupid, and the crude and overtly sexual. When a guy uses a sweet, but stupid line, we recommend that you consider talking to him; when he uses a crudely sexual one (so crude it cannot be printed here), then by all means, get rid of him immediately.

Carve this into your mind, as we will return to it over and over: One of the biggest mistakes women make is that they reject men for the wrong reasons. As we will see, plenty of perfectly good men say or do stupid things during flirting (see "The Dirty Dozen Flirting Mistakes Men Make," below). Women usually snub these men. While we do believe, quite strongly, that you must weed out guys who don't meet your criteria, you shouldn't be impulsive about it. One of the main reasons women say that there are no good men is because most women disqualify perfectly good men for the stupid, but not necessarily fatal, things men do during the initial flirting interaction. Nowhere is this more true than when a man gives you a stupid line.

When a man gives you a line, all he's really saying is that he wants to talk with you, he finds you attractive, and he doesn't know what to say. He's desperately hoping that his line, no matter how stupid, will open a conversation that you will think is worth having. And time and again, women pass over good men because their opening line wasn't good enough. What a mistake! As if your main criteria was to have a man who could create great opening lines! In fact, a man who can create great opening lines is probably nothing but trouble in a relationship, as he will be using that same wonderful line that worked on you with plenty of other women, as well. He'll leave you wondering why you always end up with jerks, when the reason is easy enough: you select men on the basis of who has the smoothest opening line. Bad move.

We suggest that you don't take any opening line—except the ones that are an open invitation to sex—as a clear sign of what a man's character is like. It might be, but it probably isn't. We suggest, instead, that you focus on how brave he was to come up and talk to you—something you, for all your willingness to reject him, haven't done for him. When you take this point of view, you can hear his line, let it go, and see it for what it is: a courageous attempt to please you, and to open up a conversation. If he looks at all interesting, give him a win by being nice in return, and have a conversation with him.

OPENING LINES YOU MIGHT USE ON HIM

A great opening line with most men is the simple word "Hi." It creates an opportunity to talk, and gets him past his need to come up with an opening line himself.

After you've said "Hi," you can ask him about anything about himself that seems out of the ordinary. If there's something unusual about his way of dressing, if he's wearing a Panama hat that looks especially good on him, or has an unusual tie or briefcase, ask him "What's the story behind that?" Get a conversation started, and you are on your way. You can also comment on some item in the news, or on an item he's carrying. Just get talking, give him wins, and don't disqualify him too quickly (more on that in a bit), and you'll have the first step of the flirting interaction underway.

OPENING GAMBITS YOU MIGHT USE

Here are some things you can do that get you into a conversation—and more—ASAP:

Ask Him for Help. Helping you, if you appear grateful for it, is an immediate win for a man. It allows him to be your knight in shining armor, here to save the day for you. So feel free to ask him for a favor or for help.

Got your hands full? Ask him to open the door, or to even help you carry something. Doing a crossword puzzle? Ask him for help with one of the clues (and be sure to thank him sincerely, even if he doesn't know the answer). Ben Franklin noted in his *Autobiography* that people become more bonded to you if you ask them to do you a favor than if you do a favor for them. You can use this to your advantage with the men you are attracted to by asking for help.

Remember to be nice when you ask a man for help, and be grateful for it. Men often complain that women seem to have a sense of entitlement, and that they don't think women show appropriate gratitude for what men do for them, even if it is small. That's pretty funny coming from most of these guys, who expect women to wait on them hand and foot once they are in a relationship. But it's the reality of their experience, so you'd better get used to it. It is true that a woman who seems ungrateful for help, or even angry about needing to ask for it, is profoundly unattractive to men. But if you give him a smile and some thanks, he'll feel like your hero, and interacting with you will make his day.

Give Him Help. Offering help to a man is not as good as getting help from a man, but it still creates a context for you to have a conversation. Just be sure to value his ideas about solutions when you are helping him and things should go fine.

One of the authors once got his car stuck on a snowy road, and a very attractive young woman stopped to help him out. They ended up going on several dates. Giving a man help can be an excellent way to create a flirting opportunity.

Admit to Being Nervous. Admitting to being nervous gives him a chance to help you—to help you not be nervous. It shows some vulnerability, and opens the conversation with an opportunity for him to help you, which he will love. After you've talked for a while, be sure to give him a win, and tell him how comfortable he's made you.

A Few Words about the "First Impression"

The importance of the first impression you make on a man is, in our opinion, highly overrated. People in general, and men in specific, are always, in every moment, looking to you for clues about what they should think of you. They are doing this the first time they meet you, and they are doing it each subsequent time they see you, as well. Therefore, if you screw up the first impression, there's a lot you can do to clean it up on the second or third interaction.

Ginny felt like she totally botched her first interaction with Larry. When they met for the first time, she felt awkward, preoccupied, and full of concern that he wouldn't like her. As a result, she laughed too loud and obnoxiously at his jokes, said things that were weird and uncomfortable, put her foot in her mouth, and just generally left the interaction feeling like a complete fool.

When we talked to her about it, she was completely depressed. "He'll never be interested in me now," she told us. "There's nothing I can do about it." We explained to her that people are deciding about you in every interaction they have with you. "If you act like nothing strange happened during that first interaction," we told her, "he will almost certainly feel that way, too. He'll place more stock in how self-assured you are while you are talking to him than he will in his memories of his first experience with you." She took our advice, and totally let go of the idea that her first impression had *anything* to do with the eventual outcome of their relationship. The next time she interacted with Larry, she put the past behind her and forgave herself for having felt uncomfortable and awkward the first time. Larry found her more interesting during their second interaction and, even though the relationship never developed any further, Ginny learned an important lesson. She learned that the first impression is not as important as the *current* impression, and that every interaction is a chance to make the current impression great.

So, if you don't feel you've made a great first impression, forgive yourself and go back for more. He hasn't written you off unless you have. Don't worry about it.

Step Two: Guiding the Conversation in the Right Direction

If you've done everything properly in step one, the man you are interested in is talking to you. If you are bright and smiling, he might even be flirting with you. Most likely he'll be screwing it up in some way, but you'll know how to handle that after reading the section below on "The Dirty Dozen Flirting Mistakes He'll Make and How to Get Things Back on Track."

His biggest blocks to thinking of you as possible romantic material are what we call *"Why Not?"* problems. A "Why not?" problem is part of the natural resistance that both you and he will have to taking things further. As a man is chatting you up for the first time, he's evaluating you even as you are evaluating him. He'll be saying to himself, "She seems like a nice woman. Why shouldn't I go out with her? Why not?" As soon as he asks himself "Why not?" he'll start to give himself answers. Why not? "Because she'll probably reject me." Why not? "Because she'll probably criticize me, like my last girlfriend." Why not? "Because she'll probably spend my money and let me buy her dinner, then tell me she just wants to be 'friends.'" A guy can generate a lot of reasons "why not," and he probably will.

Meanwhile, we are saddened to tell you that you are probably doing the same thing. You are asking, "Why not?" and giving yourself answers. You're telling yourself that he's not your type, that he has no taste, that he wears his socks inside out—whatever. You're thinking of ways to kill off the budding romance, just as he is. It's just what people do.

A part of you wants to keep your life simple, safe, and sane, and resists the complication of allowing a man into it. This part of you answers your question, "Why not?" and kills off your chances with the men you meet. "Why not" problems can be devastating, because they ultimately leave you alone and wondering where all the good men are, while the good men have been disqualified prematurely by your "Why nots."

You've got to be persistent in allowing yourself to feel the pleasure of the flirting interaction, and in making him feel good, if you are to get past the "Why not?" problem of the second step of flirting.

Handle your Desperation

One of the biggest flirt-stoppers is desperation, and it's likely to rear its ugly head in the first several steps of flirting. Nothing makes a man feel scared faster than a woman who seems desperate, lonely, or who makes it clear that she's ready for marriage and babies *right now*. A man will immediately and correctly decide that the woman isn't really interested in *him*. He will decide that she would probably be interested in any man, but only for a *relationship*. Take it from us when we tell you that men will be put off if you are that desperate and obvious.

Desperation shows up most often in three situations:

1. *When you are only pursuing one male candidate.* When you are only interviewing one male applicant, and have all your bets placed on this one guy, you are likely to get desperate. You have no backup plan, so things *must* work with the man you have targeted. This "it must work" pressure destroys your ability to say, "It doesn't matter how it goes with this man; there are lots of others to choose from." You'll get tense, and he'll notice it and get tense, too. Then you'll get more tense because you can see that you are screwing up your one and only chance. Unless you can remind yourself forcefully that there are lots of men available to you, there is a high likelihood that you will continue looking desperate.

The solution, of course, is to always be "working on" a number of men, as we've discussed before. Having a number of potential relationships "in progress" will keep desperation far away.

2. *When you are overly terrified of rejection.* When you are terrified of rejection, you also become desperate. By this time, we hope we've impressed upon you the importance of overcoming your fear of rejection, and that you are committing yourself to taking on the anti-fear practices we described in chapter 3.

3. *When your life is otherwise lonely and meaningless.* If you are lonely, and your life seems meaningless, you also appear desperate to men. You must have something that you are involved in, that gives your life meaning, above and beyond a relationship with some guy. Look deeply at yourself, at your heart's desire, at what dreams you have for your life—trips, activities, hobbies, careers, and so on—that would fulfill you without dependence on a man. If you are trying to get meaning for your life out

of your interactions with men, they will always notice it and not want to be with you.

We're not going to walk you through an entire life-overhaul here, but you'll find that the principles of being successful with men are the same principles you need to follow for success in your life. Keeping these dating principles in mind as you design your life will help you live with passion and success. You'll also be able to use the principles of planning and follow through, in creating a life you are passionate about. When you are passionate about your life, and care about something other than having a *man* in it, you won't be desperate.

AVOIDING UNNECESSARY CONFLICTS

It's important that you moderate what you talk about during your flirting interactions. Remember your desired outcome: You want this man to find you fascinating and engaging, while giving you an opportunity to test him and see if you want to take him to the next level. To this end, it is important that you avoid unnecessary conflicts while you are flirting with him. Who cares if he spouts some opinion that pisses you off? You've got bigger fish to fry.

When Jackie first went out with Kurt, she did everything properly, until Kurt started talking about his involvement in the men's movement. "Did you know that the statistics actually show that men are domestically abused by women at about the same rate women are by men?" he asked her during their first flirting interaction. Jackie disagreed with this assertion strongly, and was offended that he'd bring something as unpleasant as domestic violence up during a flirting conversation in the first place. But then she remembered her desired outcome: She wasn't there to have a difficult and ultimately useless argument, she was there to flirt and get to know this guy. She also knew that disqualifying Kurt for this flirting error would be an overreaction, so she said, "Oh, that's interesting," and changed the subject to something more to her liking.

You have to decide what's most important to you: arguing with a man, or building a relationship that works for you. If women's behavior is any indication, the average woman is more interested in fighting. (Don't worry about it—men are the same way.) The average woman gets into conflicts with men about women's and men's issues, or about why sports are so important to men. She then ends up getting rid of perfectly serviceable men for no good reason. You should be different.

If you want success with men, you must know the proper way to handle it when a guy spouts off some boneheaded, conflict-causing opinion during a flirting interaction. The correct way to handle a man's invitation to fight is to let him know that you heard him, and introduce a different topic of conversation. When Kurt spouted his opinions about men's and women's issues, Jackie did exactly the right thing. By not arguing with him, and by changing the subject, she avoided a fight, and was able to continue testing Kurt.

Of course, a point can come where the man goes beyond being a bad flirter—some men love to fight, and that's all they want to do with you. If you encounter one of these guys, you'll know it soon enough. You'll let it go the first few times he tries to start a conflict, but after a while you'll realize that fighting is all he knows how to do. Get rid of him.

If it's any consolation, he probably hasn't had sex in a long, long time.

Show Him You're Not Weird

Have you ever known a woman who was odd, or out of the ordinary, but who was still successful with men? You probably have. It may be someone you know who is tattooed all over, with green hair, and multiply-pierced. It may be someone you know who is very tough looking, decked out with black hair and a leather jacket. She may be hyper-feminine, an "earth mother," or have some other eccentricity. You notice these women seem to have made their eccentricities work for them. They are comfortable with themselves, their tattoos, piercings, green hair, new-age clothing, or whatever their style happens to be. They have no difficulty flirting with and getting men.

A woman who is "weird" in some way, and who is comfortable with it, is an inspiration to the men she meets. Men see that she is unashamed of her passions, and see her as a woman who is willing to express herself fully. These are arousing qualities to some men, who find such women "cute" or "artistic." They trust such women, because such women trust themselves. Men find flirting with these women refreshing, and their self-acceptance gives men permission to be more accepting of themselves.

A woman who isn't comfortable with her eccentricities, on the other hand, is frightening to men. Because she seems to think there is something wrong with her, men think so, too. Her shame about her passions make men see her as "weird" and untrustworthy. They don't trust her, because she doesn't trust herself. Flirting with such a woman is no fun.

The solution is to look at any of your "odd" behaviors or modes of dress, decide if you want to keep them, and, if you do, to integrate them proudly into your style. You decide if you want to keep them by asking yourself, "What message does this send about me?"

When Liz wanted to decide if she should keep her buzz-cut hairstyle, she asked that question. She not only asked herself, but also her friends and family. She found that many folks thought her short hair looked severe and intimidating. It sent the message that she wasn't feminine, or was harsh. After thinking about their feedback, Liz agreed. She let her hair grow out, got a softer look, and found she was happier. People began to interact with her differently. Men suddenly seemed to feel more comfortable around her. Flirting became easier.

But Liz's situation is unique, just as yours is unique. Some women look sexier and even more approachable with a "harsher" look, or something else that might be considered "unusual."

Often a woman appears weird to a man because she is looking for validation from him. She wants him to accept something very strange about her, as a test of how accepting he is on the whole. Or she may appear weird because she is so focused on making a statement with her appearance that she appears stuck-up or snotty. We've been over this again and again: get your validation someplace other than from men. If you are trying to get a man to validate your existence during a flirting interaction, it will make the whole thing ten times harder.

Many women accidentally come across to men as "weird" by worrying about their eccentricities during flirting interactions. They look to men to validate their oddity, and end up seeming weird and scaring men off. If you have an eccentricity, you must be different. You must be proud of it—or get rid of it—if you don't want to scare off men.

PLAYING HARD TO GET

Many women have problems playing hard to get during flirting interactions. Fortunately, there are a few simple keys that, if you keep them in mind, will make playing hard to get work every time.

The biggest problem most women have in playing hard to get is that they don't actually play hard to get. They play impossible to get. No matter how attractive you are, there's an upper limit to how hard you can be to get, and still end up being gotten. If you are very beautiful, that only makes matters worse—men are *more* likely to give up on you quickly, mistaking your being hard to get for simple rejection. Playing hard to get has to be handled very gently.

We've said it before, and we'll say it again, because it is critical that you understand it: Men live in terror of rejection by women. We know a powerful multi-millionaire, a man who owns several factories, whose employees cower at his every word. He came to us because he was lonely, and too scared to even say "Hi" to the women who attract him. He was afraid they might reject him. He is not unusual. When we do radio call-in shows, the first question we usually get is a man asking,

"How do I handle rejection from women?" Men live in fear of your rejection. Yet they pursue you anyway.

Most women who play hard to get seem to be testing men to see how far they'll go to get them. The problem with this is you only know exactly how far he'd go after he's given up. Then you've lost him, so what good did it do you to be hard to get? You've been *impossible* to get, and it's all over.

You will be different from "most women" because you will understand what playing hard to get is really about—that is, creating a constant stream of little "wins" that the man has to stretch for on his way to getting the big "win" of your heart.

Whenever you think of playing hard to get while flirting with a man, remember that it's not about making him suffer, making him work, or rejecting him just for the sheer pleasure of it.

Unless, of course, you want to be alone.

Step Three: Make the Date!

THE THREE FLIRTING SITUATIONS

How quickly you make the date depends on the kind of situation you are in when you find your target. There are three different kinds of situations in which you meet men, and each requires a different strategy.

First, there is the emergency situation. You are on a train or waiting in a line that is quickly moving forward and you have only a few minutes or moments to ask the man out, or make contact, because you will probably never see him again if you don't.

If you want anything to happen, you've got to talk to this man now, or never see him again. This can be as simple as approaching a man in a bookstore and asking him about the book he is looking at, and building the flirting interaction from there. If you are sure you'll never see him again unless you act immediately, then you have very little to lose by being extremely bold. After you've talked for a bit, you could say, "I don't usually do this, but I'm wondering: Could I give you a call sometime? Perhaps we could go out for a cup of coffee?" He may say no; he may say yes. If you are feeling especially scared, you can give him your card. You certainly have a better chance of dating him if you ask than if you don't. After all, if you don't ask, your chance is exactly zero.

The second type of situation gives you a bit more time. In this case you have a few hours, or a full day, to work on him. You might be at a party, or at a full-day class, for instance. You may have already had numerous interactions with him. In this case, before you both leave you say, "You know, you seem interesting. What would it be like if we went out for a cup of coffee sometime?" Then you set it up from there.

In the third type of situation, you work on flirting over a longer period of time. This is the man you see regularly: the man who works out at your gym, the man at the coffee shop you frequent, and so on. This is the least stressful situation, because you can work on the guy over a long period of time. You can give him all the time he needs to get used to you, to trust you, and to imagine you as a romantic part of his life. Then either he'll ask you out, or you can ask him out, when the time feels right.

It's important that you figure out which type of situation you are in with any man you are attracted to. It does you no good to be armed with flirting and seduction skills if the man of your dreams walks out of your life and you do nothing to stop him. When you figure out what class a man is in, you can plan the urgency and velocity of your flirting accordingly.

SETTING UP THE DATE

We apologize for putting so much of the responsibility for setting up the date on you. Any man who's read our other book, *How to Succeed with Women,* knows that setting up a romantic, special date should be the man's job. But in our current world of confused dating rules, you have to take matters into your own hands. Your authors are fixing this problem as fast as we can, and look forward to the day when you can sit back, hopefully under your parasol, and accept or dismiss possible suitors with a dignified wave of your lace-gloved hand. Meanwhile, you are stuck setting up your own dates properly and romantically. Sorry about that.

The upside of this problem is that you have the option of cutting to the chase, and of setting up dates that work for you without seeming weird to a man. In fact, most men will almost certainly be grateful for your help, especially if you give it gracefully.

We would love to provide you with some complicated, multi-step process for helping the man set up the date, but it really isn't that complicated once you get past any fear you might have about being the one to initiate the process. Our suggestions are simple, and if you keep them in mind, you should be fine:

Have an Idea in Mind for the Date. One of the biggest mistakes anyone can make is going into the "date set-up" conversation without a clear idea or ideas in mind of what the two of you might do together. There's nothing worse than a conversation that goes "I don't know, what do you want to do?," followed by "I don't know either. What do you want to do?" Such interchanges suck the life out of any budding relationship. You can't let that happen.

The fix is simple: Have some ideas in mind ahead of time. We'll tell you how to come up with those ideas when we talk about the "Qualifying and Middle Dates" in chapters 8 through 12. Make sure, however, that the date is as concrete as possible, and that the time and place are set.

Be Nice, Sweet, and Flexible about It. Like we said, these ideas are not complicated. When you talk about setting up the date, be nice. Don't be pushy, rude or mean. If he really can't decide, and seems to just be rejecting all of your ideas without providing any of his own, you can either put off the conversation until later, or ask him to agree on a plan "for now" until he comes up with a better idea. Most men will agree to this. If he still resists, he might be telling you he doesn't want to go out with you. Drop it, then call him later and ask him again to help you set up a date. If he is *still* unresponsive, he probably doesn't want to date you, or really could be more trouble than he is worth. We highly recommend that you be open to his ideas and his suggestions on the place and time, while insuring that the date always works for you, fits in your schedule, and is within the bounds of safety.

USING THE PHONE TO SET UP THE DATE

If you don't set up the date when you are talking to each other in person, then either he will call you, or you will call him, to set it up. Here are some general rules for using the phone to set up a date with a man:

- If you call him, it is permissible to leave a message two times. After that, hang up if you get his answering machine, and only settle for reaching him in person. Otherwise he may start to think of you as "that woman who's always calling me," and begin to get so much pleasure from having you pursue him and want him that he may *never* call you back. He may also feel uncomfortable, or concerned that you are calling him too often and that you are stalking him.

- Leave messages with specific questions and proposals on them. A general call to say "Hi" is harder for a man to return than is one that gives him something specific to talk about when he does call you back. The best way to do this is to leave messages about specific places where you think it would be fun to go together, and invitations for specific dates and times when you'd like to do those things. Say something like, "I think it might be fun to go to the planetarium together next Thursday," not, "Uh, wanna go out?"

- Don't put yourself down when leaving a message. Give yourself space to get flustered, and to be okay with it.

- Don't call to just "talk." He's not one of your girlfriends. Talking on the phone about "nothing" is not easy for most guys; it's too early in your relationship to expect it of him. Give him a break and don't expect it of him yet. Remember to give him wins as often as possible. Most men do not feel comfortable having long phone conversations, and will not experience talking about "nothing" as a win.

- At this point in your relationship, keep all phone calls short. Get him on the line, set up your date, say something nice to him to give him a win, and get off.
- Sound friendly when you leave messages.
- Never call him when you are upset with him, with an ex, or with men in general. It will cloud your ability to be kind and open with him.

If he doesn't call you back, call him again and pretend your first message never happened. Never ask why he didn't call you back—it'll make you look like a weak and whiny woman who is coming back for more. It won't make any positive difference to ask him why he didn't call you. If you did ask, he'd just make up some answer, anyway. If he's a basically unresponsive guy, you'll know it soon enough. Simply act like the first message never happened.

∽ The Dirty Dozen Flirting Mistakes Men Make, and How You Can Get Things Back on Track

One of the biggest mistakes women make is that they disqualify men too easily for making flirting mistakes. The guy is trying to say something funny, but he offends you instead. Often, men who make mistakes flirting are just playing with you the way they would play with other men: roughly, crassly, and stupidly. At its essence, this is an attempt by the man to let down his guard and include you in his style of humor, not to offend you.

The key to being able to handle men's flirting mistakes is to know how to give emotional "losses," as well as emotional "wins." Just as you are in the business of giving him emotional "wins" when he does things you like, you are also in the business of giving him emotional "losses" when he does things you don't like.

When he flirts with you in a way that offends you, it's time to give him an emotional loss. An emotional loss is the opposite of an emotional win. Instead of smiling, you scowl or frown. Instead of looking at him, you turn your head away. If there is another man there, you pay attention to the other man, instead of the flirter. You don't respond, leaving him in his own silence. You take your attention off of him, and put it onto something else. He should feel as though, for a moment, he's lost your heart.

The hardest part about giving a loss is not making it permanent. It's very easy to destroy the entire flirting interaction by giving him too big a loss. You want to correct him, but not end the budding relationship entirely. You want to sting him with a brief loss of your approval, so that he'll know that what he did was wrong, without dashing his hopes of having you altogether. Remember, he's probably not a bad person. He's just unskilled at flirting. He might be fine relationship material, but he still has some things to learn and some areas of his personality—and his approach—to polish. Withdrawing your attention and frowning will sting him, probably more than you know.

Many women are very good at giving men emotional losses. They screw up, however, when it comes time to getting things back on track. Getting things back on track is not, in and of itself, technically difficult. Rather, it is emotionally difficult. You have to be willing to forgive the man for his transgression, and to allow him back into your good graces after his brief punishment. After the transgression, and the emotional loss, you have to be willing to give him another win as soon as possible. If you don't do this, you will lose him forever.

Debra was great at this. Her flirting interactions with men were made up of carefully applied emotional wins and losses. She would smile at the man she was interested in, laugh at his jokes, respond to his innuendos, compliment him, and generally do what she could to let him know that he was doing well, and winning her heart.

When her suitor would inevitably do something stupid—such as making a joke at her expense, for instance—all that brightness would disappear like the sun during a total eclipse. "I want men to win me, and I let them, because it's so much fun," she told us. "But if he offends me, I turn off my niceness for a few moments 'til I'm sure he gets that he did something wrong." Then she gives him a win, the moment he does anything right, so he can feel her forgiveness as well as her displeasure. "It's almost funny," she says. "They get that they've crossed the line, but then when I am nice and sweet again, they seem so relieved. Then I just let things get good again."

It's important to stress how subtle these wins and losses can be. Most men who are flirting with you are scared, and are looking for any reason to call it a failure, to decide you are a bitch, and to ditch the whole effort. Therefore, your displeasure and emotional losses to him will be much more powerful than you might think. It's very easy to overdo the loss you give a man and drive him away forever.

The key to not losing the man when you give him a loss is to give him another win at the soonest possible opportunity. This does not mean the next day, or an hour later. We suggest that you make the entire episode of offense, loss, and new emotional win take *less than a minute*. Any longer than that, and you might lose the man entirely. Remember, the point is to use losses to shape his behavior, not turn him against you.

What you don't want to do is get into a fight or conflict with him about it. Confronting a man who has bumbled while flirting with you will not restore the happy flirting mood. It will only dig it deeper into heavy unpleasantness. It will likely only put him on the defense, and we all know the trouble that can cause. Just give him a brief emotional loss, get over it, and give him a win again.

Here are the dirty dozen flirting mistakes men make, and how to handle them and get things back on track:

Mistake 1: They Make Jokes about Your Mistakes

When men are together, the jokes are rougher, and are made at each other's expense. When a guy drops something, for instance, it's a funny, bonding joke for another man to say, "Way to drop that, bozo!" Among men this is great humor, an occasion for "high fives" all around. Such jokes are how men play together, and those jokes are consistently about each other's mistakes.

When a man doesn't know how to flirt with you, he may decide to use the same kind of humor with you. When you drop something, he may make a joke about it, saying something like, "Feeling a bit clumsy today, are we?" You will naturally find this offensive.

While such a joke from a man is a warning sign, it is not, in and of itself, something to disqualify him for. It *might* be a sign that he's an abusive, insensitive jerk, but it might just as easily be a sign that he doesn't know how to flirt with women, and is treating you like another guy.

The solution to most of men's flirting transgressions is the same. You've been giving him wins up to this point; now you give him a loss. As soon as he seems to understand that he did something wrong, you give him a win the moment he does something you like. Then you go on, and forget the transgression occurred.

Mistake 2: They Make Jokes about Your Appearance

This is another example of men flirting with you in the way that they flirt with each other. It may be unacceptable to you, but remember that it might not be meant as the serious an offense your feelings would have you believe.

Mr. Bright-Guy will often make a joke when you complain about your weight. You'll say something like "Oh, I've gained so much weight in the last two months, I must look like a huge cow." His snappy comeback will be something like, "Not *too* huge a cow. Mooooo!" He'll snicker, and you'll be mentally writing him off of your list of possible boyfriends.

We'd be doing a public service to men everywhere if we begged you to never complain about your weight to guys, because they really have no idea how to deal with it. They like you, and would like to make you feel better, but don't know how to do it, so they eventually end up making a joke to try to lighten things up.

However, we didn't write this book as a service to men, we wrote it to help you get the relationship of your dreams. The first thing to know, if a man makes a joke about your appearance, is that you are very likely to overreact to it. Women take their appearance much more seriously than men take their own—as you've probably noticed. His joke about your appearance probably doesn't mean as much to him as it does to you. It is yet another stupid thing that came from his mouth without any thought of the consequences. Give him a loss, and make sure he knows he's displeased you. Then remind yourself he didn't mean anything by it, let it go, and give him a win again. Get things back on track, and the loss you gave him should help keep him from making the same mistake again.

Sometimes he really *is* trying to insult you. You need to follow your gut on this. If he's a jerk and wants to keep you off-balance and lower your self-esteem, then get rid of him at once. There truly are plenty of good guys out there who aren't trying to tear you down. But don't make the mistake of getting rid of one of those good guys if he makes this mistake and is *not* one of the jerks.

Mistake 3: They Make Jokes about Violence

Guys joke about violence all the time. They often don't realize that, to a woman, having a guy they hardly know make a joke about something violent is just plain scary. Strange as it may seem, most men just don't get it. They think about this from a completely different point of view.

One of our male students learned this the hard way. He was at an all-day workshop for his business, where he met an attractive young woman. He asked her out for a drink, and as they were driving to the bar in his car, he joked, "Oh, what the heck, I think I'll just take you out into the woods and kill you." His date was rightfully terrified. After all, she didn't know him, and didn't know what he might do. *He* knew he was a safe guy, and joked with her the way he would with a guy.

If a guy jokes about killing you, the flirting interaction is over, and you should find somebody else. We see no reason why you should risk finding out later that he was *not* joking.

Most of the time, however, his jokes will be violent but not directed at you. He'll joke about punching out the waiter, or laugh like a hyena at the World Wrestling Federation show that is on TV at the bar. He'll delightedly describe a violent stunt he saw in a movie. Once again, when he brings up such topics, give him a loss, then a win again the second he brings himself back around to proper flirting behavior. If he spooks you, your gut tells you something's wrong, or he gives you the creeps, it's time to move on.

Mistake 4: They Use Physical Humor

Guys play with each other using physical humor. They play-punch each other, give each other noogies, and generally get rowdy together. Obviously, this won't work with you.

If a guy slaps you on the back or gives you a play-punch on the arm, it's time to remind him that if he's going to be with you, he has to treat a lady like a lady. Give him a big emotional loss, and, the moment he does something right, give him a win again. It is important that you give a man a loss immediately if this occurs, especially if his physical play hurts you in any way. Let him know that he is out of line, and if it continues, get rid of him.

Mistake 5: They Make Inappropriate Jokes about Sex

Guys who don't know what they are doing sometimes show their sexual interest in you by making inappropriate jokes about sex. This probably is not news. Guys come on to you the way *they'd* like to be approached—with direct sexual remarks and crude jokes. Saying, "Did heaven lose a couple of angels? Because I can see them bouncing around in your shirt," may or may not be a bad enough offense to end the flirting interaction. It is certainly the kind of mistake men are likely to make.

When a man you are interested in makes inappropriate sexual jokes with you, don't let that one joke, by itself, be enough to make you dis-qualify him. A lot of "good guys" will make this mistake because they don't know what else to do. Faced with a woman they are attracted to, wanting desperately to move things in a romantic direction, they say the things that the "cool boys" in high school said, that seemed to work for them. They make a joke, hoping you'll see their sexual interest, and share it. They want to impress you and they obviously find you attrac-tive, but they cannot express it in a manner in which you will be charmed. It's pathetic, but it's the truth.

If a man is one of the "good guys" who simply doesn't know what he is doing, you do yourself a disservice if you disqualify him over it. Give him a loss, then a win as soon as possible. Show your romantic interest in him through smiling, holding his eye contact a little "too long," and touching him.

If, on the other hand, this sexual joke is just one of many flirting errors, you can probably assume the guy is a jerk, and get rid of him. Furthermore, if it is obvious to you that the guy is only interested in you for sex, you should also disqualify him as quickly as possible.

Mistake 6: They Revert Back to Being a Teenager

Being obnoxious, making jokes about pissing, farting, and feces, are all signs of a guy who is so afraid of you that he's reverting back to what he saw the "cool boys" do to gross out the girls in junior high school. Once again, you have to step aside from your immediate revulsion and look at the context of this behavior. Does it seem like an isolated incident, or is this behavior part of an extensive backdrop of crude jokes, physical humor, and put-downs? Has he passed the other tests you have presented? Has he demonstrated the most important qualities and behaviors that you value and desire in a man? Weigh all of this when judging his digressions. If he has simply experienced a momentary fear-induced regression to the bad old days of his teenage years, giving him a momentary loss is appropriate. If he's looking like an overall jerk, and this is compounded with other inappropriate behavior, it might be wise to get rid of him.

Mistake 7: They Act Macho

Many times, men who don't know what they are doing with women will act like "tough guys" in their flirting interactions to impress you. You probably aren't turned on by his macho strutting, flexing and bragging, but, because he doesn't know what else to do, he decides that the best thing for him to do is to show you what a tough guy he is.

It's harder to handle a man whose flirting mistake is being overly macho, because if he's trying to be macho, he'll probably do it most of the time. It is probably not isolated incidents of machismo; it will probably be an unending stream of it. How do you handle this?

If you suspect that he is a wonderful guy who is strutting to try to impress you, keep your eyes open for any behavior that is softer and more sensitive. The moment he does some soft, sensitive action, reward the heck out of him. Describe what he did that you liked, and tell him "I like that gentle side of you." Smile at him. Continue to give him wins whenever he is more gentle, and losses when he is most macho. If he is a good guy, who is just trying to impress you, this approach will be a lot more effective than simply cutting him off prematurely.

Mistake 8: They are Overly "Sensitive"

The authors of this book are well known for their campaign against the "Sensitive New Age Guy," or SNAG. Being overly "sensitive" is another flirting mistake men make, and it's more like being macho than these sensitive men would like to admit.

A SNAG will try to impress you with his sensitivity during the early flirting interactions. He'll have a heavy quality, and will be hard to joke and play with, as he is always monitoring himself so he won't accidentally say something insensitive or offensive. He is very restricted in his scope of conversation and it may seem as though he is hiding something about himself from you. Instead of being romantic with you, he'll talk about how strongly he supports women's issues, and how much he resents women being paid less than men. He'll side against men in a way that seems a little creepy—as if he doesn't actually consider himself a man.

All this "sensitivity" and heaviness destroys the playful feeling of flirting interactions. But once again, if you suspect that he's a good guy with a bad technique, wait until he does something less sensitive, and praise him for it. Describe what he did that you liked, and tell him "I like that fiercer side of you." Smile at him. Continue to give him wins whenever he is more fierce, and losses when he is most aggravatingly sensitive. If he is the kind of guy you'd want to be with, and he is just putting on this SNAG face because he thinks it will impress you, this strategy will help. Don't let our disgust with this type of man taint your own ability to see the good in them (if there is any). Don't let our own judgment that SNAGs are actually Satan's children keep you from assessing them rationally against the qualities on your list.

Mistake 9: They Totally Shut Down

A lot of good guys are deathly afraid of offending or hurting women in any way. Many of the men you'd like to date have been taught by mothers, female school teachers, former girlfriends, and so on, that all men are bumbling jerks who hurt women without even knowing it. A man who's been taught this will have a very hard time playing with you and flirting during your early interactions, because he's so terrified that he'll offend or hurt you.

He'll be so terrified, in fact, that he'll get so involved in monitoring his every action that he'll totally shut down. He'll become "safe" by becoming "boring." He'll scrub out every trace of his personality to sanitize himself completely.

If you suspect that there's an interesting guy behind this dull facade, then don't write this man off. Amp up your positive reactions to anything he says. Smile brightly and ask him questions about himself. Laugh at his jokes and tell him the things you like about him.

Admittedly, a man who is deeply into being dull can be very hard to reach, and it may not be worth the effort. But if he's simply being dull as a way of hiding his fear of you, a little positive reinforcement can make all the difference. There are a lot of these dull-acting guys out there who can spring to life with a bit of encouragement and permission from you. They end up having a strong personality and become fiercely loyal to the one who captures their heart.

Mistake 10: They Talk About Things That Don't Interest You

The man who shuts down can sometimes become the man who flirts by talking about things that don't interest you. He may talk about sports or science fiction—any remote topic you couldn't care less about—but he drones on and on and on and on and on.

It's up to you to decide if this guy is worth the effort. On the up side, he may be very intelligent, but just not very good at flirting. On the down side, guys who are obsessed with talking about sports or science fiction tend to continue to be guys who are obsessed with talking about sports and science fiction. They can talk about other things, but they really do love the objects of their obsession.

The good news is, they can learn to control these behaviors. In this situation, a direct approach can be very effective. Say, "You know, I really like you, but I'd really like it if we could talk less about [whatever he is obsessing about]." This can work very well, especially if you smile while you say it and immediately offer another topic.

Mistake 11: They Don't Take Things to the Next Step

One of the most detrimental mistakes a man can make during flirting is not making any effort to take things to the next step. You are ready for him to ask you out, or to ask for your phone number. He is ready to go out with you, and should be asking you. But he is so afraid of rejection that he doesn't ask, and stymies your dating before it's even begun.

In this case, you might have to make the move. Luckily, there are some lines you can use to get him to make the move if he's scared.

- "Ask me out for coffee, and we'll talk it over." (Works very well. You are available and he knows it, but could just change the subject if he doesn't want to ask you out.)
- "Aren't you going to ask me out already?" (More risky, as he might say "no." But if you are pretty sure he wants to, but is just shy, then this line works well.)
- "Here's my card/phone number/e-mail address. I'd like it if you gave me a call sometime." (Leaves it in his court, so is less certain. Giving a shy man your e-mail address will probably work better than giving your number. E-mail is also much safer.)

Or, you could seize the bull by the horn, and ask him out yourself. "Would you like to go out for coffee sometime?" works pretty well.

Mistake 12: They Give You Mixed Signals

Last, but certainly not least, a man can confuse a flirting interaction by giving you mixed signals. You can expect that he will give you mixed signals. He will be uneven in his approachability and his ability to provide wonderful feelings for you. The key, surprising as it may sound, is to continue giving him wins when he does things you like and losses when he does things you don't like. That's it.

Some of these errors are inevitable, and almost any man will make one or more of them at some point during your flirting interactions. A man can be a great guy, love to talk about *Star Trek*, and occasionally find burps funny. Most men will seem like a mixed bag of pluses and minuses, because that's what they are. You have to soldier on with the interaction, take your chances and see how it goes. Things will get clearer the more time you spend together.

CHAPTER 7

The Eleven Tests of the Flirting Interaction

I N *How to Succeed with Women*, WE TAUGHT MEN THAT, IF THEY were looking for short-term sex, they should test the woman's interest by making their sexual interest known right away. Women who were at all open to the idea would then show interest back immediately, while women who weren't would show offense. If she was offended, the man would be able to move on to easier, if not exactly greener, pastures. He would then get through plenty of female applicants quickly, and find the ones that worked for his requirements.

You must also move through applicants quickly. There is no use in wasting your time on a man who isn't emotionally available, who can't ever be romantic, and who you don't really like. You need to discover such "fatal" shortcomings quickly, so you can move on right away to greener pastures yourself.

When you are first flirting with a man, you want to test for two things, in this order: First, you want to see if he's basically a decent guy. You want to find out if he's safe, patient, and able to be romantic. Those are the

177

kinds of qualities that most of these flirting tests look for. If he fails enough of these tests, you can move on to a guy who does have these basic important qualities without wasting your time on the second stage of testing with a man who won't measure up anyway. This stage of testing is mostly accomplished during the flirting stage of your relationship.

Second, you want to see how well he matches up with your more specific requirements and criteria. These criteria tests take place on the "qualifying dates," and during the "middle dates." Obviously, you won't need to move on to this second stage if he fails to pass the basic tests. Once he does pass these basic tests, you are in a position to start finding out about how well he matches your portrait of a dream man. If he doesn't pass these basic tests first, then you can move on without getting into more intimate probing.

Testing the man is step four of the Master Plan. Let us recap the Master Plan so far: In step one, you figured out exactly what you want in a relationship. You know that this may—and most likely will—change over time, because most goals do. But you also know that having a target will get you onto the "playing field of love" in a way that will be more effective than having no end in mind at all.

In step two, you made yourself worth winning by building your style and confidence. In step three, you found lots of male "applicants" to interview. Step three was about quantity, quantity, quantity. You learned about how men are actually everywhere, and how to find single men you could date. You learned that dating is a numbers game, and how to find the many applicants you need to sift through to find the one man who's out there, looking for you, so he can be your hero and win your heart.

Now, in step four, you are learning how to test those applicants quickly and efficiently. The setting for this testing is your flirting interactions. The outcome will depend on whether or not he passes your tests. If he passes, you can move on to the first date. If he fails, then you move on to the next applicant, until you find what you are looking for.

∞ *Why Test Men?*

Some women ask us, "Why should we have to test men? Isn't that sneaky and manipulative? Can't the man and I have a civilized, dignified conversation about what I'm looking for? Can't I just present my requirements, and ask him if he meets them?" The answer to these questions is: No.

The answer is no because men will lie to you if you ask them a direct question about their personalities when you are first getting to know them. Look, men are like everybody else. They want to put the best face on things. If you ask a man if he's interested in marriage and children, and he's mostly interested in going to bed with you, he'll say yes, because, heck! If he doesn't say yes, he'll lose you for sure. If he knows he'll lose any chance with you if he answers wrong, you can bet he'll mislead you. He'll figure that, by the time you find out the truth, you'll either have put out sexually already or be so in love with him that you'll overlook his flaws. And he's probably right. So the answer is no. You can't just ask him what his character is like. You have to test him, without him knowing you are testing him, and observe his responses and the behaviors he displays. As you develop a relationship with him, he will progressively be less afraid of you walking out on him, and will become more honest in his answers to direct questions. Some of these tests are ideal for your first interactions with him, some are better later on.

So get out your number 2 pencils, it's time for the test.

1. Testing His Attraction to You

Few people of either gender have an easy time telling when someone is attracted to them. This stems from everybody's reluctance to risk getting hurt by being "too direct" and then being rejected. Men constantly have the problem that they can't tell when women are attracted to them, while the women think they are giving signals that are profound almost to the point of being slutty. Women constantly have the problem that they can't tell when men are attracted to them, because the men are so afraid of rejection that they refuse to move a muscle to let a woman know they like her.

How can you tell when a man is attracted to you? Well, often, he won't talk to you. He'll be so intimidated by the strength of his attraction that he won't dare risk rejection by actually walking up to you and saying hello. You should understand this perfectly well, because you are probably the same way. The people we are most attracted to are the highest risk to talk with, so naturally we tend to avoid them, and thus avoid the risk. Some men who are very attracted to you will have a tendency to stay away from you.

The problem with this, of course, is that the men who are *not* attracted to you also stay away from you; so the fact that a man is avoiding you gives you almost no .guidance at all. The thing to understand from this dynamic is that just because a man isn't drowning you in attention doesn't mean he's not attracted to you. It might mean that he is. It's not the only indicator, but it's something to keep in mind.

2. Testing His Safety

As you know, safety is a paramount issue. Nothing else matters if you are not safe.

Safety is an odd thing to test. Safety is at once a feeling, and a judgment. You need to listen to your gut and follow what it says, even if it might be wrong. Being cautious means being on the lookout for both the potentials for danger and for safety at the same time.

One of the biggest challenges a man faces in getting to know you is your fear that he might be dangerous. We are not telling you to get rid of that fear—that would be a huge mistake. You should have caution when dealing with men. Dating can be dangerous. But you must learn to make fear into an ally, or even into your friend.

The problem with fear of men is that it can be overdone. It's as if part of you thinks, "If a little fear of men makes me safe, even more fear of men will make me even safer." If you are too afraid of men, you'll never be able to relax with a man enough to flirt with him, test him, get to know him, or go out with him. He'll find you suspicious and resistant and move on to someone else. At the same time, if you are too unafraid of men, you might put yourself in situations where you end up being in real danger. It's a balance every woman has to find for herself.

The best way to make fear into your ally is to give it something to do; to give it specific questions to answer and qualities to look for. If you simply have free-floating fear, you will never be able to relax and enjoy yourself. So, let's give your fear some meaningful things to do, so it can become your ally and serve your relationships.

DOES HE HAVE GOOD CHARACTER REFERENCES?

A great way to test a man's safety is to talk about him with people who know him. Ask mutual friends about the man and about his dating history. Observe him with others if you can. Find out as much about him as you can before you date. Though it isn't always possible to get references about someone, it is worth pursuing when possible.

If you meet a man at a party, talk to his friends. Once again, his friends might not be completely straightforward with you, but you can get some clues from their behavior. You can be as direct as you like. If you meet him at a party, and see that he is with friends, ask them about him when he is not around. It's best if you can find a couple, because then the man won't try to hit on you, and the woman won't be wanting the guy for herself. Tell them that their friend seems interesting, and that you would like to know more about him. See what they say. If they are cagey and seem to be withholding, then you can bet that there's something they don't want to say. If they seem free, easy and enthusiastic talking about your quarry, that's a good sign. Ask about his past relationships. See what they say. Once again, if they seem to be withholding bad news, they probably are. If they are relaxed with their responses, that's a good sign.

This test also gives you a less risky line of communication with the man you are interested in. Remember back in high school when, if you were interested in a boy, you could talk to his friends and find out if he was interested in you without having to talk to him directly? You can get the same results by talking to his friends about him as you are testing his safety. They'll tell you if he is interested in you, and will tell him that you are interested in him. People, especially couples, like to play matchmaker. It gives them the thrill of dating without the agony of defeat.

If his friends tell you that he is the perfect gentleman, that's good, but not good enough. As you'll see, the final judge of his safety will be the feelings in your own gut. But if his friends like him, it's definitely a good sign.

WHAT ARE HIS FRIENDS LIKE?

While you can't always tell everything you need to know about a guy by watching his friends, you can find out a lot. A man will be on his best behavior when he is around you. You can't know what he's like when he's not with you. But it's likely his friends' behavior will give you a clue. Don't worry if his male friends are really obnoxious—if he knows anything, he won't be like that around you. But if his friends seem dangerously unstable, into drugs, seem racist or into militia ethics, then that is obviously not a good sign.

HOW DO WOMEN WHO KNOW HIM TREAT HIM?

Do the women in his life seem to be angry or frustrated with him? Are they happy to be around him? Are they scared of him? Notice how women in his life treat him—that's how you'll be inspired to treat him if you date him.

DOES HE GET MAD EASILY?

Now you start looking at his behavior. You'll look at this even more when you test his patience, but for now, spend some time looking at his level of anger. Does he get mad easily? Does he seem to have little control over his temper? Does he have road rage when someone cuts in front of him? Does he criticize people when they make mistakes? How does he talk about his co-workers or his boss? If he treats people in a harsh manner and has a short fuse, he may be trouble. We don't have to tell you that these are bad signs.

Does He Hide Personal Information About Himself?

We're not talking about his hiding really intimate stuff, like his porn collection, from you while you are flirting. Sharing too many intimate details right away is just as spooky as sharing nothing, and just as inappropriate. But there are some things he should definitely *not* be cagey about. He shouldn't hide where he lives, for example. He shouldn't get weird if you ask him about a girlfriend or wife. And, as you get to know him better, he shouldn't hide work or home phone numbers, tell you to call him only on his cell phone or pager "because I'm home so rarely." He should not be afraid to give you his e-mail address. His unwillingness to offer you phone numbers or answer broad questions are all signs that something is "off," and you should pay attention to them.

What Does Your Gut Say?

We teach everyone we coach that they should follow their "gut-instinct" when they are deciding whether someone is safe for them. Ultimately, you are responsible for deciding if a man is safe or not, and ultimately you, not anyone else, will pay the price if you are wrong.

So, it is essential that you trust your gut feeling about a man. If it doesn't seem right, even if it looks good, pay attention to that. If your gut tells you it's a good idea even though you are somewhat frightened, then you may want to proceed. Never get caught up in someone else's estimation of a man if it disagrees with your gut feeling. His friends may be saying he's the greatest guy on earth, but if it doesn't feel right, stay away. Your gut feeling is always the bottom line when you are testing a man's safety.

3. Testing His Patience

You've got to test a man's patience. This doesn't mean you should be aggravating or thoughtless to him. You've got to test his patience intelligently, to see what kind of a man he is. He needs to prove that he really wants you as an individual, not just as a casual one-night stand. Testing his patience lets you know how he'll be through the inevitable challenges of a long-term relationship. Here are some factors to look at while you are testing a man's patience:

HOW DOES HE TREAT SERVICE PEOPLE?

One of the best places to learn about a man's level of patience is in a restaurant or other retail environment. How does he treat the people whose job it is to serve him? Is he friendly to the waitress or is he officious? Does he make life easy for the people serving him, or does he go out of his way to be obnoxious? How he treats service people can be a real clue to his level of patience.

How he treats service people can also show you if he is *too* patient. Does he accept bad service and abuse readily? Is he too wimpy to complain when complaining is the right thing to do? He might be too wimpy to be with you. A man you can walk all over will not be a man you can have a good relationship with, so you'll want to keep your eyes open for this, too.

DOES HE GET UPSET WHEN YOU ARE LATE FOR DATES?

This test works very well once you are dating, but you can also use it when first meeting. Excuse yourself for a few minutes, then come back. See if he got impatient while you were away. Is he happy to see you again, or does he seem resentful that you spent a few minutes in the bathroom?

Take a long time answering a question. See if he gets jumpy during the silence as he waits.

Once you are dating, make him wait for you to put on make-up, or show up late, and see what he does. The key is he should never become irrational or unreasonable. Even if he mentions it, he should be civil. If he gets overly upset, then you are probably going to want to part ways with him.

How Does He Respond To Others Being Late?

We suggest that, during a flirting interaction, you tell him about someone who was late to an appointment with you, and ask him what he would have done.

You can also ask him, "How do men feel when women are late?" He will tell you how *he* feels when women are late, which is what you are really after.

Is he willing to pursue you over time?

This test is the key. Is he willing to have a number of interactions with you, or does he give up easily if you don't give him everything he wants right away? If he gets impatient with pursuing you, then he probably will fail the patience test.

4. Testing His Values

You may have a set of values that you insist the man you date share with you. You may have a political leaning that any man you date must agree with. You may have a spiritual point of view that he must subscribe to, or a belief about family and children that you find absolutely essential. You can test for this belief during your flirting interactions.

The way to do this is to ask him about it—obliquely. As we've mentioned, you can't ask him directly about such things, because he'll say whatever he thinks you want to hear. You can get to the truth, however, by asking the question in a less personal way.

You do this by asking him how men feel about the value. Asking how *men* feel about something (as we mentioned above) is a safe way to find out about how your quarry feels about it. Most men are subconsciously convinced that their opinion is the same as all men's, and are happy to enlighten you about what men think while at the same time protesting that they, of course, are different. He'll tell you things about his opinions as a male spokesman that he would never tell you if you asked him *his* opinion. For instance, if you are having an initial flirting interaction with a man, and you absolutely have to be with a man who wants to be monogamous, you can say to him, "My girlfriends and I have been talking about this, and I wonder: What do men think about monogamy?" He'll spill the beans about his feelings on monogamy right away. He may say "I think most men think it's essential for relationships to work," and that tells you something about him. Or he may say "Ha! I think men hate it. Most men think of it as a trap created by women to control men—uh, not that I feel that way, of course." That tells you something else entirely.

Often this key value will be the one that the last man you were involved with lacked. Certain people get so burned by what their previous partner lacked that they make it a key test for the next person. This isn't necessarily bad, but you have to watch how you go about it, or you will look like a lunatic. If you put a personal ad in the newspaper advertising "Single female looking for a man who won't leave me, like all the others," (which is not far off from what some women do) then you are being a lunatic and need to calm down a bit.

Don't follow your impulse and approach your quarry with a direct question about it, like "My last boyfriend was scared of commitment, and I'm never going to get involved with a guy like that again. You aren't scared of commitment, are you?" Restrain yourself and follow the steps above. You'll get a much more honest answer.

5. Testing His Emotional Availability

You probably want a guy who is at least somewhat conversant with his emotions. Much to many men's displeasure, emotions, sometimes even difficult ones, are part of any relationship. You must test him for his emotional availability early, and get rid of him if he fails.

So, here's how you do it: In one of your early flirting interactions, but not the very first one (you don't want to scare him *too much*) tell him about something you find sad, and see how he responds. This can be something as simple as a recent tragedy in the news or something difficult and sad that happened to a friend. Don't make it too personal, or he'll think you are just plain weird. Don't share personal stories of being abused or assaulted, for instance. That's too heavy. But bring up something you can legitimately be sad about, tell him about it, and see how he responds.

Most men will be uncomfortable with this, and that is okay. If he really shuts down, and looks away, he may be unavailable emotionally. If he tries to fix your problem, or cheer you up, that's a better sign. At least then, you know he's willing to engage with you when an emotion comes up, rather than simply running away. You may not be crazy about the idea of being "fixed" when you are upset, but that's part of how men do things. It's a sign that he at least cares when you are sad. You can help him learn better ways of supporting you as you date him. He may also pass the test exactly as you would want. He may try to hold your hand, look at you empathetically, ask you the right questions, or just continue listening. This response is fairly unlikely, but this would be a sign of an emotionally available man.

He may also change the subject. This response is harder to sort out. Did he do this because he was afraid of the emotional content of what you said, or because he wanted to make you feel better and keep his seduction of you on a positive note? You have to decide this for yourself. If a man is a skillful seducer, he may be perfectly emotionally available, and simply be trying to cheer you up and keep his seduction on track. You'll have to listen to your intuition, and decide if he passed the test from that.

After the test, change the subject back to something positive and non-emotional right away. He's suffered enough.

6. *Testing His Ability To Produce*

You probably want a man who can produce something real and tangible in his life. A guy who does nothing but lie around on the couch (*your* couch!), eating your food and talking about how someday, somehow, he's gonna strike it rich, become famous, or whatever he fantasizes about, isn't going to be able to keep you happy. You need a man who can produce results in the real world, not one who spends his free time prac-ticing his autograph for his impending day of fame or figuring out how he'll answer tough questions when he's being interviewed by *Playboy*. The time to start testing for his ability to produce is during your initial flirting interactions.

There's a good chance he'll tell you all about his successes. It's called *bragging,* and it's something men are usually pretty good at. All you need to do is ask him about his career, and he'll probably get going. If that doesn't work, ask him what he's most proud of in his career. He'll happily tell you. If he's most proud of being the contractor for a new forty-story building, he's probably pretty good at producing real-world results. If he's most proud of being the first person in the state of Wisconsin to see *Star Wars, Episode 1,* then his real-world ability to produce might not be so good.

Another way to get at this information about him is to tell him about your material goals, and see what he says. If he responds by telling you that he'd like to date someone who has a lot of money, then you might want to steer clear. If he tells you about his goals, then you might be more interested in him.

You could also tell him about things that you want—your material desires—and see how he responds. Don't push this one too hard, though. You don't want to come across as a woman who is only look-ing for a man for his money. Also, some men who are very successful hide their wealth from the women they are interested in. Such a man wants to be loved for himself, not for what he has. You can, however, count on these men to paint at least a moderately successful picture of themselves.

7. *Testing Your Attraction to Him Over Time*

There are a lot of good reasons to do some flirting before you jump right into dating. Testing your attraction is a big one. You don't want to get so caught up in these techniques that you forget about it. We've all met people we were attracted to at first sight, who at second sight convinced us that there should never be a third.

Flirting is a great place to find out if you still like him on repeated viewings before you invest your time and emotions in going out with him. Obviously, if you start to find him unattractive during flirting, you should stop seeing him, pay attention to someone else, tell him you aren't interested in him, or give him more losses until he leaves you alone.

8. *Testing His Ability to Be Romantic*

In an ideal world, every man would have purchased and read our first book, *How to Succeed with Women*. In such a utopian world, every man would understand that it's his job to create romantic feelings and to skillfully make you feel special and delighted during flirting interactions. Then, your only job would be to give him emotional wins and losses (through your approval and disapproval) until he finally felt confident enough to ask you for the date. Sadly, there are still some men who have yet to purchase this excellent work of public service. These guys won't know a lot about romance, so you'll have to test them to see how much, or how little, they know. Here are some questions to ask yourself about his level of romance:

- Does he make me feel romantic feelings?
- Is he polite?
- Does he compliment me?

- Is he sweet?
- Does he treat me like a lady?
- Is he chivalrous?
- Does he court me?
- Do I feel happy after talking with him, or frustrated or sad?
- Is he playful?
- Is he funny?
- Does he pull out the chair for me?
- Does he open doors for me?
- Does he open the car door for me, and close it after I am in?
- Does he buy me flowers, trinkets, or little gifts?
- Does he wrap the gifts he gives me?

The more of these questions you can answer yes to, the more romantic a man he is. Remember, a man can score fairly low on the romance spectrum and still be taught to be more romantic than he is, through how you acknowledge him as you date and the wins and losses you give him. Only if he shows no romantic potential at all should you worry, because if a man can't be romantic at all, he probably also has a hard time being playful and fun.

9. Testing His Trustworthiness

Trust is earned, not freely given. The way a person earns trust is by giving his word, and keeping it. Think about it: The people you trust most are the ones who have done what they say they'll do, on a consistent basis. That is as simple as showing up when they say they will, completing tasks when they say they will, and just generally living their lives keeping their word.

Now think about people you don't trust. Perhaps there are people you know who are always late, who always have an excuse, and who rarely do what they say they will. We all know people who are like this, and we know we can't trust them.

A trustworthy man will keep his word. If he says he'll be at your home at a certain time, he is there. If he says he'll do something, he does it. A man who doesn't keep his word probably can't be trusted.

Trusting is different from liking. You may like these people very much, while at the same time knowing that they will always be late, and will not follow through on any promise they make. Remember, just because you like a man doesn't mean you can trust him. If a man seems untrustworthy, like him all you want. But don't trust him with your car keys, your wallet, or your heart. A man you can't trust will be more trouble than he is worth.

10. Asking Other Questions

You may very well also be asking yourself other questions about him during the flirting period. It's a good idea to make these questions conscious, rather than subconscious. When they are subconscious, it's hard to know when they are answered. We recommend you write a list of other questions you may have about men during the flirting interaction. This list might include questions like:

- Do I trust him?
- How much do I trust him?
- Does he have a violent temper?
- Does he want a long-term relationship?
- Is he just a player?
- How far will he go to prove himself to me?
- How demanding can I be?
- Can he stand it if I don't want sex?
- Would he be a good father?
- Is his career going well?
- Does he have a drive to succeed in the areas I think are important?
- Would my friends like him?
- Would my family like him?

11. *Testing Him Against Your Criteria*

It's often easier to test a man against your criteria later, after you've gotten back to your home and the flirting interaction is over. Pull out your list from chapter 2 and take a good look at it. Does he measure up to it? In what ways? In what ways does he fail to meet your criteria? In what ways do you not yet know if he measures up? Keep those ways in mind for the next time you see him. Has he inspired you to change your list in any way? Then let yourself make the changes.

Ultimately, you are flirting and testing, and giving wins and losses, to find that guy to have a relationship with. It's partly a search for what you know you are after, and partly a discovery of what might be possible for you. It's partly going after what you know you want, and partly discovering what you want as you undergo the process of looking. The flirting tests are designed specifically to help you weed and sort male applicants, while at the same time helping you get clearer and clearer about what you really want.

∞ *Conclusion*

We hope that in this chapter you learned the basic cause of the common female complaint, "there are no good men." There *are* good men— you've just been disqualifying them for the wrong reasons. Once you really get the truth of that, and start giving men wins and losses while you test them for the *important* factors, you'll have more available men dating you than you know what to do with. Then you can really shift your dating program into high gear, and close in on the relationship that you most desire.

For your convenience, here's a handy checklist of the tests you want to perform on a man during your flirting interactions. It can be very useful to look at this list before seeing a man, then to check it again afterwards. What did you learn?

1. Testing his attraction to you
2. Testing his safety
   - What are his character references?
   - What are his friends like?
   - How do women who know him treat him?
   - Does he get mad easily?
   - Does he hide personal information about himself?
   - What does your gut say about him?
3. Testing his patience
   - How does he treat service people?
   - Does he get upset when you are late, or when you make him wait?
   - How does he respond to others being late?
   - Is he willing to pursue you over time?
4. Testing his values
   - Ask: "How do men feel about [whatever you value]?"
5. Testing his emotional availability
   - Tell him about something sad, but not too tragic or personal.
6. Testing his ability to produce
   - Ask him about his career.
   - Ask him about what he's most proud of in his career.
   - Tell him your material goals, and see what he says.
7. Testing your attraction to him over time
   - See him over and over and see if you still like him.
8. Testing his ability to be romantic
   - To what extent does he sweep you off your feet?
9. Testing his trustworthiness
   - Does he keep his word?
10. Asking other questions
11. Testing him against your personal criteria

With the help of these tests, you'll know if you want to go to the next stage: the Qualifying Date.

CHAPTER 8

Before the Qualifying Date

JOHN WORKED OUT AT THE SAME HEALTH CLUB AS PATRICIA. AFTER flirting with him a few times, Patricia decided to make herself available for John to ask her out. Patricia talked to John every time she saw him in the club and frequently mentioned movies she wanted to see, concerts she wanted to attend, and other things that interested her. Over time she grew to like him more; he seemed cute, safe, and definitely interested in her. In one conversation, Patricia suggested that he ask her out to a nearby coffee shop, away from the noise and chaos of the club, so they could get to know each other better. How could he decline? Patricia gave him an opportunity to ask her out, though we can all see that she set up the entire thing. She let John know ahead of time that this would be only a short get-together. "I'll have only about an hour," Patricia said, "but that should be enough time for us to get to know each other a bit away from our workout routines."

Patricia set up what we call a *qualifying date*. The purpose of a qualifying date is to briefly meet with a man—just long enough to test him against your criteria and see if he is even remotely close to what you are looking for. The qualifying date is a quick and cheap way to get to know a man, and is more comfortable than a big dinner-and-movie night out, where you might feel obligated to spend more time with a guy who does not meet your criteria. We have designed the qualifying date to be brief because men associate dates with sex, and will assume a longer date has the potential to become sexual. By setting up a qualifying date you are telling a man you are interested in him, but not ready for sex. You are telling him that you are in control of the situation, and all dating will proceed at your speed. These factors will work to your benefit. The relationship will move forward or quickly die. Either way, the qualifying date puts you in control to determine the relationship's direction and the speed.

On a qualifying date, you are priming the man to possibly become your boyfriend. It is like preparing a camp stove before lighting it; done properly, you only need a few simple moves to create quite a hot little fire. Without proper preparation, you are always working too hard for what you want. With priming, you leave the first interaction prepared either to disqualify a man, or to light his fire and go for more.

This is the stage where the rubber starts to meet the road. This is the time when all your diligent preparation, all your practice in flirting with and speaking to men, your dressing for confidence, your list of criteria, and everything else is used. The qualifying date involves steps four and five of the Master Plan. Step four is "test the applicants." You started this during flirting, but will continue to do it more intensively on the qualifying dates. You continue to give men emotional wins and losses (step five) and continue the process of letting him slowly win your heart. By testing him, and letting him begin to win you (if he has shown himself worthy), you keep the relationship moving forward.

∞ *The Four Elements of a Qualifying Date*

Ann is an attractive woman in her middle 40s, divorced twice and now back in the market for a man. She has been on several dates over the past few months and her friends frequently set her up with new men. When we first met Ann she was resistant to the idea of using a system of dating. To her it seemed manipulative and contrived. We suggested that she take a new approach to dating, one that would give her a higher probability of getting exactly what she wanted. We suggested that there is important information you must get from a man—to determine your compatibility—before you can decide about future dates. We suggested that she use our program. While she was resistant to the system at first, she slowly began using it with greater and greater success.

Many women are like Ann. They prefer to take a haphazard approach, where they get to know a man without a plan, without an agenda, and are guided by the momentary fluctuations in their emotional states rather than by focusing on their long-term goals and criteria. This often leads to wasted time, hurt feelings, and regrets—much of which could be avoided if they would follow the brilliant system we have created for qualifying dates, middle dates, and beyond. There are four key elements that make up the structure of the qualifying date.

Element One: The Qualifying Date is Short

We recommend that the qualifying date last somewhere between 30 and 75 minutes, and no longer. Some women resist this idea, and stay on the date for as long as it goes well. The problem with this is they only end the date when it stops being fun, so they leave the man with a bad feeling, rather than with a good one. We strongly believe (and all of our research shows) that if you leave the man wanting more of you, rather than feeling overwhelmed by too much of you, you will have a much higher degree of success with him later. It is important that a man court you and pursue you slowly. Part of that pursuit is getting to know you slowly.

On the first few dates, it is important for you to spend a minimal amount of time with the man. It is important that you control the variables on the first few dates so that the date does not become solely about sex or about anything other than your testing him against your list. In other words, you control the tempo and the rhythm of the date so the guy does not mess things up with his agenda.

Before a date, most women are looking for reasons why a man is wrong for them. They are looking for reasons to disqualify him, even before anything happens. One of the problems in dating is that it shakes up your orderly existence, and destroys any tranquillity in your life. Add sex into the picture and all the rules change. Now instead of looking for reasons to disqualify him, you have to justify why you had sex with him in the first place. Even worse, sex will bond you quicker and confuse things that much more. Your heart will say "yes," your mind will say "no," and your head will be spinning.

Having sex too early can easily work against you. Let's say, for example, that the man does not fit your criteria, yet because of sex you feel close to him. Instead of judging him against your list and observing his bad points, you are more likely to be searching for the good in him. You are no longer capable of looking at the situation objectively. Your criteria start to seem insignificant and your passion becomes your central focus. Meanwhile, he is looking at you as a sex buddy rather than as a potential mate. Long dates early on only make all this more likely to happen. If you resolve to go on several shorter qualifying dates and a number of "middle dates" with the man, you will be more discerning before you have sex.

The qualifying date is also short because brevity allows you to invest a minimal amount of time in a man that you might not be interested in dating. We always encourage any woman we work with to go out and create a life she loves, do the things she dreams of doing, and to live wildly and passionately—even if there is no man in her life. Women who are doing what they love and following their dreams are extremely attractive to men. When a woman is in love with her life and self-confident, she is captivating to men. By keeping a date short you are saying to yourself that you do not have time to waste with jerks, or time to spend with men who do not meet your criteria. This is an important distinction for you to integrate into your dating philosophy: self-respect. R-E-S-P-E-C-T, find out what it means to you.

Element Two: The Qualifying Date Takes Place in a Coffee Shop or Other Quiet Public Place

Having the qualifying date in a public place like a coffee shop is not only safer for you, but also reminds the man that this is an informal get-together, not a date that will lead to sex. After all, what guy would want to pass up a small get-together with the lovely you? And a date in a coffee shop is very conducive for "just talking"—for you, this means testing the man against your list. A formal dinner, conversely, prompts an entirely different set of expectations about where the date will go. Besides, the distraction of the food takes your mind off the job at hand. A movie date is even worse. Imagine asking the man your questions during a high-speed action flick. Good luck. Having a coffee date allows you to talk to one another in a relaxed atmosphere, where there is little else to do but focus on becoming aquainted.

It is also important that you choose a place where you will not run into your friends or his. If you know that a certain coffee shop is a hangout for him and his friends, do not go there. Suggest a neutral place. You do not need the distractions of friends—yours or his.

THE WORST PLACES TO HAVE A QUALIFYING DATE (STRICTLY FORBIDDEN)

Some places are much worse for qualifying dates than others. We are forbidding you to go to places that are not conducive for testing a man against your list. These places provide too much pressure, will likely seem weird and uncomfortable, or be too serious and formal for a qualifying date. These places will prevent you from accomplishing your goals. Coffee shops and their equivalent are the only places we can recommend because they are the most conducive for the qualifying date goals.

Avoid the following settings for qualifying dates at all costs:

- Weddings
- New Year's Eve parties
- Family events
- The beach
- Funerals (duh!)

When you talk to a man about arranging a qualifying date, you must have a suitable place in mind. Be sure to pick the place before calling him. Specificity will greatly increase the chances of his showing up—and besides, you know that guys hate asking for directions. It is always better to tell him exactly where the place is, even if he claims to know.

Element Three: It Is Not a Time to Be Competitive

One of the biggest turn-offs for a man is a woman who constantly has to prove her independence or strength around him. This usually happens when a woman is insecure and feels a need to prove herself. To be clear: We are not saying you should be a mousy woman who waits for a man to talk before speaking, or someone who is anything but the powerful woman you are. When you are getting to know a man, however, it is important that you avoid being overly competitive. If you are, he will either let you win just as a ploy to get sex or the worst aspects of his personality will emerge and he will do anything possible to defeat you. Either way, you won't like the results.

Loren went on a qualifying date with Sam. The date was going wonderfully. They were drinking iced coffee at a romantic coffee shop in the early afternoon. The conversation was deeply personal. They were getting along famously. Loren was testing him against her criteria and he was passing all the tests. Then she made a fatal error in judgment. Loren began asking him odd questions about his history with sports, and began badgering him about wanting to arm wrestle (she was a weight lifter). He refused, and she began teasing him that he probably wasn't strong enough to win. Next, she suggested that they play card games. She beat Sam every time. She was a bad winner and gloated over each victory. Sam sank down in his chair looking quite defeated and, not surprisingly, he never called Loren again.

Maybe you are saying to yourself that you would never do such a thing. The truth is, women frequently act like this, to one degree or another, on dates. Both our male students and our personal experience with women tell us this is so, and it usually leads to disaster. From bowling to arm wrestling, from playing pool to cards, darts to backgammon, from Monopoly to Scrabble, it is all potential for trouble, especially on qualifying dates.

Competing with a man will often bring out his worst qualities. It is as if there were a primal urge in men to win no matter what (this is the urge that he *should* be directing toward winning your heart). While it is a mistake to put him in a place where he will defeat you, it might be even worse if you defeat him. Wait until the relationship is much more stable before getting into competitive activities with a man you are interested in. If we sound regressive in our approach, we are not. We are sharing a useful tip with you. Men have told us that an overly competitive activity has often been the end of a perfectly good date. Many women, too, have told us that after competing with a man she wasn't as enthusiastic about him as she had been before the competition.

We do not want you to think that all competitive games with men are bad. We are stressing the importance of not doing anything on a qualifying date that could lead to trouble. It is possible to play competitive games with a man and have a wonderfully romantic time doing so. Such games simply need to start later, after you know each other better. On a qualifying date, a competitive game is too risky.

The other question this raises is, why would you want or need to compete with a man in the first place? Is it just for fun, or do you hold a grudge against men for being mean to you? Do you want to even the score by humiliating any man you can? Do you have an exaggerated need to prove to a man that you do not need him, that you are a powerful woman, and that he hasn't got any kind of a hold on you? If so, you need to reexamine whether you really want a romantic relationship with a man. Competing with your man will not lead to a fulfilling relationship, nor will it be any fun.

Remember, you want to use a man's need to win in the way it was meant to be used: in the quest he really should be on, the quest to win your heart. Instead of giving him wins or losses through competitive activities, remember to let him win your heart, one step at a time, the way we taught in the flirting chapter.

Element Four: The Qualifying Date is Not a Time to Socialize

As we have said before, the qualifying date is not a time to do whatever you feel like doing and talk about anything that you feel like talking about. This date is an opportunity to test the man. Test him. Test him. Test him. Get it? The qualifying date is not a time to socialize. By socialize we mean, hang out and talk without a purpose. This is the last thing you want to be doing before you've seen if he meets your criteria. Hanging out without a purpose is something you do with your friends and family members, not a potential mate on your first real date.

In the minds of most men, dating and friendship are two different things. You cannot be both a friend and a romantic partner to a man—it will not work. Men see you as either a potential sex-partner, or as a friend. Very rarely will a man see you as something in-between. It's like drinking and driving: You either drink, or you drive. You can't do both. There is no in-between. You must decide whether a man is going to be a friend or a potential boyfriend and stick with it. Just hanging out and talking without an outcome in mind will not fulfill the purpose of the qualifying date. It will be treating him like a friend when you should be testing him as a potential lover. It will cause confusion and trouble, waste your time, and leave you wondering, when you find you have another male "friend," where the good men are.

As a note of encouragement, we do not mean you should be overly business-like or have a bad time, either. Any man will be uncomfortable if he feels as though he is being interviewed for a job (even though that is exactly what you are doing). Talk to him about topics you are interested in. Let the conversation develop naturally. At the same time, pepper in questions that will test him against your criteria. Do not be obvious, but do control the tone and the speed of the interaction. No matter what else is going on, in the back of your mind you should always focus on your list. From there you can either disqualify the guy and move on to the next applicant, or further explore the potential of this man. You maintain control by not letting the qualifying date degenerate into simply socializing.

∞ The Four Expectations that Cause Trouble on the Qualifying Date

There are a host of ways you may blow the qualifying date. Women can easily mess things up by having unreasonable expectations that ruin the date. It is important to understand your own biases so that you can compensate for them and avoid screwing it up. Expectations on the date can often cause you to have a terrible time. They can blind you to the man you are with because of your own preconceived notions. The wrong expectations will get in the way of accomplishing your goals on the date, and will create added tension that will hinder your experience. Here are the four expectations that cause trouble on qualifying dates, and how to handle them.

1. Expecting Him to Be a Jerk

Many women approach dates with so much past hurt and pain from failed relationships that they expect all men to be jerks. They go on a qualifying date and wait for a man to do something they do not like so they can justify their point of view: all men are jerks. This will kill any opportunity of connecting with a man, let alone falling in love. Expecting men to be jerks places so many barriers between you and men that even if a guy is interested in you he has to jump through so many hoops and work so hard—with so few wins along the way—that ninety-nine percent of men will give up and you will remain alone, forever. Men who have been with women who expect all men to be jerks feel harshly judged, and uncomfortable. They report that they leave the relationship or date as quickly as possible.

Simply put, most men worth dating are unwilling to deal with a woman who thinks all men are jerks. The only men who are routinely willing to put up with it are the men who *are* jerks. They do not care what you think of them. All they are after is sex. They do not mind hurting you. They justify the suffering they cause you by telling themselves that you deserve it, for having such a low opinion of men. If you think that all men are jerks, the only men you will attract are the ones you should avoid. It is a problem.

The solution to dealing with this expectation is to be clear about your criteria, and to use that criteria in selecting men. This will help in separating your past experiences from your new goals. When you deal with men solely from your past, you lose track of what you want in the long-term. By judging a man against your criteria (rather than against your past experiences), you are assessing him objectively rather than subjectively. When you deal with him from your criteria, you begin to explore whether you are compatible, rather than exploring just exactly how he is a jerk, like your ex.

Another perceptual tool that may help you is to list all the men you have ever dated and known who you feel wronged you, treated you poorly, did not respect you, or who hurt you in some way. List how old you were, and what the specific incidents were. Also list how you felt after each experience. Next, look over the list and note any men you can forgive, and how you could do so. Also note the men you are *unwilling* to forgive at the moment, and write something about what it would take for you to forgive those men.

From there we recommend you write down a description of the experience or the name of the person on a piece of paper and burn it. Do a little ritual to release you from this past hurt. Enjoy watching the paper, and your past pain, burn. People often find this activity gives their forgiveness some permanence. It creates a real event—the burning of the paper—to which they can refer as the moment when a particular person was forgiven. This exercise is not a heal-all or a cure-all, but it can help you release past hurts.

If your life is dictated by bad experiences in your past, your life will be much harder. In case you have not noticed, male/female relationships can be uncomfortable and difficult. The different perspectives you and a man bring to a relationship can stretch you to your breaking point, even without dredging up the past. It is important that you make peace with your past so that you can increase your chances of healthy and satisfying relationships with men in the present and the future. Forgiveness is not a touchy-feely new-age solution. When you forgive someone in your heart you are free from the constraints of the past and you increase your capacity to love and receive love. The freedom this forgiveness provides makes you more attractive to men. We all know people who are always angry and who are bitter people. They are not particularly attractive and are usually difficult and scary to be around. And then there are people who are happy, and who have a forgiving nature. They are easy to be around, are sweet, and very approachable. Think of it this way: If you were a man, which type of woman would you want to date?

You may also want to continue to explore the idea of giving men wins, and how you can use this more effectively in your dating. Any man can give you ample reasons to dislike him or to think of him as a jerk, if that is what you want to have happen. When you shift your focus onto making a man into a winner (more on this when we discuss the "middle dates"), it will keep your mind focused on what is important. It will keep you focused on developing a long-term relationship, rather than dwelling in the past or going down a dark tunnel of resentment.

We believe it is silly to ignore the past, and not learn from it. Being naive will not help anything, and we are not encouraging you to put on a happy face when you may have had some bad experiences with men. At the same time, being nasty or rude will not increase your chances of getting a man who will love you. It is a balancing act. You must learn to be aware of the good and the bad in a man at the same time.

2. Expecting to Have a Bad Time

Gina was Ms. Pessimistic. She wanted a boyfriend more than anything, but was so self-critical and self-absorbed that it was hard for her to relax around men. She was sweet and funny when she felt comfortable, but was usually so nervous and so consumed with concerns that she rarely dated or even flirted with men. Gina would focus on all the reasons why a man would dislike her, and why she would inevitably have a bad time on dates, until her concerns would snowball and stop her from even talking to men. If you are like Gina and share this expectation, then it will be nearly impossible for you to be with men. If you expect to have a bad time and expect to be painfully uncomfortable, you will, and the man will likely feel uncomfortable when he is around you.

All of us get nervous and can be self-critical at times. It is as though there were a chatterbox in our heads that never shuts up and offers us puerile, moronic, and useless information. "It's not going to work. Why would he ever like me? I'm too fat. I suck. My hair is a mess today. My last boyfriend said I was worthless. I'm stupid. My butt is too big. I'm not a good conversationalist." This voice has one unswerving mission: to keep you out of action at the battle-front called dating.

The voice may convince *you*. But we know it is always wrong. Yes, always. You think you are too fat? One of the most extremely overweight women we know has a long-standing relationship with a man who loves her, who goes out of his way to delight her, and who, as she puts it, "has never shamed me about my weight." We know women who met their current boyfriends on bad-hair days, or who had former boyfriends tell them that they were worthless, who now have men in their lives who think that they are priceless jewels. We know women who think they are bad conversationalists who have learned how to talk with men, and who have successful relationships. They all had the same negative inner voices that you have. And they all learned that those negative voices are always wrong.

The question is how you deal with the noise in your head, and how it taints your perceptions. There are several tools you can use to begin to dissolve your self-criticism, which we will teach you here. We are not dumb enough to tell you just to get over it. There are no simple solutions, but there are things that can help. First, it's worth understanding that your critical inner voice—that voice that tells you to not even try, or that no matter what you do, you will have a bad time—is only trying to help you.

Think about it. From an evolutionary perspective, it pays to avoid trying new things. The bold people, the ones who were fearless and who tried new things, were not the ones who survived to have children.

They got themselves into dangerous situations, and were killed. If bold fearlessness had been an essential survival trait, then that trait would be incredibly common, because traits essential for survival tend to outlive all the other traits that are less important for survival.

In the long run, timidity is better for the survival of the human race than is an overwhelming drive to do new and scary things. On some deep, reptilian level, your mind knows this. When you try to do something new, and get out of your nice, safe, comfort zone, it resists, and tells you everything that can possibly go wrong. It magnifies your every flaw, and gives you dramatic previews of the kind of pain you may expect to experience if you don't give up. All this leads you to become so convinced that you will have a bad time, that you stop. This makes your brain happy, because you are staying in the safe and familiar zone.

When you understand this, you can put your resistance into perspective. Thank your resistance for trying to protect you. Remind yourself that talking to a man is not *that* dangerous. Then do it.

You might also try having an internal conversation in which you lay out your concerns one at a time. Like Gina, you may think you are fundamentally undesirable and unlovable. We recommend that you list your concerns and explore their validity. Your list might look like this:

- I weigh too much
- My hair doesn't look right
- I am too old
- I do not make enough money
- Men always leave me

. . . and so on.

Next, pretend you were giving advice to a close friend. This is her list of concerns. How would you respond to her list if she showed it to you? Her list would probably seem silly and overly dramatic to you.

Go through your fears, one at a time, from the point of view of a friend:

Fear: "I weigh too much." A *friend answers:* "It is true that you aren't a skinny toothpick, like a model. But you also know it's true that most men don't like really skinny women, and that plenty of men like women who are more curvy and voluptuous. When you compare yourself to supermodels, you really are comparing yourself to women who most men think are just too thin, anyway. Also, you know plenty of women who are heavy who have relationships. You also know that you tend to think you look worse than you actually do. Plenty of women of your weight have great relationships! So get off it, and get out there!"

Fear: "My hair doesn't look right." *A friend answers:* "That's an incredibly lame excuse! Oh, I know that you feel more attractive when your hair is longer [or whatever the complaint of the day about your hair is], but it actually looks good! And remember, a great relationship was never built on hair alone! Besides, it's your smile that blows men away, anyway!"

Fear: "I'm too old." *A friend answers:* "That's ridiculous! You may be getting older, but men are getting older, too, and they are getting more financially successful. It is true that a lot of them are married, but a lot are divorced, too. And don't forget younger men. Mary Tyler Moore's husband is more than fifteen years younger than she is. So it can be done!"

As you work your way though your fears and complaints, you will feel more and more empowered to take action. At the same time, you will see the extent to which these convictions you have been carrying around are actually little more than excuses. You will see that women overcome such problems and meet men every day. If they can do it, you can too!

The only rule of this game is that you are not allowed to end on a negative interpretation of your life. You must keep at it until you come up with something that is truly positive.

You see, just because your brain tells you bad things about yourself—that you can't pursue a man, for example—you don't have to believe it. Just because your mind can come up with a worst-case scenario and paint it for you in vivid detail, does not mean that you are required to believe that the scenario will come true. Free yourself from the bonds of having to believe the worst. You do not need to. Believe some of the more positive interpretations for your life. It will be okay. Do not worry about it.

You might also review what we told you earlier about being in "the zone," which is another tool to help get you through your expectation that you will have a bad time, and into a realm of pure success with men.

3. Expecting Him to Be a Meal Ticket

The classic gold-digger takes every opportunity to use her beauty and charm to get men to pay for her in any way she can. The gold-digger lives as a prima donna and relates to men as though they were a pack of supplicants whose only purpose is to bring her life's finest. We know you are probably not one of these women. Successful gold-diggers are rare, and do not regularly buy books called *How to Succeed with Men*.

However, many women we know or have interviewed are gold-diggers to lesser degrees. To be clear: We want you to get what you want in relationships with men. If your heart's desire is to marry a rich man and have him support you forever, go for it. That is a great goal. But even if that's your one goal in life, having a prima donna attitude and being demanding of men from the start will probably not work. Many good guys will not be willing to play this game. Even men with lots of money may be turned off by this attitude. Most men enjoy the experience of providing for a woman and bringing her joy, but no one likes to feel like they are being used. When you expect a man to be a meal ticket, it is like being with a man who expects you to give him sex and who doesn't want to get to know you first. It is similarly uncomfortable for the man.

You may not like the solution: Do not be a gold-digger. Do not think of a man in terms of how he can support you financially, and you will be on your way to a much better relationship. Begin relating to him in terms of how he can win your heart. Think about how you can make him into a winner. Place your attention on how related you feel, or do not feel, to a man and on how much fun you have when you are together, rather than on his net worth (more on this in the *"Middle Dates"* chapter). Step into his shoes and begin to experience the date from his perspective. What is it like being with a woman who is demanding? From his perspective, your being financially demanding makes you much less appealing, unless you have a extremely terrific body, and he thinks he can get his hands on it.

4. Expecting Him to Fawn All Over You: "You're So Vain"

In a way, this is the opposite of the expectation that you will have a bad time. Some women expect a man to feel so privileged to be in her presence that he should do nothing but fawn over her. Sara, a statuesque blond with Nordic good looks, was shocked when her date just wanted to hang out and get to know her. She felt upset and aggravated that he didn't frequently comment on her beauty and her brilliance. She expected him to compliment her for every detail of her personality and every time she did anything even remotely sweet. If you are like Sara, you are creating an impossible situation for men. When a woman wants an unlimited supply of acknowledgment, a man cannot possibly fulfill her. If you need to be complimented and acknowledged for everything you do, no matter how small, it will likely drive the man crazy. You are setting every man up to fail, because no one can ever give you enough praise and compliments.

Women who have an overwhelming need for constant compliments usually have someone to forgive from their past. If you are such a woman, you probably have had men in your history who never gave you the kind of acknowledgment you deserved, and you are still trying to make up for their lack. We suggest you try the forgiveness exercises we talked about above. When you have forgiven the men who did not acknowledge you in the past, you won't be so needy for an infinite amount of acknowledgment today.

∞ The Four Ways to Prepare for a Qualifying Date

Joan was the type of woman who became terrified before any date and could hardly speak. She didn't feel like herself, and when the date ended she thought she would never see the man again. Joan came to us for help about where to meet qualified men and about how to prepare herself so that the dates would go more smoothly. With our encouragement, she routinely attended literary discussion groups—a natural place for her to meet men. At one of the discussions she met Clint, an English professor. They talked for a while after the discussion and he asked her out for coffee. Joan was nervous before the qualifying date and sought our advice on how to prepare. We shared with her specific tools for getting emotionally ready before and during the date, as well as questions to ask him, and ways to create specific outcomes for the date. Our advice helped her focus on what was most important to her—testing the man. She followed our advice, the date went smoothly, and they soon dated again. Because she prepared properly for the date, it went well.

1. Have Faith

In an earlier chapter we talked about being in "the zone." When you are in "the zone," you are in a state in which you are both committed to your goal, and free of your goal, simultaneously. You really care how things turn out and, in a way, don't care how they turn out, at the same time. You are able to let go of your concerns, and trust that everything will work out fine. We suggest you remind yourself to have faith before you go out on a qualifying date with a man. Remember, everything will work out okay. Remind yourself to have faith that the date will go fine. Having faith will help you release your concerns and have a better time on the date.

2. Have a Backup Plan

From the standpoint of safety and emotional stability, we insist that you create a backup plan for the date. A backup plan does two things. First, it gives you options in case the man does not show up for the qualifying date. Second, it gives you plans on how to escape if the guy turns out to be a creep, or if you find out that you really do not like him.

Stephanie had planned a wonderful date with Seth: an elaborate nature walk followed by a gourmet picnic. The date would end with an outdoor music concert featuring a jazz trio playing under the stars. Stephanie could not wait and told all her friends about the date. She had even shopped for a new sundress and was ready to show it off.

On Saturday morning Stephanie woke up to disappointment—it was raining and it looked like an all-day storm. When she turned on the weather report the meteorologist mentioned a tornado warning for the area. Her plans were ruined. Stephanie was embarrassed at how upset she felt, but she had been looking forward to the date all week. She sat on her bed glum and depressed. Instead of changing her plans and planning another activity or attending another event, she decided to cancel the date. Stephanie had no idea what could even come close to her original plans. This can easily happen to you if you do not have a backup plan, because any plan can be foiled at the last minute.

The solution? Never make plans with anyone and never leave the house? No! The solution is to always have a few backup plans, so that if something goes wrong you can always switch to plan b, c, or even d. While the rain was a disappointment, after the storms passed, the couple could have visited a museum or an indoor botanical garden, a lovely restaurant or a movie, a coffee shop with a cushy couch to kiss on, a bookstore with an erotica section, etc. The point is that a backup plan can salvage a date gone awry.

Wait—there could be even more trouble to prepare for. He might not even bother to show up for the qualifying date. Yes, that "wonderful" guy may turn out to be a chicken or a jerk. As you begin to date a variety of men you will eventually encounter a few guys who won't show up for dates. This happens to any woman who dates aggressively. The most important thing to remember is that it isn't personal. This advice is easier said than followed, we realize. Let's make it easier by taking this one step further: Take nothing a man does personally. Every behavior he displays or does not display is about his own reactions and thought processes, and has very little to do with you. When a man does not show up, it doesn't mean he doesn't like you or that he isn't attracted to you. It usually means he is scared or a space cadet. Do not worry about it.

The solution is to always bring a book or something to do in case the guy is truant or tardy. Bringing along something else to do makes you look busier and more in demand. It shows that you are up to things in your life, are not desperately waiting for some man to come and entertain you and save you from your normally boring existence—even if you are. If your date does not show up, leave after twenty minutes or so. The best solution is to do whatever you want to do at that point and reward yourself for being brave enough to show up for the date. You get to read, drink coffee, flirt with the business guy reading the paper nearby, and leave whenever you want.

We recommend that you never let a guy blow you off for more than three dates, no matter how cute, rich, sweet, or charming he may be. And three is bordering on the ridiculous. After three strikes he really should be out. Don't arrange any more dates with him. This is very important because when a man blows you off he is demonstrating his lack of integrity, his carelessness, and his inability to follow through with what he says he will do. If he can't show up on time, or even call, what else will he fail to do once things get more intimate? When you are overly forgiving toward a man, you demonstrate weak boundaries. You tell him that he can walk all over you. Do not send that message.

Being late is another story entirely. Some women really do not care about punctuality, while others rank it as extremely important. You must decide for yourself. If being on time is an important part of your criteria and values, do not hesitate to disqualify a man if he is always late and doesn't call. If you are much more laid back about this matter, then act accordingly. The key is to do things that match your long-term desires.

Once again, physical safety is another essential issue to explore. We are not lawyers, bodyguards, or martial arts experts, so we cannot give advice on how to handle specific situations from the standpoint of legality and safety. However, we always recommend that you take matters of physical safety very seriously. You may want to carry mace or be trained in self-defense, take a rape prevention course, or learn more about date rape. We mention this not to scare you or make you paranoid, but simply to alert you to this very horrible issue. Knowledge and preparation are often the best prevention. We also mention these preventative measures as actions you can take to increase your comfort and confidence when you are with men.

For safety reasons, we always recommend that you set the qualifying date at a public place. Furthermore, never go out with a man if your gut tells you to avoid him. If you do date a man in spite of your concerns, make a pact with a girlfriend that you will call her every hour to check in. If you do not feel completely comfortable with a man, be sure to meet in a public place where you know there is an easy escape route. And remember not to go home with a man until you feel very comfortable with him. The essence of our advice is to take things slowly and let the man prove his trustworthiness as you test him over time. If you are careful from the start, have a backup plan, and always trust your gut when it comes to safety issues, you make it much more likely that you will be fine.

3. Create Goals For the Qualifying Date

Before the date, we recommend that you review your list of criteria and decide on three or four characteristics to look for. If patience is really important to you, then be a bit late and see how he reacts. If economic security is important, test for that by ordering at the same time he does, and see if he pays. Ask him about his career and begin to ascertain his income. How does he measure up? Have concrete goals for each date in terms of things you are testing him on and qualities he must demonstrate. Having specific goals for the date is essential in moving from the qualifying date to the middle date. Having goals is a way of testing a man for your criteria and either moving things forward or getting rid of the guy. Without goals, the date will wander directionless and you will be no further toward your ultimate goal. If you have no goals, he will (if he has any sense) use the opportunity to seduce you, perhaps faster than you would have otherwise liked.

4. Use The Before-the-Date Checklist

- Dress in a way you feel comfortable and powerful
- Review your list of criteria
- Bring reading material or something to do in case the man is late
- Remind yourself to have faith
- Plan to stay only 30–75 minutes
- Have money
- Have your outcomes clearly in mind
- Leave home on time to arrive on time
- Create a backup plan
- Create a possible plan for a follow-up date

∞ Conclusion

So now you are prepared for the date. Let's review the Louis and Copeland master preparation: You are clear about the four elements of a qualifying date. You are clear that the date is designed to be short (30 to 75 minutes). You are clear that it is not a time to be competitive with a man and that it is not a time to just socialize. You know that it takes place in a coffee shop or another location that is conducive to talking. From there you have explored the expectations that cause trouble on the date and how to deal with them. You have mentally prepared yourself. You have a backup plan in place in case he doesn't show up or in case you don't feel safe with him. You have gone through the before-the-date checklist. You are prepared and ready to go!

CHAPTER 9

On the Qualifying Date

Congratulations, you've graduated to the big leagues. If you have gotten this far in the dating game, you are miles ahead of the competition and years ahead of where you were when you began this project. You are learning the inside track to dating the man of your dreams and constructing a relationship that will fill you with delight. Give yourself a round of applause and know that your authors are leading the crowd in a standing ovation. Now prepare yourself to jump into the date, and into the unknown.

In the last chapter you prepared yourself for the date. It is now show time. This is an opportunity to put all the learning and practice into play. It's time to go for it!

∞ Tests to Run on Him

You are now becoming a master of testing men. Even after everything we said about testing in the "Flirting" chapter, you may still be resistant to the idea of testing a man. Maybe you still believe it is a form of manipulative behavior or a way to reduce intimacy by being conniving and sneaky. Many women associate testing with moral judgments of right and wrong. But that is far from what we are teaching you. We are not advocating judgment based on morality or on any criteria except what you are looking for in a mate. Testing is not about being mean, cruel, or nasty, but simply about getting what you want in a relationship and disqualifying men if they are not potential candidates.

We believe testing is a way for you to have integrity with men. It is a way for you to create win/win situations so both of you get what you want. When you feel yourself resisting the testing process, remember: You deserve the life you want, the love you want, and the man you want. In fact, we believe that it is your birthright to have your dream relationship manifested into reality. By settling for second best you are not helping anyone.

The Nine Tests of the Qualifying Date

Now that you understand why you must test a man on the qualifying date, we will expand your horizons once more. When we talked about flirting we discussed in detail the type of tests we recommend you run on the man during the flirting interaction. We also discussed how you can construct questions or create situations in which you can observe a man's reactions and behavior. In the flirting chapters you learned that when testing a man, you look for specific and concrete behaviors. You do not base your decisions on your emotions. In the flirting interaction you had an opportunity to begin the testing process. On the qualifying date you have the opportunity to flesh out your previous answers and get more conclusive evidence and information about the man. Think of yourself as a scientist and the man as your scientific problem. The goal in your research is to come up with a better understanding of who he is and what he might be like in a relationship. On the qualifying date you repeat some or all of the tests again and continue to uncover information about the man. To review, here are the nine tests:

1. TEST HIS ATTRACTION TO YOU
- Does he smile at you?
- Does he seem to want to be around you more?

2. TEST HIS SAFETY
- Does he get mad easily?
- Does he hide personal information about himself?
- What does your gut say about him?

3. TEST HIS PATIENCE
- How does he treat service people?
- Does he get upset when you are late?

4. TEST HIS VALUES
- How does he feel about . . . [whatever you value]?
- How do "men" feel about . . . [whatever you value]?

5. TEST HIS EMOTIONAL AVAILABILITY
- Tell him about something sad, but not too tragic or personal.

6. TEST HIS ABILITY TO PRODUCE
- Ask him about his career.
- Ask him about what he is most proud of in his career.
- Tell him your material goals, note his reaction.

7. TEST YOUR ATTRACTION TO HIM OVER TIME
- Is he still attractive to you after several dates?

8. TEST HIS ABILITY TO BE ROMANTIC
- To what extent does he sweep you off your feet?

9. TEST HIS TRUSTWORTHINESS
- Does he keep his word?

Go back to your list and pick out the four or five qualities or behaviors a man must demonstrate before you will consider having a relationship with him. These are the qualities that are non-negotiable. It is crucial that you test a man against these qualities before you move on to a middle date. If he doesn't demonstrate the basic traits, do not waste your time. A man must pass these tests before you move on to the next phase.

After the date is over you will go back and look at your criteria and compare the guy's responses to your requirements. You will then review your four or five desirable qualities in a man and determine if your date had them. From there, you decide if you will see him again.

If he fails these tests, either change your criteria or disqualify him. Get out your list and look at your priorities in behaviors. Remember, you do not have time to waste dating losers with whom there is no future. You are meeting enough men to have a lot of men to test; don't settle.

∞ Money On the Date

So who pays for the date? We are in confusing times for men and women. We have male students who have been criticized by women when they open a door or offer to pay for a date! We have other students who are so used to going dutch on every date that much of the romance is absent from the dating process. What are your expectations regarding money on a date? Do you want to pay? Should he? Dozens of men have asked us what they should do about this. We have even heard of a men's rights advocate who came up with a dating contract that states if a man pays for a date, the woman must have sex with him or refund the price of the date! On the other hand, we know women who feel so strongly about equality that they will never let a man pay for anything. For the record, we always tell our male students that it's the man's job to pay for the date. Who knows what your date will think about it?

In our experience the best solution is to do whatever makes you feel comfortable. We have worked with women who have such a sense of fairness that they feel obligated to have sex with a man simply because he pays for dinner at an expensive restaurant. If you know that you will feel obligated to be sexual with a man, or even spend more time with him than you would otherwise, pay your half. Perhaps you feel no obligation in these situations. In that case, go for it. Let him shower you with gifts and take you to expensive places; just make sure to let him win your heart in the process. There is no ideal solution to the question of who pays. Our most emphatic recommendation is that you do whatever makes you feel most comfortable. Act in the manner that makes you feel free of obligations and in a manner that allows you the space to test a man during the date.

∞ The Man Handler: Controlling the Sexual Speed of the Date

Cindy's date with Marc went wonderfully. He passed every test and she had one of the most enjoyable qualifying dates of her life. Cindy gave Marc a win anytime she could. During the date she thanked him for bringing sugar for her coffee, listened intently to his stories, commented positively on his appearance, and listened to his opinions on politics. Before he left, she let him kiss her. Cindy rewarded Marc with wins every time he behaved in ways that she appreciated.

When you reward men with wins, it is important that you do so in proportion to how much pleasure they have brought you. Many women reward the jerks. They sleep with guys who make a few smooth moves and talk seductively. They fail to offer wins commensurate with the level of pleasure and romance the man is producing for them. Instead of rewarding a man when he is honest, sweet, romantic, and nurturing, they reward the guys who are flashy and shallow. The result is always the same: Women end up having relationships that lack substance, romance, and love.

Let's also look at the other side of this story. We have worked with women who almost never give men wins. It is as though they have no ability to be gracious, sweet, soft, or polite. It is easy (and even fun!) to give men only losses. At the time of this writing, one of the top popular songs is Shania Twain's, "That don't impress me much." In this song, the central character meets a variety of men, all of whom show their best features, all of which she slams with "that don't impress me much." None of them has a chance of winning her. Such women simply do not see the point in making men into winners. If you fall into this category, and easily treat even the sweetest man coldly, you will remain alone. We've said it before, and we are going to keep repeating it throughout this book: If a man cannot win around you, he will move on to someone with whom he can. End of story.

There are three situations you may find yourself in on a qualifying date. You may like him and want things to move forward; you may want to proceed with caution; or you may dislike the guy and want to leave. Use the qualifying date to move the relationship forward, to slow things down, or to cut the guy off completely.

1. If You Like Him and Want to Go Forward

If you are very interested in a man, it is important that you let him win around you—a lot. It is important that you give him small wins during the date as a way to help him fall in love with you and feel like a winner in your presence. It is important to start this habit early on in a relationship.

Can you recall a time in which you felt baffled by a man's behavior and you were unsure about how to respond or how to interpret his signals? Have you ever wondered why men do not understand you and what you really want from them? We all get confused about the opposite sex. Sometimes it seems as though it's impossible to understand even the most basic communication from the opposite sex. This is why it is crucial that you give the man clear wins if you want to keep moving things forward. A win tells him he is doing the right thing, that he is doing his job, and leaves him feeling happy. A loss tells him he has made a mistake and gives him an opportunity to redirect his focus onto another win. It is pretty simple at this stage; give a man wins when he does things you like and losses when he makes mistakes. When you give men wins they will want to be around you. It can be that simple.

2. If You Want to Slow Things Down

If you want to slow things down, it is important that you decrease the frequency and the intensity of the wins you give a man. If you slow down your willingness to give him wins, he will most likely slow down and decrease the intensity of his pursuit. Sex is the ultimate win (we hope you realize this by now). If you really want to slow things down, dramatically decrease the frequency of sexual contact of any kind. It is hard for a man to experience a loss when he is having hot pumping sex with you whenever he wants. That is why it makes sense to cease or to avoid beginning your sexual contact if you want to slow down the relationship and build the bonding process.

Another way to slow things down is to go on more qualifying dates and to focus more on testing him than on romance. For you, a qualifying date is a time to continue testing him and a time to get a clearer idea of whether you want to move forward. You can then increase the number of wins you give him once you decide if you are interested in pursuing the relationship further.

3. If You Aren't Interested in Him at All

If you are not interested in the man and no longer want to see him: *Stop giving him wins!* Give him losses.

If you are not interested, you can be honest with him, or slightly stretch the truth to make it easier on him. You can stop returning his phone calls and avoid him, period. Some women, out of guilt, avoid being blunt because they don't want to hurt a man's feelings. That does not work. When you are not candid with a man, he does not know what to think. If you are wavering and unsure of yourself, he may think you are just afraid to get involved, and keep pursuing you. The best way to cut things off is to be honest but polite, and leave no room on his end for misinterpretation.

We know it always sucks to be in the position of cutting off the relationship, but those are the breaks, kid. As you know, it sucks to be on the receiving end of a break up, too. In an ideal world nothing bad or uncomfortable would happen, but, as you have no doubt noticed, things are not always idyllic. Remember to value yourself, your time, and your heart. Instead of wasting time with a guy who does not meet your criteria, you could be pursuing the ultimate romantic, juicy, and loving relationship.

If you use these three levels of wins, you will be able to control the momentum of the date. You will be able to keep your romance moving forward, slow it down, or even stop it. You will be able to give yourself the time you need to test the man thoroughly before you move forward and you will know how to move things to the next level.

⊙ *Don't Leave Him at a Loss*

When Diane went out with Jim for the first time she discussed every topic she thought of. She discussed her support of capital punishment. She expressed to Jim that her experience with men over forty was that they were all just a pack of horny animals who wanted sex without commitment. She discussed her hatred of the media and the news. She went on and on, commenting on every strange and controversial topic under the sun. Jim ended the date early, convinced that Diane was a psycho. Sharing your extreme opinions is a good way to kill your chances with a man. At best you come across as a nut, and at worst a dangerous criminal or a member of a violent cult. Read the following section so that you can avoid the mistakes Diane made on her date.

The first question to ask yourself when saying something that could be interpreted as controversial or extreme is "why am I saying this?" We recommend that you consider whether asking a question will give a man a win, or give a man a loss and create more distance between the two of you.

Here are a few other questions to examine when deciding on a topic of conversation:

- How will this further my goal of testing him?
- How will he respond to this?
- What will he think of me if I ask this?
- Will he feel uncomfortable if I ask this?
- What message am I sending to this man as a woman who would talk about this so early in a relationship?
- Does talking about this make me into the woman I am committed to becoming?

Whenever you enter a conversation early on in a relationship, especially on the qualifying dates, you must consider such questions. We have seen even the most sophisticated women make the mistake of bringing up controversial topics on the qualifying date. Such women might discuss past boyfriends and husbands, former lovers, men who have harmed them, their menstrual cycle, why men are jerks, or other awkward topics. If you are the kind of woman who loves to discuss these sorts of things when you are out with a man, we ask you again to remember your goal, and ask yourself, what is the point of doing so? How does this give a man a win? How does it give him a chance to pass or fail a test? How is the man you are out with supposed to react or respond to your words?

It may be hard for the man to respond to you when you discuss weird or extreme views. It will be hard for him to come up with something that will produce a win. If you tend to bring up topics that leave men at a loss, you may want to consider changing your approach. We have dug deep into our vault of stories from men and have come up with a few of the most common conversations which will kill a date no matter how well things are going.

Obsessions

Some women share their obsessions on the qualifying date. This is a sure way to give a man a case of the creeps. Do not share your devotion to a particular pop star or a particular sexual fetish. This will lead to trouble. A love of men's feet, for instance, will not win points with most men. Sharing stories about guys you stalked and are still obsessed with will only lead to more trouble, as well. This ties back to our discussion of romantic conversations. Remember, we said that if you describe a feeling, the person listening has to go inside and experience that feeling, just to understand what you are talking about. When you describe an obsession, a man will imagine being with such an unbalanced woman, and may feel all the bad feelings possible in that situation. You are telling the man to stay away from you. You are telling a man that you could become obsessed with him, and this will make you seem like more of a hassle than you might be worth. And so, he will avoid you. People don't usually need their lives to be *more* crazy. They need them to be more calm. If you come across as eccentric and obsessed, he will lose interest.

Your Ex

Why are you talking about former boyfriends or husbands on the qualifying date? What good could this possibly accomplish? If you talk about your ex-husband or your ex-boyfriend, it looks as if you still want to be with him, it makes your date uncomfortable, and makes him wonder why he is even talking to you. It sucks for him to have to hear about this other guy because he automatically becomes competition. This will reduce his odds of wanting to date you. He might be thinking, "Well, I like her, she is attractive, I can imagine us together—but what about her ex?" In the end, it is more important to focus on the man you are out with. Any comparison between former dates and the guy on the qualifying date is unnecessary, and rude.

The Deficiencies of Other Men

Another great way to ruin a date is to tell the man who is with you about how creepy men are and about the various ways men have hurt you. This again is a wonderful way to turn off any man and make him feel defensive and even ashamed. He does not need for you to tell him about how boyfriend number twenty-two went hunting, how horrible it is to kill little animals, and how men are so bad for having a predatory instinct. Your current date does not need to know how boyfriend number eleven didn't bathe, and how horrible it is that men have poor hygiene habits. He does not need to know all the ways in which you are angry with "the patriarchy" for not treating you fairly. When you describe the deficiencies of other men in even the most innocent ways, your date will take it personally, as he will not be able ignore that he is part of that horrid class you so love to hate: men.

Marriage

Some women are careless and discuss the importance of marriage on the qualifying date. Usually women who are frustrated that they are not married will mention marriage as though a man would pledge eternal love and propose right there on the date. Although commitment or marriage are important, presenting it too early is a recipe for scaring off a man. It makes you look desperate. When you mention marriage or the "C" word on the qualifying date, you will come across as weird, insecure, and no fun. He doesn't care that casual dating worked for you when you were in your twenties, but now that your biological clock is ticking you are ready to be married. This will just put him off. If you have a tendency to want to discuss marriage and commitment issues on the qualifying date, chill out—there will be time for this conversation later. Don't worry though, this book will teach you how to present the commitment conversation to a man in a step-by-step manner, when the time is right. It does not, however, belong on the first few dates.

Your Desire to Have Babies

Just because your biological clock is ticking away does not mean every man who comes into contact with you needs to hear about it. We know you want to have babies. We know that you *really* want to have babies. Just as talking about marriage and commitment on the qualifying date is inappropriate, so is talking about children. Talking about your desire for children is better suited for the middle dates or when you examine the potential of a long-term relationship with a man. Talking about kids is best brought up within the context of long-term goals, long *after* you have gotten to know him better and extensively tested him. If you want to know how he feels about children, watch his behavior. When a nearby baby cries, does he seem annoyed? Or interested? When you are around children, does he play with them? Or does he avoid them?

If you insist on asking a man direct questions about kids on the first few dates he will probably lie, and give you the answer that he thinks you want to hear. Why? Because (once again) if a man knows he will lose all chance with you if he is totally honest, he will mislead you, in the hopes that he can seduce you. This is why asking a man directly if he wants to have children is not an effective way to gather his true opinions. You must watch his behavior around children, and keep learning about his character.

If you already have kids, of course you must tell him right away. Often this will come up while you are flirting. If a man doesn't want to date you because you have kids, move on to the next guy. Do not dwell on what might have been. Change your focus, explain the whole thing as his problem, and move on.

Body Issues

Some women love to share the most intimate details about their physical imperfections on the qualifying date. Specifically, many women love to share how fat they feel and how a particular body part looks fat. Other women discuss their clothes size and how small they wish they were, or how small they were back in high school. Then they whine to a man and ask him if he thinks a particular body part looks chubby, Rubenesque, unattractive, or pick any other synonym for fat. A man can never win in this situation. Can you see why? If he actually thinks she is fat in those places she will become upset. If he says no, then she assumes he is lying and she badgers him. It can go on and on like this with no hope for the guy.

Each and every one of our male students has had this sort of experience. A woman who is delightful and a wonderful date suddenly goes down the dark tunnel, where she begins whining and complaining about how fat she is, and how (whatever body part she feels bad about) is not right. These sorts of complaints and this type of search for approval does not belong on the qualifying date. Let your long-term mate listen to you and comfort you. Now is not the time to begin this inevitably long, slow and torturous conversation.

Women also love to complain about their hair—the famed "bad hair day." Do not look to men to comment on your hair. Most will not even notice whether there is a variance in color, length, or style. Men will look at you and think about sex, not noticing imperfections with your bangs, uneven strands near your ears, or any other hair-related issues. The bottom line is that men will likely not even know enough about hair styles to have an intelligent conversation with you about them.

Men are either hot for you or not, and your hair has very little to do with it, no matter how it looks.

Shall we continue? Men have recounted situations in which a woman describes how her skin breaks out when she is excited, how her right knee hurts when it rains outside, how her makeup doesn't look quite right, how one of her breasts is larger than the other, how the mole on right shoulder blade catches her bra strap, how she wishes she were taller, how she has an eczema patch on the small of her back, and so on. Once again, why tell a man this? What men are left with is that you are insecure and probably a high-maintenance woman. Besides, why draw attention to your imperfections? The qualifying date is about making a good impression in a short period of time, not alienating the guy or making him wonder about your faults.

After a guy gets to know you better and begins falling in love with you, physical imperfections will be less significant. At the beginning of a relationship, however, they may seem important, especially if you point them out. Even when you really want to tell a man about a physical problem or discuss fat parts of your body, do not do it. Repeat after us, "I will not discuss imperfections or concerns about my body with the men I date." Complain to your girlfriends about these issues instead, and leave guys alone until you are in a committed relationship. At that point you can drive him crazy all you want. Listen to what we say here: We are absolutely right on this issue.

Times You've Lied, Stolen, or Cheated

Some women feel such a strong need to be honest with men that they confess every dishonest thing they have ever done in their life within the first thirty-five minutes of meeting. Maybe they think it is a bonding experience to share times when they have lied, shoplifted, cheated in poker, manipulated a police officer, or whatever their offenses happen to be. When you mention times you have been dishonest or times you have stolen or cheated, the man may wonder if you will commit those crimes against him. Honesty is noble, but it is also important to be tactful and to be aware of the potential effect of confessing things about yourself prematurely. He'll start to watch his wallet when he's around you. You will scare him. Once again, after you have been with a man for a while and have a solid relationship, talking about criminal and manipulative behavior may be cathartic and even funny; on the qualifying date, however, the guy may just as easily think you are dangerous. It may leave him wondering about your police record and whether you are going to steal his television.

Mental Illness

It is amazing what things people share in the name of emotional honesty. We all know people who have been manic-depressive, attempted suicide, or suffered emotional breakdowns. Mental illness strikes many wonderful people and the pain involved is truly horrible for themselves, their families, and their friends. At the same time, there is still a huge social stigma, especially with men, around being hospitalized for mental problems. Sharing this information may be an important part of an individual's healing journey, but men will likely be scared by the gravity of these conditions, and not understand that they can be controlled, if you disclose them on the first date.

This type of problem is much too complicated to discuss casually on a qualifying date. We suggest that you first test the man for his ability to be compassionate before bringing up this topic; otherwise he may hurt you with an insensitive response, and both of you will likely feel uncomfortable. Most men would have no idea how to respond if you began talking about having bi-polar disorder or panic attacks, for instance. As a result, it is best to wait until the middle dates before bringing up these topics, long after you have decided that you want to be in a committed relationship with him. It should be noted that most of our male students have proven to be very supportive of their girlfriends and mates in their healing processes once they are in a committed relationship.

∞ Rules for Sharing Feelings

"What about feelings?" you ask. "Isn't it important that I be emotionally available and honest with men at all times? Isn't it important that I take emotional risks and let the man get to know the inner me?" Well, yes and no. Being vulnerable and candid is crucial to the success of any long-term relationship. But we are talking about the qualifying date here, and it is simply too premature to raise these sorts of issues. Most men won't have a framework in which to hold your emotional vulnerability. They may interpret it to mean that they have done something wrong, or hurt your feelings. Mentioning extreme fears and emotional pain will likely put the man off and leave him unclear about how to respond.

At the same time, we are not suggesting that you always operate as a perfectly happy, Pollyanna-like, expressionless automaton, devoid of any real emotions. You have to figure out how to be honest without being extreme. By testing a man and his emotional availability, you can judge how far to take things with him. Create the situation so that you can be emotionally expressive, he can win in the process, and you both can feel satisfied by the interaction. When you are able to be emotional in a way that he can handle, you both will be happy and feel like winners.

What to Share

Now that we have thoroughly covered what not to share, it is only fair that we explore the other side: what to share. First of all, remember that you are with the guy for only 30 to 75 minutes and you want to leave him wanting more of you, not bored and wanting to get away. During that time it is important to focus on testing, having fun, and talking in a relaxed manner. Talk about what truly interests you and learn what he is like. Even more important than what he says is his attention to you. Take mental notes on his answers to your questions and on how he treats you. Here are some questions that may be useful for you to explore as you get to know him.

- Even if he doesn't like swing dancing, for instance, how open is he to learning?
- Even if he hasn't heard of macrobiotics, how open is he to hearing about it and discussing the details with you?
- How open is he to learning about you?
- Do you feel judged around him, or is he supportive from the start?
- Is he someone who rarely looks into your eyes, or is he paying attention and does he seem awake and easy to engage in conversations?
- How open is he in talking about himself and answering personal questions?
- Does he bore you with details of his horrible work life, or does he take you on a flirtatious and romantic conversational trip?

The conversation should be fairly light and easy going, but not solely about the weather and sports, either. Always remember your goal of testing him, and you will be fine. And if you do blow it, there are always other men out there who are candidates to be your long-term mate.

∞ *How to Listen So He Wins*

Barbara is a master at giving men wins. She is encouraging and attractive without being subservient or ditzy. Barbara is able to talk to men about their lives, jobs, and so on, and gives them wins by validating their experiences. She easily and non-intrusively compliments men on their accomplishments and also validates them when they treat her well. Barbara may compliment a man on his appearance, when he makes her laugh or smile, and when he does little things for her like buy coffee or open doors. Men are able to win in her presence because she feels free to acknowledge and compliment them. Men feel proud and special to be around her, because her happiness makes them, in turn, also feel happy. The result is that men love doing things for Barbara because she makes them feel good for doing so.

How to Listen and Act So He Wins

1. Validate specific things he says about himself and his life that seem interesting to you.
2. Compliment him when he treats you in ways you appreciate.
3. Compliment when he exhibits behaviors that are on your list.
4. Ask him personal questions about himself and validate him when he answers.
5. Make specific requests of men (like opening a jar lid, opening a door, buying you coffee).
6. Compliment his good intentions, even if the result was not what you expected.

∞ To Kiss Or Not To Kiss

If a man wins enough on the date, he will probably want to kiss you. (Actually, he will probably want much more). When a man is attracted to you he may act strangely. He may stare at you with a dazed look on his face, appear awkward and embarrassed, touch you frequently, keep his distance, be in your physical space, or exhibit a host of other odd and contradictory behaviors. Most likely he will be contemplating when he should make his move and try to kiss you. When it comes time to kiss, it is best for you to be clear about your willingness or unwillingness to do so. He will be looking to you to decide when he gets to kiss you. That said, we will now give you the lowdown on how to handle the first kiss.

Mary had a wonderful time with Bob on their qualifying date. He told wonderful stories about going on photo expeditions to France and the Greek islands. After the qualifying date she felt so attracted to him and so happy that she could hardly contain her desire to kiss him and run her hands through his dark curly hair. In the end, Mary decided to give him a big hug and a peck on the cheek instead, because she wanted to make sure they moved slowly into a relationship. She thought about her long-term goals and decided to avoid adding to the whirlwind of emotions she was experiencing. After weighing her options she decided it would be too overwhelming to kiss him and decided to wait until the next date.

If the date goes well, you need to figure out how to end it. Is it best to go for the hot French kiss-fest, a gentle peck on the cheek, a hug, handshake, or simple good-bye? The decision is yours. Most likely, the man will want to kiss you, but will be looking to you for signals on how far to go and what to do. You control the speed of any sensual activity and the guy knows this. Your behavior and your approachability will set the tone for the good-bye. See chapter 11 "Charming a Man on the Middle Dates," to learn how to heat up your man and get to that first kiss quicker.

Our advice is to take the long-term perspective and weigh the consequences. In the end, do what you think is best for yourself. We have known women who have gone to bed with a man on the qualifying date, had a great time, and who had everything work out perfectly from then on. We've also known women who have had horrid results after having sex on the qualifying date. Some women have kissed passionately after a qualifying date and had it set the tone for a wonderfully nurturing relationship. Others kissed passionately during a qualifying date and felt it caused the relationship to end too quickly. In the final analysis you alone must weigh your desires versus your long-term goals. You must measure your level of comfort with the particular man, and your comfort with yourself, if you go for it. Listen to your gut; it will be a good indicator on how to proceed.

∞ Creating the Next Date

Carole worked at an advertising firm and hadn't had a boyfriend in two years. She came to us looking for the solution to her dating woes. We put her on the program you have been reading about—meeting and dating men, then qualifying or disqualifying each one for his long-term potential. One of her first qualifying dates was with Gary. He had a decent career, but was a bit shorter than she liked, and seemed awkward. Carole decided to proceed anyway. From the start, however, she had mixed feelings about dating Gary. His shorter height was a big turn off. But it was more than just the height issue; Gary was rude at times and seemed interested only in sex. She tested him and he passed more than half of the tests that she threw out during a qualifying date. At the end of the date she was pretty sure he was history, but she wanted to see him once more just to be sure. After the next qualifying date, she had no doubt that Gary was disqualified.

Even though Gary didn't work out (thank God), we praised Carole for the way she tested him and the way she searched for information until she could base her decision on the data, having Gary pass or fail the test. She followed the rules for the qualifying date and even went back for more research just to make sure her initial assessment of Gary was correct. Carole neither wasted time being vague about how Gary should proceed, nor did she spend time with a man who had no future potential with her. And, of course, she didn't sleep with him and hopelessly confuse matters.

After a qualifying date you have only three options:

1. If he passed very few of your criteria, disqualify him.
2. If you are unclear about your attraction to him, or he has passed enough of your tests that you are unsure about his suitability, go out with him on another qualifying date.
3. If he has passed enough of the qualifications on your list and the essential tests listed earlier, set up a middle date.

Whether you want to proceed to a middle date or another qualifying date, it will be much easier to set a date before you leave the qualifying date. Have a date and time in mind. Make sure to contact him within one week to set up either type of date; if you wait any longer it will be much less likely to happen. Before you set up the date be clear about what information you want from him. In the case of another qualifying date, focus on what information or behaviors you need from him to choose to move to the middle dates and what information or behaviors will eliminate him from your list of potential applicants. With this information in front of you, you can more easily construct appropriate tests for him. In the case of a middle date, it is assumed that you have elected to move forward because he meets enough of your basic criteria. However, you will still need to test him. The next chapter on middle dates will thoroughly prepare you.

⚭ The Three Signs to Break Off the Date Early

Some dates are meant to be broken off early. There is no reason for you to hang out with jerks or to waste your time in uncomfortable situations. There are both jerks and non-jerks in this world. We are telling you, once and for all, that you do not have to spend time with the jerks. Some men will break cardinal rules during the qualifying date. They quickly tell you through their actions that they are not boyfriend material. Do not waste your time: get rid of such guys. There is no reason for you to stick around and have a bad time. Here are a few signs that it is definitely time to end the date.

Sign Number One: You Are Having a Bad Time

Dating is risky business. It means going off into the unknown. A man might seem interesting when you first meet him, and become a boring jerk later on. It might seem as though you have a lot in common on the phone, only to find out that he is a sex-crazed pervert on the qualifying date. Whatever the problem, if you are having a bad time with a man, feel free to end the date early. If the guy has been offensive to you, if you clearly are not interested and you have no intention of dating him again, end the date early. Simply stating, "I don't think this is going anywhere," may work, as would, "I am sorry, but I have to run now." There is no reason to explain yourself, be overly apologetic or to waste any more of your time.

Because this is a qualifying date, you set it up to be short. You can tell him about a real or fictional commitment you have—he should not be expecting to spend the whole day with you, anyway. Excuse yourself politely, and leave.

We suggest you never get into justifying or giving complicated reasons for why you have to end a date with a man. If he is a jerk, he does not deserve the truth, especially if telling him the truth is awkward, or if you are afraid that the truth might make him dangerously angry. You are not a social service agency; you do not have the responsibility to tell a man everything you think about him at every moment in a misguided effort to help him change and grow. If he asks you to stay, and you've told him that you have another appointment, go. If he asks you why you won't stay, do not explain why your friend would be angry if you were late, or any other reason that he might be able to counter. A jerk will try to learn your reasons for leaving, and argue with you about them, hoping he can wear you down. Don't fall for it. Tell him that you have another appointment, and that you keep your appointments. Do not allow yourself to get into an argument about the minutia of your day. If you must leave, leave.

Though it seems completely illogical, you can also have a bad time when you like the guy a lot and are overwhelmed by your attraction to him. In these situations you may begin questioning whether you are good enough for him. You might work yourself up into a terrible state of nervousness in which the probability of a relationship with him seems smaller and smaller as you get weirder and weirder. It often comes down to feeling uncomfortable with the idea that you might get exactly what you want. It can be scary. After all, if a guy who is a loser doesn't want you, who cares? But if a guy who might be a winner rejects you, that could really hurt. If you are scared because the guy seems to fit so many of your requirements, remember to have faith. When you focus your attention and energy on having the relationship of your dreams by visualizing and pursuing the man on your list, he will likely show up in your life. Remember that you have attracted this man and this situation to you. If you feel uncomfortable, be willing to stay in the situation anyway. Be willing to get what you want in life. It will likely clear up as you get more comfortable with him and with your own power.

Sign Number Two: Your Instincts Tell You He Is Dangerous

If you do not feel safe with a man, leave the date immediately. Safety is something you should never ignore. Some men are violent, dangerous, and so on. The problem is that there is no Reader's Digest guide to understanding dangerous men. They come from all economic backgrounds and races. It is much more important to be safe and possibly lose a good guy and a fun date than to risk being harmed by a dangerous guy.

Sign Number Three: He Fails the Tests

Why bother pursuing a man who fails your important tests during the flirting interaction and the qualifying date? Your criteria should include items that are requirements as well as other behaviors or details that would be wonderful extras. Perhaps generosity is a requirement, but being wealthy would be an extra feature, like a deluxe chrome package on your new car. In this case, a man could be generous with you but not have an abundance of money. Your priorities may also shift as you spend more time with the man—remember how we keep telling you to look at and revise your list after interacting with a man? The details seem less important and his character shines through. However you choose to measure a man, it is important that you observe the whole man (his behavior, looks, etc.) and factor in how much you like and trust him. It is also important to think about how compatible you are and how much fun you have when you are with him. At the beginning of the relationship, your list will likely shift. If a guy fails your most basic tests, however, it is a definite sign to end the relationship.

∞ The Boneheaded Mistakes Men Make

We all know that dates have the potential for great joy, romance, and ecstasy. At the same time, they present an equal opportunity for screwups and bad times. All dates have the potential to fail. Let's look at some of the common problems men make on first dates, and at how to handle them.

Boneheaded Mistake One: His Conversation Bores You

He talks incessantly about science fiction, the history of fiber optics in the telecommunications industry, sports, work, or any other boring topic.

We first mentioned this problem when we talked about flirting, but guess what? This behavior might show up on the qualifying date, as well! When Paula first went out with Mike she had no idea just how bad a date could be. Not only did Mike talk endlessly, but he was boring. He droned on and on about the newest models of computers and how many megabytes of RAM were available, the features, the Internet connection speed, the type of ports it featured, the dot pitch of the monitor, and on and on and on until she thought she would either scream, strangle him, or do both simultaneously. How many times have you been out with a man when he began discussing a topic that you had absolutely no knowledge of and no interest in, yet he talked about it for hours and would not stop? We know this happens all the time.

Why do men do this? Lots of men are uncomfortable around women and don't want to appear stupid and vulnerable, so they talk about what they know best: work or sports, for example. First of all, remember that while he may be boring, he isn't necessarily a bad guy, so you should not automatically disqualify him. Have some compassion for the guy, but have compassion for your ear drums, too. You can switch the topic of conversation, but remember that he isn't likely droning on because he is trying to dominate the conversation, rather he is probably nervous and doesn't know what else to talk about. He may still very much fit within your criteria. He talks on and on only because he wants to impress you, not bore you.

We recommend that you be honest with a man and unafraid to interrupt him as you attempt to switch the topic of conversation. Maybe he doesn't know he is talking too much or that you are not interested. It is hard to tell what is going on in his head and when you pretend to be interested you are only encouraging him to talk more. Think about it this way: In some ways it is good for him to talk about boring topics because it gives you an opportunity to test him for how he reacts to being interrupted. Some men will apologize and switch the topic, others will mumble under their breath and talk about something else, and others will become ashamed and not even look at you. This is good information to use as you decide whether you want to see him again.

Boneheaded Mistake Two: He Doesn't Show Up For the Date

Congratulations, you have had a no-show. This is good because it builds character. Okay—that is a bit sarcastic. It stinks, but it does help you practice overcoming rejection, and that is good. We hope you have planned for this ahead of time, as we have suggested, by bringing a book to read and something else do in case he didn't show. We suggest you give him only one more chance to redeem himself, or possibly two—after that he is on the bad list and must be avoided. Remember, don't jump to conclusions, don't take it personally, or obsess about what you did wrong to make this happen. The truth is that you do not know what happened. You do not know if he forgot, or if his cat was sick and had to go to the veterinarian, if his car broke down, or what. In the best of all possible worlds he left you a message on your answering machine apologizing profusely and is sending over flowers to make it up to you, but this is reality we are talking about here. He probably won't handle it so well.

Here are our recommendations on how to handle a no-show. If you are angry with him, do not call him until you have calmed down. After you have some distance from the experience, call him and ask what happened. Do not yell at him or accuse him, because this will cause him to avoid you. Many women will be angry with a man and chew him out and then are surprised when he avoids them; give him the benefit of the doubt. If he is a good guy, the trouble will be worth it. It is permissible to leave one message on his answering machine, but talk to him as soon as possible. In most cases the situation will be cleared up by asking him what happened. If you like his excuse, you can give him another chance. If he misses another date, consider him history. Blowing off a woman is a clear sign that a man is undependable, doesn't have integrity, and probably cannot be trusted with bigger responsibilities.

Boneheaded Mistake Three: He Stumbles Through Romantic Interactions and You Feel Sorry For Him

Yes, many men will not know how to have a romantic conversation or an intimate encounter. This may be a good sign. Most of the men you want to have a long-term relationship with are not slick and full of smooth moves. Good, honest, earnest, and hard-working guys are not master seducers or sly womanizers. They will stumble, fall on their face occasionally, and they will blow it. This is normal, and will happen at any level of commitment with a man—from casual dating to marriage. Get used to it. That does not mean that every man who is uncomfortable and stumbles while with you is a good guy or that he matches your criteria; most won't. It does mean that you shouldn't disqualify a guy just because he says something stupid or makes a mistake. Give men some space to blunder and the ones worth developing a relationship with will learn to treat you romantically and sensitively. Having a forgiving nature doesn't mean you don't have boundaries or that you accept abusive behavior, but it does mean that you give a man the benefit of the doubt, and are responsive when he attempts to be romantic, even if he is a bit clumsy.

Boneheaded Mistake Four: He Pushes Too Hard and Too Fast with Sexual Overtures

Lisa found Justin attractive and intriguing. She was twenty-three and a grad student. Justin was in his early twenties and seemed shy. He had short blond hair, a muscular body, and a cute, boyish face. She noticed him months ago and always flirted with him when she saw him at school and around campus. One day he asked her out. Lisa suggested they go out for coffee a few days later. During the date Justin seemed distant to Lisa. He didn't talk much and seemed preoccupied. The date ended abruptly when Justin said he had to go to work. Lisa walked out of the coffee house with him. The minute they stepped out on the street, Justin grabbed her and began kissing her with no prior warning or sign. Lisa reacted quickly; she slapped him and stormed off.

Some men will move too fast with sexual advances and you will need to decide ahead of time how you want to handle it. Most men will make the first move and will then respect the speed at which you want to proceed. Your response depends on your criteria and what you eventually want from a man. Justin, for instance, deeply offended Lisa and she vowed to never see him again. If she had some warning that Justin was going to kiss her, or if he had done so more gently and more romantically, Lisa would have allowed him to continue. Once again, you have to decide what is offensive to you and to what extent you are offended. Remember, a man might go for the first sexual move because he has misinterpreted your behavior. When he botches something up, you decide if you will forgive him. It comes down to how safe you feel with the guy, how out of line you think he was, and what you want.

⚭ *Drugs and Alcohol*

This is a big problem in the dating scene. How do you handle it? We recommend that you be very clear about your views on these issues as part of determining your criteria. What are your views on drug use? Do you think it is wrong for people to smoke marijuana, for instance? Could you date someone who is a pot smoker? What about other drugs? And where do you stand on drinking alcohol?

You need to ask yourself some questions. Are you willing to date someone who casually uses illegal drugs? In what situations aren't you willing to do so? Be clear on this matter and the possible repercussions so that you can interact with a man based on considered criteria rather than reactions to his behavior. If you determine that you cannot date a drug user, then stick to your decision. Do not enter a debate. And more importantly, never go into a relationship with the hopes of reforming a man. This is nearly impossible. If you are going to date someone who uses illegal drugs, do so without any hopes of changing him; only of accepting him.

Drug addiction and alcoholism are serious matters. You should observe a man's drug and alcohol use in terms of his potential for addiction. On the one hand, be aware. On the other, avoid overreacting and jumping to conclusions. Some women will accuse a man of being an alcoholic if he wants a beer during dinner. Other women are in such denial that they let a man do heroin for years and never confront him or discuss the effects of his drug use on their relationship. You must be aware of signs and symptoms of addiction. Once you are in a committed relationship you will likely support your partner in getting help, counseling, or therapy. If you learn about this type of behavior early in a relationship it is best to decide whether you are willing to date someone who abuses drugs or alcohol.

∽ *After the Date*

After the date, the most important thing to do is to find ways to interpret the date as a success. Most singles tend to judge themselves harshly and ignore the aspects of the date that went well. Instead, they agonize over the mistakes, the moments they felt nervous, the few times they made dumb comments, or spilled coffee on their new pants. In terms of your training and development you must find things to feel proud about. Maybe it was a major accomplishment just to be out with a man. Perhaps it was a triumph that you ended the date early because you weren't interested in him, whereas in the past you would have stayed and been bored. Write your list in your journal. Find ways to make the date a success in your mind. This will increase your self-confidence for the next time.

It will also be useful to take the time to examine the "After-the-Date" checklists and the "Wins Test," rate his performance on the tests, and complete the study questions (all coming up at the end of this chapter). Spending time reflecting on the date will reveal the gaps in your skills and also the places where you are starting to develop mastery. You can then reevaluate your list and create a game plan for the next date and the next man.

Here is a series of tests and lists that you can use to examine your date's compatibility with you.

Wins Test

Ask yourself:

- Were you willing to give the guy wins? Why or why not?
- What were specific examples of letting him win?
- Was he receptive when you let him win?
- Did you give him wins in proportion to how well he produced for you?

Passing the Tests: Yes or No

Answer these questions with as many specific and concrete examples as possible.

1. TESTING HIS ATTRACTION TO YOU

Did you test him? Yes or no? How do you know?

2. TESTING HIS SAFETY LEVEL

Do you feel safe with him? How was this tested and demonstrated?

3. TESTING HIS PATIENCE

Did you test him in this area? Yes or no? Is patience an important virtue in your ideal man? How did you test him for patience?

4. TESTING HIS VALUES

Did you test him? Yes or no? How do you know if his values are compatible with yours?

5. TESTING HIS EMOTIONAL AVAILABILITY

Did you test him? Yes or no? Is he emotionally available? Could he be emotionally available with minimal effort and training from you?

6. TESTING HIS ABILITY TO PRODUCE

Did you test him? Yes or no? How do you know? What do you want him to produce for you?

7. TESTING HIS ABILITY TO BE ROMANTIC

Did you test him? Yes or no? Is he romantically inclined? Could you train him to be romantically inclined with minimal effort?

8. TESTING HOW MUCH YOU LIKE HIM AS YOU GET TO KNOW HIM BETTER

Do you want to see him again? Yes or no? Did you set up a follow-up date?

9. TESTING FOR OTHER CRITERIA

Check other criteria from your list and write whether he was tested for those areas, and whether he passed the tests. List the best and worst parts of the date. List the ways in which he blew it. List the ways in which you blew it.

After-the-Date Checklist

DID YOU DO THE FOLLOWING?

- Give the guy at least two wins.
- Arrive on time.
- Prepare a backup plan.
- Bring work or a book to read.
- Give the guy wins in proportion to how well he produced on the date.
- End the date after 30 to 75 minutes.
- Test the man.
- Date at a coffee shop.
- Create goals before the date.
- Bring money for the date to avoid any hassles.
- Listen to him in such as way that left him winning.

DID YOU REMEMBER NOT TO DO THE FOLLOWING?

- Compete with the guy.
- Share stories about your ex.

- Come to the date just to hang out and socialize.
- Kiss the guy just because he pulled out a wad of cash.
- Mention illegal activities you've been involved with and jail stories.
- Talk about marriage or commitment.
- Let the guy insult you.
- Share obsessions.

Testing the Man: Conclusion in Action

Lynn did everything correctly on her qualifying date with Michael. When Michael asked her out to dinner she suggested they meet at a coffee shop. She did not want to spend hours with Michael before she found out if he met her criteria; she wanted only an hour of his time. Before the date she sat down with her list and picked a few of the criteria to test him on: humor, sweetness, safety, romance, and intellect. She came to the date with a few ideas on how to test him for these qualities.

When Michael arrived at the coffee shop, Lynn was absorbed in her favorite magazine. Her first test was to see if Michael would be punctual. He passed the first test perfectly. Michael approached the table with a big smile and looked deeply into Lynn's eyes. She appreciated his boldness. When she put her hand out for a handshake, Michael kissed it lightly. It seemed sweet to Lynn, not tacky or forced or overtly sexual, but rather a sign of respect and romance.

After Michael ordered a cup of coffee Lynn got lost in their conversation. She asked him questions about his job and made sure to give him wins during their discussion. She smiled often and looked deep into his eyes to demonstrate her attraction to him. Lynn also kept her eye on her watch; otherwise, she knew the date could go on well into the night.

She spent time talking to Michael about her favorite books and her favorite movies as a way to test his intellect. He was an English major in college and they discussed medieval literature and Greek mythology.

When he passed the test to her satisfaction, Lynn noted it in her internal notebook and smiled that much more.

Even though they seemed to be getting along so well, Lynn made sure to also test Michael for safety. She asked him for his work and home phone numbers to test his willingness to give personal information. Michael gave her his business card and his e-mail, too. He passed the initial safety test without any trouble.

Lynn watched how Michael treated her throughout the date. She noticed that he focused on her during the date, not checking out the young women in short skirts and halter tops at a nearby table. She noted that he treated all the employees politely. She used these observations as a way to test him for sweetness.

Lynn noticed that Michael appeared to pay attention to her when she talked and truly seemed interested in what she was saying. He seemed genuine, so he passed another test, but Lynn knew she would continue to test him for sincerity over time. Lynn could tell by the way he listened to her that he was definitely interested in her romantically. Kissing her hand was another demonstration of his romantic potential. At the same time she didn't feel objectified or viewed as a sex object. She found Michael intriguing and exciting.

Lynn ended the date after approximately an hour. She wanted to continue talking to Michael, but knew the date should end on time. At the end of the date she decided that Michael had passed enough tests to justify going on a middle date. Before the date, she had researched a few potential locations and events to attend for middle dates. Lynn mentioned that she wanted to go to the local public gardens. Michael asked her out and they set up the middle date before leaving the coffee shop.

As Michael got up to leave he seemed unsure how to say good bye. Lynn wanted to kiss him but she decided it would be best to wait until the next date. She hugged him and pressed her breasts into Michael's chest. He kissed her softly on the cheek. Lynn sighed to herself. She knew he wanted her and the feeling was mutual. Lynn could not wait until their next date.

Lynn was successful on the qualifying date because she kept focused on the theme of the date: testing the man. She didn't let herself get swept up in the romance and the sexual tension. She made it a priority to value her goals over her temporary desires. In the end, Lynn came out a winner.

CHAPTER 10

Preparing for the Middle Date

L ET'S REVIEW OUR STORY SO FAR, SHALL WE?

You knew that you wanted more success with men than you've been having. You wisely decided to buy this book. Then you discovered our ten-step Master Plan for getting a guy and building the relationship of your dreams.

Step one of the ten-step Master Plan was getting absolutely crystal clear about what you want. You created a picture of the ideal man and of the ideal relationship. You learned that this picture may change, and most probably will, as you move through the dating process. You learned that changing your picture is okay, because having a destination in mind—even if you change that destination as you travel—will get you where you really want to go better than having no destination in mind at all. You learned that once you are on the road, things start to happen— odd coincidences, chance meetings, and the strange miracles that often start the best relationships. You learned that going for something specific puts you in a position where such miracles are more likely to occur.

In step two, you made yourself worth winning. You tackled the twin demons of personal style and confidence. You learned how to control the messages you send to men through how you dress and behave, and how your ability to endure rejection is the key to finding the right man for a long-term relationship.

In step three (interviewing men), you learned how to find and interview male applicants. You learned that men are everywhere, and found out how to create your life so that you are constantly around them. In step four (testing men), you learned that your natural tendency is to disqualify men for the wrong reasons. You learned how you've probably disqualified men simply because they were bad flirters or had poor opening lines. Worse, you learned that you have probably kept dating men who were the most expert flirters and who had the best opening lines, in spite of the fact that those men were most likely to keep using those skills—on other women. You learned how to compensate for the clueless flirting skills of otherwise wonderful men. Also in step four, you learned how to test men to find out which ones are attracted to you, safe, patient, emotionally available, romantic, able to produce, and who share at least some of your values. You used these clues, rather than the strength of his flirting or opening lines, to decide if you wanted to proceed to the first date. You learned how to get him to ask you out, how to ask him out, and how to set up the first date.

In step five you learned how to give a man emotional wins and losses, and how to use this to control the direction and velocity of your flirting interactions. You learned how to make a man feel like a winner—not so much in competitions, but as a winner of your heart. You learned that making a man into a winner keeps him coming back for more.

You then started step six, "spend time with a man," and had your first date. You learned that the first date is the "qualifying date," a "fact-finding mission" about him and his values. You learned how to test a man on the first date, what to expect from him, and how to pace the date by giving him wins and losses. And you learned how to handle the inevitable problems of the first date, so that the second date—and beyond—has any chance of happening at all.

Now, you've been through the qualifying date (or dates), and you are ready to come back for more. So is he. You are entering the middle dates—the time before you present him with a commitment deal, and turn the "dating" into a "relationship" at last.

The middle dates involve steps five and six of the Master Plan. During the middle dates, you go more deeply into each of these steps. You go more deeply into step five by continuing to give the man wins and losses. The man learns that, with you, he is a winner and a provider—especially when he gives you the feelings you like by being romantic and considerate. The middle dates also let you go more deeply into step six, spending time with the man. You are getting closer, and possibly becoming sexual. You are also getting to know much more about what the man is like.

These are the dates where you are seducing each other, where you are deciding whether or not to become romantic and sexual partners with each other. Most of the information you'll get from this chapter is about the middle dates *before* they become sexual. There are two reasons for this. First, some women will want to wait until they have a commitment deal in place (see chapters 14 and 15) before they get sexual with a man. Second, strange as it may sound, once you have become sexual, your relationship usually starts to settle down a bit. After things have become sexual, you'll notice that you start to "hang out" together in a way that you were not doing during the first few middle dates. You are more comfortable together, and start to get into routines and establish traditions together. This chapter will focus mostly on the first few dates that happen *after* the qualifying date (or dates), before you are really comfortable together. You will use these middle dates to set up what the relationship will be like, and to begin creating your future together.

∞ The Seven Components of a Successful Middle Date

1. The Middle Date is Longer than a Qualifying Date

The middle date takes place over many hours. While your qualifying date is short, your middle date is longer. On the qualifying date you want to get in, find out if he's a possible keeper, and get out again, wasting as little time as possible. You want to find out about him, and leave him wanting more. On the middle date, you are beginning the process of exploration. You are finding out what he is like, what you are like when you are with him, and what kind of rhythms you have together. This takes more time, and if you've gotten to a middle date with a man, you've probably decided that he deserves it.

2. The Middle Date Makes the Man Feel Like a Winner

We've talked about how important it is to a man to feel that he's winning your heart. If you get nothing else from this book, get that. If your words and actions constantly tell a guy he's a loser, you will *always* be alone. If your heart is impossible to win, and he never feels like he can win with you, you will *always* be alone. If you ignore everything else we teach you in this book, you will still be successful with men if you become expert at finding the ways in which men are winners and letting them know that you notice them. If you learn everything else that we teach you, but don't leave the man feeling like a winner, you will remain alone, no matter what else you do.

3. The Middle Date Makes the Man Feel Like a Provider

To this conversation we are now adding the word *provider*. A man feels good—like a real man, a masculine man, a *man with big cahunas*, when he feels like he has provided something for a woman he likes. (Helpful reminder: He likes you if you make him feel like a winner.) But being a provider can take many forms. It does *not*, repeat, *not*, necessarily mean spending up his money. There are a lot of ways that a man can provide for you. Spending money on you is only one of them.

Let's look at the issue of money from the standpoint of a man feeling like a winner and a provider. We've all known women who have gone out with men they weren't interested in for no more reason than to get an expensive meal at a guy's expense. Men have a pretty good idea of when this has happened. As we've mentioned before, we're not here to tell you that this is right or wrong. We are here to say that going out with a guy just to visit a fine restaurant won't get you the kind of relationship that you are committed to having. When you use a guy as a meal ticket, don't think he doesn't know you are doing it, because, on some level, he does. He doesn't feel like a big strong provider. He just feels like a chump. He may even feel angry. Because spending money on you hasn't left him feeling like a winner, he'll look for another way to win. It's likely he'll start to see your relationship as an exchange: money (in the form of expensive food) for sex. Then he'll really start being a jerk, and you will have to deal with it.

This is not to say that every time a guy is a jerk about money and sex, it's because of you. Guys have a nearly infinite capacity to be jerks all on their own, without your help, but it is easier for a guy to justify using you for sex if he feels like you are using him for money.

Is this to say that you shouldn't let a man buy you dinner? Of course not—buying a woman dinner is part of dating. But you should make him feel like a winner and a provider for doing it, or he will start looking for his own ways of feeling like a winner. You need to let him know he's your hero. How? By acknowledging what he provides.

WHAT DOES A MAN PROVIDE?

There are many ways a man can provide for you, and you must notice and acknowledge them. Ask yourself this: Is it more important that a man have lots of money, or that he have a great personality, an ability to share his feelings, and that you feel good around him? You will probably answer that providing money is not nearly as important as providing a great personality, an ability to share his feelings and to make you feel good. His personality, his ability to share his feelings, and how good all that makes you feel are things he is providing for you. You must become an expert at noticing and acknowledging what he provides if you want to succeed in a long-term relationship with a man.

Making a man feel like a provider is a three-step process. First, you must notice what he is providing for you. Second, you must acknowledge what he is doing that makes you feel provided for. Third, you must tell him how his providing for you makes you feel. For instance, when Betty went out with Chuck on their first middle date, they took a cab from her place to the local zoo. At the end of the ride the driver tried to rip them off. Chuck was firm with the driver and got the price much closer to what it should have been.

Betty noticed that Chuck had provided for her (step one), and decided that this was a perfect opportunity to make Chuck feel like a provider. As the cab drove away, she told him, "I really appreciate that you didn't let him rip us off. You were brave to talk to him and get him to reduce the price." That was step two, telling him what he was providing. She then went on to step three, telling him what he provided for *her* by doing that. She said "I feel so safe and taken care of when I'm with a man who can be so courageous. Thank you." Chuck felt like a total hero, committed himself to being courageous in the future, and thought that Betty was about the coolest woman he had ever known.

Let's go over these steps one at a time:

Step One: Notice What He Is Providing For You. Different men provide different things at different times. Some of the things men provide
are big and dramatic, some are small and easy to ignore. Here's a partial
list of what a man might provide, to start inspiring your ability to notice.

You may notice that a man:

- shows up on time
- is good looking
- pays for things
- has a good personality
- makes you feel happy
- makes you feel excited
- makes you feel relaxed
- makes you feel at peace
- takes care of your feelings
- risks his safety to protect you
- would be willing to risk himself to protect you
- is a gentleman
- takes care of you
- risks rejection for you
- pulls out a chair for you
- opens a door for you

Step Two: Acknowledge What He Is Doing That Provides For You.
It does no good to notice what a man provides for you if you don't
acknowledge it to him. It's not enough to tell him that he makes you
feel good, or safe, or trusting, or excited. You also have to tell him
precisely what he did to make you feel that way. This is what step two
is about.

When you acknowledge what he is doing that provides for you, you
are telling him what kind of actions make you feel good, and the kind of
actions you'd like to see more of. This is where you say, "I like the way
you talk about your feelings," or, "I like the way you asserted yourself
with the cab driver when he tried to rip you off."

Step Three: Tell Him How His Providing For You Makes You Feel. In step three, you really hammer the acknowledgment home by telling him what you got out of what he did to provide for you. After telling him "I like the way you talk about your feelings," tell him what it provides for you: "because it makes me feel happy." After telling him, "I like the way you asserted yourself with the cab driver when he tried to rip you off," finish by telling him, "That made me feel safe."

You can make a man feel like a provider about big things or about little things. It doesn't matter. You can notice he opened the car door for you and closed it after you got in (step one). You can tell him "I noticed that you opened and closed the car door for me. I think that's very sweet." (Step two.) Then you can complete the circuit by telling him what that gave you, by saying "It really makes me feel good inside to be treated like a lady. Thank you." (Step three.)

What He Should Be Doing. While you are giving him a feeling of being a provider and a winner, he, if he has any sense, is working on giving you feelings of romance and of being special. He will certainly do this if he's one of our students. If he's not one of our students, then his natural inclination might be to do nothing at all. We can't let that happen.

Fortunately, if you are making him feel like a provider and a winner, you will be different from almost any other woman he's ever dated. You'll be seeing and appreciating things that few, if any, other women have seen or appreciated. You'll be telling him about what you appreciate, and about what it provides for you. That will *certainly* be different from almost any other woman he's been with. And he'll feel good about it.

By giving a man experiences of being a provider and a winner during the middle dates, you help him feel bonded to you and he looks forward to seeing you again. These good feelings will inspire him to treat you differently from the way he's treated other women. Just as you would feel inspired if you were treated like a princess by a man, he will be inspired, by feeling like a hero, to go out of his way to make you feel good. As you give him wins for those actions, he'll do them even more.

4. The Middle Dates Are Out-of-the-Ordinary

The middle dates are romantic dates. You are moving out of the mode of qualifying, and into the mode of creating special, intimate feelings together. To this end, you need to do things that are out-of-the-ordinary. We'll go over this in more detail when we show you how to set up a date. Remember, you want to create memorable experiences for the two of you to share. One way to create such experiences is to break out of the normal routine and go places you've never been, or to places you only go on special occasions, such as when company is in town. If you do such things with your date, the experience will seem new, exciting, bold, and adventurous.

The date can take place at a museum, a sporting event (only if you know he likes sports, and you do, too), a concert, a special restaurant, or any other out-of-the-ordinary place that you are both likely to enjoy. You can go to the museum to look at Egyptian artifacts, or to a little nearby town for a meal in a quaint diner. If your city has good tourist attractions, don't hesitate to use them for your dates. We know a woman in New York City who got a lot of dating mileage out of suggesting her dates take her out on a cruise around the Statue of Liberty. It never failed to be a romantic date. A woman we know who lives in St. Louis has good luck suggesting that she and her dates go on an adventure up the St. Louis Arch. "It's always fun, and out-of-the-ordinary," she says. "A nice meal afterwards, and the date is a success!"

For "Extra Credit"

As you get to know him better, you can also go somewhere that speaks to one of his interests or hobbies. One woman we know began dating a man who, through the course of conversation, mentioned that he was very "into" reading about Benjamin Franklin and the Revolutionary War. Because they both lived in Philadelphia, she asked him if he would take her to the Ben Franklin Museum and to see Independence Hall. He was thrilled, and took her the next Saturday. She was interested, and had a good time listening to him hold forth about the Revolutionary War. When she got bored, she just suggested that they move on to the next display. He told her that she was unlike any woman he had ever known—not because she was interested in what he was interested in, but because she was interested enough in *him* to care about what he loved.

Men are like this: Men have hidden loves and joys, and there are places they go to learn about and share what they love. The man you are dating loves something. He may love cars, or action films. He may love Civil War reenactments. He may love collecting comic books. If you want extra bonus relationship credit, then your job is to look for this thing, this love, whatever it may be. When you hear him talk about something that makes him light up, ask him more about it. If his excitement is providing good feelings for you, tell him, "I can see that you really love this topic. It makes me feel good to see you so lit up about it." This is a huge win, and will make him feel like a very special provider for you.

When Denise started dating Sam, she noticed that he really liked collecting and reading old cartoon books. He had many of them all but memorized, and he, along with a friend of his who was also into it, would make up games quizzing each other about them. It was completely pointless—except that it gave Sam pleasure, and it was something that he loved. So Denise wisely noticed that these cartoon books were very important to Sam.

When a vintage comic display came to their local museum, Denise asked Sam to go to it with her. He had a terrific time sharing what he loved with her, and she had fun being with him while he was so enthusiastic. "That was when he really bonded to me," she told us later. "I loved him even when he was being passionate about something silly. I don't think any woman had ever done that for him before, and it really made me special to him. There was no way he was going to leave me after that."

We're not telling you to lie, or to show an interest when you don't really feel one. That could lead to you spending each and every weekend with his hobbies, which would probably get pretty boring. We are telling you to admire him in his passion. If Sam asked Denise if she *really* liked old comic books, she'd say, "I'm not so into the comic books, no. But I do like being with a man who can show such passion. I think it's neat, and I like that about you. It makes me feel like I'm with a man who has passion about his life." In this way she would bond him to her—after all, she's the first woman to ever like him when he was expressing his passion—without lying or having to pretend that it was her favorite thing in the world.

5. The Middle Date Is Not Just a Time to Socialize

Pop quiz: What's the difference between hanging out with your female friends, and being on a date with a man? Answer: While being with your friends is about socializing, being with a man is only partly so. On the middle date, as on the qualifying date, you are a woman with a mission. You are continuing to test the man, giving him wins and losses as you do. While it is critical that you have fun, fun is not the only thing there is. You are still focused on your goal of creating the relationship of your dreams. You are focused on finding out whether this man will fit your criteria, or if it's time to move on. So don't forget to look at your list of desired qualities in a man before and after your dates. Keep testing him against your criteria. Keep noticing his character. Have fun, but don't forget that you are building a relationship.

6. The Middle Date Is on a Flexible Schedule

As you will recall, qualifying dates have a definite format: They are short. They are about discovering what a man is like, his likes and dislikes, and to start to find out about his values. You want to get in, find out if there might be a future, and get the heck out again, wasting minimal amounts of time along the way.

Middle dates follow a completely different formula. While they are still goal-driven, the pace is slower and less intense. The goal of the middle dates is to have experiences with the man that allow you to get to know him, and there are many paths to that end. While you have a plan for a middle date, you also should be flexible about it. You should be willing to deviate from your plan, if that seems like the right thing to do. If some unexpected opportunity comes up for the two of you, you should be flexible enough to take it.

When Amy went with Danny to an art opening (her suggestion), she never expected that they would be invited back to the artist's studio for drinks and a private show with a few of the artist's friends. In fact, she expected that they would go on to the restaurant where they had reservations. But when the artist invited them, they ended up having a wonderful experience together that they both would remember for a long time. You must be flexible on your dates, so that spontaneous, wonderful things can happen that will help you get to know your man better and bring you closer together.

7. The Middle Date Has a Back-Up Plan

Things can and do go wrong, so it's always worth having a back-up plan. If you planned to go to the local horticultural gardens, what will you do if it rains? If you planned to go the museum to see the Degas exhibit, what will you do if the lines are too long? Don't be too uptight about it—just spend a few moments before each date coming up with some options for you and your date if your primary plan falls through.

∞ Middle Date Tests

That's right! Testing isn't over. The testing has simply shifted. During your flirting interactions, you tested the man for the basics: mostly, safety and attraction. On your qualifying date (or dates), you continued your testing of the basics: Is he patient? Is he romantic? How does he feel about commitment? You also added in a few tests from your personal criteria. On the middle dates, it's time to start testing him for the more important factors—the basic values that you have decided must be in evidence for you to consider a man for the long term.

On the middle dates, you must remember your criteria even if you don't want to. You'll be setting up dates that are romantic, and giving him opportunities to sweep you off your feet. As all this is going on, you must not lose sight of testing him, even as your emotions may be telling you to throw caution to the wind.

On the middle dates, you test the man less by questioning him, and more by watching him. You start to explore his *character*, which is somewhat difficult. When you first met the man, and were flirting with him, you also spent some time, if you could, finding out about his *reputation* by asking other people about him. While reputation is what other people think of him, character is what he is actually like. You'll be watching him to get an overall grasp of the kind of person he is.

Remember this: Any behavior he feels comfortable doing to someone else, he will probably eventually feel comfortable doing to you. If he tells you about how he cheated on, lied to, or manipulated his ex, you can be pretty sure he will feel comfortable doing those things to you. If he seems to have no sense of business ethics, it's worth noticing that he probably won't have much of a sense of ethics with you, either.

You also need to keep listening to what he is actually saying to you. During the middle dates, some women get so swept away that they enter the fog of "it will be different with me." This can happen even when a man shows every sign that he will be the way he is, and the way he has always been, for the rest of his life. You have to keep paying attention. How many times have you consoled a crying girlfriend who, after a relationship was over, said something like "I should have known he'd never commit to me. He often said he wasn't the marrying type." Probably at least once. If you actually listen to what the man tells you about himself, and watch his behavior from the point of view of your criteria, it will be easier to decide if you should keep dating the man, or move on to someone else. Don't let a man who doesn't fit at least the basics of your list become your "one and only hope" for love and relationship.

Jennifer was an expert at this. She had a precise list, and was absolutely ruthless about it. She did a lot of dating while she was looking for a relationship, and didn't hesitate to disqualify men for the reasons that were important to her. She was 5'11", and simply would not date a man shorter than she was. End of story. She was a nonsmoker, and she didn't care how many other wonderful qualities a man might have—if he smoked, he was out. There were other factors she was more flexible about—age, weight, and occupation, for instance. She stuck to her criteria, and when she discovered a man didn't fit the most important ones, she got rid of him right away, no matter what her emotions said, so she wouldn't become overly attached to the "wrong" man.

By the time a man got onto a middle date with Jennifer, she knew he was, at least potentially, a "keeper." But the first two middle dates were the end of many potential bad relationships for her. She says about one man, "He even bragged to me about how he always got away with cheating on his taxes, and about how he lied his way through an audit! I knew if he felt good about lying to the government, he would feel good about lying to me someday. After that date, I told him, 'Thank you, but I'm not interested anymore.'"

Testing during the middle dates involves not getting so swept away that you ignore the obvious signs of a man's deeper character. You keep listening to what he says to you, and watch how he behaves in real life. You keep referring to your criteria, and keep up your willingness to walk away from a man who will never fulfill you.

∞ Things to Do Before a Middle Date

Setting up the Middle Date

Once again, you can't count on him for anything. Whether it's after the qualifying date or after a middle date, making sure your next date is romantic is still up to you. After taking a wonderful walk at the zoo (which you suggested), followed by a wonderful dinner and some passionate kissing at your doorstep, most guys won't know enough to plan another romantic date with you. They'll ask their buddies what to do and, if you are lucky, *not* come up with two tickets to the see the local ice hockey team in action. It is true that by some strange miracle he might come up with a romantic idea. But you shouldn't leave it in his hands.

Remember, the fact that he doesn't know a lot about being romantic doesn't mean that he can't be taught. And the fact that you may have to teach him about romance doesn't mean that he won't get the idea, or that he's a bad guy to have a relationship with. Once he's all trained up, he'll probably be just fine. While your girlfriends are complaining about the lack of good men, you'll be in a good relationship because you were able to use intelligence in your selection process, and were able to find and exploit a "diamond in the rough."

Still, on the middle dates your "diamond" will need some polishing, and it's up to you to gently provide it. Ask yourself, what kind of experience might I find romantic? That's the kind of thing you want to suggest. Here's a list of possible "middle date" activities. Which might you like to do? Which might you find romantic? Which might be available where you live? After you decide on one, you must suggest it to your man when you are setting up your next date.

Potential Places to Suggest

- A movie in an out-of-the-way or artistic theater
- Nature (if you feel safe with him)
- A road trip to a nearby quaint little town or exciting city
- A part of town that is safe, that neither of you frequents
- A museum
- A concert
- A wonderful restaurant
- A tour
- A park where you can feed bread to the birds
- An ice cream parlor
- An amusement park
- A botanical garden
- A drive in the country
- A planetarium
- A dance club
- A drive-in movie
- A play
- A zoo
- An aquarium
- Cooking together at your place or his (only if he wants to!)
- A wine-tasting party
- A bike ride
- A comedy club
- Any "tourist attraction" that you only go to when you have friends in town

You can add to this list—it's just here to give you inspiration. A middle date activity is one where you do something you wouldn't ordinarily do, or go somewhere you wouldn't ordinarily go. It has no purpose outside of being something cultured, pleasant, adventuresome or urbane that you can do together. It should be a "bonus" activity in life—something you could go your whole life without doing, but also something that could add to your life if you did it.

Before you set up the next date with your guy, take a look at the above list. Scan it. Is there a museum in town you'd like to go to? Are they having a special traveling exhibit you might want to see? Find out about it, and get enough details so that you can be specific about it when mentioning it to your man. Is there a nature preserve in the area? Are they having a special "bird walk"? You may want to suggest to him that the two of you go. You may even choose several possibilities. Then, when it's time to set up the next date (more on this in a moment), you'll have several romantic suggestions, all ready to go.

Figuring Out When and Where to Set up the Next Date

ON THE DATE?

One of the best times to set up the next date is before you finish up the date you are currently on. This can work especially well early on in the relationship. You've spent some time with him, he seems to be testing well, but you are afraid that he might still slip away, so you decide to go for setting something up right then. This is perfectly legitimate. Just know that he might not be able to set up your next date at that moment. He might not know his schedule. He might not have his datebook with him. Just because he says he doesn't know at the time doesn't mean he is rejecting you. Simply get in touch by phone later, and wrap it up then. If you can wrap it up in person, however, it is often easier to do so.

ON THE PHONE?

Yes, you can call him to set up the next date. Yes, you can dial his number. We've discovered in our studies that most people, both women and men, put far too much significance on calling. We are constantly asked,

"Is it okay for me to call?" and "How long should I wait before I call?" The answers are, 1) it is okay for you to call, and, 2) you can call whenever you want. Don't wait; don't worry that you will bug him.

The main objection that both women and men have to calling is that they don't want to appear desperate. This fear keeps them from taking the risks innate in reaching out to people, and they inevitably end up alone. Or they get into useless conversations: "Have I waited long enough? It's been a day. Should I wait another day? Yeah, that's what I'll do. Waiting one day after seeing him isn't enough. I should give him a chance to call me, if he's interested. I don't want to look desperate." It's a weird power-struggle, and it's entirely made up. The whole thing is just a rationalization to keep you from doing the two simple things it takes to get the next date on the road. You can do these things at any time, without appearing desperate. Ready for the two things you must do?

1. Dial his number.

2. Talk.

That's all there is to it! Remember, the biggest single cause of appearing desperate is being afraid of appearing desperate. To call without seeming desperate, all you have to do is let go of the idea that calling is a desperate thing to do. It is not. It is empowering. He will probably feel flattered. If you want to set up a date, all you have to do is dial his number and talk. Allow us to liberate you from that whole universe of fear in which you are desperate if you call him, or in which calling him at the wrong moment will ruin things. You made all that up. There is no such thing as calling "too soon." Just make the call. Don't worry about it.

Once you have him on the phone, just present your ideas of what you might do, and when you might do it. Smile as you talk to him—it changes how your voice sounds, and makes it more pleasant to listen to. Don't spend too much time on the phone (unless he really is a big talker). Save your chatting for when you see him next, on the date you are setting up.

Add Romantic Details to the Next Date

Think of a wonderful romantic moment you've had. It might have been a walk on a beach with a loved one at sunset. It might have been laying in bed with a lover, hearing the sound of him breathing and watching the beautiful dance of the morning sunlight coming through the window. Whatever that moment is, it's a sure bet that it was probably made wonderful by the *details.* Every little detail was "just right."

Romance is in the details, and romantic moments are moments where all of the details *are* "just right." The walk on the beach is perfect, the temperature is perfect, the sunset is perfect, the feeling of the sand between your toes is perfect. Or, lying in bed, the sun is perfect, the way the light falls, just so, is perfect, the crinkle of the sheets is perfect . . . all the "little things" are in place, and there is nothing to cause any problems, nothing to distract you at all.

After you've set up your next date, it's worth keeping the details in mind. Ask yourself, "What details can I add to this date to make it even more romantic and fun?" If you are going for a walk in a nature preserve, you might want to bring crackers and cheese and a bottle of wine. If you are going to a museum, you might want to look and see what restaurants are nearby. Just keep asking yourself what might make it more fun, memorable, and special. Then, when it comes time for the date, consider putting those details into it.

Create Your Sexual Limit for the Date

On the middle dates, you need to control the pace of sexual adventuring. As we've mentioned, you do this by giving him wins and losses, each in their proper measure.

Many women have told us that they benefit from setting their sexual limit for the date *before* the date even happens. Marcie told us, "I know I want to go more slowly, but once I start kissing a guy I get so turned on that I'm tempted to go too far too fast." She found that setting a sexual limit for herself before the date started helped her keep the relationship moving at a pace that worked better in the long run. "I know I'd get into bed too quickly, before I knew whether or not the guy was a long-term possibility," she says. "That worked for me when I was in my twenties, but now my biological clock is ticking, and I can't afford to waste time getting involved with a guy who is unlikely to stick around."

If you decide to create a sexual limit for your date, we recommend that you tell a female friend about the limit you have set and promise her that you won't cross it. The reason is that promises made to other people work much better than promises made to yourself. When Marcie tells Janet that she promises to only go to "first base" with a guy, she knows when she's on the date that she'll lose face before her friend if she breaks her promise. If she only promises to herself, however, she can easily say "Eh, who would know?" and let her self go farther than was actually in her own best interest. Promising to someone else keeps the promise alive, and helps you keep the limit you've set for the date.

You are now ready to go on your middle date. You understand what it is about, how it will go, and what your purpose is. You've reminded yourself of your desired outcome, and set your limits for the date. You might be a bit apprehensive about the date, but don't worry. Your buddies are here to show you the way through, and beyond, the middle dates.

Let's do it!

CHAPTER 11

Charming a Man on the Middle Date

Y OU'VE PREPARED YOURSELF FOR THE DATE, YOU'VE FOUND A GREAT place to go, and you've gotten it all set up. You are meeting your quarry, or he is coming to pick you up. You see each other, your eyes lock, and the date has begun!

It's all well and good to like a guy, enjoy his company, and to have him like you. But it's not enough. To get a relationship happening, you must have romance. And romance, to a guy, means seduction. Get ready for the keys to seducing a man.

☞ Assessing How "Fast" You Want to Be

There are specific things you can do to heat up a guy and speed up the seduction, while at the same time not seeming slutty or cheap. How many of these things you do, and how quickly you do them, depends wholly on how quickly you want the seduction to proceed.

When Maria first started dating David, she was very attracted to him, but she also had concerns. He lived in the same four-unit apartment building that she did; if their relationship didn't go well, it could be awkward every time she saw him. But she was attracted to him, and thought there might be some possibility for a relationship. She talked to him every chance she got, and, when she got a new dresser and needed help moving it up to her apartment, she used the "asking for help" opening gambit and knocked on his door. He helped her move the dresser, and she asked him if he'd like to stay for a beer "to thank him." After chatting for a while, she wondered aloud if he'd like to get some dinner with her. He agreed, and they went out for a date.

Maria became even more attracted to David as the evening wore on, but she remembered that getting too sexual too fast with this largely untested man could lead to significant complications in their duplex. Accordingly, she decided to use the moves we'll teach you here more slowly and more sparingly. She decided she'd make her interest and availability known, but also make it clear that she wasn't "easy."

Donna, on the other hand, wanted to get sexual with Larry much more quickly. They both happened to be staying in the same hotel, each on a business trip to Houston. She discovered that he lived in Tucson. She herself lived in Chicago. She wasn't interested in a relationship with him, but knew she wanted to have sex with him, that night. She decided to use the moves we'll teach you here fully and maximally.

How much you use these moves will depend on the pace at which you want to go. They are like a spice that you might add to your interaction; unless you truly want sex right now, you shouldn't use too much spice. Like food, the more you spice an interaction with a man, the hotter it will get.

∞ The Easy Ways to Seduce a Man

Remember, no matter how blatant you are, some men will still be gunshy and unwilling to make the first move. Often these guys got burned early on in their dating careers. Many men have had experiences of women giving "clear signals" that turned out to be anything but. This especially happens during the teen years, and sadly, many men never get over such experiences. One of our students, Stanley, told us about a woman he dated when he was a teenager who flirted with him, went on dates with him, and even kissed him goodnight. When he went for more passionate kisses she became enraged, asking "Why do men always think I want to get involved with them?!" Another man knew a girl who spent an evening lying on his couch, her head in his lap, telling him all of her sexual fantasies, only to become furious when he tried to kiss her.

It only takes a few incidents like these to permanently scramble a guy's ability to read women's signals accurately—and most men have had at least one such experience, usually more. That's why you have to rely on a number of signals, each one of which you have to amplify far beyond what you might think is necessary to get through to your normal, shell-shocked guy, that you are interested in him.

If you're not a woman who normally does flirty, seductive things, take heart. One of the wonderful things about dating is that you spend time with men who don't know you. A man who doesn't know you doesn't know that you don't normally flirt, or act seductively. Things you do that might feel strange to you won't feel strange to him. He'll figure, "Hey, that's just the way she is." He'll probably even like it.

So go ahead and try out these seduction moves. They may seem odd to you, but trust us: They'll be just fine with him.

Be "Winnable"

Once again, you must be winnable. If a man can't win with you, any relationship you might develop will go directly to Hell. And once again (we are saying it over and over so that you will get it), being winnable doesn't mean that the man defeats you, or that you let him win in every little competition you have together. It means that he can win your heart, your approval, your admiration. If it's not possible for a man to win your heart, your approval and your admiration, you've doomed the relationship before it even starts. So, when you are seducing a man, you *must* be winnable.

Don't Give Him Wins for No Reason

The more wins you give a man, the more he will probably like you. But remember, wins have to *seem* like wins to the guy, not just like "give-aways." Rewarding a man extensively for doing absolutely nothing can be counter-productive. If he doesn't feel like he's doing anything to earn a win (because it's all being handed to him), he won't have any reason to feel like a winner. That would be bad.

You are always walking a line between being too easy to win and being too hard to win. If you are too easy, he won't feel special. He'll think that you would give yourself to anybody. If you make yourself too hard to win, you run the risk that he'll think you are either un-winnable or not worth the effort. Neither of these outcomes is acceptable.

When you give a man a win, it should be for something he's provided for you—usually a feeling. Just continue your habit of noticing the good feelings he gives you, or the things you admire about him, and comment on them. Tell him what you admire about him or his behavior, and what it gives you. "I really like the way you dress. It makes me feel so good to be with a stylish man." "Thank you for taking me here." "You are so smart (gush)." "You are so romantic." "You have sexy eyes." When you give him wins for what he provides, he feels like a real winner, and that makes him like you more. After all, you are a woman who can be won. Most men have never met such women, and will think you are a rare treat—and you will be.

Use Seduction Words

Some words are more sensual and seductive than others. Words like "urine," "foreclosure" or "bill collector" are less sensual than words like "seduced," "attracted," or "sultry." To turn a date with a man into a seduction, you must use romantic words as much as you can, without looking weird. That means using them more than you are probably comfortable with, while allowing other conversation to happen as well.

Here's a list of romantic words and phrases. You may find others to add to this partial list:

Seduced

Attracted

Crazy about

Romance

Hot

Kinky

Dreamy

Sexy

Passionate

Feeling in your body

Exquisite

Exotic

Erotic

Magical

Special

In their own little world together

Warning! As you may know, there is one word that is a seduction word for women, but at the same time an *anti*-seduction word for men. That word is "love." "Love," as in "in love," and "falling in love," and "falling in love and getting married and being committed to each other forever and ever," would be seduction phrases if a man used them on you, but they are usually *not* seductive when you use them on a man. Leave them alone until later in the relationship. We'll show you how to bring "love" into your vocabulary later in this chapter.

Look into His Eyes for "Too Long"

As we said in the flirting chapter, looking into a man's eyes for "too long" creates a moment of intimacy that shows him your romantic interest. You should look into his eyes when you are talking with him, at least from time to time. It's not a staring contest, though. Remember: hard, long stares are usually considered more aggressive than seductive. But even if you are in the habit of never looking into a man's eyes when you interact with him, you should start to do it at least occasionally. It shows him you aren't scared, and if you do it in a relaxed manner, shows him you are willing to be open and honest with him.

If you want to increase the speed of the seduction, then hold his eyes for "too long." At least once during the date, you should establish eye contact, and hold it for a second or so longer than is comfortable, then look away to some other part of his face. This is especially intimate and romantic. It's a subtle way of getting him to open up his "personal space" to you and prepares him to open up even more, later. It shows your romantic interest blatantly, but it's over before he can become uncomfortable with it.

Check out His Body

Wait, wait! Before you ogle him like a hot hunk at a Chippendale's show, let us explain to you how to check out a man's body without looking cheap; it's a subtle art. On the one hand, a man might think you are too easy if you look at his body too obviously. On the other hand, if you don't check him out at all, he may think that you aren't interested in him sexually. You handle this problem by looking at his body quickly. Start by looking in his eyes, then quickly, in a second or two, let your eyes sweep over his body. Then return to his eyes. Do this once or twice as you converse with him, and he will start to get the idea.

Touch him Casually

Men notice women who touch them. The woman who touches his hand while she speaks, or who touches his arm to emphasize a certain point, has much more seductive power than a woman who keeps religiously to her own territory, acting as if touching would break some critical boundary. Touching a man casually and non-intrusively establishes a precedent that will make more intimate touching seem natural later. It gets him used to accepting your touch, and gives him a preview of the excitement that might be his if he wins you.

These touches are quick, and gentle, and are over before he has a chance to get uncomfortable with them. You might touch (or even squeeze) his arm for a moment when talking, to emphasize a particular point, or touch his back while you are walking to your table in a restaurant.

Sometimes women get flustered, and find they have forgotten how to do this simple thing. It's easy; as you gesture during conversation, there are times when your hand is far away from your body. Those are the moments to push that hand a bit farther, and to touch him.

Touch His Hand

This is a bit more intrusive, a bit more intimate. You simply put your hand on his for a moment to emphasize some point you are making, hold it there an instant too long, look into his eyes, then take it away.

Wink at Him

Winking creates a little moment of intimacy between you and someone else. A woman who winks at a man shares a special connection, a momentary little world just for her and the object of her affections. When you wink at a man, you do it to make him feel special. Make the wink fast; You're not lowering a garage door here. And smile—it's not some big significant event; it's just a wink.

Whisper to Him

Whispering to him is powerful for a number of reasons. First, when you whisper, you command his attention more fully. If he doesn't pay attention, he'll miss what you are saying. Second, when you whisper, you create a little world that is for the two of you alone. Third, you have to get closer to him to whisper, and he has to get closer to you to listen to what you are whispering. If you lean across the table to whisper something, your mouth gets perilously close to his ear (not to mention the possible increase in seduction value if you happen to be wearing a low-cut blouse when you do this leaning). It's intimate, yet easy to do, and easy for him to accept. It doesn't seem strange or odd. This all makes it easier for him to make romantic approaches later, or to accept yours if you choose to make them.

Keep Your Body Powerful

Sitting, standing, walking and moving as if you are fascinated and fascinating will go a long way toward conveying the kind of vitality and vivaciousness that men are attracted to. Just keep asking yourself, "How would I be sitting if I was totally turned on by my life, fascinating, and fascinated to be here?" Then sit and move in that fashion.

Ask Sensual Questions and Conduct Seductive Conversations

When seducing a man, you want him to be thinking romantic and sexual thoughts about you, and you want him to act on those thoughts.

You probably don't want to be too blatantly sexual—it might scare him off, it might make you seem too "cheap," or he might painfully reject your none-too-subtle advances. You have to find a more crafty and sensitive way to get him thinking along the same lines as you are.

What we are about to teach you will not be necessary in every seduction situation. Asking sensual questions and conducting seductive conversations is not necessary if the man you are with is all heated up and ready to go to bed with you at the drop of a hat. But we know that, despite what many men think, women don't always live in the atmosphere of sexual availability that men fantasize they do. We know that sometimes you are with a guy, and you don't know if he desires you or not. We know that sometimes you are with a guy who might need some seducing. When you are in those situations, sensual questions and seductive conversations are your secret weapons to get his mind moving in the right direction. This technique is also very useful for women who are shy, because it will give you questions and comments that you can memorize, and practice out loud, which will make it easier to speak seductively to your man when the time comes.

ABOUT SEDUCTIVE CONVERSATIONS

Have you ever been with someone who was describing something disgusting? Perhaps a friend had been sick, and later described to you, in intimate, loving detail, every step and every nuance of how it felt to be about to throw up. Can you remember how you felt as he or she described that sickness? Didn't you start to feel kind of sick, too?

Or have you ever wished someone would stop describing some horrible event or accident, because, as you hear it described, you are starting to feel how it must have felt to be there? You probably have. It is a simple principle: *to describe a feeling to someone makes them experience that feeling*. That's why you feel sick when your friend describes getting ill, or you feel queasy when someone talks about a disgusting accident or bloody car crash.

To seduce a man who isn't all primed and ready to jump you already, you must take advantage of this principle, only in reverse. You must describe the feelings you want him to have—romance, attraction, taking risks, arousal, lust—in lush and lavish detail. You must also get him to describe those feelings, through your questioning. As you and he describe and talk about these feelings, he'll start to experience them.

The principle is simple: When someone describes something to you, you must imagine it to be able to understand what that person is talking about. If I'm describing my new car to you, and tell you that it's a red mini-van, you can't help but imagine it. Even if I tell you *not* to imagine it, you have to imagine it in order to know what not to think about.

The same thing happens when you describe a feeling to a man, or get him to describe one to you. Whether or not he wants to feel the feeling you are describing, he must feel it to begin to know what you are talking about. The extent to which he feels it is dependent on how well you describe it. We'll show you exactly how to do this in a moment.

About Sensual Questions

The way you conduct seductive conversations is by asking sensual questions. Asking the proper sensual questions is one of the fastest ways to achieve your goal of getting him thinking romantically about you. This isn't just "making conversation." This is where the rubber hits the road.

Most sensual questions have three parts:

1. The excuse,
2. The description,
3. The question.

While this isn't always true, and the three parts aren't always in this order, if you follow this pattern you'll easily be able to create sensual questions which will get you and your quarry into seductive conversations.

The *excuse* is the part where you briefly explain why you are about to ask the question. The excuse is something like, "A friend of mine and I were talking about this, and I wonder about your opinion on it . . ." or,

"I saw a TV show last night that got me thinking about the idea of attraction . . ." or, "I've been having a lot of fun lately asking people this question about romance . . ."

The second part is the *description*. Before asking the sensual question, briefly describe the feeling you want him to experience. This might be, "It was so romantic, the way they felt drawn together, the chemistry slowly building until they had that electric, passionate first kiss." It might be, "your heart just opened up, and you could feel your inevitable passion with this incredible woman."

The third part is the *question* itself. It is, "What was your first kiss like?," or, "What's the most romantic thing you ever experienced?" Put it all together, and it looks like this:

- "You know, I saw a TV show last night where these two teenagers fell in love and were having their first kiss. It was so hot, the way they felt drawn together, the chemistry slowly building until they had that electric, passionate first kiss. It got me thinking . . . I'd be curious, what was your first kiss like?"

- "Do you remember the first time you fell in love? Everything seemed so fresh and new and amazing, remember? It was like that first time when you really understood that someone wanted you, all of you, just the way you are. If you don't mind me asking, what was that like for you?"

- "My friend John was just telling me about the most passionate, intense date he was ever on. It was amazing. Imagine this: you are out with a woman you really like and find really attractive. You are sitting in this gorgeous outdoor restaurant, overlooking a lake. You can hear her clothes rustling when she moves. She smells good, and her smell is so close to you that you can almost taste her. You feel like you don't even need to eat, just sit there and breathe that wonderful fragrance of her skin. Anyway, that's how he put it. And you have this incredible date as the sun goes down over the water, the stars come out and then the moon rises, and the two of you feel so connected. And then you start to touch, feeling such total lust and passion, you know what I mean? What would you say was your most passionate moment ever?"

- "I was having this discussion with my friend, and I wonder what you think. Do you believe in love at first sight? Where you see someone and you just feel that 'click,' and it's like, even though you are meeting for the first time, you feel like you've known her forever? Or does that feeling of attraction just build inside of you, slowly? Have either of these ever happened to you?"

- "Do you believe in destiny, like certain connections or interactions are pre-destined to happen? I am sure you know the feeling when you see someone and you just feel that 'click,' and even though you are meeting for the first time, you feel like you've known her all your life? Has that ever happened to you?"

- "My friend Robert is falling in love. It's so fun to watch. He was telling me about meeting this woman and feeling like he'd known her all his life. He felt like, 'Oh, it's you,' even though they had just met. Have you ever met someone and just felt like you'd known her forever?"

- "I've been thinking how great it would be to take a vacation, and so I've been asking people what they've done that they really loved. It's been fascinating to hear about people's ideal vacation experiences. What's your absolute fantasy vacation?"

- "You know, it's interesting how different people feel special in different ways. I mean, it's like each person has his or her own code for feeling special, connected, and really loved. I'm curious; how do you know when a woman really appreciates you?"

If these questions seem too personal, you can always ask questions about *men*, rather than about him (just as you did during the flirting tests). He'll tell you the same kind of answer, either way. For instance, instead of asking, "how do you know when a woman really appreciates you," you can ask, "how does a man know when a woman really appreciates him?" The answer will be the same either way you phrase it.

Women tend to think the mood has to be "just right" before they'll ask questions like these. It's a tricky issue, because the mood that is right for these questions is created by questions precisely like these. By asking these questions, and questions like them, you help build the sensual mood that makes this kind of seductive talk appropriate. You've just gotta jump in and start asking them.

Also—and most especially if you are shy, and do not usually know what to say to men—don't be afraid to memorize these questions word for word, exactly the way we've said them here. There's a huge difference between asking about a first kiss the way we put it here and saying, "Hey, what was your first kiss like?," with no excuse or description.

You also won't want to fire these questions off in a row. It'll sound odd. You're not interrogating him. Be subtle and stay on task with these questions and it will greatly speed up the seduction process.

Have Answers to Those Sensual Questions Prepared

As you ask your sensual questions, you'll find that, aside from answering them, your date will often also ask them back to you. That's where seductive conversations come from—a man and a woman sharing sensual, seductive questions and answers back and forth between them. So you'll ask your question, he'll give you an answer, and then say "How about you? What was *your* best kiss like?"

The common mistake in this situation is to tell him about your most romantic moment as you experienced it. This is all well and good, but it doesn't necessarily advance the seduction. If you want to move the seduction forward, you must answer this question by describing your sensual experience, or a generic romantic experience, from his point of view. This gives you another opportunity to describe sensual feelings of attraction to him, and gets him even more into thinking about being sensual with you.

Here's how you do it. Suppose you asked your date "What's it like when you feel really special and appreciated?" He answers, and finishes up with, "Well, I guess that was it. What's it like when you feel special and appreciated?" Follow these guidelines, and you'll be golden:

Answer the question from his point of view. The way you do this is to use the phrase, "You know what it's like when you . . . ?" For example, you'd answer, "It's great when I feel special and appreciated. You know what it's like when you feel like someone is seeing you as you really are? Like they deeply care about you and just think you are really great?" It's also useful to describe those feelings in the present tense. This makes it easier for him to have those feelings *now*, not simply to imagine having had them, once upon a time. Say "It's like you can let go and be sensual," rather than, "It's like you felt you could let go and be sensual." Both will work, but using the present tense works better, so you might as well use it.

Describe the feeling you want him to have. Now describe the feelings you want him to have, from his point of view. You might say "It's like you feel as though you are melting into that other person, it's so great. You feel so connected, so much passion, it's like you've known each other for years. Those are the most passionate moments for me."

Be general in what you reveal. If you describe a specific experience, do not describe the man you were with, or how crazy you were about him. This will only put your current date off. Say, "It was an incredible evening. You can imagine what it was like: walking under the open stars, the air is the perfect temperature and smelling like flowers. Then later, great wine and candlelight. Just perfect, you know? And such great kissing! You know how it is when you have your lips pressed against your lover's lips, and you never want it to stop?" Don't say, "I was with Johnny. What a man! He was so awesome—an amazing body, and he used to drive me around on the back of his Harley. He was the only man I've ever had multiple orgasms with!" This will annihilate your current seduction. Keep your descriptions general so that your date can feel included.

Turn Sensual Questions into Seductive Conversations

If you want him to feel passionately attracted and strangely fascinated, you'll have to design conversations about passionate and fascinating topics. You can turn your sensual questions into seductive conversations—both through your answers to the questions, when he asks them back to you, and by asking conversation-extending questions. For instance, if you ask a man, "What was the most passionate kiss you've ever had?" he may tell you "It was with this girl when I was in high school." Don't let him stop there! Even though he's answered your question, you want him to elaborate, for two reasons. First, you want him to talk about his romantic experience so he'll remember how it felt, and start feeling that feeling now, with you. By expanding on the memory, part of him will go back to that experience and begin to relive it. Second, you want to get data to use should you chose to continue to seduce him. If he's willing to tell you what worked on him before, you bet you want to listen! Here's a list of conversation-extending questions you can ask to keep seductive conversations going:

"Wow. What was it about it that made you feel the best?"

"I am very impressed. Will you tell me more of the details?"

"Fascinating. Tell me more about [some part of the experience]."

"How did that make you feel?"

"That's amazing. Have you felt that way since?"

The Three Steps to Practicing Talking on the Date

When faced with a real live man, you might be nervous. It makes sense to practice whatever you can beforehand, so it's easier to do. For this reason, we suggest you practice your sensual questions and answers *out loud* before the date. We know it sounds silly, but it can really make a difference in how well you lead seductive conversations when it really counts. By practicing ahead of time, you will get used to saying seductive things and begin to relax and speak with an easier flow. Use the following three steps of practice, and the sensual questions will melt any man in sight.

First, practice the questions, as they are written above, out loud until you think you can say at least a few of them by heart. Second, imagine his responses. Practice saying the conversation-extending questions out loud, as well. Third, practice answering all of your own sensual questions, in case he asks them back to you. If you are willing to practice out loud, you'll find it makes a huge difference on the date.

Remember, not all dates require that you go to such lengths to conduct seductive conversations. If he's already hot for you, and you think he has enough nerve to go for the first kiss (or if you are going for it with him!) then sensual questions and seductive conversations might be overkill. But if, for some reason, the seduction needs a nudge, this will help.

Have Fun

Like "have a good attitude," "have fun" is one of those commands that people like to give you without ever telling you how to do it. We suggest that, on the middle dates, you remember that one of the purposes of going is to have fun, and that if the opportunity arises to actually enjoy yourself, you should take it. Study all these guidelines before the date, but then let yourself relax and forget them from time to time. If you've studied first, your brain will be able to keep you on track. This shouldn't be laborious. Noticing opportunities for enjoyment, and taking them, can help. All these moves work together to create a functional seduction.

When Lisa went out with Adam for their third date, she was ready to move forward with him. He had passed most of her tests and he seemed like relationship material. Even though he hadn't been the best flirter to ever walk the face of the earth, Lisa was able to compensate for his occasional thoughtlessness, and was happy to be discovering the wonderful, warm, bright and funny man Adam was. By the time they had gone out several times, she wanted to make things more romantic. She had looked into his eyes during their first few encounters; now she stepped up the seduction, holding his eyes for a bit "too long" in what she hoped was a smoldering glance. Lisa became even more "winnable" than she had been before, openly admiring him and telling him what his admirable qualities provided for her. She increased her use of seduction words, and even conducted seductive conversations, asking him about his first kiss, his most romantic moment, and even—in a moment of daring—about the most exotic lover he had ever had. Lisa checked out his body once or twice on the date, knowing that he was seeing her look at him. She touched him casually, and squeezed his hand as she laughed at one of his jokes. She winked at him, and leaned over to whisper into his ear (she could feel him vibrating, at that point, and thought he was full of the desire to kiss her). All through the date she kept her body powerful, sitting, standing and moving like a powerful, turned-on, fascinated and fascinating woman. She let herself have a good time through it all, and didn't get caught up in taking the date too seriously.

As she did all this, Adam was warming up as well. He started to touch her more, holding her gaze, and even leaving his hand on hers for a few moments. By the end of the date, he kissed her, and Lisa was able to take it as far as she wanted to go.

After the Date

Making It a Success in Your Own Mind

When Suzanne goes out on a date with a guy and, afterwards, doesn't feel like he likes her, or doesn't feel that there is a possible future with him, she beats herself up. "Why can't I ever get a man to like me?" she moans. "After all the work I do, I never end up with anything. I bet I'll never have a relationship again. Also, I'm too fat." Her catastrophizing and pessimism make it impossible for her to think she's succeeded at any aspect of the date she's been on. At the beginning of your training in creating and maintaining great long-term relationships, such a way of thinking is impractical. You can't afford to stay in such pessimism. You must learn to make *every* interaction with a man into a success, whether he likes you or not, and whether you have any chance of building a relationship with him or not.

You, and you alone, must decide what your definition of a successful date will be. If you are like Suzanne, and you only see a date as successful if the guy is falling all over himself for you while at the same time being an ideal partner for a future long-term relationship, you are making dating much more difficult for yourself than it actually needs to be. The bottom line is that your definition of a successful date should leave you feeling good after any interaction with a man. Your definition of success must help you learn whatever you can from a date, and leave you charged up for your next encounter.

The average woman seems to think that to have success with men, she must be able to meet and coyly get a date with a brilliant, thoughtful neurosurgeon who loves kids and isn't obsessed by his work, all in one afternoon. Alternatively, she thinks that everything about her behavior and appearance must be letter-perfect. These are much too stringent definitions of success, and they will not get you the kind of life, or relationship, that you want. Besides, these goals are unrealistic, even for the most smooth, beautiful woman on the planet. Even she makes mistakes, botches up dates, and is occasionally rejected. At the same time, there are women who think of themselves as overweight and awkward who are in very successful relationships. What these successful women know that you may not is how to make even the most potentially humiliating "failures" into successes.

We suggest that you adopt this definition: If you learned something from your interaction with a man, it was a success. This isn't just "fancy footwork" thinking, either. If you learned *anything* from an experience, you'll be able to handle that situation better the next time it comes up with another man. And it almost certainly *will* come up again.

Becky takes a very different approach than Suzanne does. No matter what kind of a date Becky has, she finds a way to make it into a success. If she goes out with a man who turns out to be a total raving egotist, in love with his fancy car, and full of tales of his success "smashing the other guy" in business, she still makes it into a success for herself. She may take the opportunity to learn new ways to identify such men earlier, or she may try to use the date as an opportunity to try a new approach. If, after three dates with a man, he confesses that, though he didn't feel like he could be honest about it earlier, he now has to tell her that he's married, she may use the experience to discover a crucial step she was missing in her testing phase, or notice how she skipped testing entirely with him because he seemed "so cute." She'll learn not to make that mistake again, and that lesson will make the date a success, even though it didn't end in the way she would have liked.

Committing yourself to making each date with a man a success by learning something worth knowing also keeps you from becoming a victim in your interactions with men. Becky knows that if she learns something worth knowing from the guy who confesses that he's married, she's not a victim. She's a learning, growing woman, and her dating is a success. And along the same lines, it's no fair having what you "learned" be something destructive like, "I learned all men are liars" or, "I learned I'll always be alone." You have to have learned something *worth knowing*. Reinforcements for your pessimism, and reasons why you are doomed, are not worth knowing. You have to learn something good.

We suggest that you think of every learning experience with a man as a success, and that you not rest after any interaction unless and until you have discovered what you have learned. Just keep asking yourself, "What did I learn from this?" and eventually you will figure it out. This way, you ensure your future success. You keep yourself moving forward, rather than allowing yourself to become dejected and to give up. By making every date a success, you drive yourself relentlessly toward inevitably having the relationship you desire.

After the Middle Date Checklist

After the middle date, it makes sense to look back and see how you did. Here's a list of important middle date ingredients. Which of them did you use?

On the middle date, did you:

- make the date longer than the qualifying date?
- make the man feel special?
- make the man feel like a provider?
- admire something about the man, and tell him what it provides for you?
- get out of your normal routines and environments?
- find out about his passion?
- admire his passion?
- have a back-up plan?
- have flexibility on the date?
- test him against your criteria?
- keep an eye open for his character?
- notice if he is comfortable with other people?
- test his relationship with commitment?
- set up the date at a suitably romantic spot?
- add romantic details to the date?
- have a sexual limit for the date?
- know how "fast" you wanted to be?
- make yourself "winnable"?
- use seduction words?
- ask sensual questions, and create seductive conversations?
- look into his eyes for "too long"?

- check out his body?
- touch him casually?
- touch his hand?
- wink at him?
- whisper to him?
- keep your posture and movement powerful?
- have fun?
- not just socialize?
- not complain about other men to him?
- not talk about downbeat topics, violence, etc.?
- not rely on him for certainty that the date is going well?
- not take the thoughtless things he did personally?

Asking yourself these questions after a middle date is a good way to keep yourself focused on what is most important to you. It keeps you from drifting off your purpose.

Deciding if the Relationship Has a Future

One of the most important things you can do after a date is to check the man against your list of qualifications, and see how he measures up. Your natural proclivity may be to avoid this step. You may want to just "let the relationship flow," or you may be scared of finding out that the guy has nothing to do with the list of desirable qualities you've created. Don't worry about that, we'll handle it. But do take a look at your list after a middle date. It's critical that you spend at least a few minutes grounded in reality, no matter how wonderful and romantic the date seemed.

This is where you may think about changing your list, or about getting rid of the man and moving on to someone else. For instance, if you really like the guy, but he's not in the age bracket you had written on your list, you may decide that age is a requirement you are willing to change. Or you may decide it's one you aren't willing to change. If you aren't willing to change the requirement, know this: If you keep dating him, and get into a relationship with him, you will be "de facto" changing your requirement anyway. If it's really so critically important that he be in alignment with your requirement, then you have to ditch him and move on; the sooner, the better.

You may very likely decide that you do like the guy, and are willing to change your requirement. That's fine. Change it on your list. Then continue your assessment of the guy, until you get all the way through your list. If the man meets (or or inspires you to change) enough of your requirements, he might have long-term potential. Then you can go back to feeling all romantic and mushy. You might be on your way.

CHAPTER 12

Zen and the Art of Man Maintenance

CONGRATULATIONS! YOU'VE FLIRTED, YOU'VE HAD QUALIFYING DATES, and now you have at least one guy in the "middle date" zone. Now you must study maintenance.

Maintenance is anything you do to keep the good feeling going between interactions with a man. Maintenance keeps the budding relationship from disappearing into the morass called "your life."

◌ Maintenance and Your Excuses

Maintenance may not come naturally to you. You may have to make yourself do it. For some women it's like doing your taxes, or getting the oil changed in your car.

Many women find excuses for not putting time into maintaining their budding relationships, especially at the very beginning. Instead, they come up with excuses. Women like Suzanne tell themselves, "I'd call him to say hi, but I'm really busy right now. Things are swamped at work, and geez! I need to lose ten pounds before I can really pursue men. Besides, it's the man's job to pursue the woman. If I call him, I'll look weird! Damn this patriarchal culture that won't give women the power to pursue men!" As you can see, we've heard all the excuses.

Other women don't keep up the maintenance because they want a relationship to "just happen," and are offended by the idea that you might have to do something for a romance to occur. If you are one of these women, we invite you to look at the possibility that you are as afraid as any of your sisters, and that you need to own up to that fear, and get on with it.

You make these excuses for one reason, and one reason only: because you are scared to reach out to another human being, and are afraid of getting hurt. There's nothing wrong with being afraid of that, but you absolutely must not let it stop you. If you don't maintain that initial connection with a man, your mutual fears of looking desperate, being rejected, and getting hurt will pull the whole possible relationship down on top of you in a tumble of excuses about being "too busy" or "too fat."

☜ *Frequency of Maintenance*

When you take maintenance actions in a relationship with a man, you are applying what behaviorists call "reinforcement." A "reinforcement" is a reward—something that feels good—that the subject gets for performing a certain behavior. For instance, giving a dog a treat each time he comes when you call his name, reinforces the behavior of coming when you call. In time, the dog will look forward to coming when you call, because he knows that obeying you will mean he'll get a reinforcement that he likes.

The thing to understand is that if you give the dog a treat every single time he comes when you call, he will actually start to get lazy. He'll figure, "Eh, why should I hurry? I can get over there in my own good time, and take the treat." Constant reinforcement stops being effective after a while.

You may have noticed this in your own relationships. Have you ever had someone who consistently goes out of his or her way to make you feel special? Suppose that one morning, out of the blue, someone at your work place brought you a cup of excellent coffee when you first sat down at your desk. You'd probably feel pretty special, and you'd be happy to see that person later in the day. You would have associated seeing that person with the good feelings you got from the gift.

But now imagine if that person brought you coffee every single day, like clockwork, and never missed a day. At first, you'd probably appreciate it Then you'd notice it less. Eventually you'd hardly notice it at all. You might even start complaining when the coffee wasn't exactly the way you liked it, or get angry if he or she missed a day. You'd naturally go from being delighted by the constant gifts, to seeing them as a regular part of life, or even as something you intrinsically deserve. This is a natural reaction to constant, unvarying reinforcement.

If you constantly shower a man with gifts and attention, or give him wins without his earning them, you risk the same thing happening. At first, it's important to reinforce a man constantly; it gets him in the habit of being happy about seeing you. But after a while, if your praise and attention are going to stay effective, you must start bestowing them a little more irregularly. This is what behavior experts call a "variable schedule of reinforcement." You don't send him a card every week, or every date. You don't always have a little snack for him when he comes over to your house. You don't always show up to flirt with him at the same time, or on the same day of the week. You vary your schedule of making him feel extra-good, and thus keep the interaction exciting and fresh for him.

Tina puts a variable schedule of reinforcement to good use. "When I first start dating a man, I go out of my way to make him feel good a lot," she says. "But in time, I know I can start scaling back. As long as I keep making him feel good often, I get better results if I don't reinforce him ecial gifts or presents every single time I see him." The classic watch out for is any reinforcing behavior that begins to look like a habit to you. Keep an eye open for things you *always* do to make him feel special. Don't *always* bring him food, don't *always* visit his work place once every three days. Vary your schedule of reinforcement, and you'll have a lot more success.

∞ The Six Maintenance Keys that Keep You Securely in a Man's Heart and Thoughts

We've helped you to understand what maintenance is, why it's important, and how often to do it. Now let's give you some specific things you can do to maintain your budding romantic relationships.

Each of these activities are things you would naturally do if you were falling in love, and had chemistry driving you both crazy with attraction and lust. If you are still just building up to that state, be warned—these actions will not only increase his attraction to you, but they will also increase your attraction to him. Don't be surprised if you start to really like him as you do these maintenance activities.

1. Love notes

Let's compare and contrast the effective love notes men write to women with the effective love notes women write to men. A love note written to a woman should be brief, poetic, and lovely. It should talk about wonderful feelings, bonding, and the incredible sensations of becoming more intimate and connected. Meanwhile, a love note to a man should be brief, a little poetic, and, if at all possible, say something about sex.

Yes, sex. While we usually counsel men to not say anything overtly sexual in their love notes, you should probably say something at least a little racy, or your love note will have about as much appeal to him as curling up for the evening with a bag of rice cakes to watch a chick-flick like *Steel Magnolias.* It will all be very nice, but won't have much relevance to his life. If you can't bring in sex, at least bring in passion. There are four parts to the standard maintenance love note. Here's how you put it together:

FIRST, ACKNOWLEDGE HOW WONDERFUL HE IS

Complement him on something masculine. The more specific the compliment, the better. For example, writing "Your steely gray eyes reflect the power and passion I feel burning inside of you every time I touch you" is probably better than commenting that he has "real nice eyes."

SECOND, ACKNOWLEDGE HOW GREAT HE MAKES YOU FEEL

Once again, you are giving him the experience of being a competent provider by thanking him for the great feelings he is giving you. You might tell him something as simple as "being with you makes me feel so special. I just want to thank you for that."

THIRD, SAY SOMETHING SEXUAL, OR AT LEAST PASSIONATE

This is where the rubber hits the road. Of course he's happy that he makes you feel good, and glad to be a competent provider. Of course he's happy that he's winning your heart, and pleased to see that you are winnable. But in a love note, none of that is enough. You have to say something sexual to keep his interest alive, and to keep him pursuing you.

You might say, "I keep thinking of your lips against mine, and how great your body felt against me during that first kiss. I keep re-living it over and over and am looking forward to more." or, "I keep wondering how good you will feel when we are ultimately connected."

How sexual you get in the love note should be related to how far you want to go with him the next time you see him. If you think the next time you'll see him you'll end up having sex with him, you can be more racy. You might say "I'm so looking forward to making dinner for you this Friday. I'm great at breakfasts, too!" If you expect that the next time you'll see him you'll share your first kiss, or perhaps some making out for the first time, you'll want to be more demure. In that situation, you might say, "I hope your lips are as sweet when they're kissing me as they are when they're speaking to me." Either way, you've said something sexual that will wake him up, open his eyes, and get his juices flowing for your next time together.

Fourth, Tell Him You Are Looking Forward to Next Time You See Him

After saying something sexual, tell him that you can't wait to see him again. After a note like that, he'll be primed and ready to go.

2. E-mail

Always ask men you are interested in if they have an e-mail address, and if they check it. E-mail is the perfect medium in which to write romantic letters that will flatter and arouse him, without seeming too overwhelming at the same time.

You can conduct romantic conversations via e-mail, and have the "home court advantage" of being able to pick your words carefully and review them thoroughly before he ever sees them. You can write him love notes through e-mail, or, if he likes to write e-mail, ask the romantic questions we showed you earlier in this chapter. E-mail is an excellent place to maintain your budding relationship by telling stories of your first kiss, how it felt when you first knew you were in love, etc.

There are several warnings you should take heed of about men and e-mail, however. For men more than women, the Internet is first and foremost the international pornography superhighway. Your man may not be a good writer, and might not be used to writing long e-mails, but he probably will be very used to thinking of his Internet connection as a direct connection to sex. This might make him move faster into talking about sex than you might like. After all, sex is the main thing he thinks about when he's online, so he will naturally tend to drag you to that same level.

Second, the medium of e-mail itself might get you talking about explicit sexual acts faster than you might want to. It's fun, it's exciting, and it seems unreal, so why not let yourself go and give him something really sizzling in his e-mail box? The reason is that you are dating this guy. He's not some stranger you're never going to meet. Getting too hot in e-mails *will* make things hotter and heavier in your budding relationship, perhaps faster than you would like.

The solution is to keep an eye on yourself when swapping romantic e-mail with a man you are dating. It's okay to give him some sexual vibes in the notes you send him, but just remember, however far you go in e-mail will probably be how far you go in person.

When you use e-mail with a man, remember the rules of creating love notes, listed above. If he's into sending e-mail, then by all means write back and forth with him. And remember not to go farther with him sexually via e-mail than you would in person.

3. Flowers

When Jim first started dating Sandy, she sent him flowers after the first time they had sex. Far from making him feel weird about the relationship, it made him feel great. "I felt like enough of a winner and a provider with her, I didn't need to prove it by rejecting her gift," he told us. "And she was so cool about it, I didn't feel guilty for not doing it first."

There's no need to spend a lot of money on flowers for a guy. A simple ten dollar bouquet or a daisy, a note, and a handful of chocolate candies will go as far as (or farther than) sixty dollars worth of roses, and cost you a lot less.

Speaking of roses, you should probably not send a guy roses early in a relationship (or ever, probably). Most men have seen how powerful the gift of roses is for women. They've seen how meaningful roses seem to be. If you get a guy a rose, or roses, the odds are he'll wonder what it means. He won't *know* what it means, but he'll suspect it must mean something. He'll worry that it's *significant*, that he's being seen as a more serious relationship object than he wants to be. The solution? Don't give him roses. Problem solved.

You can give a guy flowers in person, drop them off at his house, drop them off at his work, or have them delivered. If you drop them off at his house, go over when you are sure he won't be there, or call first and tell him you want to drop something by; can you come over for a minute? When you do see him to deliver flowers (either at work or at his home), only stay for a minute. Don't stretch it out into a longer visit unless he insists. We suggest you pop in, leave him with a great feeling, and pop out again. If you stay around, you are likely to start thinking of your needs, your emotions, and getting him to praise you for your great gift. All that is well and good, but it's not maintenance. In maintenance you think about *his* feelings, so you want to get in quickly, make him feel good, and get out again.

4. Gifts and Cards

Guys don't do gifts the way women do. The cute little gift you'd buy is probably just another useless trinket to him, something else that he'll have to store, and a harbinger of what it will be like when you finally are living together, and all your stuff is chronically in his way. Okay, perhaps it's not that bad, but men and women do handle gifts differently. This difference was summed up in an early *Dilbert* cartoon. The first frame shows a woman receiving a card from a man. She says, "Oh, this is so wonderful! I'll cherish it forever!" as she holds it close to her heart. The second frame shows the guy getting a card from a woman. He reads it, feels good, and says, "Thanks!" In the last frame, he's crunching the card into the trash can while she watches, aghast. Crunch, crunch, crunch. That will probably be the final destination of any card you give him. He'll enjoy it, then throw it away. If you give him a little trinket, though, he won't know what to do with it. He can't throw it away, it's a real thing! At the same time, what's he supposed to do with the agate stone or "Special Moments" figurine you gave him? Put it on the coffee table? You've got to be kidding!

So what's the point? Don't give him gifts? No, but you might want to give him gifts that he'll find useful, or gifts that will turn into trash all on their own. As we said, men think cards are trash already, so they are a perfect vehicle for your love notes. Flower arrangements are also great, because they turn into garbage in a week or two, all on their own. He can enjoy them, then get them out of his life.

A man will appreciate it if you buy him something he will find useful, but there are several caveats to this rule. First, you must get him something that *he* will find useful, versus something that you will find useful when you are at his house. A tea-strainer is not a great gift for a man if you are the only person who drinks tea at his house. You can buy him the strainer, but don't think of it as a gift.

Second, if you are going to buy something for a man that he finds useful, be warned: He may well already have it, or have a specific idea in mind about which model and make of the item he wants to get.

In many ways, food is the ideal gift for a guy. It's useful, because he can eat it. He knows where to put it—into his mouth. And it turns into trash after it's been enjoyed. Give him some great food item with a note telling him to think of you while he enjoys it, and you'll have succeeded in giving a romantic gift to a guy.

5. Continuing to Let Him Win Your Heart and Continuing to Show Him How He Is a Provider for You

By now, this part should be second nature. You maintain a man by continuing to make him into a winner and a provider in your eyes. You don't stop doing this just because you are on middle dates—actually, you'll do this for the rest of your relationship. That will be for the rest of your life, so you might as well get used to it.

6. Sex

Sex is the ultimate reinforcement for a man, and, obviously, a key to keeping your relationship alive. It is also the ultimate win that you can give a man. That probably is not a big surprise to you. You know what to do.

Getting Less Formal

Introducing: The Family!

When should you introduce your family to him? For most people, introducing a boyfriend to the family is a big deal. It will usually seem like a big deal and signify that your relationship is deepening; that the relationship has long term potential. Because of the high significance factor, we recommend you delay introducing a man to your family at least a few months, until the relationship has proven to endure for a bit of time. We do not want you to create a scenario with your family in which you bring home a new man every month, claiming to them ahead of time that he is "the one." This will cost you their blessing and support. Wait until the relationship has proven itself before moving it to the next level by introducing him to your family.

Dealing with His Friends and Your Friends

Introducing your man to your friends and having you meet his friends has much less significance than having you meet his family. In fact, meeting his friends can often be a good way to test him. How willing is he to introduce you to his friends? How well does he treat you when you are with his friends? How does he treat his friends, and how do they treat him? This can show you a lot about his character.

Introducing him to your friends can cause trouble, however. The biggest problem is that your friends may not like him, and then influence you to dislike him, even if he is a great guy. Tony was one of our students, and he had this experience. He dated Shannah for three weeks and had been on four middle dates. She adored him. They had hot sex, lots in common, he passed her tests, and life was great. Shannah introduced him to her best friend Gwen, and that is when the trouble began. Gwen didn't like Tony. She didn't trust him, she didn't like that he was self-employed, she disliked the jewelry he wore, she didn't like the way he unbuttoned his shirt when they went out, and she thought he was too harsh when he left messages on Shannah's answering machine. All of Gwen's observations made Shannah question her attraction and relationship with Tony, and she ended up breaking up with him.

Your friends can often support you in judging a man's character and his level of trustworthiness, but can also be very harsh critics and find little things about a man to criticize and pick on. You must decide if your friends are capable of being honest, yet supportive. If they are not, do not introduce him to them until things are much more solid. If you feel that they can be objective, introduce him right away.

Saying "I Love You"

Men get confused. They confuse monogamy with marriage (we'll get to that later, when we talk about the Commitment Deal), and they confuse the word "love" with being trapped in a static, clingy relationship. And they are right. (Just kidding.)

Don't think he doesn't love you just because he doesn't say he loves you. He probably does. We believe that men actually fall in love more easily than women do—that's why they have to learn to shut off their feelings so much more effectively than women do. For men, the kind of emotional passion that comes with sex is scary. They get too connected, too quickly for their own liking. They learn to keep their emotional distance so they don't get too vulnerable. And they succeed at keeping this distance, all too well.

Whether or not you buy this line of reasoning, when a man hears you say, "I love you," it often doesn't strike him as a gift. More likely, it seems like an obligation. To most men, hearing an "I love you" now leads to hearing "why don't you love me better?" down the line. If he's learned that "love" with a woman means obligation and not measuring up, his response to "I love you" will be to run away, fast.

The best way to keep "I love you" from being a big deal is to decide, in your own mind, that it's not going to be a big deal. Don't make the saying of "I love you" heavy and significant. All that will do is terrify him. Say it in some delighted moment in an offhand way, and then go on as if nothing had happened.

Remember, when you are with a guy, he is looking to you for reassurance that everything is okay—not so much from your words, but from your behavior. Nowhere is this more true than around the phrase "I love you." If you are sharing a moment of laughter and delight, and you say "I love you" as the two of you are giggling, it won't overwhelm him. On the other hand, if you pin him down with your stare, say "I love you" significantly, and then wait expectantly, he's going to feel trapped. Do him a favor. Don't trap him with "I love you." It sort of blows the point of the whole thing, anyway.

If you try to force a man to tell you that he loves you, you will inevitably get something like this, which Valerie heard after trying to force an "I love you" out of her recalcitrant boyfriend: "Of course I love you. I wouldn't be with you—an average looking, middle-aged woman—when I could have a hotter, younger woman, if I didn't love you." She forced the issue, and she got slammed, hard. That'll happen to you, too, if you try to force a man into saying "I love you."

If you want a man who says "I love you" more than the man you are with says it, applying pressure to him to say it more will not work at all. If your man doesn't say "I love you" as much as you'd like, we suggest you start looking for places in your life where he is saying "I love you," but not in so many words. What does he do that tells you he loves you? Notice those things, and take some of the significance off of the words "I love you." If you can't find any such things, then you should consider that perhaps he doesn't love you, and that you should move on. If you can find such things, then love him the way he is, and don't force the "I love you" issue.

∞ The Seven Steps of Fighting with a Man

Problems do occur on middle dates. Given how much time you are spending together and the increasing expectations in the air, you both may be more tense than usual. He will be off in his own world thinking of stupid things he's said, worrying about whether you are having fun, and wondering when he'll get to see you naked. You will probably be off in your world thinking of all the reasons why you may or may not become a long-term couple, whether he is having fun, and wondering what he'll think when he sees you naked. All this can create trouble.

The two of you together might have an upsetting experience, and you and he may need to talk about it. He might get angry about something. You might get angry about something. No matter what happens to upset your relationship, the solution is the same. You must hear what he has to say without telling him he's wrong. Present your side, if you feel it's necessary, get things resolved, and move on. We'll get much more into handling trouble later. For now, here are the basics of handling fighting on a middle date:

1. Listen to Him

When most men are upset, they need someone (you) to listen to them. If they can express the problem, concern, or misunderstanding early enough, it will likely go away easily. We recommend that you just listen without interrupting him, and without telling him why he is wrong. When you listen to him without correcting him, he is likely to calm down quickly.

2. Repeat Back What You Heard

A man not only wants to know you listened to him, but he also wants to make sure you completely understood everything he said. When you repeat back what you heard him say, it gives you an opportunity to clarify anything you may have misunderstood, and an opportunity to demonstrate that you really are listening. This will also help calm him down.

Often when we listen to someone, we don't really hear what they say. Repeating back what a man says clarifies things. It makes sense to start with, "Let me repeat that back, so I'm sure I understand what you are saying." This keeps you from adding in your own distortions, which it is completely natural to do. If he says something patently ridiculous, like "I just get really upset when you take a business call at home when we are together," you are likely to distort it. You are likely to say "I understand. Let me repeat that back. You're saying that you are too much of a baby to support me in my career." This is, in fact, *not* what he said. That's your interpretation of what he said. He will correct you, and you can keep refining it until you actually do understand what he said. Eventually, you'll get that he wasn't saying he was a baby, or that he doesn't support you, or that he doesn't care about you, or any of the things that you added to what he said. Eventually, you'll understand that what he said was that he gets really upset when you take a business call at home when you are together. Nothing more.

There's a real power in repeating back what a man says to you, until you actually get it right. As long as you think he's telling you he is a baby, or doesn't care about you, or whatever other meanings you might add to his communication, you'll be responding to something other than what he actually said. As long as you are responding to something other than what he said, you are sowing the seeds of massive miscommunication. When you respond to what he actually said, however, you are calming the waters of conflict. You are helping him feel heard, and that will smooth things considerably.

3. Thank Him

Even if you feel angry about what he is telling you, or if you think he is twisting what actually happened in his own dark, demented way, thank him for taking the time (and the risk) to talk to you about it. In his world, he is taking a risk by telling you what is bugging him. Most men are trained to hold it all in, until they explode. By getting it off his chest, he is likely to feel more relaxed and more connected to you. As he becomes more relaxed, he'll become less defensive.

4. Give Him Your Side

After, and only after, you have repeated back what he said without distortion, and thanked him, should you move on to this step.

Most of the time, you really don't need to say much. Of course he's distorting what happened. Of course he's being unreasonable. But most of the time, you can just let it go (see step six). Much of the time you'll find it makes more sense to make the emotional sacrifice of choosing to not say everything you think, and get on with your relationship.

On the other hand, sometimes there are things that must be said. Here are some simple guidelines for communicating "cleanly" with a man.

Agree on the Data

It's no good arguing about something that you can't agree actually happened. If you are upset that he showed up late, and he claims that he showed up at the agreed-upon time, you don't have much of a basis for fighting about his being inconsiderate. You then have to let it go, or fight about the time he said he'd arrive. If you can't agree on the facts, then the facts are what you have to talk about.

Don't Refer to Your Opinions as Facts

This is a real relationship-killer. It's not a *fact* that he's inconsiderate. That is your opinion. The fact is (if you can agree on it), that he said he'd show up at 6:30, and didn't show up until nine. Saying, "It drives me crazy when you are so inconsiderate" is more likely to spark a fight than saying, "When you say you'll be here at 6:30 and you don't show up 'til nine, I think you are really inconsiderate."

The difference is that, when you state your opinions as opinions, you are saying what you think, plain and simple. When you state your opinions as facts, you are stating The Truth, from God's point of view. Naturally, he will object to that. As would you, if he did it. It's not a "fact" that he's being a jerk, or that he's inconsiderate, or that he says things for the sole purpose of hurting you. Those are your opinions, your judgments. They may or may not be true, but they *are not facts*. For some reason, people get calmer when you acknowledge your opinions as your own, just as they get angrier when you treat your opinions as God's holy truth. Keep your opinions as your own, and you'll calm a fight; state your opinions as God's opinion, and you'll fan the flames of conflict every time.

State Your Feelings

We suggest that, when fighting with a man, you keep it simple when talking about your feelings. You might want to stick to the basics: Happy, sad, afraid, angry, and ashamed should cover all the ground you'll need. Get more complicated with a man at your own risk.

5. Make Promises, Apologies, and Requests

If you follow the previous four steps, he will probably calm down. If you think it's appropriate, you can promise to not to do whatever he is upset about again. It is also important to apologize for anything "out of line" that you did to cause him to be upset. The devastating effects of your thoughtless remarks or actions can often be healed by a simple apology. If it's the right thing to do, then apologize.

Make requests: Tell him what you want, and ask him what he wants from you. Your requests may be simple, such as "I want you to show up when you say you will," or more emotional, like "I want to feel close to you." With most guys, you are going to be better off with requests of specific behaviors that he can agree to. You can also ask for promises and apologies, if you wish.

6. Let It All Go

Given that he was upset, you are likely to be, also. We strongly recommend that you let go of the fight as soon as you can, and get on to other things.

Any relationship that lasts will require some emotional sacrifice from time to time. You won't always get the "last word" in an argument, or get to say every single thing that's bugging you. Think long term: What's more important, saying everything you think and feel at every moment, or creating a long term relationship that can really last? The better you get at making this sacrifice, and at letting it all go after a fight, the better your relationship will be.

7. Change the Subject

If he's said most of what he has to say, and you've said most of what you had to say, then it's time to move on, as quickly as you can. We're not telling you to brush conflicts under the rug, but it is important that you allow conflicts to end when it's time for them to end. One of the biggest mistakes some women make is that they won't allow a conflict to be over. They want to dig into it, over and over and over. Don't be like that. Give the guy—and yourself—a break, and let the conflict finally be over.

∞ *Conclusion*

The middle dates are where you start deciding what's up and what's what in your budding relationship. It's where you get deeper into testing, and where you really start to take time to be with and get to know a man.

You've figured out what you want. You've figured out where the men are, and have interviewed lots of them. You've disqualified men for the *right* reasons, and stopped disqualifying them because they weren't perfect flirters, or because they didn't have ideal opening lines. You've given men wins and losses, gone with men on qualifying dates, and now are having middle dates with one or more men. Over time, you begin to focus your attention on one man. You get closer. Perhaps you become sexual. You think perhaps you are falling in love.

But wait! This still isn't a relationship! He's not committed. He's not monogamous. And you can't help but notice, he's also not particularly perfect in every detail, either. We'll now give you a little break to think about the problems a man can cause; then we can go on to creating and closing your commitment deal. From there, it's on into your relationship!

CHAPTER 13

Problems and Trouble

"If the commitment is not there, it's time to walk away."
—Larry Flynt, *Esquire*, March, 1999

TROUBLE, CONFLICT, FIGHTING, AND PROBLEMS. THEY ARE AN inevitable part of almost any relationship. Every interaction with a man—every degree of commitment in a relationship with a man—poses the opportunity for problems to arise. This chapter will bring you down to the depths of hell—the problems and trouble spots in a relationship—and back up again. We will shed light on the areas in which you will likely cause trouble in relationships, and then look at the ways in which a man will likely cause trouble, too. Think of this chapter as your survival kit for any type of conflict or trouble situation you might encounter with a man. Let's get started.

Dates from Hell

Date Number One

When Zoe went to meet Jacob for their first date, she was nervous. Jacob was a muscular, attractive, and intelligent professor she had met a few weeks before at a party. They had a strong connection and spent many hours talking about political issues, art, and fashion. Jacob seemed like the quintessential Renaissance man. He seemed interested in Zoe, but she wasn't sure. They set up a coffee date before they left the party and Zoe's interest in him grew as the day of their date came closer.

Zoe looked great for the date. She wore a tight skirt and a top which revealed a bit of cleavage. She felt sexy. She arrived early to the coffee shop and waited patiently for Jacob. He arrived right on time . . . with another woman.

"This is my girlfriend Lynn," he told Zoe. "I figured you wouldn't mind if I brought her along."

"Of course not," Zoe responded, realizing instantly that her plans had been completely fouled up. The three of them sat down, and Zoe immediately noticed that Lynn was acting possessive and demanding about Jacob.

Jacob looked at Zoe and said, "Our conversation was so fascinating at the party that I realized Lynn and you would probably have a lot in common." Zoe was uncomfortable and miserable. The three of them talked in a forced manner about boring political issues. A few minutes later, Jacob got up from the table and said, "I have to prepare for my course tomorrow. I was hoping Lynn and you could get to know each other better. Lynn needs some new friends." Jacob walked out the door leaving Zoe to endure one of the most horrible hours of her life, talking to Lynn about her life and her relationship issues with Jacob. "I felt like a fool. I had put on a sexy outfit. I had visions of getting to know Jacob better. What a jerk." Needless to say, Zoe never saw either of them again.

Date Number Two

Daria was new to dating. She was in her early twenties, and had always been too shy and scared to date. Daria was a nerd in high school, and had never taken dating seriously. While she had dated a few men, Daria had always been passive during the process; she let men decide everything and made no requests of them.

Daria met Sam in a college chemistry course. He was nineteen, exotic looking, and, for reasons she could not explain, seemed to really like her. On their first date, they went to a restaurant. "We had a wonderful meal," Daria commented. "But then he said, 'You are paying for half, aren't you?'" Daria didn't have any money. "The date went downhill from there. He was angry I didn't pay my half, and we never were able to relax together after that." The date ended awkwardly and they never spoke again.

Date Number Three

Sue had been dating Max for a few weeks. He was a political activist and was involved in many anti-hate groups. They had a date set up for a Thursday night. "He took me to see *Schindler's List*," she told us. "It was horrible. I cried the whole time. I was upset about the movie, and even more upset that he would take me to such an intense movie so early on in our relationship. It was the most unromantic date of my life." She never called him again.

Date Number Four

Anna met Mike while she was roller-blading. He was beautiful. He looked like a professional weight lifter, with an incredible chest and face. Mike was charming and flirtatious as hell. Anna was thrilled to be going on a date with this Chippendale dancer-type guy, but there was one problem.

"When we went out, Mike flirted with every woman in the place. It was horrible to be with a man who wanted to talk and flirt with every other woman in the place, except me. It was truly humiliating. That was the last time I ever saw Mike."

Date Number Five

Thirty-six, tall and tan, Henry had taken great care of his body. He was an insurance agent, and they met when Rebecca came in to update her policy. After a coffee date, Henry walked her to her car. They kissed, and ended up back at her apartment. They were making out on the couch when Henry got weird: "All of a sudden he tried to rip off my top. When I stopped him, he started begging me to have sex with him. It was terrible. He was pathetic. I made him leave, and even canceled my insurance policy with his company."

There is no shortage of dates from Hell. A recent *Cosmopolitan* magazine article gave a few examples of stupid things men have said or done on first dates:

- The man who asked his date, "Why is it that all the good women are taken?"
- The man who said, "I'm so intrigued by the mind of a serial killer. The rage and passion he must feel while actually killing someone is fascinating to me."
- The man who offended (and mystified) his date by saying, "I shower four times a day. I have to."
- The man who felt compelled to admit, "When I have sex with a woman, I always have to imagine I'm with someone else."
- The man who said about marriage, "I'm not a big fan of the institution myself."

- The man who said about his ex-girlfriend, "Some people just *need* hitting."
- The man who invited a woman for dinner at his house and, at the end of the date said, "To keep this relationship devoid of any sense of anyone owing anyone anything, why don't you pay your half." He then presented her with an itemized bill of everything he spent on the groceries.

The Maintenance Spectrum

By now, you are surely aware that all relationships require some maintenance. Everyone needs certain things to happen in order to feel like someone cares about them. Taking care of these needs is called *maintenance*, and you must do it to keep your man happy.

Men vary greatly in what they need you to do in order for them to feel appreciated. Some men's needs are fairly simple. If you are considerate, and do not treat them like dirt, they feel appreciated and attracted to you. Others require constant compliments, reassurance, and attention. Some even need to fight with you and have regular conflict in order to feel that the relationship is right for them. Men need varying degrees of maintenance.

You have probably heard women talk about men as being "low-maintenance" or "high-maintenance." This is a very useful distinction to make. Here is how you tell the difference, early on, between low-maintenance men, high-maintenance, and men who need too much effort to be worth the trouble.

Low-Maintenance Men

The low-maintenance man is a gift to women. He doesn't require much to feel happy with you. His needs are simple and easy to figure out. He will even help you, by telling you exactly what he needs, and meaning it.

Here is what you need to know about him:

- He takes very little in life personally. The low-maintenance man will not jump on you every time you make a mistake or thoughtless remark. When he is upset, he lets it go easily and is therefore easy to be with.

- He contains his feelings well. If he is upset, he will not make a scene, and won't take it out on you. He takes responsibility for his feelings.

- He makes an effort to be reasonable, and is able to compromise and listen to your issues and problems, then express his own.

- He accepts you on your own terms. He is not looking to change or fix you. Rather, he is happy with you and your quirks.

- He doesn't "flip out." If he feels anxious, upset, or stressed, he handles it responsibly, and often you never even know about it.

- He feels he has more to learn about life. He is open to learning new things, and does not jump to conclusions. He isn't overly attached to his own opinions.

- His feelings in the moment are fairly insignificant to him. He is emotional, but makes life-decisions from a rational and logical base.

- He is highly romantic. He frequently does the "little things" for you that make you happy, and keeps romance a priority in the relationship.

- He does not expect you to know what he needs. He does not play mind games with you, or become upset when you don't read his mind. He is forthcoming with his opinions and his desires.

- He is emotionally consistent, and does not have massive mood swings.

- He isn't overly concerned about what other people think of him.

- He genuinely cares about you, and likes women. He does not harbor resentment toward all women.

- He is generative and creative, and is not dependent on you as his source of support and entertainment.
- He rarely complains, and rarely whines.
- He is able to be spontaneous and have fun with you, and is happy to spend time with you on romantic adventures.

Medium-Maintenance Men

You are more likely to encounter medium-maintenance men than low-maintenance men. The medium-maintenance man has more needs and takes more things you say and do personally than does the low-maintenance man. He is more work. He makes more mistakes. At the same time, he is not so wrapped up in his own feelings that he is impossible to deal with. Here's what you need to know about the medium-maintenance man:

- He takes some things in life personally. There are some topics you would be better off avoiding, like your hatred of sports, or your attraction to other men.
- He occasionally takes his feelings out on you. If he is in a bad mood he sometimes takes it out on you, and can be nasty or start a fight. He will usually apologize for it afterwards, though, even by purchasing flowers for you or taking you to a nice restaurant.
- He is sometimes unreasonable.
- He does "flip out," but feels badly about it later. After he has an emotional scene, he apologizes and does what it takes to make things right again.
- He sometimes forgets to treat you like a lady. He is inconsistent with his romantic pursuit of you, and does not consistently buy you flowers or take you out.
- He can be sensitive about his finances and his career.
- He is moderately creative and moderately whiny.

- He likes sex, but sometimes is self-centered in the bedroom. Sometimes he only pleasures himself, then rolls over and is instantly asleep.
- He has moods, but is mostly stable. One day he may be happy, the next day angry, upset, or worried.
- He worries sometimes about how he looks to other people, and what other people think about *you*.

Too Hot to Handle (High-Maintenance)

The high-maintenance man is out of control. He has little control over his moods and behaviors, and has constant problems with everything, most especially you.

The high-maintenance man is characterized by his belief that he has the right to be as difficult as he likes. He is incredibly impulsive and irregular, and *you* have to deal with it. If he feels like yelling at a dangerous-looking stranger, he does it, and you have to handle the consequences. If he feels like screaming, crying, pouting, or generally acting like a baby, he would never dream of containing himself. He thinks nothing of yelling at you during dinner at a nice restaurant and creating a scene. After all, he reasons, if he cannot completely express his feelings at every moment, you must be trying to repress him. Here is what you need to know about the high-maintenance man:

- He takes everything in life personally. If it rains out when he wants to go on a walk, he is angry at the weather.
- He takes his feelings out on you. If it is raining out when he wants to take a walk, he takes out his anger on you. If he is in a bad mood for any reason, he takes it out on you.
- He feels he has the right to be unreasonable. He never makes any attempt to be reasonable, and you have to just live with it.
- He feels he has the right to "flip out." If he feels anxious, upset, or

stressed, he does whatever he feels like, wherever he might be, and you have to handle it.

- He feels he understands "God's opinion" about everything, and is happy to set you straight at all times about what you are doing wrong. He loves to lecture you about everything in detail and backs it up with his vast knowledge of how the world really works.
- He is insulted by everything you do.
- He believes his feelings and opinions in the moment are the most important thing in the universe. He can never just "get over it," and get on with life. He has to process or fight about everything right now.
- It is impossible to give him feedback. If you tell him anything about his behavior, he will not listen and will change the subject, or he will yell or create a scene. He seems to think that any problem is because of you and takes no responsibility for anything in the relationship.
- He generates nothing and is not creative, but complains constantly about being bored.
- He is incredibly jealous, and gets upset when you talk or look at other men when you are with him.
- He becomes furious if you do not instantly and automatically know what he needs at all times. Your inability to be psychic with his needs is proof, in his mind, of your insensitivity.
- He is incredibly inconsistent. One minute he will be happy, the next, sad, crying, or yelling.
- He believes there is only one right way to do things, and you are doing it wrong.
- He is unreasonably demanding in the bedroom without giving your needs any thought.
- He worries continuously about how he looks to other people, and what other people think about *you*.
- He is very picky and judgmental about your behavior.

- He has an explosive temper.
- He dates women, but doesn't really like them. He sees women as a necessary evil.

Which type of man do you tend to date? Is he the ultra-demanding high-maintenance type? Is he the medium-maintenance, fairly-demanding type? Or is he the angelic low-maintenance man who seems to be a true gift from God? Understanding which degree of maintenance a potential date will likely need is useful early on because it allows you to determine if he will be worth the trouble. Once you assess the type of man you have on your hands, you then have an idea of what to expect from him. Only you can determine if you can handle a high-maintenance man (even though we strongly suggest you avoid them). You might also look at why you seem to consistently date a certain type of man, and what you can do to change.

∞ The Eight Secrets of Handling the Problems Men Cause

The biggest trap women fall into with men is that they handle the problems men cause incorrectly. Instead of diffusing problems, they often end up making things worse. You have surely had this experience: You are with a man, and he seems upset. You try to help, and end up fighting with him. He then complains that you aren't listening to him, that you are judging or criticizing him, and you don't understand his point of view. This fight probably happened because you were unaware of the following eight secrets of handling the problems men cause. Follow these rules, and your fighting days are over.

1. The Magical Cure for a Man's Problem

One way to cause conflict with a man is to try to fix things for him. Women who try to fix a man's problem will get themselves into unending trouble. Solving a man's problem is a big mistake, because if you do, he will make *you* the problem. Here is how it works:

Men handle problems differently than women do. When men have problems, they want to solve them on their own, pure and simple. In fact, they may even feel powerful and strong knowing that they are solving problems alone, through their own brute strength and will. When you try to help out, even when your help is sincere and loving, a man will likely feel as though you are questioning his masculinity. He'll be afraid of becoming a wimp who needs women to take care of him. Meanwhile, women tend to share their feelings about problems. Men don't. If a man is designing a computer program, for instance, and can't get it to work, it is uncommon for another man to ask him, "How do you feel about that?" and spend time sharing how it felt when he had a similar problem with a program he was writing. Men roll up their sleeves, get in there, and try to fix it.

Similarly, men don't tend to indulge each other in complaining about relationships. If two guys are at the gym, and one says, "I met this hot woman, but she hasn't called me!" the other one won't commiserate about how bad that must feel. Instead, He will more likely say, "What's the matter, forget how to use a phone? Call her up, you idiot!" Problem solved; on to other topics of conversation.

This difference between men and women is shown clearly in a recent *Cathy* comic strip. Cathy's car has broken down on a winter morning, and she cannot leave the house to get to work. She calls her boyfriend, Irving, and he says he will come over to help her. As she waits for him, a fantasy forms in her mind. "He'll come over, and we'll be so happy to see each other. We'll drink coffee, eat morning buns, and be brought together by this car problem. Everything else will disappear, and we'll be laughing and happy and in love on this cold winter morning."

At that moment, Irving enters. "I called a tow truck, it'll be here in ten minutes," he tells her. "I also called a cab, so you'll be able to get to work. I must go, big meeting this morning." Whoosh, gone, and Cathy is left sulking in the final frame, "Men have no idea how to handle problems." Women like to feel their way through problems. Men like to solve them, preferably alone.

When a man comes to talk to you about his problem, you must not solve it. Let us repeat that, because it seems so strange: When a man comes to you with a problem, you must not solve it. If a man presents you with a problem, and you try to solve it, he will almost certainly be angry with you. He will likely accuse you of not listening, or of being a nag. That is the thanks you will get for trying to help a man by solving his problems.

When a man comes to you with a problem, be thankful. As long as he has that problem, he won't be making *you* his problem, and you are in the clear. Instead of fixing it, we advise you to listen to him, be with him, and let him know you have faith in his ability to solve the problem on his own.

One day Karen's boyfriend Leo was upset because of a work problem. "I didn't know what to say," she told us, "but I remembered not to solve his problem. I gave him a kiss on the lips, and told him that I knew he was powerful enough to handle any problem at work. I smiled at Leo and allowed him to tell me about all of his work troubles. " He vented his feelings for five or ten minutes, and eventually he stopped. "Later Leo told me, 'I can't believe how wonderful you were! You were just so perfect when I was so upset!' That blew me away, because I didn't actually do anything!" If Karen had tried to "solve" his problem, Leo wouldn't have thought she was being supportive and wonderful. He probably would have felt resentful that she was trying to give him unsolicited advice, and a fight would have ensued.

You must try to be like Karen and tell a man you support him in coming up with his own solutions to his problems, while also being available to him for support and encouragement. Here are a few magical phrases to use with any troubled man:

- "I know you are so strong, you can handle anything."

- "I have complete faith in you," followed by a deep kiss.
- "I am sure you know how to handle this problem."
- "I support you in handling this in any way that makes sense to you."
- "You can do it, I am sure of that."

Do not worry if you find yourself repeating these phrases over and over. By reinforcing that you support him and have faith in his abilities, you give him space to find a solution to any problem. When you reward him with a win in the form of a kiss, hug, or any sexual act, he feels powerful and self-confident, and then gathers the energy to take action to solve his problem.

2. Fighting With a Man Is Like Defusing a Bomb

One of our students was a military demolitions expert. He told us about working with bombs. "Most of the time, you handle a bomb by sending in some sort of robot to just blow it up. No problem if you're not nearby. The real problem comes when you have to get in there and defuse it. You really want to be patient, not jump to conclusions, and remember what you are up to when you are defusing a bomb."

It occurred to us that in describing defusing a bomb he was giving us an analogy for fighting with a man. If you can get someone else to take the blast, so much the better, but most of the time, you will have to do your fighting with men yourself.

Fighting with a man is a delicate procedure. Like defusing a bomb, you can't let your mind wander from the most important thing. When you fight with a man, the most important thing is to end it quickly, and with a minimum of stress. If you get caught up in some detail of the fight, or let your anger take over, you will lose the fight, even if you technically "win" it. You might be able to badger him into admitting that you are right and he is wrong, but you won't have created harmony, and you won't be receiving a reward later.

3. Keep Asking Yourself, "What's Most Important to Me?"

It is easy to lose your head in a fight with a man. He says things that hook you, and make you want to defend yourself. This is almost as big a mistake as trying to solve a man's problem. Consistently remember what your desired outcome is. If you are in the early stages of your relationship with a man, and your relationship is not quite solid, we strongly urge you to avoid fighting with him altogether. If you must fight, remember what is most important to you. Is it more important to you to make him see that you are right, or is it more important for him to desire you? Your answer to this question will guide your behavior in a fight with a man.

On Annette's first date with Paul, she started telling him about her favorite women's magazine. Paul commented that all women's magazines are dumb and are only created to sell products and manipulate women. He told her "My one wish in life is that women would stop acting as though women's magazines and fashion are so important." At this point, Annette needed to ask herself, "What's most important to me? Having a relationship with Paul, or arguing?" If she had asked herself this question, she probably would not have made the mistake she made, by responding, "You jerk! I don't know what you're so huffy about. It's only the coolest women's magazine around—everybody thinks so." Naturally, he took offense at this. "Oh, everybody likes this magazine, do they? Well, I think only women who are mindless and superficial value fashion magazines over ideas and intellect." They started having a fight. "What are we doing?" she asked herself. "What happened?" It was a good question.

It is important to realize that taking offense at what someone says is a choice. Have you ever been insulted by someone, and simply let it roll off your back? Perhaps you thought to yourself, "It isn't worth it," and simply went on with your life. At that moment, your commitment to something else—having the life you want, perhaps—was more important than proving to someone that you wouldn't allow them to insult you.

If you want romantic success with men and you have never been able to avoid being offended by a dumb comment a man has said, you had better learn how quickly. Men will give you plenty of opportunities to get angry. You must choose not to take the bait, and choose not to get offended by anything they say. It may be helpful, when you feel upset, to imagine that the person rather than being an adult, is only a child. Imagine if a six-year-old kid told you the same thing. It may seem obnoxious and annoying, but wouldn't have the same impact as a man you are interested in dating. If you can "pretend" he is a six-year-old kid being silly, it will help you keep your mind on the seduction.

One of our students, Bonnie, made such a choice with Ivan. She met Ivan when a mutual friend took them both sailing on his boat. Ivan was in his late twenties, and looked good in his bikini bathing suit. "He was cute enough," Bonnie told us, "and so I decided he'd be worth some effort to date." Their mutual friend mentioned that Bonnie had just had several articles published in an academic journal. Bonnie happened to have a copy of the article with her, and she showed it to Ivan. "Men usually respond positively to it," she told us. "But Ivan started finding all these errors in how it was typeset, and talking about how it wasn't put together and written properly. It really upset me—after all, what had he ever done that he could talk about? But I kept asking myself, 'What's most important to me,' and I realized that I didn't care what he thought of the article. Bonnie avoided arguing with Ivan, and they discussed other topics. They spent the remainder of the cruise talking and getting to know one another. They went on several dates and she really enjoyed being with him. "If I'd fought with him about the article, I never would have been able to date him," she told us. "It really made a difference to ask myself what was most important."

4. Never Reason With an Upset Man

If you are with a man and he is upset, this is also the time he is likely to be unreasonable and difficult to be around. This is true for everyone. When *you* are most upset, *you* are most likely to be unreasonable, too. Reason and logic will only make an upset man more upset. Have you ever tried pointing out the lack of logic in an upset man's thinking? How well has it worked for you? Our guess is, not at all.

When a man is upset, your job is *not* to influence him. Your job is to influence yourself. You must get yourself to stay calm, remain clear of his upset, and avoid trying to get him to see reason. Let him be upset without having him take his anger out on you. Keep asking yourself what you are committed to, and go with your commitment, rather than with your emotional reaction.

5. Don't Take Anything Personally

Gina was on a middle date with Tony. Their date was going fine until Tony said, "It must be hard not really living in the real world. I mean, since you only work at the University and around egg-heads all the time, it must make it hard to relate to real people." Not in the real world? Only work at the University? This might be an insult, or it might not be. Unfortunately, Gina decided to take it as one. "Well, what's that supposed to mean? I'm in the real world!" she said to Tony. She had taken something he said personally, and allowed a possible fight to begin.

Think back to a fight you have had with a man. Most of the time, the conversation will have been going along fine. You two were talking and there was no problem. Suddenly, someone said something stupid that could be considered insulting. The other person took it personally, and a fight ensued. Sometimes the man you are with will say boneheaded things that sound like insults to you. Sometimes you will say the same sorts of dumb things to him. If you take something a man says or does personally, you lose sight of your outcome, and your goals will not be accomplished.

You must remember what your desired outcome is when you are out with a man, especially in a stressful situation. It is incredibly easy to take something a man says or does personally, let yourself become insulted, and then start a fight. Here is a list of things a man will do that you should not take personally. As you go out on dates, you will no doubt find other things to add to this list.

- Not calling you back
- Showing up late, or not showing up at all
- Canceling or changing dates at the last minute
- Not appreciating all the nice things you do for him
- Being cold, distant, insulted, or difficult to talk to
- Not responding to your flirtatious advances
- Ignoring you when you say hello

6. Handling Male Rudeness Gracefully

So how should you handle these difficult behaviors, if you can't take them personally? Little things, like not calling you back, you don't really have to deal with if you simply take on the responsibility of always doing the calling. Ditto with a man you have just met seeming cold, or difficult to talk to. Handling his rudeness is your job. But truly rude behavior, like missing several dates in a row, must be dealt with. If you let a man seriously inconvenience you without responding, he will simply do it again, and may even pull worse stunts on you. You must respond.

The secret is to know how to handle male rudeness without getting into a fight. You want to handle it so he becomes crystal clear about the rules of dating you. He must learn what is acceptable and what is not. When you tell a man clearly what is acceptable and what is not, he then gets to choose how he will conduct himself. You do not have to be mad, or out of control. No man will respect a woman he thinks is acting psycho. Men will be scared by this sort of behavior, and they will want to stay clear of you.

Male/female relationships are always a balancing act. Setting boundaries with men is important. Define acceptable and unacceptable behaviors clearly. Use wins and losses to enforce your decisions. If you do not take a man's behavior personally, you will be able to give him wins when he does something you like and understand how to give him losses when he does things you do not like. In the end, you will be much more effective, and he will respect you more for it.

Lyle missed a date with Cindy and didn't call to apologize. She didn't take it personally. She reasoned that Lyle was pushing her, to see what he could get away with. Because she didn't take Lyle's behavior personally, Cindy was able to talk to him on the phone without starting a fight. Instead of fighting, she said, "Listen, I like you and everything, but you've missed a date with me and didn't even call to apologize. I have a rule you need to know about: if you miss another date, I can never talk to you again. So if you want to go out with me, you've gotta show up, and this time bring flowers." Her voice was firm, she did not yell, and she did not apologize. She set a boundary, and instead of whining about how rude he was, she gave him a simple choice: show up, or get lost. He showed up for their next qualifying date, flowers in hand, and they ended up having a wonderful evening. "He was pushing to see how far he could go," Cindy told us. "I wouldn't have talked to him again if he missed another date, but I'm glad he showed up. We had a wonderful time." By not taking Lyle's behavior personally, getting depressed, or caught up in his feelings, Cindy was able to handle the situation effectively.

7. Listen So a Man Feels Like He Is Heard

In chapter 12, the "Seven Steps of Fighting With a Man," we offered tips on listening so a man feels like he is heard. This technique has proven to be effective in resolving conflicts with men because it allows both parties the opportunity to state their points of view and then move on to resolution quickly and efficiently.

8. Never Explain Yourself

When you are having a conflict with a man, you will be tempted to explain and justify who you are and why you do the things you do. No matter how upset you feel, do not explain yourself. When you explain and justify yourself, you create more fuel for the fire, and the fight will usually intensify rather than calm down. Instead, a good rule of thumb is to answer questions only. If he asks you why you did something, answer his question, but do not feel as though you owe him an explanation for every aspect of your behavior just because he is upset with you.

You are not dating this guy to get your validation in life from him. You are getting validation in other places, remember? A man is an addition to your life, there to add love to your life, not to be the central thing that makes you feel good. If you are trying to get validation from men, you will become dependent and easily upset when he inevitably offends or hurts you. Simply remember what is most important to you, answer relevant questions, get through the conflict without explaining yourself, and things will calm down quickly.

⚭ The Ways Men Fight and How to Handle Them

People fight in different ways, and each person tends to be consistent in his or her way of fighting. There are two basic modes that men default to. They either yell, or they manipulate. Let's discuss each one of these modes in detail, and show you how to handle men when they go into them.

Ol' Yeller

Men who default to yelling do not just get upset—they get *angry*. Subconsciously, they figure they can control you if they can scare you with their anger. If they cannot, they will either respect you more, or get out of your life. Either way, you win, so it is worth learning how to handle men who default to yelling.

HOW TO SPOT HIM EARLY ON

The yeller is a warrior by nature. He likes to fight, looks tough, and will often take offense at the slightest thing you say. He might be rude to waitresses, love telling you violent stories, or brag about conflicts he has been in. He might be abusive and critical in conversations and during minor conflicts. If you find yourself having to walk on eggshells to keep him from getting angry, you are with Ol' Yeller.

HOW TO FIGHT WITH HIM

Ol' Yeller wants to scare you into submission. Subconsciously, he figures that if he is unreasonable enough, he can get his way. You cannot win a fight with Ol' Yeller. The solution is to avoid conflicts with him, and leave the situation any time you feel he is being abusive.

Warning: Men who love to scream and be rude may also become violent. If you ever sense that a situation is becoming dangerous, get out immediately.

The Manipulator

You have probably heard the saying "Don't get mad, get even." The manipulator lives by this code. The manipulator will attempt to take control of you indirectly and thereby even the score. Manipulators are control-freaks. They don't feel safe unless they are able to manipulate and control everything around them. This tendency of theirs is exacerbated by conflict, because conflict is a direct challenge to their control.

While Ol' Yeller tries to control you with anger, the manipulator tries to control you with mind games. The Manipulator is especially pre-occupied with being "right," and having "logical" arguments that prove his correctness. He will have justifications and arguments for why he is right, but will drive you crazy in a fight because his "logical" arguments will not be logical. He will irrationally insist that he is making sense, all the while questioning your sanity as you get angrier and angrier with his inconsistency. The Manipulator will portray himself as the soul of sanity, a man sadly drawn into having to defend himself from your unreasonable attack. This will make you even crazier, proving even more, in his mind, that you are unreasonable and therefore wrong. When he points out to you how crazy you are acting, you are liable to lose your mind entirely. This is not a pretty sight.

How to Spot Him Early On

The Manipulator is often very intelligent, and may be in a field that requires a lot of "civilized" conflict, like law, academia, management, or administration. He may well be highly educated. These signs alone, however, are not enough; many men who are not manipulators share these characteristics, and many men who are manipulators do not.

When you are on a date with a manipulator, he needs everything to be "just so." He is very particular about his needs and his comfort. It is often important for him to reject your ideas, just so he can prove that he has the power to do so. His "reasons" occur to you as incredibly lame. He's practicing his technique. Watch out.

The Manipulator is hard to please. There is always something just a little wrong with everything. Complaining and being irritated, for him, is a way of establishing control. He may send back food at a restaurant, or require a drink with a particular brand of gin. If they do not have that brand, he will, with a heavy sigh, have nothing at all. He may complain about details of the way you dress. You will notice that you feel like he is particularly controlling and persnickety. That is because he is a manipulator.

HOW TO FIGHT WITH HIM

Don't Argue with Him. Watch out. The Manipulator can drive you crazy. The only way to keep from going insane with a manipulator is to avoid falling into the trap of arguing about the nonsense he is spewing forth. Arguing will never work, and will only drive you insane. His rebuttals will only perpetuate the fight. What the Manipulator wants is control, not logic. He is afraid that if he loses control, something bad will happen to him. Pretending to care about logic and reason is his way of getting that control. He gets to drive you crazy, then act like you are an illogical, nasty, out-of-control nut-case. If you argue with him about his logic, he has won immediately, and it is all over for you.

Tell Him He is Right. Tell the Manipulator that he is right as much as you can stomach doing it. If there is some small point that he is correct about, tell him, and emphasize that he is right about it. "You are right that this relationship is very important to us both," you might say. "That's very, very right." Try not to sound sarcastic. You are trying to give him as much control as you can, so he will calm down, without letting him control *you*.

Apologize for Not Being Logical. It is also very powerful to tell the Manipulator that you are sorry that your feelings are not logical. He can insist that your feelings should be logical, but you can always come back with, "I guess that's not the way I am." As long as you do not get drawn into an argument about whether or not you should be more logical, you are safe. "It's just important to me to be able to go out with my ex-boyfriend as a friend," you might say. "I'm sorry it doesn't make any sense. I know how frustrating that must be. But it really is how I feel, and I don't think that's going to change."

Tell Him how Important He Is to You. Keep in mind that he is not a bad guy. He is just scared of being out of control. It can help calm him down if he hears how important he is to you. If he is not important to you, you can find something about your relationship that is. You can almost always truthfully say, "I hope you know, it's important to me that you feel good and happy." Of course it is important—he is much easier to be with, and you get more of what you want, when he's happy. Just hearing that will often calm the Manipulator down.

Change the Scene. You probably are not going to get anywhere useful in an argument with the Manipulator, so you might as well get it over with as quickly as possible. See if you can leave, or get the two of you doing something else that does not allow you to argue, like seeing a movie or being with other people.

America's Most Wanted: More Ways Men Fight. We already examined the two primary ways men fight; by yelling and manipulating. There is a host of other ways men fight that you should also be aware of. As you read this list, remember that you also fall into these categories to some degree. We all have our own strategies for handling conflict. Understanding different styles of conflict and how to handle them are the most important parts of resolving trouble.

THE DISAPPEARING MAN

Some men become so upset and scared when they get into an argument, or an all-out fight, that they leave. They will withdraw emotionally and psychologically and then become silent, distant, and look spaced out. Or a Disappearing Man will leave the scene. He'll get in his car, and simply leave. The Disappearing Man probably grew up thinking that fighting and conflict should be avoided. Now, as an adult, he avoids fighting at all costs. The Disappearing Man is scared of hurting you, and fears his own anger and the potential for damaging those he loves. Instead of handling conflict and talking about problems, he goes and sulks in a dark corner, alone. While these men are usually loyal partners, men who disappear during conflicts can become high-maintenance.

The solution? The Disappearing Man must be treated sensitively and gently during conflict. We recommend that you always allow the Disappearing Man to leave the scene without harassing him or trying to prevent him from leaving. Later, after you have both calmed down, discuss what happened calmly and ask him why he felt upset. You might want to create a formal agreement with the Disappearing Man that if he leaves, you will talk to him, at least on the phone, within twelve hours to discuss what happened. If you can find ways to handle fighting with the Disappearing Man, he can become a wonderful and loyal love partner.

THE CRY BABY

We admit to having a bias against the Cry Baby. These men are overly emotional when you fight with them, cry, and become overly dramatic. The Cry Baby is manipulative with his tears. He typically uses crying to deflect your anger. Suddenly, instead of dealing with why you are angry and exploring solutions, the Cry Baby will tear up, pull on your heartstrings, and exploit your capacity for sympathy. He does this rather than deal with the consequences of his actions, or have a clean fight with you.

Fighting with a Cry Baby can be exhausting because you will want to comfort him. When fighting with a crier, your needs become less significant than his. He demands attention because he is crying (sniff). How can you be so angry? Can't you see how upset he is? (Sniff sniff.) The moment you comfort the Cry Baby and stop being with your own feelings of upset, the Cry Baby wins the fight and is no longer accountable for his actions.

The solution is to deal with the Cry Baby by holding him to account for his actions, while trying your best to avoid falling for his emotional ploys. If you can't contain your maternal instincts with the Cry Baby, it is crucial that you always go back within twelve hours after the drama has passed and discuss, resolve, and complete the fight. You must also continue to clarify what exactly *you* want from the Cry Baby, and never sell out your own needs just because he is crying.

THE APOLOGIZER

Some men will try to avoid fighting by being so overly apologetic that you do not want to fight with them anymore. The Apologizer is all too willing to take responsibility for any conflict you might have. These men use apologizing as a technique to get you to leave them alone. They will flagellate themselves for behaving so badly and treating you so disrespectfully. At the same time, their apologies will not be comforting; they will seem manipulative and insincere.

You must use specific requests and pinpoint specific problems you have when you are dealing with an Apologizer. Since he will try to shrug off all responsibility for conflicts by trying to get you to shut up by apologizing, then returning to his same old ways, you must make sure he also makes specific promises about changing his behavior and listening to the reasons why you are upset. If the Apologizer is interested in having a long-term relationship with you, you must force him to talk out problems and learn to communicate more effectively during conflicts. If an Apologizer cannot work out problems with you, get rid of him.

∞ The Three Classic Types of Men to Avoid

Let's face it, some men should be avoided. Your life will work better, you will be happier, and you can save time by avoiding the true jerks out there. The three, classics you should avoid are The SNAG (Sensitive New Age Guy), the Jerk, and the Pervert. You must know and understand these types of men so that you can easily spot them, and avoid having them mess up your life.

Craziness and difficulty in men exist on a continuum. It is not always easy to tell when a man is so crazy and difficult that you should avoid him. Here are the general warning signs that you are in the presence of a psycho guy:

He Tells You Intimate Details Right Away

Some men will try to bond with you by sharing inappropriately intimate details about their lives right away. They might confess to bizarre sexual fantasies, addictions, problems, strange experiences, or anything else which seems out of context so early in a relationship. When a man is too open, and reveals too much about himself prematurely, it is a sign that he has weak boundaries. As a result, he likely has a difficult time dealing with intimacy with you, and will tend to be *too* honest. A man who attempts to be an open book will also tend to tell you every thought, feeling, idea, memory, or anything else that comes into his little head. He can be trouble, and a very high-maintenance man to be around. Be on the lookout when a man begins sharing intimate details in the early stages of a relationship, and keep an eye on him for potential trouble.

He Has Been in Many Abusive Relationships

Some men have been in many abusive relationships. They are either masochistic, and love it when women hurt them and take advantage of them, or they are sadistic and love to hurt women. When a man is used to abuse, either sadistic or masochistic, there is never room to simply get along and love each other without the threats and underlying abuse in the background. When a man is a victim (masochistic) he will eventually make you into a perpetrator, and find ways for you to hurt him. When a man is a sadistic abuser, he will eventually find ways that you have crossed him and will punish you. Either way, the man who loves abuse should be avoided. Dating him will only lead to unnecessary pain and trouble.

He Is Obsessive/Compulsive

Obsessive and compulsive men are often artists and creative types who become fixated on a woman or an object and dedicate their life, or their attention, to it. Obsessive and compulsive men will often say, "I'm a really obsessive person," or, "I've never let go of anything that didn't have claw marks from me holding on." It may seem strange that someone would show you such a disturbing part of his psyche right away. It is a warning sign to stay away, unless you want him obsessed with *you*. While some of these men will have a propensity for developing an unhealthy obsession with you, others with the tendency for compulsive and obsessive behavior will make perfectly good boyfriends. They will be quirky and bizarre, but not dangerous.

A 'Red Flag' Goes Off Inside of You

This is the most important guideline of all. Women often ignore their own intuition when it looks like they might have an opportunity to be with a man. They pursue relationships even when it is with creepy men who they *know* will cause them unending problems. Do not let yourself be fooled by the high of a few ecstatic dates, or by a romantic man. If a "red flag" goes off inside of you, and you have a bad feeling about a man, be a powerful, confident woman and *stay away from him*. If you are smart enough to apply the technology in this book consistently, you will get the relationship you have always wanted. You do not need to humiliate yourself, or put yourself in danger by being with psychos. We say it again: if you have a bad feeling about a man, *stay away from him*. Listen to yourself, and trust your instincts.

The three types of men to avoid have these characteristics in abundance. Let's look at them more closely, one at a time:

1. The SNAG

The Sensitive New-Age Guy, or SNAG, tries to seduce women by being nice, helpful, artistic, and sensitive to women's issues. He wears crystals and lets his hair grow long. He may pretend to be a peaceful musician and play the drums, or enjoy practicing guitar in the woods. The SNAG pretends, even to himself, that he is not a rutting sex-crazed beast, like other men. He is all full of light and goodness and has no vitality or male presence. When he does something mean to a woman, *and he does*, he does it totally without awareness. Furthermore, he never takes responsibility for all the people he offends and hurts.

The SNAG is like the emotional Cry Baby, except worse. The SNAG is particularly dangerous because he will take your side, and criticize *all* men as a group, as though he were different or better. The SNAG may also take the form of the new age spiritual jerk, who looks down at you for not being "above" your anger with him. The SNAG acts as if prayer and meditation are the cure for all issues and arguments. He might even avoid conflict under the guise that it isn't "spiritual." He might also use quotations from holy books as ways to manipulate you. The SNAG hides behind his smile and meditative appearance, and is often angry and very judgmental.

SNAGs all share a similar sense of smug superiority to other men. They tend to be so full of themselves that they judge others for not being as evolved as they are. When you fight with a SNAG, you must be concrete and specific in order to resolve conflicts. If he can come back to earth long enough to have a conversation about the here and now, create agreements with him to handle the issues that caused the conflicts.

2. The Jerk

The Jerk is a complex problem. He is identifiable because he is undependable and inconsistent. One day, he will take you on a ride on his Harley in the country and make love to you in the woods. Then you will not hear from him for three weeks. One day he will lavishly shower you with gifts, the next moment he will be angry about some off-the-wall thing you did last week. While the Jerk has the capacity to love you and be wonderful, you never know what will cause him to become upset, and you never know how he will act or react. You cannot make plans around the Jerk, because he could break them with a moment's notice. If you are naive, you will think you have the power to be the one who can tame the Jerk, but you can't. The Jerk has the power to break your heart. While he can be a hot lover, and a good time, the hassle and inconsistency will not give you the relationship you desire in the long run.

3. The Pervert

All men are preoccupied with sex. That is normal. The Pervert is much worse. He seems to be holding dark secrets from the world and often seems suspicious and sneaky. The pervert usually seems to be lying, even about the most mundane topics. In the bedroom, the pervert may hint at wanting to experiment with various kinky sex fantasies, but will be unwilling to be specific. The Pervert might also seem overly embarrassed when you discuss sex with him, even when you discuss your own sexual fantasies. It is likely that the Pervert has many sexual fantasies which he hasn't told anyone ever before and he hides them from the world. What makes things worse for the Pervert is that he probably judges himself very harshly, lives in guilt about his desires, fears you will judge him, and worries that he will eventually be "found out."

The Pervert might also seem obsessed with your body and obsessed with talking and discussing sex with you. He might constantly try to touch and kiss you. The Pervert might seem overly pushy when it comes to sex. When you are out with the Pervert you might have the sense that he does not care about you and is only using you for sex. When you feel scared being sexual with a man, you may be with a pervert. When a man seems to be lying to you and seems to be hiding the truth from you, he's probably a pervert and it is best to confront him directly about his behavior. If he does not give you an answer you feel good about, get rid of him. It will probably not be worth dealing with a Pervert because he will be very high-maintenance.

These are the men you should avoid because they are too much trouble. It is good to start noticing such men and to practice keeping away from them. By avoiding the most psycho cases, you will save yourself much suffering.

∞ The Eighteen Problem Men and How to Handle Them

Are you ready for more problems and trouble? We figured that you would probably appreciate a virtual feast of trouble all in one place, so let's continue to explore the world of troubled men. Some men will do anything to kill their chances of having a successful relationship. Here are more problem men that you are likely to encounter in the dating world, along with how to handle their bad behaviors. Here's the list of problem men:

The Special Boy

Like the Sensitive New Age Guy, the Special Boy prides himself on not being like other men. He often has one or two "special" relationships, usually platonically with women. He often dresses in an unusual way, or wears very "special" items of clothing. Most women avoid him because he sends out a message that he is immature. They say that there is something weird about him. Those women who do not avoid him may like him, but only as a friend. If you are dating a Special Boy, you will be happier if you get him to concentrate on being more like other men than on being different from them. You will be happier if you help him to stay grounded and in the present moment, rather than letting him float in the sky, dreaming about his plans which will never come to fruition anyway.

The Feminist Man

This well-meaning man has taken on the women's freedom struggle as his own, but there is a subtext to his behavior that is disturbing to most women. He is easily able to talk about how men are the problem in the world, and how "all men" hurt women in various ways. It is as if he doesn't think of himself as a man. He may even say that he doesn't, preferring the term "person." The Feminist Man is deeply ashamed of his maleness, his sexual fantasies, and his masculinity. On top of all this, he is slimy, and secretly thinks he can get sex by apologizing for being male. The Feminist Man may seem to be on your side, but he will eventually betray you.

The Woman's Friend

As we have said before, you must limit your number of male friendships, because they get you in the habit of being friends with men rather than lovers.

Some men are in such denial of their male identity that they surround themselves with women. They think that having several female friends is the equivalent to having several female lovers. This ploy rarely works. A man who has mostly female friends is desperately denying his masculinity and could turn out to be a difficult boyfriend. He will probably turn out to be a submissive jerk who will end up betraying you.

The Beaten Down Man

Some guys have been beaten down by life and seem to have no vitality left. The Beaten Down Man has given up on life. He has no energy, no vitality, and barely makes it through each day. He seems slumped, stressed, and depressed. Life is too hard for him. The Beaten Down Man is not attractive to women because he is not generative and vital. He is overly serious, angry, sarcastic, and resentful.

The Beaten Down Man will likely suck the energy right out of you. He is pessimistic and loves to depress anyone who will listen to his horrible stories about his horrible life. If you start dating a Beaten Down Man he will likely depress you and bring you down.

The Beer-Drinking Jerk

The Beer Drinking Jerk's behaviors exist on a continuum. This continuum is related to age and physical attractiveness. If he is an attractive 22-year-old weight lifter, you might think his being a drunken jerk is cute. If he is in his forties with a huge beer gut, and all he wants to do is watch TV, eat hot dogs, and drink more beer, than you have trouble on your hands. Sure he will be monogamous. But so what? A man in his 40s who is a Beer Drinking Jerk is not going anywhere in life. What you see on that couch is what you will get from this type of guy. He will end up boring you to tears, and be unwilling to change. Unless you are a Beer Drinking Jerk-ette, avoid this type of guy or you will be sadly disappointed.

The Know-It-All

Everyone hates know-it-alls. Women hate it when men lecture them or talk down to them, both things the classic Know-It-All loves to do. This guy will have an answer for everything. He often works with computers, or in another technical field. He believes that the more knowledge he can share, the better a person he is. The Know-It-All believes that the more technical language he uses in a conversation, the more people will respect him. He often uses his knowledge to one-up himself over some-one else. This helps him feel good about himself. When he shows off his knowledge as a source of self-esteem to you, he is actually showing off his insecurity.

One of the biggest problems in dating a Know-It-All is that he will talk and talk and talk some more, all about topics you could care less about. The only way to survive a relationship with a Know-It-All is to get him to shut up. If he can understand that you love him for who he is, not for what he knows, he may be able to calm down and relate without hiding behind his arsenal of knowledge. If a man is willing to shut up when he is with you, keep him. Otherwise run away as quickly as you can.

The Control Freak

The Control Freak must control every little detail of every interaction. It is difficult for him to go at anyone else's speed, or follow your lead without criticizing or making smart-aleck comments. The Control Freak requires you to meet him on his own turf, and will become difficult when you want him to do anything he does not want to do. The Control Freak will refuse to compromise with you, because he must control every situation.

The Control Freak will also try to control you. He may call you every twenty minutes to make sure you are not with another man, or he may want you to work with him so he can keep an eye on you all day long. He might try to tell you how to dress, what to eat, and even what to read.

If you are an insecure woman with self-esteem issues, you might find the control freak an attractive option. But in the end, even a woman with terrible self-esteem will rebel. Even if you decide to put up with him, the Control Freak will not sustain your relationship because he's a nut-case. Our advice is to stay away from this one and move on quickly to a man who will appreciate you.

The Androgynous Boy

Some men favor the feminized, non-masculine look. Even though the Androgynous Boy is hated by other men, he puts out an air of smugness and superiority. He might have dreadlocks, wear a dress, have both of his ears pierced, or dress like a woman in other subtle ways. However he dresses, the Androgynous Boy must prove to the world that he is different and special.

While the Androgynous Boy is cute in a boyish sort of way, and some women will be attracted to him, most people will be repelled. Sadly, this type of man is hard to take seriously. The Androgynous Boy tends to be irresponsible, undependable, and flaky. If your ideal man looks like a woman and hasn't yet gone through puberty, then go out and get an Androgynous Boy. Otherwise, don't fall for the Androgynous Boy.

The Comedian

The Comedian performs for women. He believes that if he is funny enough and entertaining enough, women will sleep with him and ultimately love him. While most people value humor in a friend and a love partner, humor alone is not enough to sustain a relationship. Comedians show a high level of insecurity through their constant need to make people laugh and their need to be the center of attention. It is as if they are always asking for some sort of validation from others that they should be getting from themselves. If you date a Comedian, you will end up relating to him as an entertainment machine, and expect him to perform for you. You won't relate to him as a man with whom you can have an honest, intimate, and passionate relationship.

The Geek Boy

Get out the pocket protector and the industrial glasses, it's time for the Geek Boy. The Geek Boy's main problem is that he is more comfortable with machines than he is with people, especially women. The Geek is sometimes ridiculously uncomfortable with women. He retreats into the world of computers or machines, where he feels he understands what is going on. While he is loyal and caring, he probably still needs to learn how to provide romantic feelings and experiences for you. Furthermore, he is unlikely to have any clue about providing for you in any way. Geeks are usually horrid conversationalists and have denied their sex drive for so long, that they take a long time to warm up. If you have a Geek Boy on your hands, prepare for a lot of work to reform him.

The Therapist

The Therapist thinks that if he can only solve a woman's problems, she will want to make love to him. The Therapist acts as if he is Mr. Compassionate, but all the while he is plotting to seduce you. He will listen to your most intimate issues and offer good advice—sometimes. He seems extra nice, but also a bit weird. You probably wonder why he is spending so much time with you helping you through your personal crises. The Therapist is usually a good guy who is lonely, but also wants to sleep with you. The Therapist thinks you will bed him if he gives you good enough advice.

Dating therapist types is usually a big pain in the rear end. They will analyze you, and have opinions about your behavior. They might interpret your dreams, and attempt to offer psychological interpretations for your behaviors and your decisions. The downfall of all therapist types is that they will give you unsolicited advice on your life, and their feedback will eventually become a drag to be around no matter how "useful" it seems. No one wants to have a patient/client relationship with her boyfriend. If you need therapy, see a therapist. If you want a man, date one and avoid the psycho-babble interactions.

The Twelve-Stepper

The Twelve-Step program is a wonderful fellowship that has saved many lives, and we are not here to put it down. But it is worth mentioning that men deeply involved in the "program" can create predictable problems when they are with women. If you tend to date men in the program, it is a good idea to know what to watch out for.

The Twelve-Stepper tends to take life a little too seriously. He screws up interacting with you by needing to talk too much about his emotional pain, and by his need to appear "vulnerable" by sharing his childhood traumas. He might also turn you off with his need to think of everything in terms of addiction. If you want a drink, he might ask if there is a history of alcoholism in your family. If you light a cigarette, he might try to lecture you on the addictive perils of nicotine. Pleasure, it seems, is inherently suspect to him, and you might get really tired of his comments quickly.

The Slave

The Slave thinks that any positive attention from a woman is a sign that he is on his way to having sex with her. To this end he does everything for a woman that she could possibly want. If she is hungry, he makes her dinner. If she needs his help moving furniture, he makes an elaborate show of canceling his plans so he can be at her beck and call. He figures that her occasional compliments about how "sweet" he is, along with the obvious sacrifices he makes for her, will eventually and inevitably add up to sex for him. The Slave keeps being her servant as he awaits that day.

The truth is that women hate Slave men, even as they use them mercilessly as handymen, cash machines, and secretaries. The day of sexual reward will always remain in the future, and the Slave will never get what he wants. It is like the *Dilbert* cartoon where Dilbert has a date with a woman to "grout the tile in her bathroom." That is not a date, it is being an idiot. When you date a Slave, he will eventually become boring. If you are looking for a soul mate you will never find mutual respect by dating a slave. If you are looking to exploit a man, date a Slave.

The Whiner

The Whiner is like the Beaten Down By Life guy, only worse off. Rather than suffer in silence about what the world has done to him, the Whiner makes sure everybody knows about it. He sends a loud and clear message to women that says, "I am immature and you want to stay away from me." If you are wise, you will get the message, and want nothing to do with him.

The Whiner might have had an especially rough life, and it may even be true that he has much to complain about. However, the Whiner has no ability to function maturely in the world, and has no ability to be responsible for his problems. In fact, whiners love their problems. They hide safely behind the protective shield of whining. The trouble will start when you begin to feel sorry for the Whiner. You might try to rescue the Whiner from his problems. However, the Whiner will eventually abuse your eardrums with his horrible stories about his hard and horrid life. This will get to be too irritating, fast.

Like the Slave, the Whiner thinks that if he gets a positive, compassionate response from a woman, then he *must* be on the road to sleeping with her. Like the Slave, he mistakes any positive reaction for arousal.

The only difference is that, while the Slave seeks a "you're so sweet, you make me so happy" reaction, the Whiner seeks an "I feel so sorry for you" compassionate reaction. Neither approach should work with you.

Take our advice and don't be fooled by a Whiner!

The Man on the Rebound

Here is the bottom line: The Man on the Rebound is trouble. He wants only two things from you:

1. To have sex with you, and

2. To cry on your shoulder while he uses you to take care of him.

When you date a man who is on the rebound, he will likely be in a depressed state and is probably questioning his ability to get a woman. The Man on the Rebound is looking for sex, and may not have had sex in a long time. He will use you as a "transitory object." In other words, you will be a short-term sex babe while he recovers from his last relationship. He will cry on your shoulder and sleep with you. You will bond with each other. You will fall for him, and then he will want to break up after a few months, or he will sleep with someone behind your back and *then* break up with you. Either way, the Man on the Rebound is trouble.

Let's review the motives of this problem type. He wants only two things:

1. Sex, and

2. To cry on your shoulder while he uses you to take care of him.

Need we say more?

El Cheapo

El Cheapo is not a cartoon character; he is real. El Cheapo is a tightwad in the worst way. He is so obsessed with saving money that he takes the romance out of anything that might cost money. The idea of going to a movie, for instance, upsets El Cheapo. Before he can go—if he can go at all—he must lecture you about how the price of movies has gone up over the past few years. In the process, he kills the fun for you, and the joy of dating.

Under the guise of being fiscally responsible and frugal, El Cheapo will avoid paying for dates, avoid taking you out, and even avoid buying necessary items for himself. El Cheapo will likely dress out of fashion, wear ripped-up clothes, wear glasses that are twenty-two years old, and only own threadbare furniture because the new stuff "costs too much." At the same time, El Cheapo will likely have a fairly high-paying job and be saving all of his money for the next world economic crisis, or for some emergency that will never occur.

If you want to be taken out and lavishly showered with gifts, too bad. El Cheapo will require you to pay your half, always. If you are a completely non-materialistic woman, this type of guy might really appeal to you, but if you want material goods and occasional spectacular charms, get rid of El Cheapo today.

The Hater

We have worked with many men who hate the world. In fact, their mantra seems to be, "I hate unconditionally." The Hater is the classic angry man multiplied by one hundred. He has strong opinions about everything, and at any moment he is usually hating someone or something. Discussing politics? He hates all politicians. Wanna go out for ice cream? He hates ice cream. He hates sports, a particular musical band, his ex, or even a color. The hater will inevitably hate you, and your ideas about how a relationship should go. The hater is unlikely to be physically violent, but will probably be emotionally violent and abusive. When you fight with the Hater, he will likely tell you that he hates it when you tell him about a certain feeling or idea. He will also hate some aspect of your argument. The Hater is a high-drama, intense man. If you are a sensitive woman, or feel uncomfortable around anger, stay away from the Hater.

The Redneck

Many of our students end up dating men who seem perfectly normal on the outside, but end up being redneck morons. The Redneck comes in many forms. He can be a racist jerk, believe in the KKK, be a militia member, or part of the white power movement. The Redneck might also be a bar fighter who picks on gay men, Jews, or kids who have tattoos, piercings, and purple hair. The Redneck hates groups of people and takes pride in acting tough and intimidating toward any minority he doesn't like.

Some women put up with the Redneck and his racist tendencies. These women believe that they can tame the Redneck, but the Redneck will never reform his ways. While he might be committed to you, and even marriage-minded, he will continue to be abusive, and even violent, toward any group he hates.

We cannot recommend strongly enough that you get away from this sort of garbage quickly. He *isn't* going to change.

The Twenty-five Problem Women

While it sure is fun to look at all the ways men can be jerks, we have to look at how you can be a problem, too. You will probably be on the following list somewhere, in some form. The point we want you to get is that we *all* have tendencies which are less than flattering to the opposite sex. If we can be aware of our tendencies and work on decreasing the intensity and frequency with which we express them, we can be perfectly fine relationship partners. Here is a list of problem women. How many of them describe you?

- *The Rich Bitch*
- *The Alcoholic/Druggie*
- *The Therapist*
- *The Princess*
- *The "I hate you for loving me"*
- *The Bar-fighter/Cat-fighter*
- *The Depressive*
- *The Angry Feminist*
- *The Arguer*
- *The Complainer*
- *The Religious Moralist*
- *The Drama Queen*
- *The Nag*
- *The Wounded Bird*
- *The Stalker*
- *The Anorexic*
- *The Hypochondriac*
- *The Enabler/Rescuer*
- *The Weird Performance Artist*
- *The Control Freak*
- *The Know-It-All*
- *The Look-Gooder*
- *The Earth Mother*
- *The Conflict Instigator*

Breaking up Is Easy to Do

Should you find yourself in a relationship with one of the problem men we have described, you will probably have to break up with him. Breaking up is one of the worst parts of dating, but is sometimes necessary. Here's the basic information you need to know in order to prepare for and execute a successful breakup conversation.

Why Break Up?

Bad relationships are like broken-down cars. They get worse and worse, and constantly need more repair. At a certain point it makes more sense to junk the vehicle and get a new one. The other option is for you to maintain the car over the long haul, regularly doing the required maintenance to keep it in good condition. Even then it may be a lemon. If you are willing to do the work necessary to keep the car running, and it's not a lemon to start with, you can keep your car going indefinitely. If you aren't, then it's time to call it quits.

Diagnosing Where You Are in the Commitment Game

The longer you date a man, the harder and more painful it will be to break up. The more you get to know one another, the higher the investment, and the greater the loss when the relationship ends. We have developed a method to diagnose your level of existing commitment. These six types of commitment will help you identify your degree of commitment and the predicted level of difficulty you will have in breaking up.

THE SIX TYPES OF COMMITMENT

1. The One-Night Stand. Eventually everyone has a one-night stand. There is no investment in a relationship on either side. The experience is purely sexual for both of you. After the experience you might feel a range of emotions, from guilt to the desire to see him again. The man, on the other hand, most likely had a good time and would be perfectly happy *not* seeing you again. The best way to "end it" is to simply never talk to him again.

When you have a one-night stand, you give up the expectation that you will see him again. While the relationship *might* become more, he most likely will not want you to see you again. If he does, it will only be for sexual reasons. Either way, do not expect one-night stands to be anything more than pure sex. In the morning go home and avoid thinking about him again.

2. The Acquaintance. By acquaintance, we are referring to a man you have dated a few times. While a one-night stand is primarily sexual, an acquaintance is someone you have invested time in getting to know. While you might like him, and even have found things you share in common, not enough time has elapsed for you to become attached to one another. If you find yourself realizing that the relationship has no potential, break up with him quickly. Do not prolong the breakup conversation. That will only make life worse for both of you. Tell him that the relationship has no long-term potential, and that you are ready to move on.

3. You Have Dated for a Few Weeks. If you have been on four or five dates with a man, he definitely likes you. Otherwise, he probably would not have invested the time and money to take you out. After a few dates, your level of attraction is probably somewhere between finding each other sweet and interesting, and wanting to rip each other's clothes off and jump into bed. After four or five dates the "relationship" is definitely evolving into something intimate and more intense. However, if you have tested the man over the past month and are clear that he does not have long-term potential, it is best to break up.

After a month of dating, we recommend you break up in person. By this time he has started having secret fantasies of having you as his girlfriend, even if he would never admit to hoping so. If you are having sex, breaking up will be more difficult. Some relationship experts believe that men become attached to women more quickly than women become attached to men. If you have had sex a few times, the man is definitely getting used to being around you and is already considering dating you for the long-term.

Breaking up after a few weeks will probably be difficult for both of you. The first few weeks and months of a relationship often feel magical.

Breaking up while the ecstatic feeling is present is more difficult. However, if the man is not what you are looking for, breaking up is inevitable. There is no way to be diplomatic about breaking up, so we recommend you be honest with him about why you do not think the relationship has future potential. Be diplomatic. Avoid giving him harsh criticism and feedback. Don't be cruel. Break up, but make the process as gentle as possible.

4. You Have Slept with Him a Few Times and Realized the Relationship Was Becoming Problematic. After you have sex a few times, the nicest guy can sometimes turn into a psycho jerk. Maybe you didn't notice his psycho qualities at first. Maybe you were so swept up with his charm that you ignored the warnings. In any case, it is important to get away from such a man quickly. The longer you are with a problem man, the harder it is to break up and the more trouble he will cause you down the road.

Breaking up with a troubled man can be difficult. He will most likely have a strong emotional reaction. It is important that you watch out for safety issues when breaking up. Psychos can react violently or cause huge scenes. It is best to simply say that you are not ready to be in a relationship, or that you realize you cannot give him what he wants in a relationship and from a woman. You certainly cannot tell him that he is a psycho jerk from hell, or anything else that nasty. If you are afraid he will become violent, break up in a public place where there are other people around.

5. He Is an Occasional Sex Partner. Some women love to have a man they can be friends with, have sex with, but not have a committed relationship with. We have had many students, male and female, who have had these kinds of sex partners. Sometimes their sexual interactions went on for years. Sometimes they turned into long-term relationships.

If you are breaking up with a sex partner, first examine why you are dismantling the relationship. Do you feel that he is preventing you from meeting your ideal long-term mate? If so, get rid of him. Is it impossible that you could have a long-term relationship with him? If so, what has prevented you from doing so?

One reason to break up is if, after informally dating for a while, he wants "more" and you don't. At first, being occasional sex partners was working well, but after a while, he began to fall for you and wanted to create a serious relationship. Meanwhile, you wanted it to remain informal.

The other reason to call it quits is if you meet another man and begin a committed relationship. In this case, the occasional sex partner will have to go. A simple phone call or in-person conversation will likely do. Just be honest, and the break up will probably be easy. He will likely understand, and may perhaps even congratulate you.

6. Dated for Over Three Months. For all practical purposes, after three months you *are* in a relationship, and you *are* his girlfriend. Even if you do not think so, he most certainly does. A break up at this stage must be well planned. He will be hurt, and there won't be anything you can do about it, short of selling yourself out and staying in the relationship. You both may have big emotional reactions and need to grieve together, or apart. You must get support from girlfriends during this process, because you may be seduced into staying with him by your guilt or grief. After three months, you are more attached to one another than you realize.

The Six Warning Signs that It Is Time to End It

We all have blind spots. Before working with us, one of Sandy's blind spots was understanding how her behavior could attract or repel men. Men and women have many blind spots in relationships. It is common for women to ignore warning signs that their relationship is failing. These warning signs are examples of blind spots. Since they are blind spots, women do not register them as significant, and even downplay the possibility of the dangers and hazards involved.

What follows are some of the warning signs that your relationship is in jeopardy. If you are currently experiencing one or more of these signs in your relationship, you should seriously consider ending it. Many of our students had horrible consequences when they stayed in a dangerous and abusive relationship. If one or more of the warning signs applies to you and your relationship, breakup quickly and avoid the inevitable headaches and heartaches.

YOU DON'T LIKE YOURSELF WHEN YOU ARE WITH HIM

Some men probably bring out the worst in you. They bring out your worst temper, worst qualities, worst thoughts, worst feelings, worst everything. Some women do not take responsibility for their anger. Instead, they blame the man, claiming he is doing something to elicit their bad feelings. Even though you may dislike him, and even though he may bring out your worst qualities, *he* probably is not doing anything. You simply react to him and do not like yourself when you are with him. Take responsibility for *your* part of the situation.

Hara, for instance, was dating a political activist named Jim. Half of the time they got along well. Even when they were getting along she always felt as if she had to hold back her thoughts and opinions from him. Hara constantly felt afraid that if she was honest, they would get into a heated argument. Jim could share his opinions with her, however—and he did this *all* the time. Since she was constantly *dishonest* with Jim, she eventually began feeling meek and timid around him. Hara hated herself for acting that way, and the relationship continued to get worse.

As you can guess, the relationship quickly failed. If Hara had paid attention to her fear and how uncomfortable she felt around him, and remembered that there are plenty of other men to date, she would have saved herself a lot of hassle and broken up much quicker.

If you do not like how you act around a particular man, either change your behavioral patterns, or get out of the relationship. The cost is simply too high to stay in a messed-up situation. Remember, if you feel bad around him, it is *your* responsibility to get out, not his.

He Doesn't Like You

It may sound funny, but many women report dating or marrying men who dislike them. Men have reported the same thing: being in relationships with women who seem to dislike them. In these situations, the couple stays together because there are qualities about each other that they like and enjoy, but on the whole, one party dislikes the other. The disdain for the other comes across in the form of constant criticizing, complaining, and general nastiness.

Some women stay in bad relationships like these, usually sidestepping the pain it causes them, or the constant blows to their self-esteem. There is no reason to continue dating someone who does not treat you with respect.

One of the fundamental values we teach in this book is that your self-esteem and confidence as a woman are essential to success in any area of your life. If a man, a job, or anything else hurts you, cease the activity or relationship immediately. If you are not empowered by the relationship, get out.

He Has Constant Emotional Problems

Bill was usually lovable. He was sweet, sincere, charming, and had a great job. At the same time, he was highly emotional and had constant emotional outbursts. It was nearly impossible to predict what would set him off. When he was angry, he would swear and throw things at anyone within firing range. When he was sad, he would hyperventilate and sob. His full range of emotional outbursts scared Darlene. She really liked him, but felt that his emotional problems prevented her from getting to know him, and ever feeling comfortable.

Bill is a member of a group of men who are lovable, yet are so out-of-control emotionally that they are hard to date. Even though Darlene liked Bill, we still advised her to break up with him. He was too wild and too unpredictable to be in a relationship with. While it may sound harsh, the best way to protect yourself, if you are dating an overly-emotional man, is to break up. Be gentle in the breakup process, and do everything you can to stay friends.

HE IS TOO DEMANDING

Some men act as if you have no other purpose in life than to serve them. Maybe they frequently call you at work, and ask you to spend inordinate amounts of time talking when you should be working. Maybe they stop by your home at all hours of the night, and bang on the door, wanting to have sex. Or, maybe they call and want you to pick up a long list of grocery items, including beer and pizza.

Some women have an easy time setting limits with demanding men. When a man tries to interfere with their work schedule, comes over at odd hours of the night, and makes other demands, they simply tell him "no." End of story. The majority of women, however, mess up their schedules and their lives to cater to a man.

The problems start when your schedule starts getting thrown off because you are spending time doing things for him that should be spent on your own life. The first solution is to start religiously using the magic word "no" in all your conversations with him. It may take a while to get your life back in order, but if you are strong-willed and are not afraid of saying "no," it is imaginable that you could keep things going. If this does not work, or if he becomes even *more* demanding in the face of your refusals, then it is time to split up. If a man is demanding in the early phases of a relationship, he is likely to get worse over time.

YOU DON'T RESPECT HIM

Why are you with a man you do not respect? Is it that he is cute, rich, a stepping stone for your career, or what? You are in for real trouble if you date men you do not respect. There is nothing that will harm your self-esteem more. When you date a man you do not respect it will eventually weigh on you and chip away at your confidence. What does it say about you, that you have to date a man you do not respect? This question will probably come back to haunt you. If you do not respect a man you are dating, it is not worth pursing the relationship because the costs will be high to your self-esteem, sense of personal integrity, and your confidence with men.

He Wants to Come Between You and Your Girlfriends or Family

As we have said many times, close female friends and family are very important. The lone rangers in life, who only spend time alone or with their man, will eventually bottom out. The nurturing, teasing, and ability-to-be-straight-with-one-another type of camaraderie and support women give each other is unique and necessary for your mental health. A woman who succeeds with men has other women and family members she can talk to, get support from, and confide in.

When a man tries to come between you and your friends, he is trying to control your life. He is trying to cut off your contact with others in a similar situation. He is cutting off your mainline to feminine energy and your independence. Why is he doing this? What threat do your friends and family pose to the relationship? A man who loves and supports you would *never* try to come between you and your friends and family; he would support your outside relationships.

The bottom line is that no man is worth cutting off your friends for. The men may come and go, but close female friendships can last forever.

The Five Components of a Successful Breakup Conversation

If you decide that you must break up, here is a model for the breakup conversation that will help you break things off in a clean, clear, and benevolent manner, *and* will leave both of you able to move on faster.

1. The breakup conversation must include a time for you tell him everything that did not work about the relationship.
2. The breakup conversation must include everything that did work in the relationship.

3. The breakup conversation must include time for him to tell you what worked and did not work about the relationship.

4. The breakup conversation must allow time for you to acknowledge the ways in which he contributed to you while you were together. You must give him ways to win during the breakup conversation.

5. If possible, forgive him for anything he did to you, or for anything you have been angry about.

If you include these five components in your breakup conversation, both of you will have an opportunity to share with the other about what worked about the relationship and what didn't work. When both of you have an opportunity to share with the other your feelings and experiences, it will be easier to break up and move on.

How to Handle the Top Problems Men Cause

You can no longer use any excuses for getting into relationships with extremely difficult, demanding, and unstable men. We have shown you the different types of men to avoid, and the types to go for. If you apply yourself to mastering the techniques in this book, you will eventually have a wonderful man with whom you want to have a long-term relationship.

But just as you think the relationship is going smoothly . . . watch out! Trouble rears its ugly head even in the most "together" men. To help you handle those inevitable breakdowns on the road to relationship fulfillment, we are providing this emergency tool kit of ways to handle the common problems men cause.

Q: What Should I Do When He Is Moody?

A: Many men think that they have a right to be moody, and a right to be as difficult as they want to be when they feel in a mood. As one man told us, "I don't care if I am difficult to women!"

When a man is moody, you must ask yourself what is most important to you, and remember to not take his behavior personally. The most critical thing to know when dealing with a moody man is how to avoid rewarding him for being in a bad mood. If a man is in a bad mood, and you tip-toe around him, kowtow to his every demand, and are extra-nice to him, all you are doing is training him that being in a bad mood is a great way to get you to treat him better. Guess what? Next time, he will get into a mood quicker, and stay there longer, because of your training.

The four keys for handling a man's bad mood are:

1. Acknowledge it;

2. Show some compassion for his problems;

3. Stay up-beat and happy;

4. Get away from him as soon as you can. Let him work through his mood, and get together with you later when he is feeling better.

Here are some things you can say to take you through each of these steps:

1. Acknowledge the mood. "Had a bad day, eh?" "Not feeling so good today, eh?" "Having a rough time, eh?"

2. Show some compassion for his mood. The key here is: *never* try to solve his problem. Just listen to him, and show some compassion. You might say: "Sounds rough. I know how bad a bad mood can be." "Wow, I'm sorry you are having a hard time."

3. Stay up-beat. This is critical. You must go on with your life, little-affected by his bad mood. Otherwise, you are simply indulging his moods, and rewarding him for being down. Make it clear to him that his mood is not going to change yours.

4. Get away from him as soon as you can. If he is really down, he will either want to sort it out with your help, sort it out alone, or take it out on you. If he wants your help, do not offer solutions: Just ask him clarifying questions so he can get clear on what he is upset about. Hopefully, he is not upset because of *you*. If he wants to sort it out alone, or take it out on you, get away from him. You'll be happier later that you got away.

Q: *What Should I Do When He Criticizes Me?*

A: There are different degrees of criticism, from big to small. You have to balance your experience of being criticized against how much you like him, and how mean he is when he criticizes you. If the criticism is small and you really like him, you may want to listen to what he has to say, and then let it go. The best way to let criticism go is to not defend yourself. Simply say something like, "Oh, that's interesting that you feel that way," or, "I didn't know you felt that way." *Never* justify yourself when he is criticizing you, or explain yourself. That will get you into a conversation, or even an argument, about it. Remember your desired outcome. You are there to have a relationship, not prove how right you are, and how much you are above his criticism. If you acknowledge it, and let it go, his criticism can go away as fast as it arrived.

It sometimes works best to nip criticism in the bud. He may not even know he is criticizing you, and may need you to call his attention to it. You might calmly, but firmly say, "Hey, you've never spoken to me like that before, and I didn't like it. Please don't talk to me like that again." If he is very critical, this will only start a fight, but you shouldn't be spending much time with very critical men, anyway. As Madonna says, "Respect yourself."

Q: *What Should I Do If He Hits Me?*

A: If you can get out of the situation safely, leave instantly. Say nothing. Ignore everything he says. Be out of his house or apartment within thirty seconds. We mean it. If you feel as though your safety is in jeopardy and the man is unwilling to leave your apartment, or he will not let you leave his apartment, call the police immediately. Domestic abuse is very real and very serious. Do not let things escalate, and do not let him get away with hurting you.

Q: *What Should I Do When I Feel Jealous?*

A: THE FOUR-STEP PROCESS FOR HANDLING JEALOUSY

The first question to ask yourself is, why do you feel jealous? Is it because there is concrete evidence that your boyfriend or fiancé is having sex with someone else? Is he merely flirting? Is he checking out other women in front of you? Or is it an irrational and unfounded fear?

Jealousy can become a harmful wedge between a man and a woman. Jealousy can quickly snowball into a horrible drama that should only exist in your worst nightmares. The best way to handle jealousy is to follow our four-step process:

1. Vent your jealous feelings with a girlfriend. By venting your fears and concerns, you can see the parts that seem real, and the parts that seem unreal. After you have vented your feelings with a friend, you will be in a better state to talk to your man.

2. Ask specific questions. After you have calmed down, have a conversation with your man where you ask him questions about the specific incidents that made you feel jealous. Perhaps you felt jealous when he talked to a waitress at dinner last week, and it seemed like he was flirting with her. Or, maybe you felt jealous when he was checking out women in bikinis on the beach when you were sunbathing a few days go. You might have felt jealous when he hugged his friend Amy, and he seemed turned on.

   No matter what the incident was that triggered your jealous feelings, ask him questions about specific incidents. Next, listen to his answers to your questions without interrupting him.

   When you ask him questions about specific incidents rather than make blanket statements or ask broad questions, he can respond and you can handle your jealousy.

3. Clarify. After he explains what happened, you then decide what to do next. Perhaps after he answers your questions you are no longer upset. You can drop the whole thing and go have fun with

him. Case closed. If you are still upset with him, however, after he answers your questions, you must then decide if you have any other questions for him to answer. Ask him additional questions, but do not put him on trial and force him to defend himself. Remember to listen intently to what he is saying, and seek to understand his experience and thoughts.

This process will work best if you can step into his shoes and understand his experience. Then you can look for ways to avoid feeling jealous in the future. If this process turns into a fight, you will likely withdraw, sulk, cry, and create more damage, while doing nothing to solve jealousy in the future. When you clarify his behavior and understand his experience, you can move on quickly and set the stage for handling jealousy in the future.

4. Make specific requests. Once you are clear about what specifically happened and why it made you feel upset, you can then find a solution that will protect you from feeling jealous in the future. Perhaps he told you that even though he watches women on the beach, he does it only for fun. He has no desire to be with any other woman than you, and he promises to never cheat on you. After you understand that his behavior poses no threat to your relationship, you can then make specific requests of how you would like him to behave differently in the future. For instance, "I know you love me, and I am committed to our relationship. I would really appreciate it, if you would avoid checking out other women in front of me. It upsets me, I feel jealous, and it causes me to feel distant from you. Would you do that for me (smiling coyly)?"

By being specific in your requests of him, it gives him little to fight with you about. When you make specific requests, it takes the pressure off him to justify his position and his behavior. He can look at your proposal and either accept, decline, or counter offer. Either way, you are creating solutions to your jealousy problems, and empowering both you and him in the process.

Q: I Am Dating A Man Who Refuses to Wear Condoms. What Should I Do?

A: When a man tells you that condoms are not necessary, an alarm should instantly go off in your head. You can be sure that the man is incredibly stupid. If you listen to his moronic suggestions, you are not only risking your future health, but future plans, if you have an unexpected pregnancy.

Birth control and prevention against STDs is *your* responsibility. The days of unprotected sex are gone. So should be your days of depending on a man to provide protection during sex. Here is the bottom line: if you are not in a monogamous relationship, and you have unprotected sex, you have a huge chance of contracting VD. No man likes condoms. They definitely decrease the sensitivity and the sensation during intercourse, but so what? Even though condoms are unpleasant, they are the law of the jungle. If the man you are dating does not want to wear condoms, then do not have sex with him. If a man complains like a baby that condoms are horrible, you probably want to get rid of him. If you are in a long-term committed relationship, only then can you consider having unprotected sex and using other forms of birth control.

Before you start having sex without condoms, both of you *must* be tested for STDs and HIV. If both of you are clean, then you might consider having unprotected sex. Without condoms, you are still risking disease and pregnancy, but the decision is up to you. We recommend you do what you feel comfortable with, not buckle to a man's desires. We also recommend that you have a discussion, not while in bed, about what you will do if you get pregnant.

If you are not in a committed relationship, we recommend you use the adage, "No glove, no love" and avoid having unprotected sex.

∞ *Conclusion*

You are now ready to handle the problems men cause. You can spot the men you should avoid, and understand the common modes of male fighting. You understand the maintenance spectrum and now know how to spot a high-maintenance man, a medium-maintenance man, and a low-maintenance man. You now know to avoid trying to solve a man's problems. You now know never to reason with an upset man, and you know never to take anything personally when fighting with a man. You have looked at the problems you cause in dating, and have seen some of the steps you can take to stop creating problems in the future.

You then explored the three classic men to avoid, the eighteen problem men, and you even saw the ways in which *you* cause trouble for the men you date.

One of the most difficult problems in dating is handling breaking up. You examined why to break up and how to do so. Next, you learned the six types of commitment and the six different ways to break up. You then learned the six warning signs that it is time to break up, and finally, you learned the five elements of a proper breakup conversation.

We then discussed several different problematic situations and how to handle them. You learned how to handle your jealousy, how to deal with men who hate condoms, how to handle male rudeness, how to handle it when a man criticizes you, and how to handle domestic abuse.

While the information in this chapter may not make your relationship problem-free, it will, if used as directed, help you keep the peace with the man you love, and help you get rid of the ones you can't.

CHAPTER 14

The Commitment Deal: Preparing for the Commitment Conversation

L ET'S LOOK AT OUR TEN-STEP MASTER PLAN ONCE AGAIN. WE'VE COME a long way, and are about to take a very important step in the next two chapters. It's worth making sure we are fully grounded in where we've been, and what we've done so far, before moving on.

In step one, you got clear about what you wanted in a man and in a relationship. You developed a picture of the kind of man and the kind of relationship that you wanted. You learned how to create a structure that would lead you toward having the relationship you wanted, and how to keep records that would keep you on track. In step two, you made yourself worth winning by building a personal style and confidence that sent a message to men that you are worth winning. In step three, you interviewed a lot of applicants. We taught you how successful women think about meeting men, how to set up your life so that there is an abundance of men for you to interact with, and gave you a long list of places where you could meet and interact with eligible men. In step four, we taught you how to test these men. You tested them through your flirting interactions and on your qualifying dates with them. You learned how to handle the boneheaded mistakes that men inevitably make, and how to distinguish between the errors they make that are serious, and the errors they make that you can forgive—and still have hope for a positive long-term relationship. You learned how to test men for safety, patience, generosity, integrity, and a host of other factors. You learned how to test these men against your personal list of important criteria. You either rejected men when they failed to live up to your criteria, or you consciously changed your list of requirements as you learned that certain criteria were less important than you originally thought.

In step five, you learned to give men emotional wins and losses, which you have been practicing in all your flirting and dating interactions. Remember, you give wins and losses to control the speed of the seduction, to let the man know what behaviors you approve of and disapprove of, and to reward him for doing things you like. More importantly, you give him wins so that the man will start to experience the exhilarating process of winning your heart. As he began to win your heart, and as he saw that you were actually winnable, he became more enthusiastic about you, and the relationship progressed.

In step six, you selected a man to start spending more time with. You started having middle dates, began to get comfortable with the man, and probably started a sexual relationship. You had a variety of seductive dates, as well as plenty of time to get to know the man by just hanging out. As your relationship with this man deepened, you both experienced some degree of falling in love. You handled problems as they arose (step seven), and are now starting to ask yourself, "Where is this relationship going? Does it have a future? Does he want to be with me for the long-term? Isn't it time we got more serious?" You may even be finding yourself getting a little angry that he hasn't discussed these things with you of his own accord by now. You may start thinking that it's time for you to tell him, "We need to talk about our relationship."

Careful, now! We'd hate to have you spoil a good thing by going about a "relationship conversation" in the wrong way. We don't want you to come this far, only to mess it up at this delicate juncture. How you handle your "relationship conversation" will make all the difference in what kind of committed, long-term relationship you end up in—or even if you end up in one at all.

We'll talk about handling long-term relationships later. First, you must get one started. A great many men are looking for a committed, long-term relationship. If you happen to be dating one of those men, and if you've followed the Plan so far, you've become worth winning, helped him win your heart step-by-step, and made him feel like a wonderful provider. You've had good experiences together and handled problems marvelously. Some men, under these circumstances, will bring up commitment and talk about the long-term without your help or prodding. However, if you aren't with one of these men, or the man you are with isn't moving toward commitment fast enough, then it's time you learned about preparing for the commitment conversation.

∞ The Commitment Deal

Most women try to get a man to commit in ways that ultimately don't work. Often the commitment conversation is little more than an ultimatum from the woman to the man: Say you'll commit to me, or I'm leaving you. This approach may get a man to *say* he's committed to you, but it usually doesn't work for the long term. Because the man isn't really invested in the idea of being exclusive with you (he's just afraid that you'll leave), he'll have a tendency to simply tell you what you want to hear. He'll make half-hearted efforts to appear committed to you, and resent you for forcing a commitment down his throat.

This is what happened to Janine. She had been dating Leo for ten months, and found herself getting increasingly irritated that he wasn't bringing up the subject of their long-term potential. "He was just cruising day to day, not thinking about the future at all," she told us. "He was perfectly happy to have sex with me and hang out with me—and he was a good guy, and all—but it got to the point where even seeing him was upsetting. He made it worse by not realizing that anything was wrong, or that it was high time we talked about our relationship. It was driving me nuts!"

Finally she couldn't contain herself any longer, and confronted him. "Look," she told him, just as they were drifting off to sleep one night. "We've got to talk about our relationship." Leo was shocked by the urgency in her voice. It seemed so sudden to him. Of course, his surprise only made Janine more upset. "Where are we going?" she asked him urgently. "Are you willing to commit to me, or not? I can't stand all this uncertainty anymore!" Leo tried to put her off, asking if they couldn't please talk about it tomorrow, and telling her that he'd have to think about this commitment thing and get back to her about it. Janine saw this for the brush-off that it was, and pressed harder. "Why should you have to think about it? Haven't you been thinking while you've been with me all these months?" Predictably, this interaction didn't get Janine the outcome she desired. She told us, "He didn't get back to me about it, so I had to bring it up again and again. He seemed so evasive and nervous when we'd talk about it I began to wonder if he really loved me at all, or if he was just using me for sex. Finally I told him that if he didn't commit to me, I was going to have to leave him. He then told me he was committed, but he seemed so uncertain about it. He wasn't enthusiastic, that's for sure. Also, I feel bad, like I had to force it out of him. I love Leo, and don't want to have to treat him like that. But I didn't know what else to do."

Janine didn't know how to prepare her man for talking about a commitment, nor how to present that conversation in a way that worked. The result was a strained relationship and an unreliable commitment from him. This kind of thing happens to women all the time. We can't let it happen to you.

A *commitment deal* is essential to a commitment conversation. A commitment deal is essentially a list of what you are willing to give up, the sacrifices you are willing to make, if your man will commit to your relationship. If you want to understand the importance of a commitment deal, you have to start by looking at your relationship from your man's point of view.

∞ What Commitment Looks Like to You, and What Commitment Looks Like to Him

What is a relationship commitment? It varies from woman to woman, man to man, and relationship to relationship. Usually a relationship commitment involves monogamy, exclusivity, and a shared belief in the possibility (at least) of a lifetime exclusive romantic involvement with one another. It is a stepping stone in a progression that, if all goes well, leads to marriage, shared financial commitments, having children and creating a family. Then, it's on to growing old together, and sharing every day of the rest of your lives with one another.

Men and women have different relationships with this vision, and you must understand and be compassionate about those differences if you want to be able to present a commitment deal to a man that he will embrace with enthusiasm. First, you must understand this: the romantic picture of lifetime involvement is most women's primary relationship fantasy, not men's. Since you were a little girl, the likelihood is that you have had fantasies about the one man for you, the perfect relationship that would last forever, and that man with whom you would have children, buy a house, and build your future. You may have spent time imagining your wedding, your family, and the home you would build together. You've been on the lookout for the man you hoped you would know, from that first moment, was "the one." When you decide that it's time to have a relationship conversation with a man, it is this fantasy that you are attempting to fulfill. Even the most together woman has this fantasy to some degree—certainly more than most men do.

Men, as you may have gathered, have a different fantasy. He probably

hasn't spent his life dreaming of that one woman with whom he can settle down and have children. He's probably not spent any time at all fantasizing about his wedding day, what kind of house he wants with his
wife, or what he'll name his kids. His fantasies about women have run in
another direction entirely, and those relationship fantasies are fundamentally incompatible with yours. Simply put, while you have been fantasizing about the one permanent relationship for you, his ultimate relationship fantasy has been about having sex with a variety of young,
beautiful women. He's been fantasizing about this since he was thirteen
years old with a ferocious and unwavering consistency. While for you, a
committed relationship means fulfilling your lifelong dream and aspira-
tion, the odds are that for him a committed relationship means never,
ever getting what he has fantasized about and desired for most of his life.
Even though there are many men who desire a committed, long-term
relationship, they still fantasize about their ultimate sex scenario.

You must respect this difference between his ultimate fantasy and
yours. Simply deriding a man's ultimate fantasy or being very, very offended by it will never get a man to whole-heartedly commit himself to
you. One of the most terrible errors that a woman can make when trying
to get a man to commit is to degrade and put down what he has fantasized
about for years and years. Such a woman seems to think that her ultimate
fantasy of a life-long monogamous relationship is perfectly reasonable,
while her man's fantasy of the sex life of his dreams is offensive, childish,
stupid, immature, juvenile, and ridiculous. She takes aim at a very
personal and precious part of the man she claims to love—his ultimate
relationship fantasy—and shames and humiliates him for it. Then she is
surprised when he isn't eager about giving up that fantasy to fulfill hers.

What Men Give Up

The solution to all this is to create a commitment conversation that
is respectful of what the man will be giving up in order to be with

you. Here's a partial list of what men give up in order to commit to a relationship with you, so you can start to see things from his point of view:

OTHER WOMEN

Unless you are one of the seven women in the world who want a non-monogamous, committed relationship, you are expecting the man who commits to you to give up dating other women. No problem, you might say—you've been dating him for months, and you know he hasn't been seeing anyone else anyway.

Not so fast! For most men, giving up the *possibility* of other women is just as bad as giving up the other women for real. Many men believe, in the back of their minds where they would never admit it to anyone else, that one day they will magically become a super-stud and have hot sex with the most beautiful women in the world. At the very least, some part of them nourishes this hope. If a man hopes for this, and then commits to being monogamous with you, what'll he do when the centerfolds and exotic dancers come knocking at his door? Once again, this may seem patently ridiculous to you, but to him it is very real, even though he will never admit it. When a man gives up the possibility of other women in order to be with you, he is making a very real sacrifice, *at least in his own mind*. If you want a commitment from your man that will last, you would do well to respect this sacrifice.

BEING COMPLETELY IN CHARGE OF HIS OWN FINANCES

While a man might not be co-mingling his finances with you immediately after you first become committed to each other, he can see where all this is heading, and on some level it frightens him. He likes to be able to spend his money any way he likes: on himself. Once again, you'll get farther with him if you respect the sacrifice he is considering by committing to you than you will by deriding it or accusing him of being afraid of commitment.

NOT HAVING TO THINK ABOUT HAVING KIDS

When a man starts down the commitment road with you, all sorts of frightening possibilities come up for him. One of them is the possibility of having kids. Even a guy who wants to have kids usually wants to have them "someday." Getting closer to that "someday" is *not* a top priority for him. So when he faces commitment with you, he faces having to give up the freedom of putting kids in his "someday, maybe" file. Suddenly you are getting yourself involved in the conversation, too, and he's losing some of his control.

FREEDOM FROM BEING TRAPPED

As long as he's not committed to the relationship, he doesn't have to worry about getting trapped by it. He feels free to be there, because he knows he can leave any time.

Once he commits to you, he loses the freedom to leave whenever things get difficult. If you "go nuts" on him, or stop giving him an abundant sex life, he will be more trapped (at least in his own mind) than he was when you were more casually dating. When you ask him to commit to you, you are asking him to give up this freedom. It's scary for him, and a good thing for you to be able to be compassionate about.

OTHER FACTORS

Each man is an individual, and has individual fears and concerns about getting into a committed relationship. As you design your commitment deal and have your commitment conversation, you'll need to address these concerns, as well as the others we have listed here.

The Four Ways You Must Prepare for Your Commitment Conversation

If you are sensitive to the power of his ultimate fantasy over him and respectful of the sacrifices you are asking him to think about making, you will automatically do better than most other women during your commitment conversation. You won't put him down, and that respectfulness will help him feel free to commit himself to you. For us, however, this sensitivity is only one of the key elements of turning a relationship conversation into a full-blown commitment deal.

Once you have the sensitivity and compassion to what he'll be giving up, you must prepare yourself for your commitment conversation. You'll use all of the following information in the next chapter.

1. FIGURE OUT WHAT HE'S AFRAID OF

As we said, all men are different, and these fears will vary from one man to another. Most men are afraid of what we've already discussed. He may also be afraid of:

- having to support you financially
- having kids he has to support financially
- giving up his freedom to do what he wants, when he wants
- not seeing his friends as much
- having to give up his hobbies to spend more time with you
- having his hobbies or loves ridiculed by you
- failing at the relationship, and having an awful break-up
- you will take up so much time it will hurt his career
- you will make more and more demands on his time
- having to give up his dreams in order to be with you—no longer being able to tour in that rock band he's always wanted to start, for instance
- the sex going bad once he's made a commitment
- getting married, then getting financially hurt in a divorce
- having you "go nuts" on him, and being stuck with it
- you trying to change and "reform" him
- current small issues becoming big later
- you becoming a domineering "mom" figure to him

All these appear as real threats to him, if he gets involved in a committed relationship with you.

Think about the man you are dating. What is the biggest loss he fears he will have to face if he commits to you? What is the second biggest loss? What is the third biggest loss? Is the biggest loss the possibility of dating other women? Write it down. Is the second biggest a fear that he won't have time with his friends anymore? Write that down, too. Make as long a list as you need to cover all of the fears and concerns you think he will face by becoming committed to you. In the next chapter, you'll learn how to address these fears during your commitment conversation. For now, simply note the sacrifices and losses your man might think you are asking him to make, and the fears that you think will come up for him around your commitment conversation.

2. Figure Out What You'd Like from Him

Here are some things that women have told us they'd like from their men. Which ones might apply to you?

- He doesn't date other women.
- He doesn't sleep with other women.
- He spends at least two evenings a week with me.
- He admits publicly that we are a couple.
- He touches me and is affectionate in public.
- He isn't looking for someone to replace me.
- He doesn't check out other women when I'm around.
- He doesn't go see exotic dancers.
- He doesn't flirt with other women on the Internet.
- He doesn't flirt with other women, ever.
- He gets rid of all his pornography; I am enough for him.
- He takes me out at least once a week, and pays for everything.
- He buys me presents at least twice a month.
- He plans events with me, months in advance.
- He stops partying with his friends so much; he shows more responsibility.
- He calls me practically every day.

- He goes out of his way to help me if I need it.
- He takes care of me when I get the flu.

Everything on this list should be verifiable in reality. "He doesn't think about other women" isn't verifiable, unless you are willing to make your relationship into a nightmare of interrogation about what he is thinking. Even then, he could lie to you. "He doesn't check out other women when I'm around" is verifiable. You can see if he is doing it or not. "He takes me out" is too vague, and hard to verify as well. Takes you out how often? Once a year? Once in your life? It's better to say "He takes me out for an evening at least twice a month." That is something you can easily verify.

We aren't suggesting that you take every item in our example as a suggestion of what you should expect from a man (more about this in a moment). It is simply important that you make this list so you can know what you are after and take the next step in creating your commitment conversation.

3. Figure Out What on Your List is Essential, and What You Can Give Up

Some of the things you want from your man are more important than others. Some of them are critical: He absolutely must be monogamous with you, for instance, or he must never yell at you.

While some items on your list are essential, some other items on your list are more like conveniences. Not having them met might be uncomfortable, but you could live with it if the most important commitments were in place. These are the things you can give up, in order to make him happier with the sacrifices he is making to be with you. Rose told us about how she used this principle when she was creating her commitment deal with Scott. "I knew that Scott was good at dating, and was pretty slick with the ladies," she told us. "I knew that giving all that up to be monogamous with me would be hard for him to do. I figured that, if he was going to give up other women to be with me, the very least I could do was to not be upset when he owned pornography or went to see strippers, even though I find all that stuff pretty disgusting, myself." Rose honored the sacrifice she was asking Scott to make (being monogamous with her) by making a sacrifice herself.

Think about what you might be able to give up from your list. Karen put on her list that she wanted from Richard to never smoke cigars around her; smoking a cigar happened to be something Richard really loved to do after a good meal out. Karen decided that, if he were willing to commit to her, she would give up her right to be upset about his cigar smoking, and to not complain about it when he did smoke—as long as he didn't do it in her house.

Kathy said that one of the things she wanted from Martin was that he would be affectionate in public with her—something that Martin, for whatever reason, found difficult to do. This really bugged Kathy, because she thought it meant that he was embarrassed to be seen with her, a charge Martin categorically denied. She decided that, if he would commit to her, she would give up her need to be touched by him in public, and that she wouldn't bug him about it again. It was a sacrifice she found she was willing to make in the face of the sacrifices she was asking of him.

Look: having a man commit to you is not enough. If you want to have a successful long-term relationship, that commitment must be freely given. It cannot be extorted from him and have any lasting power. His resentment about being forced will eventually surface and create distance in your relationship. You must have a man who commits to your relationship powerfully and of his own free will. He must see how joining forces with you will add to his life, not just demand more sacrifices of him with no thanks whatsoever.

Richard commits to Karen not just because she lets him smoke the occasional cigar. Martin commits to Kathy not just because he doesn't have to touch her in public. Scott committed to Rose not just because she doesn't give him grief for looking at pornography or visiting strip clubs. These actions are signs of a deep respect for who these men really are. These women showed the men that they care about them as more than just "commitment objects." They've actually taken the trouble to figure out what the commitment might cost the man they are with, and have taken steps to address it.

Understand this: *Men are not used to women who appreciate the sacrifices they make when they commit.* If you are one of those women who does, you will touch a man's heart like no other woman ever has. Your commitment deal will have power with him because it won't be simply about forcing a commitment so you can "know where the relationship is going," no matter what the psychological cost is to him. You'll be creating a real partnership between the two of you. You'll be showing him that you care about him in a way that he will be able to understand on a visceral level.

And that, more than anything else, will make him responsive to your commitment deal offer.

4. MAKE A LIST OF WHAT HE PROVIDES FOR YOU

During your commitment conversation you'll be telling him about what he provides for you. In order to do this, you must make a list in advance, so that you can tell him what he's been providing for you off the top of your head.

Take a few moments now to write down what your man has been providing for you. If you need a refresher in learning how to see a man as a provider, review chapter 10.

∞ *Preparing for Your Commitment Deal Conversation*

In a way, creating a commitment conversation is like painting a house. When you think of painting a house, you probably think about dipping the brush or the roller into paint, bringing the brush to the wall, and spreading the paint on it. The reality is, the application of paint is often a very small part of the "painting-a-house" project. Most of your time is spent preparing the surface for the paint. It's spent inspecting the walls, washing them, scraping off the old paint, dealing with colonies of spiders, and replacing rotting wood. Once you have the surface all prepared, the actual house-painting—the glamorous part of the project—goes quickly and easily.

Relationship and commitment conversations are much the same way. While there are specific strategies for approaching a commitment conversation (which we will cover in the next chapter), the *preparations* you make beforehand are the most critical part. Imagine trying to paint a house without preparing the surface first. It would be a disaster. Yet this is what most women do when they go to have a relationship and commitment conversation with a man. They've done next to nothing to prepare for the conversation. Perhaps they've complained about the lack of commitment to their girlfriends; that's usually all the preparation they've done. They haven't put themselves in a state of compassion for the ultimate fantasies they are going to ask their men to consider giving up. They may even be angry that they have to bring up the conversation at all. They chose times to talk when the man is tired or distracted. They have no concept of commitment deals whatsoever, and go in with only demands or ultimatums. Is it any wonder that relationship and commitment conversations seem so awkward?

There are some simple steps you can take to "prepare the surface" for your commitment conversation. If you do these, your man will be more receptive to the conversation, or perhaps even bring it up himself.

Keep Giving Him Wins

It's still important for a man to feel like a winner with you. It's easy for couples to slip into the habits of picking at each other's flaws, or of making each other wrong for many little things in their day-to-day lives. You must not do this. Don't succumb to the temptation to stop giving him wins. If you want a committed relationship, you must keep finding ways that your man is a winner and a provider, and you must keep letting him know that you recognize what he provides for you. You must keep delighting in what he loves, even when it's silly. If a man feels like a loser with you, he will naturally resist commitment, and resist any conversation about it. If he feels like a winner and a provider, he has every reason to want to be with you. It will make your conversation much easier.

Keep Being Worth Winning

Both men and women tend to let their looks and behaviors slide once they get into a consistent relationship. Don't let this happen to you. We suggest that you keep exploring your personal style, both for the pleasure that it will bring you, and as a way of continually delighting your partner. Keep exploring what you love, and creating a life that you are excited about living, whether there is a man in it with you or not.

Be a Great Sexual Partner

The biggest win you can give a man is a great sex life. If a man is sexually satisfied, he's *much* more likely to be responsive to your commitment conversation than if he is not.

Finding out what a man fantasizes about, and being willing to play-act his fantasies in bed bonds a man powerfully to you. Listening to his fantasies without judgment or disgust also connects him to you more intimately. While a good sex-life is not always a sign that a man will be open to committing to you—he may just be using you for short term sex—having a *bad* sex life works against any commitment you may create.

Always Be Looking for Ways to Improve the Relationship

We'll go over this in more detail when we talk about long-term relationships, and keeping the commitment deal closed, in chapter 16. For now, let's just say that your man will be more open to a commitment conversation if you have made a habit of always looking for ways to improve the relationship. This means figuring out activities that you enjoy doing, and doing them together. For instance, Carol and Steve figured out early on that they enjoyed getting away to romantic bed-and-breakfasts together. Knowing full well that Steve would forget about setting up such romantic get-aways if left to his own devices, Carol took it upon herself to make sure they got away for at least one night a month on a romantic B&B getaway. In this way she kept creating new and wonderful ways for them both to enjoy and appreciate the relationship.

∞ The 15 Commitment Killers

Just as it is important to do the proper things to lead up to the commitment conversation, it is equally important to avoid the "commitment killers" before your commitment deal conversation.

The commitment killers are behaviors that make you hard to be around, and so make it hard for a man to commit to you. "But wait a minute," we hear you cry. "Don't men do these things, too?" Of course they do. Most men have an extraordinary repertoire of ways to put you off, and to make you not want to be with them. For more on that, review chapter 13.

For now, it's worth noting this: By and large, if a man offends a woman, she will want to change him. She will want to talk about what happened, express her feelings about his offense, and in some way mold his behavior so that he will not do it again. Once a dating relationship has been established, a woman is more likely to try to change the offensive behaviors she finds in her man than she is to think about leaving because of them.

Men are different. When a woman offends a man, he doesn't particularly want to change her. He wants to get away from her. Therefore, when your man offends you, it doesn't have nearly the impact on your desired long-term relationship than when you offend him. He doesn't harbor the fantasy that he can change you, so when you are hard to be with, it drives him away from the relationship.

The behaviors you must avoid are the *commitment killers*. They are behaviors which, if you do enough of them, will guarantee he will be uncomfortable and uncooperative in a commitment deal conversation. If you notice you indulge in some of these behaviors, you may want to stop. The key commitment killers are:

1. *Taking everything in life personally.* A woman who takes everything in life personally is hard to be around. This kind of woman is angry and inconsolable if it's raining outside when she wants to take a walk, or enraged if her favorite restaurant is closed when she wants to eat there. If the normal difficulties of life seem like a personal affront to you, a man will be less likely to want to commit to you.

2. *Taking your frustrations out on your man.* If you then take out your anger—about the restaurant being closed or the fact that it's raining out—on your man, you are driving him away even more, and making it even less likely that he will accept your commitment deal. If you have a random bad mood, and make yourself feel better by taking it out on him, you are destroying your long-term chances, too.

3. *Feeling you have the right to be unreasonable.* Not everything in every relationship has to be rational and logical. But, if you are often wildly unreasonable, figuring that he'll just have to live with it, you lower your chances of commitment.

4. *Feeling you have the right to "flip out."* If you scream or "go nuts"

when you are upset or stressed, and don't make any effort to control yourself, the harsh reality is that whatever man you are with will be less likely to want to commit to you. We all have times when we become stressed out and carry on. The key comes in your willingness to attempt to control your behavior, even when you are upset, and in your willingness to apologize after becoming upset. If you are unwilling to attempt to control your behavior when you are upset, it will be much harder for a man to commit to you.

5. *Feeling you understand "God's opinion" about everything.* If you are too eager to set your man straight on the ultimate truth about anything and everything, he will feel like you don't value his intelligence or opinions, and he will be right. This feeling will make him less likely to commit to you.

6. *Being overly insulted by common male behavior.* Men do offensive things. It's the nature of the beast. You are right to give him a loss when he does so. A frown or the withdrawal of attention can work wonders to change his behavior and help him understand what he's allowed to do around you, and what he is not.

    The key question is, how long do you keep giving him that loss before you return to giving him a win? As you may recall, we suggest that you give a man a loss, then a win again as quickly as possible. If you won't let the man win you again after he's offended you, then you are being overly insulted and driving the man away.

7. *Having to process or fight about everything "right now."* If you can never get over a difficulty quickly, and have to "process" or fight about every little thing immediately, it will be harder for him to commit to you. This isn't to say that there aren't some things that need to be discussed immediately. But if you find you are creating embarrassing scenes in public, or when you are with

other couples, because you insist on fighting over something *right now*, then you may be driving your man away.

8. *Being difficult to give feedback to.* No one likes to hear difficult feedback about their behavior. Some people prevent others from giving them feedback by flipping out, screaming, being overly argumentative, or crying instead of listening and taking it in. If you feel you have the right to do this, you are driving your man away.

9. *Expecting him to entertain you.* Any person, male or female, who is not creative, or who often complains about being bored, and wants other people to entertain him or her, tends to drive people away. If you behave as if a man needs to entertain you, it will be harder for him to commit to you, too.

10. *Being incredibly sensitive.* A woman who gets extremely upset when her man looks at another woman, for instance, might want to consider that she might be incredibly sensitive. Women who have extreme sensitivity or who are overly obsessed with their own comfort are harder for a man to commit to.

11. *Being hot and cold sexually.* Men like to have some sort of idea of what they are going to get if they approach you sexually. If one night you are an incredibly hot vixen, and the next become furious when he shows any sexual interest at all, you make it harder for him to accept your commitment deal.

12. *Expecting your man to be psychic.* Most men don't "just know" what to do to make you feel good. Very often our male students complain to us that women tell them that, as men, they should do more of the "little things" and be more romantic. However, when the men ask their women for examples of the kind of behavior they desire, the women respond with some variation of "If I have to tell you, it doesn't count."

Let's be clear and tell you that we actually agree with these women. It is the man's job to show enough persistence and adaptability to figure out, at least on occasion, what will make a woman happy. But if you constantly expect a man to be psychic and punish him for failing at it, he's much more likely to simply throw up his hands and walk away from the relationship. If his inability to be psychic is proof, in your mind, of his insensitivity, you are driving him away.

13. *Being emotionally inconsistent.* Guys like consistency. They like for things to get set up, and stay the same forever. Rarely does a man decide to re-arrange his furniture "just to see what it looks like" or move around pictures on the wall "because I was ready for a change." Consistency rules with men, and a woman who is emotionally inconsistent—happy one minute then enraged, crying, or terrified the next—is harder for a man to freely commit to.

14. *Being hyper-critical.* Acting as though there's only one right way to do things, and consistently believing that your man is doing it wrong, will drive your man away.

15. *Worrying too much about what other people think.* This is a cousin of being hyper-critical. If you are overly concerned about what other people think about you, you will eventually extend this concern into worry about what other people think about your relationship, and what other people think about your man. You'll start pressuring him to change his behavior based on these worries about what other people might think. This will make you hard to be with, and drive him away.

If you engage in some of these behaviors, do not lose heart. Remember, rarely does any one thing make or break a relationship. A relationship is made up of thousands of interactions, each one of which either adds to or subtracts from the total sense of connection, comfort, trust, and love between two individuals. A healthy relationship can take the beating that a few of these commitment killers, acted out occasionally, might cause.

However, if you recognized yourself over and over in this list, you might want to think about ways to improve your behavior. Would *you* want to commit to someone who took everything personally, who took his frustrations out on you, who was unapologetically unreasonable, who flipped out regularly, who was completely opinionated, hard to give feedback to, emotionally hyper-sensitive, inconsistent sexually, constantly critical of you, and so on? Of course not. You might be able to forgive one or two of these behaviors occasionally, but if most of them showed up often, you'd be looking for another man.

If you did see yourself a lot in this list, don't worry—these are all qualities that you *can* change. There's nothing shameful about you. You are not a bad person, and these behaviors are not *you*. They are just a bunch of bad habits. You can change them.

Recognition of a problem is always the first step in solving the problem, and most problems are smaller than our emotions about them would have us think they are. If you saw yourself over and over on this list, and want to develop habits that are more like those a man would commit enthusiastically to, we suggest you seek the help of a qualified counselor. If you saw yourself a few times on this list, don't worry about it—the awareness itself will probably help you change those behaviors easily. You'll see yourself beginning one of them, and notice. You'll say to yourself, "Wow, is this really what I want to do, knowing as I do that it will drive my man away, and make him less likely to want to commit to me? Is acting out this behavior that important to me?" You'll probably find that it isn't, and easily choose a more profitable way of interacting.

∞ The Eight Signs that He Is Ready for the Commitment Conversation

You've been continuing to have middle dates with your partner. You spend time together, experience the world together, make love together. You bond. You begin to feel that the time is finally ripe for the commitment conversation. Here's how you can tell if that feeling is correct:

1. *There is de-facto monogamy.* You may not have had a commitment conversation, but you aren't dating anyone else, and you are pretty sure that he's not dating anyone else, either.

2. *You "hang out" together.* Losing the "event" feeling of dating is an inevitable part of building a relationship. It's not so good if this feeling goes away during *all* of your dates—that might be a sign of the spark going out of your relationship. It is natural, however, for informal "hanging out" to occur. If you find you are hanging out a lot, it's getting to be time for the commitment conversation.

3. *Your lives are enmeshed.* Your stuff is at his house. His stuff is at your house. You have your own toothbrush in his bathroom, some of your clothes are in his closet, and so on. He has the same at your home.

4. *You've developed "rituals."* Do you always go out for a fish fry on Friday night? Do you watch your favorite TV show together? Do you always go square dancing on the second Tuesday of each month? Do you have a favorite restaurant you regularly go to together? If so, you've developed rituals, and are becoming ready for the commitment conversation.

5. *Seeing him is a normal part of your routine.* It's become easy for you to get together, or you have times that you are together without even having to think about it. If you always see each other on Wednesday and Saturday nights, for instance, you are in a routine with him. The same is true if you ride to work together, or meet regularly at the gym. If you are developing stable routines, he is becoming ripe for your commitment talk.

6. *You talk on the phone daily.* If chatting with him on the phone once or twice daily is a normal part of your routine, it's a good sign for your commitment conversation.

7. *You do things for each other to make each other's lives easier.* Do you pick up each other's dry cleaning, or give rides to each other's kids? Do you run errands for each other? This is a good sign, as well.

8. *You help each other figure out your lives.* One of the most wonderful things a relationship partner can do is help you figure out your life. If you discuss your problems with each other, helping each other find solutions and design strategies, you are becoming close enough for a commitment conversation.

⌘ *Conclusion*

You've now done the preparatory work for the commitment conversation. You've developed your compassion, and learned about what a man gives up when he commits himself to a relationship with you. You've learned about how his ultimate fantasy is probably different from yours, and about how committing to you usually means sacrificing his fantasy to give you what you dream about. You followed the four steps of preparing for your commitment conversation. You figured out what he would be most hesitant to give up and figured out what you want from him. You've discovered which factors of commitment you could give up in order to make his sacrifices easier for him, and which factors are critical. You will learn to use this key information during the commitment conversation in the next chapter.

You've prepared him for the commitment conversation by continuing to make him feel like a winner and a provider. You've continuously complimented him on how he provides for you emotionally, and continued to let him be a winner of your heart. You've also continued to develop yourself and your personal style, so that you continue to be worth winning. You've been a great sex partner and have continually been on the lookout for new ways for the two of you to experience pleasure in your relationship. You've looked at your own behavior to see if you accidentally indulge in any of the "commitment killer" behaviors. If you found that you did, you've become aware of the problem, and, because of your awareness, are more likely to be able to catch these behaviors early and eventually avoid them.

You are now ready to move on to having the *commitment conversation*. In the next chapter, you will learn how to have a commitment conversation with a man in a way that makes him see that you are developing a shared vision, rather than merely forcing him to acquiesce to your relationship demands. Then, it's on to having and enjoying the relationship of your dreams.

CHAPTER 15

The Commitment Conversation

H AVE YOU EVER BEEN KISSED BY A GUY WHEN YOU WERE COMPLETELY unprepared for it, and not at all interested in it? Women tell us that it's the worst. He's awkwardly trying to force something on you that you don't want. At the same time, he's trying to get something from you that you don't want to give. The whole thing seems sudden, unwelcome, and awkward. You are so surprised and freaked out that you don't know what to say and don't know what to do.

This is how many men feel when women first start talking about commitment and "the relationship." They feel the same way you do when a man awkwardly lunges at you for a kiss you do not want. In *How to Succeed with Women* we taught men that the key to getting that first kiss is having the preparatory work done before you even think about going for any kind of kiss at all. We taught men that when they do the right things from the start of the date, leading up to that kiss, the woman welcomes it and even desires it. We teach men to be romantic and charming from the first moment they meet a woman, so that, even if

391

she doesn't want the kiss, she isn't surprised by it. The preparatory work is the essential key to making the kiss seem natural.

The same is true for a woman approaching a commitment conversation with a man. If you haven't done the proper pre-work (as we described in the previous chapter) your attempt to discuss commitment will be as unwelcome to him as an unexpected kiss from a platonic male friend would be to you.

Once again, it's like lighting a camp stove. If you just lunge at the stove with a lit match, of course it won't light. If the stove doesn't light, the problem isn't with the match you are using, how you are holding it, or the way you struck the match on the box. It's not a defective camp stove and it's not afraid of commitment. You just haven't primed it properly. If you focus your thinking on what you are doing wrong during the lighting stage, when the problem is that you haven't primed the stove properly, nothing you do will work. You need to realize that lighting the stove itself is trivial if you have primed it properly.

In the previous chapter we talked about the steps necessary to prime the stove of your man's commitment. This chapter assumes that you have followed through on those things. It assumes that he feels like a winner and a provider, that he thinks you are worth winning, that he is excited by your sex life (at whatever level of involvement that may be) and that you are always learning new ways to delight in the relationship together. It assumes that you have taken the time to become compassionate about what he is giving up, and have thought about what you are willing to give up in order to be with him. It assumes you aren't killing your chances for commitment on a regular basis.

If all this is true, then you have primed your man properly. That doesn't assure he will be completely comfortable with talking about commitment, any more than being wonderfully romantic to a woman assures she'll be completely comfortable when a man goes for the first kiss. What is assured is that if you don't prime him properly, as we showed you how to do in the last chapter, he almost certainly will *not* be ready for the commitment conversation. If you have done those things, he probably will be more open to it.

So, assuming you've primed your man properly, when, where and how should you start your commitment conversation?

⌒ *When Not to Start a Commitment Conversation*

Both men and women have strong impulses to initiate relationship conversations at the worst possible times. Usually this happens because the person initiating the conversation is either upset or afraid, and hopes the conversation will help. Additionally, sometimes that person chooses a time when the target of the conversation is more vulnerable, under the mistaken impression that this vulnerability will make the conversation go more easily. It won't.

Women complain that men resist relationship conversations, and it's true that they do. But it's also true that men resist these conversations a lot more if you try to start them at the wrong times.

Let's save you a lot of trouble and telling you when *not* to initiate a relationship conversation:

When He Is Going to Sleep

Women who want to have relationship conversations late at night, in bed and right before going to sleep, drive men nuts. Men hate it when women do this. Of course, it doesn't matter to us if men hate it. If starting relationship conversations late at night worked to get you what you wanted, we'd tell you to do it. After all, this book isn't about pleasing men, it's about getting you the relationship of your dreams.

Sadly, springing a relationship talk on an unsuspecting man when he is exhausted doesn't work. It doesn't give you what you want. It makes him angry. He suspects that you are trying to "attack him when he's at his weakest." He resents that you are keeping him awake with a whole bunch of urgent questions that you've spent a lot of time thinking about, which he's just now hearing for the first time. He'll resist this conversation every step of the way.

When He Is Stressed or Upset

Same as above. He'll resist you if you bring up your relationship when he's stressed and overwhelmed or upset by something else. You have to make the emotional sacrifice and wait for the right moment.

When You Are Stressed or Upset

When you are stressed or upset it isn't a good context for a healthy conversation about the future of your relationship. When you are filled with dissatisfaction about not knowing where the relationship is going, for instance, and bring it up because you can't endure not knowing one second longer, you are likely to be abrupt and abrasive. You won't be at your best. You'll be demanding and overly emotional, possibly angry or crying. Ideally, the commitment conversation should be an act of free creation between the two of you. The feelings accompanying it should be light and even pleasurable as you create a possible future together. If you are stressed, angry or unhappy when you bring it up, the conversation will become (at least to him) about making you feel better. He'll say whatever he has to in order to calm you down or get you to stop crying. He'll make promises he can't or won't keep just to get you to shut up, and he'll try to change the subject as soon as he can. Once again, you must wait until you are not upset to talk about your relationship.

In the Middle of a Fight

In the middle of a fight is the worst time to bring up issues of commitment and your long-term vision of a relationship together. He'll be more likely to want to leave you when you are fighting, and you'll be more likely to issue ultimatums that might drive him away. The commitment conversation is about creating a long-term vision together, not about forcing him to give you what you want. You will never, *ever* create a mutually empowering vision for your relationship while you are having a fight. Wait, wait, wait.

The Best Time to Start a Commitment Conversation

The first thing we want you to do is to get over the idea that your relationship conversation has to be a big, heavy, scary operation. When you use our method, it's not like going to the dentist. He'll have less fear because of the way you present yourself during the conversation, and because of how you've been behaving in the relationship (see the previous chapter). He won't be filled with resistance because you have chosen a bad time for the talk. You'll have avoided the common pitfalls that add work to conversations about love.

Of course, some men will still resist. Some men have been burned in relationship conversations over and over, and all they need to hear is the phrase "talk about our relationship" and they run away terrified (which is why we'll teach you how to conduct the conversation without saying that). Men who don't expect or desire to be with you long-term will also resist any relationship conversation. Men who've felt trapped by women in the past will be afraid, too. Later in this chapter we'll show you how to handle this fear. For now, you must choose the right time for the conversation.

A Time When You Both Have Some Time

You'll want to choose a moment when you are both relaxed and hanging out. Lying on the couch on a Sunday afternoon can be ideal. Ditto if you are taking a walk in the park, or out in the woods.

When you are on a drive can also work, if 1) you don't have a history of fighting in the car and 2) the drive itself is not stressful. If you have a history of fighting in the car with this man, then you should avoid any possible conflict in it from now on. Sadly, after you've had a few bad experiences in the car it can start to seem like "the place to fight." Don't bring up your relationship in the car unless you never fight there.

Also, if the drive is stressful, any talk you have will be stressful, too. Only bring up your relationship in the car if the drive itself is easy, beautiful, and fun.

A Time When Neither of You Are Stressed, Tired, or Upset

This means not before bed, and not when either of you are overwhelmed by work (or even *at* work). Handle stress and high emotion separately from your relationship conversation.

A Time When He Isn't Absorbed in Something Else

You may have plenty of time one Sunday to have a relationship conversation, but he may be watching the Superbowl on television. No matter how well you present your commitment conversation at that time, he will be resistant. Make sure he isn't absorbed in some other activity when you bring the conversation up.

A Time When You Are Feeling Good Together

Ultimately, the most important factor in bringing up your relationship conversation will be the feeling the two of you are sharing in the moment. If you seem to be in a relaxed flow together, and have some free time, then it's a good time for the conversation.

∞ The Fourteen Steps of a Successful Commitment Conversation

Now it's time for you to have your commitment conversation. There are a lot of wrong ways to have this conversation. As you will see, most women create commitment conversations that make men's fears and resistance worse, not better. Using our method you will open his heart and clear away his fears about the commitment conversation.

There are a lot of steps in the process. You may not need to use all of them. We are showing you how to handle a man who is very afraid of committing to you. If your man is very open to commitment, you may find that this conversation goes quickly and well, and that you are able to skip steps.

However, it is worth learning this format. You will find it to be a fundamentally different way of talking about commitment than any you have tried before.

1. Acknowledge What He Provides for You

If you've been continuing to make your man feel like a provider (and we hope you have), you'll have some facility at this already. You'll also have your list of ways he provides for you that you made in the last chapter. You'll begin your commitment conversation by listing these for him, from memory.

As we've said before, men aren't used to feeling acknowledged by the women in their lives. From a male point of view, women mostly criticize men for not being more like women. This may be hard to believe, but we ask you to accept, at least for the purpose of this conversation, that it's true. When you acknowledge what a man provides for you, he feels like a *real man* on some primal, visceral level.

That feeling of acknowledgment is the purpose of this step. You want your man to feel like a winner when he goes into this conversation. You want him to feel like the woman in his life is grateful for what he gives her, not greedy and grasping and demanding ever more. It relaxes him to hear about how great he is, and makes him more open for the conversation to come.

This step might look like this:

"You know, you've given a lot to me, provided a lot for me, and I really want to acknowledge you for it. You really make me feel like a lady, and I appreciate that. You really make me feel pretty and sexy, and you turn me on a lot. I really appreciate the way you always open the car door for me, and close it after I get in, and all the little things you do for me. You buy me things and take me out, and I'm always proud to be seen with you. You've been developing your business and becoming more financially successful all the time—you know that's not why I love you, but it does make me proud of you, and feeling proud of you provides something wonderful for me."

2. Acknowledge the Sacrifices He's Made

This is more of the same. You want him to feel like you are the one woman who really sees him for what he provides, both through what he gives, and what he gives up. When you acknowledge the sacrifices he's made, he sees that you appreciate what he does for you, rather than downplaying what he does and demanding more.

This step might look like this:

"I want you to know that I'm aware that you've made sacrifices for me, as well. I know that you don't go out with your buddies as much as you used to. I know that you clean up your apartment more because I like it that way. I know you work out to look good for me, and that you bought all those new clothes. You even cook for me sometimes! Those are things that most men never do to make a woman happy. It know it isn't always easy, and I want you to know I appreciate it."

Having said that, look at what you've done so far: You've treated this man substantively differently than any other woman ever has during a commitment conversation. Rather than attacking him with dissatisfaction and demands, you have been acknowledging him. As a result, he'll be more open and receptive to your next step.

3. Ask Him for the Favor of Advice

Next, you ask him for advice. This is the step where you start talking about your relationship, and begin moving toward making your commitment deal. But he doesn't need to know that, yet. Most men would rather hear that they need a root canal than to hear a woman say "We need to talk about our relationship." So instead of "needing to talk," you *ask him for advice*. While he might not be crazy about talking about relationship agreements (to put it mildly), he *loves* giving advice. You can use this to your advantage during your commitment conversation.

This step is simple. You might say:

"I'm wondering if I can ask you for another favor. I need some advice about our relationship."

Instead of fighting you or being on the defensive, he'll be "all ears" to listen to your problem and try to fix it.

4. Let Him Know You Have Other Options than Just Being with Him

This is where the rubber starts hitting the road. You want to let him know that you have other options than just being with him. You don't want to present this as a threat, however. Rather, it's a conundrum that you need his help in figuring out. Saying that you need his advice on whether or not you should be dating other men will get a much better response than demanding to know if he's willing to be monogamous because you can't stand the uncertainty of not knowing anymore. Asking him for advice on whether you should be allowing other men to pursue you puts him in the driver's seat of the conversation. Rather than having to answer your relationship demands, he has to figure out how much he wants you to be exclusive to him. You might say:

"I need some advice about our relationship. We've been together for [time] now, and other men are making it clear they'd like to ask me out and are being really nice to me. I'm not sure what to do."

This step is a stumbling block for some women because it asks you to imply that other men are interested in you. What if that doesn't appear to be true in your life? What if there are no other men (that you are aware of) vying for your heart? What should you do then?

We believe it's critical that the man you are dating know that you could be a scarce commodity, even if you aren't one at this exact moment. First of all, you don't know for sure that there aren't men who are interested in you. There are almost certainly more men who are interested in you than you know, and they are staying away from you because you are in a relationship: the guy who flirts with you at the coffee shop, the man at your finance class who was interested in studying with you, the guy who you talk to at the gym. You may have gotten out of the habit of thinking of such men as potential dating partners, but they are. Remember this during the commitment conversation: You could be a scarce commodity, if you aren't actively feeling like one already.

Furthermore, we believe that if you follow the steps in this book, you *will* have other men pursuing you. So it is true that you could do what it takes to have other men. That's what he really needs to know.

If you don't see any other male options in your life, this might be one of those times when you tell a small white lie, if you are comfortable with that. Tell him that David Copeland and Ron Louis keep asking you out, and you need his advice about what to do. Use us as an excuse—it's an added service we provide. No extra charge.

5. Handle His Answer

At this point, he will probably ask you what *you* want to do. You've told him other men are flirting with you, and, because you don't have any agreement with your current man, you don't know what to do. You've asked for his advice.

He will probably respond with the same question for you. He'll ask, "Do you want to date other men?" Notice that now you have *him* asking *you* the kind of question you have probably been wanting to ask him. You've done an end run around his resistance to the commitment conversation, and have him questioning you about the relationship. He's starting to wonder what kind of a deal he wants to make with you, rather than simply having to respond to your demands.

So he will probably ask you if you want to date other men. There are several other responses he might make.

He May Ask about Your Other Suitors

He may ask, "Who else is interested in you? Do I know him?" If he's the jealous type, he may even play a guessing game: "Is it Fred? Is it Lucas? Who is it?" If your man is the jealous type you should be very vague when you first present the idea of other men to him. If he's so jealous that you are afraid he might go nuts at the idea of another man, and that scares you, then you shouldn't be having a commitment conversation with him. You should be breaking up with him. No relationship with a man is worth risking your safety. There are simply too many other fish in the sea to waste your time on one who might be unpredictably dangerous.

If you are concerned your man might get hung up on the "who is it" question, be especially vague when you make it clear to him that you have other options. Say something like "It's just a feeling I get when I'm around guys that gives me that idea. Men come up and talk to me, and flirt with me, and I'm not sure what to do about it. I must be putting out the vibes, though I don't mean to."

He May Tell You that You Should Date Other Men

You do run a risk when you present a commitment conversation as a conversation, rather than as an ultimatum. You run the risk that he doesn't want to commit to you, and that he'll tell you. When you tell him that you have other options and you don't know what to do, he might say, "I think you should date other men. I want to date other women, too."

This is a harsh reality, but we believe you are better off hearing about it now than forcing a weak commitment with open threats and finding out later that he didn't really mean it.

If you get this response from your man, try offering him a short-term try-it-out commitment. "Some of these other guys seem fairly interesting, but the truth is, in my ideal world, we would be together. I'd like to find a way. I think you and I make a pretty good couple, and I'd like us to just try it for a while, just for now, to see how it works." See if he'll accept it.

If he can't go for trying out a commitment "just for now, to see how it is for us to be a couple," (or at least agree to think about it), then you might want to consider getting rid of him. If he can't agree to a commitment this loose and temporary, then he's not interested in you for the long-term. It's sad, but you'll have to face it.

6. Respond to His Advice

He probably didn't take either of those routes, though. The odds are, he asked you what *you* wanted to do. This is *probing,* a natural part of the male advice-giving process. He'll ask, "Do you want to date other men?" You might say:

"I guess the truth is that I don't, if we set up our relationship that way."

This is an important sentence. You tell him that you don't want to date other men, *but only if you set up your relationship that way.* If you don't set up your relationship to be exclusive, you don't intend to think of it as exclusive. You are telling him, "let's make a deal."

Saying that you want the relationship to be exclusive if you set it up to be exclusive, is much more powerful than merely saying that you don't want to date other men. Take it from us: he's perfectly happy in a relationship where you are committed to not dating other men, while he makes no commitments whatsoever. That is why you must stress the importance of mutually deciding to set up your relationship as exclusive, or not.

7. Tell Him Your Reservations about Committing Longer-term

The question you've asked him to advise you about—whether you should be accepting other men's interest or not—opens up the commitment deal conversation. It leaves him with the question: Do I want to commit to this woman, or not? The important thing is that he is asking *himself* this question. You are not asking it. You are simply asking for advice! Asking him for advice, rather than confronting him with questions about the relationship leaves you in the clear.

The moment he asks himself if he wants to commit to you or not, he will be confronted by his reservations and fears about committing himself to you for the longer-term. You must make a move to intercept and handle these fears or they will derail your commitment deal. He won't tell you about these fears. He won't volunteer them to you. You must press on and handle them, even before he can think of them.

The best way to get your man to feel that he is safe committing to you, even though he has fears, is to do what you can to help him feel understood. If you understand or even *share* his fears and concerns, he won't worry that you will attack him for having them. He won't have to put up his defenses.

Women complain that men don't show women their vulnerability.

Of course this is true, but not to the extent you might think. Men show women vulnerability all the time, only to get shot down for it. When your man is experiencing his fear about committing himself to you, he is very vulnerable. If in any way you tell him that his fears are stupid or immature, you are attacking him while he's vulnerable. If you confront him about "having an issue with commitment" you are attacking him when he is vulnerable. He will close up like a clam. Later when you want him to open up for you again, he'll subconsciously remember what it was like the last time he opened up to you. His emotions will remain firmly shut.

The way out of this (at least for the commitment conversation) is to show him that you understand or even share his fears and reservations. These fears and reservations are on the list you made in the last chapter—the things he'll be most afraid of in a commitment to you. Use this list to identify his top fears. Next, you must find the places in your own psyche where you share those fears, no matter to how small a degree. You must then show him that you can share his fears and reservations about a committed relationship.

For instance, you may notice from your list that he's afraid of giving up his freedom. He's afraid that if you commit to each other, he'll be trapped if something goes wrong. You may be able to find a place in yourself where you share that fear. During this phase of your commitment conversation, you'll tell him about it. You may discover from your list that he's afraid that if he commits to you, he'll miss out on experiencing other women. During this part of the commitment conversation, you may share with him the part of you that is afraid that if you commit to him, you'll miss out on other men. You may discover from your list that he's afraid that if he commits to you, the relationship will take up so much of his time that he won't be able to get anything else done. During this part of the commitment conversation you may share with him the part of you that has that fear, as well.

This part of your commitment conversation might sound like this:

"I like you a lot—you know that—but I have some reservations about getting into a more serious relationship, too. I'm concerned that if I commit to our relationship, the spark might go out of it, then I'd be trapped, do you know what I mean? Also, I do sometimes worry—what if we aren't the right people for each other? And sometimes I worry that our relationship will take up too much time if we get more involved— you know how demanding both of our jobs can be."

By doing this you have shown him that you can share and understand his fears. You can relate to where he's coming from. This gives him psychic space to open up to you.

8. Tell Him about the Sacrifices You Are Willing to Make

In this step you are showing him that you are willing to make some sacrifices, just as you are expecting him to do. You get these sacrifices off of the list you made in the last chapter of non-essential but desirable commitment qualities. You offer these as things you might have to give up if you became more committed to him.

This is where you offer your commitment deal. By telling him what you are willing to give up, you make some concessions that make it easier for him to make some concessions to you. You are offering to make certain sacrifices. Will he be willing to give you what you want in return?

This part of the commitment conversation might sound like this:

"I also see, at the same time, that there's stuff that I'd have to look at giving up if we had a more committed relationship than we do now. I think I'd have to let it be okay that you like pornography, and not give you any grief if you went to see exotic dancers occasionally. I'd have to put up with your cigar smoking at restaurants without complaining about it. I'd have to learn to live with the fact that you don't like to touch me in public, and stop complaining about it. I know you'd have to probably make sacrifices if we became more committed, too. Can you give me some advice? What do you think I should do?"

You've laid out your problem: You are a scarce commodity, and other men are interested in you (or at least would be, if you gave them the chance). You've told him about hesitations he could relate to, and offered him sacrifices you'd be willing to make. Finally, you've asked him what he thinks you should do. You've offered the deal. It's time to start closing it.

9. Close the Commitment Deal

Now you start pushing for a commitment, gently. You've asked him what he thinks you should do. He'll probably say something like, "Well, I'm not so crazy about you dating other men." That's when you say:

"Perhaps we should try out saying that we have a monogamous, more committed relationship for a while, just to see how it works out."

It's important how you put this. If your man is really afraid of commitment, the "for a while, just to see how it works out" part of your statement is critical. If he's not commitment-phobic, you might not need to say it.

10. Assure Him He's Not Making a Serious Long-Term Commitment by Making This Commitment to You

Now you need to handle his fear that he is locking himself into a long-term, committed, marriage-style relationship with you, just by having this conversation. If he is at all afraid of commitment, your trying to close the commitment deal will scare him off. You must say what is necessary to convince him that you aren't nailing him down to be with you forever—you are simply making a monogamy and "we are a couple" commitment *for now*. The fact that it will probably last a very long time, and be upgraded into a more serious commitment in the future shouldn't come into the discussion.

You might say:

"I know I'm not ready to commit for a serious long-term relationship with you. Maybe someday, but not now. We really don't know each other well enough to make such a big step. But I do think it's a good idea to commit to each other for now, and see how it feels down the line."

He'll likely respond with something like, "Yea, that sounds okay."

11. Rephrase the Commitment

Now you feed it back to him. Say something like:

"Then I'll make sure that these guys know that I'm in a committed, monogamous 'couple' relationship, and that they should leave me alone."

He'll probably think that's a pretty good idea.

12. Begin to Construct Your Future Together

Now you move on to creating a future together. You might start this part of the conversation by saying something like this:

"You know, I think it might be helpful to think about the future that would really make us both happy. Can I ask you another question? If you were in an ideal relationship—not necessarily with me, just an ideal relationship—what would you want it to be like in a year? Or maybe five years? What might you want to have created? What might you want to have done?"

He will almost certainly not have an answer, and will probably turn the question back on you, asking you what *you* would see in a relationship in the future. You should tell him.

Begin this part of the conversation by describing at least some future possibilities that you know he would like for himself. If you know travel is important to him, and it's important to you too, then say so. If you know having a good sex life is important to him, and it's important to you, too, mention that. You might say something like:

"Well, I'd want a relationship where we had a lot of fun together, that's for sure. I would want the man I'm with to be really satisfied with me. I'd want him to be happy with me, to have enjoyed being with me, and to be totally thrilled with our sex life. I'd want us to both have been very supportive of each other's careers. I'd want us to have taken some time to travel together, and to have experienced new things."

After telling him all this, ask him the question: "I'd be curious—what kind of thing might you dream about?"

13. Brainstorm Together

Now you'll get into a give-and-take conversation about a possible future for your relationship. (You'll see what this might look like in the complete example following this section.) There are a few guidelines for this conversation:

Keep Bringing It back to Him

He'll try to get out of talking about it by telling you that he doesn't know the answers to your questions about the future. He says this because it is true—he really hasn't thought about it. You must give him examples of what might be possible, then ask him what he thinks again.

Use "Softeners"

You don't want to be demanding in your speaking with him. That's why you use "softeners." Softeners are phrases that show him that you are asking him to share, not commanding him to. Phrases like, "I'd be curious to know," or "if you'd care to share" are softeners. Use them liberally when questioning him.

Remind Him that It's Not Personal

If your man has real fear about commitment, you may have to remind him that you aren't asking him about a long-term relationship with *you*. You're asking him about his *ideal* long-term relationship. That way, he'll give you valuable data about a relationship you could create together without being afraid that he's committing himself long-term to *you* by doing so.

14. *Reward Him!*

He's done enough, don't push him any further. There's lots of other stuff you could ask for, but you really need to simply reward him for what he's done so far. Look at what you've done, and what he's made it through: You initiated a relationship and commitment conversation. You got him to agree to a be monogamous couple. You've really done enough for one day.

In the future you will work on upgrading your commitment—getting more specifics from him, getting him to do more of what you desire, and doing more of what makes a long-term relationship work for him. For now, it's time to reward him.

If you want your man to have good feelings when he thinks about this conversation, do what it takes to make him feel really good at the end of it. This may be a good time to make love in a way that he really enjoys. Congratulations! You made it through your commitment conversation!

∞ The Commitment Deal Conversation: A Play in One Act

Here's what the whole commitment deal conversation might look like:

You: "You know, you've given a lot to me, provided a lot for me, and I really want to acknowledge you for it. You really make me feel like a lady, and I appreciate that. You really make me feel pretty and sexy, and you turn me on a lot. I really appreciate the way you always open the car door for me, and close it after I get in, and all the little things you do for me. You buy me things and take me out, and I'm always proud to be seen with you. You've been developing your business and becoming more financially successful all the time—you know that's not why I love you, but it does make me proud of you, and that feeling provides something wonderful for me."

Him: "Wow, thanks. I'm glad you appreciate it."

You: "I want you to know that I'm aware that you've made sacrifices for me, as well. I know that you don't go out with your buddies as much as you used to. I know that you clean up your apartment more because I like it that way. I know you work out to look good for me, and that you bought all those new clothes. You even cook for me sometimes! Those are things that most men never do to make a woman happy. It know it isn't always easy, and I want you to know I appreciate it."

Him: "That's really sweet. Thank you. You are most welcome."

You: "I'm wondering if I can ask you for another favor. I need some advice about our relationship."

Him: "Of course. What can I help you with?"

You: "We've been together for seven months now, and other men are making it clear they'd like to ask me out and are being really nice to me. I'm not sure what to do. I need some advice."

Him: "Wow, that's pretty heavy. I'm not sure what to say. Do you want to go out with other guys?"

You: "I guess the truth is that I don't, if we set up our relationship that way. I like you a lot—you know that—but I have some reservations about getting into a more serious relationship, too. I'm concerned that if I commit to our relationship, the spark might go out of it, then I'd be trapped, do you know what I mean? Also, I do sometimes worry—what if we aren't the right people for each other? And sometimes I worry that our relationship will take up too much time if we get more involved—you know how demanding both of our jobs can be. I also see, at the same time, that there's stuff that I'd have to look at giving up if we had a more committed relationship than we do now. I think I'd have to let it be okay that you like pornography, and not give you any grief if you went to see exotic dancers occasionally. I'd have to put up with your cigar smoking at restaurants without complaining about it. I know you'd have to probably make sacrifices if we became more committed, too. Can you give me some advice? What do you think I should do?"

Him: "Well, I'm certainly not crazy about you dating other guys."

You: "Perhaps we should try out saying that we have a monogamous, more committed relationship for a while, just to see how it works out."

Him: "I think that might be a good idea. You know, to try it out."

You: "I know I'm not ready to commit to a *serious* long-term relationship with you. Maybe someday, but not now. We really don't know each other well enough to make such a big step. But I do think it's a good idea to commit to each other for now, and see how it feels down the line."

Him: "Okay, let's do that, and see how it feels. I don't think you need to worry so much about it."

You: "Then I'll make sure that these guys know that I'm in a committed, monogamous 'couple' relationship, and that they should leave me alone."

Him: "Sounds good to me."

Her. "You know, I think it might be helpful to think about the future that would really make us both happy. Can I ask you another question? If you were in an ideal relationship—not necessarily with me, just an ideal relationship—what would you want it to be like in a year? Or maybe five years? What might you want to have created? What might you want to have done?"

Him: "Wow, that's quite a question. I'm not sure what to say. What would you want?"

You: "Well, I'd want a relationship where we had a lot of fun together, that's for sure. I would want the man I'm with to be really satisfied with me. I'd want him to be happy with me, to have enjoyed being with me, and to be totally thrilled with our sex life. I'd want us to both have been very supportive of each other's careers. I'd want us to have taken some time to travel together, and to have experienced new things. I'd be curious—what kind of thing might you dream about?"

Him: "I really haven't thought about it. I liked what you said."

You: "That's great. What parts did you like most, if I may ask?"

Him: "Well, I liked the part about fun, and travel. You know I'm really into airplanes, and I'd think it was great to be in a relationship where we went to the Experimental Aviation show just about every year. And I liked the sex part—I'm glad that's important to you! It's important to me, too."

You: "I'd like a relationship where we keep exploring new things sexually, and have more and more fun. And I thought it was great when we went to the Air show last summer! If you were standing five years in the future, looking back at a great relationship, what else might you be looking back on that made it wonderful?"

Him: "I also think of lots of time together just hanging out with our friends, having wonderful meals together . . ."

You: "I know what you mean! Enjoying ourselves and just being together."

Him: "Yeah! I'd also look back on having enough time for my hobbies, too. I wouldn't want the relationship to keep me from my woodworking."

You: "I could support you in that. I could also see having a relationship where we really supported each other in taking care of our bodies."

Him: "We could work out together, and learn more about healthy cooking. We could even take a cooking class!"

You: "That might be fun! You are so wonderful! I love you!"

[You begin kissing him as we *fade out* . . .]

∽ *Conclusion*

We know that we've dumped a lot of information on you in these last two chapters. We know that it's detailed and step-by-step. We wrote it this way because we are committed to helping you have relationship conversations that really work, and because we know it takes time to peel off a man's fears and concerns and open him up for a commitment conversation.

Of course, there is no single template that will cover everything that can occur when you are interacting with another human being. You may find that some steps work wonderfully for you, and that some steps don't seem to work with the man you are dating. You may find that he's not resistant to the commitment conversation, so you don't have to do as much pre-work to handle his various fears and concerns. But if you need a model for speaking diplomatically and sensitively about creating a committed relationship with a man, this chapter will serve you admirably.

And, of course, this is not the only conversation about commitment you'll ever need to have. As you keep on creating your future together over the weeks and months to come, you'll need to upgrade your commitment deal by returning to this conversation. Remember to use a structure like the one we presented here: Be compassionate for whatever you are asking him to give up. Prepare for the conversation properly, and have it at the proper time. Acknowledge him for what he provides for you, and for the sacrifices he's made for you. Tell him your concerns about taking things to the next level, and offer him the sacrifices you are willing to make. Ask him for advice, and keep creating your future together.

You've successfully completed steps eight and nine of your Master Plan: You've presented him with a commitment deal, and closed that deal. You now have a committed relationship.

Your next step is clear, and it's the final step of the Plan: Keeping the commitment deal closed.

CHAPTER 16

Loving a Man for the Long Term

GREAT LONG-TERM RELATIONSHIPS RARELY "JUST HAPPEN." YOU have to do things to create them, and to keep them growing and fun. Maintaining a long-term relationship is like maintaining your body. It's like going to the gym: If you are committed to keeping your body healthy, one workout a month will hardly suffice. Long-term relationships are also like dieting: Following your diet one day a month won't keep the weight off. Keeping your long-term relationship alive and happy demands continuous focus and attention.

The good news is that, while going to the gym may seem like work at first, after you are in the habit of going it becomes energizing and a lot of fun. Keeping your relationship exciting is the same way. At first it may seem like work, but after you start to see the results, it becomes energizing and fun. It's worth taking those first steps to keep your long-term relationship alive.

You'll notice that some of the things we tell you to do might seem unfair. "Why should I do all this work if he doesn't?" you might ask. The answer is simple: If you don't take action to make your relationship into the kind of relationship you want, your relationship will turn into a waiting game. You'll both start spending your time waiting for the other person to do something nice first, and your loving connection will degenerate into a nightmare of scorekeeping about who has been doing more. If you take some simple actions, however—even if you have to take them first—your generosity will inspire your partner, and help keep the relationship alive.

⌾ The Seven Keys to Keeping a Long-Term Relationship Happy, Exciting and Hot

1. Keep Doing the "Little Things"

Many women start taking the men they are with for granted after they've been together for a while. One man tells us this story: "Before we got married, Rachel always made me dinner one night a week. It was so wonderful to come home to hot food, music on the stereo, candles, and a glass of wine all waiting for me. It always made me feel so good, like she really cared about me.

"After we got into a long-term relationship, all that suddenly changed. She stopped ever making any meals that were special. When I finally asked her why she stopped cooking for me, she just told me to not be so sexist, and quoted me statistics about how women do more housework than men." This did nothing to keep their relationship alive.

Much of the time, your change in behavior isn't that dramatic. The change is gradual as you stop doing the "little things" because you stop feeling like doing them. Early on in the relationship, you wanted to do the "little things" that made your man happy. You were so wrapped up in love with him that you didn't even have to think about going out of your way to make him happy. You just did whatever it took. You seemed to have infinite energy to do the little things that pleased him because you were so in love.

The problem is this: At the beginning of a relationship, you are naturally enthusiastic about the man you are with. That natural enthusiasm gives you plenty of energy to please him. You feel like doing the little things that keep a relationship going. You do them, and continue to make him happy.

Sadly and inevitably, you will begin to lose your desire to do those little things as time goes on. Here's how it works:

As you get to know him better and begin to see some of his flaws, you will naturally tend to become just a little complacent with him. As you get to know him better, you feel less like doing the little things, so more and more often you don't do them. As you do fewer of the little things, your sense of his being special diminishes, and you feel even less like putting in the effort. In time, you stop doing the little things entirely. After all, you no longer feel like it! Congratulations. You have killed your relationship, and soon will be complaining that the spark has died. Before you know it, you'll be looking for another man to take your boyfriend's place.

You fell into the relationship complacency trap. Because you relied on your *feelings* to guide how much you did the little things, you inevitably did them less and less. The less you did them, the more tepid the relationship became. The more tepid it became, the less doing the little things appealed to you.

The solution is not to let your feelings be your guide for when you do the little things that please him. If you want the relationship to stay alive and continue to be exciting, energizing and fun, you must commit yourself to doing the little things whether you feel like doing them or not. Schedule time in your daily planner if you must. Just get those little things done.

Women who are in successful long-term relationships understand that the good feelings of the relationship are created by doing the little things, not vice-versa. As a result, these women commit themselves to continuously finding ways to delight their partners, as if the relationship was new and fresh.

Deb and Kevin have been married for nine years. They are the wonder of all of their friends, most of whom have been married and divorced at least once in that time period. Their relationship seems alive and growing, while those of their friends are failing. The reason the relationship is doing so well is because both Kevin and Deb always do the little things.

For instance, we were at their house when Deb decided to run out to get some tapioca to go along with the meal Kevin was making. We went along. She noticed a football video that Kevin wanted was on sale at the grocery store. "I think Kevin would love this," she told us. "I'll get it for him."

Kevin was delighted about the gift. He felt loved because Deb did a little thing to keep the relationship alive. He, in turn, looked for ways to make her happy. Why shouldn't he? After all, she took the time to make him happy. He wanted to respond in kind.

The number one key to maintaining long-term relationships is the understanding that the seduction is *never* over. You must *always* continue doing the little things. We can't possibly emphasize this enough. If you want your relationship to last, you must keep doing the little things.

2. Support Him Fully

You must be a constant source of support for your man or your relationship will die. He must know and trust that you will stand by his side, no matter what. It is that type of trust and support that keeps the bond between you strong.

Over the course of your relationship, you will both be discovering who you are on a deeper level and what you are really like. To the extent that all of life is a process of self-discovery, relationships are a process of self-discovery, too. We don't mean to get too psychological on you here, but this is important to understand if you want to have a long-term relationship that lasts.

Another way to put this is to say that both you and your man will always be growing, learning, and becoming different people than you were when you first met. In the face of this fact, you have a choice. You can either support him as he grows and develops, or you can resist his growth. If you support him fully, he will be more likely to support you fully. If you don't support him fully, he will eventually break up with you. It's your choice.

This is how Lisa lost her last boyfriend. Clem was always interested in changing and growing. He had a full-time job, but took classes at night. After they had been dating for about a year, he started taking art classes that really excited him. "I feel like I'm finally starting to find myself," he confided in Lisa. "I think I might be an artist, deep inside. It's really fulfilling something in me that nothing else ever has."

Instead of supporting him in these new interests, Lisa got scared. "More fulfilling than me?" she immediately asked. "How about that. I must tell you I'm worried about you becoming an artist. Where will you get money? I can't support you. Besides, I don't trust those artist types, especially the dancers. They're all gonna try to get into your pants, anyway. And what about those artist's models? They pose nude, right? Promise me that you won't cheat on me, okay? Promise me right now!"

For the next two months, every time Clem brought up anything about his newfound passion, Lisa responded in the same unsupportive way. It all finally ended when Clem told her that he was sleeping with a woman from one of his art classes. "She understands me, and is supportive of what I'm doing," he told her. Lisa was enraged, and complained to all of her friends that she was right all along—those artistic types stole her man. The truth was that she drove him away by being completely unsupportive of his passion. In the face of her lack of support, he found a woman who was supportive.

Of course it can be scary when someone you love becomes enthusiastic about something you know nothing about. Certainly you might get tense if your boyfriend is suddenly around different people from those you hang around with, or pursuing something that seems silly to you. In spite of all that, you must be supportive of his self-discovery if you want to maintain the relationship. This will cause your relationship to get better, rather than allowing it to "grow apart."

When Daniel got a puppy and became passionately interested in dog training, Susan became interested, too. While she knew it was really *his* hobby, she made herself get involved and found ways to enjoy it. The truth was she didn't naturally like dogs much, and would rather have been hanging out at home than going with Daniel to dog training classes. Susan made herself become interested in dog training because she knew that was the best way she could keep their relationship alive and growing. She also knew that his interests were a wonderful way for her to go outside of her normal routine. By getting interested in her man's interests she kept herself growing and got out of her normal routine.

Being supportive of your man is critically important to the long-term success of your romance. If you start trying to block his growth, rather than support it, you will end up alone.

3. Listen To Him

We went over communication basics in chapter 12 when we talked about the seven steps of fighting with a man. You may want to review that communication process, and really get yourself to the point where you can use it in a relationship. As a brief reminder, the seven steps are:

1. Listen to him,
2. Repeat back what you heard,
3. Thank him,
4. Give him your side,

5. Make promises and apologies,

6. Let it all go, and

7. Change the subject.

4. Maintain Your Own Sanity

Many women make the mistake of thinking that their relationship with a man will satisfy all of their emotional needs. While a relationship with a man will satisfy many of your needs, it will *never* satisfy all of them. When you try to make a single relationship meet all of your needs, you unfairly burden the relationship and the man. It creates stress, which you only make worse because your needs are not being met. Certain things that women tend to let slide once they have a man are actually more important in long-term relationships. Here are the things you must do to maintain your sanity in a relationship:

HAVE FEMALE FRIENDS

You must continue to have female friends if you want your long-term relationship to work. At the beginning of a relationship it is easy to lose track of your other friends. You can get away with this for a while, but once the relationship becomes more settled, it is essential that you re-establish contact with your female friends and keep them in your life. Ideally, you'd never lose touch with them at any stage of a relationship.

Friendships with other women give you a space away from your man to kick back and get into all the parts of yourself that you normally don't let out around him. If you don't have these friendships, you run the risk of starting to treat your man the way you would a female friend. You will start expecting him to be more like a woman than a man, and you will start being more offended by his maleness than you were previously. Keeping women friends in your life prevents this from happening.

Women friends will also give you feedback in a way that your man can't. They can also give you great guidance about your relationship that you or your man would never think of. When Molly was having hard times with Jacob, she counted on her female friends to give her clear, "straight from the hip" feedback about how things looked from the outside. This feedback made all the difference in Molly's ability to restore life to her otherwise failing relationship.

Do what it takes to keep your friendships with women alive.

DON'T SHARE EVERYTHING WITH HIM

Many of your thoughts are not useful in building a long-term relationship. Your longing for a man who is taller and more muscular, or your occasional thoughts about leaving him are not always smart to share with him. Ditto on some of the conversations you have with your women friends. There's no need to tell him things that will upset him, yet have no bearing on the relationship. You just have to let go of some of your thoughts and not share them.

When Maureen has a man in her life, she feels it is absolutely necessary to share every thought, feeling, or sensation she has with him. She doesn't understand that many of the thoughts and feelings she has are basically insignificant to their relationship. She strongly believes she's being dishonest if she doesn't tell him every little thing that pops into her head.

For instance, she was once out having dinner with her man when a stunningly beautiful, sexy man stepped out of a limo right outside the window by their table. Maureen gawked openly. Her boyfriend immediately said, "He's rich and really muscular and attractive. Would you rather be with him than me?" Bound by her idea of "honesty," she answered, "In a lot of ways I think I probably would." Predictably, this started a fight between them.

Maureen got caught in the "honesty" trap. She should have known to say something like, "Sure, he's got a lot going for him, but you have everything it takes to enthrall me completely. I love looking into your eyes, kissing your lips . . . and I'm so grateful to be with you." Maureen allowed herself to get drawn into a conversation about her boyfriend's merits, relative to those of the rich and sexy hunk who got out of the limo. Because of her need to be "honest" and share everything, she tells him about how much she would like to be with a man who was so successful and who had such a great body. She ends up in a fight that she started by sharing her every thought.

No matter what man you commit yourself to, he is going to have qualities that bug you. Listing them to him is not honest; it is destructive. His little flaws in personality are probably not going to change, and sharing your feelings about them probably won't make a positive difference. Complain to your women friends about these flaws, and let go of them when you are with him.

It does no good to share unimportant and disruptive thoughts and desires with the man you are committed to. Tell him what is important, but don't go generating trouble when you don't have to.

KEEP BUILDING A LIFE YOU LOVE

Just because you have a man in your life doesn't mean that you can now start getting your sense of validation from him and him alone. The same rule applies to you now that applied to you when you were dating: Get your sense of validation from your life, not from men. The way you do this is by continuing to make yourself worth winning.

Remember, you want him to be a wonderful part of your life, not the centerpiece of it. You must continue to have goals for your life, and you must continue pursuing them. You must continue to do the things that make your life the way you want it to be. You must continue to explore your personal style, and continue to pursue what you love. Look at it this way: Your passion about your life is probably part of the reason your man fell in love with you in the first place. If you let that go after you are in a committed relationship, you won't be the woman he fell in love with. In time, that simple fact will destroy your relationship.

5. Don't Try to Change His Maleness

As we said in chapter 14 when a woman is offended by her man's behavior, she is likely to try to change him. At the same time, when a man is offended by a woman's behavior, he is likely to want to leave her. Therefore, he has much less tolerance for your trying to change him than you have stamina to try to make him change. This quandary causes a lot of trouble in long-term relationships.

This tendency is worst when women try to change behaviors that are inherently male. Burping, farting, liking violent films or pornography—these are inherent male behaviors that are not going to change any time soon. If you try to change these behaviors in your man, you will be trying to make him less of a man and more of a woman. Such an attempt will not be good for your relationship's long-term survival.

Instead of trying to change basic male obnoxiousness, make it clear to your man that you are not against such behaviors—you'd just prefer that he act them out away from you. Give him a loss (then a win again as soon as you can) when he does one of these things, but don't make a big girly dramatic display out of it. If you get too dramatic about him farting or burping, for instance, he'll start to laugh at you. You'll give him what behaviorists call a "drama reward," and he'll end up doing it again just to see you spaz out.

Take it easy. Give him a loss, then a win again as soon as possible. Respectfully and seriously request that he do such things elsewhere. Don't make him wrong or shame him, don't tell him he's disgusting and shouldn't be that way. Just ask that he not do such obnoxious, guy things around you, and get on with your life.

6. Keep Your Sex Life Happening

You can't afford to let your sex life die. Once again, keeping it lively is dependent on your choices, not your feelings. If you stick with your feelings, after a few years your desire will start to wane, even with the hottest of men. You must take the consistent actions that keep your sex life lively. You must commit yourself to staying interested sexually. We recommend that you always and forever experiment with new types of sexual play and always strive to keep your sex life fresh.

You must not let your sexual relationship die because your sex life is the thing that separates your relationship with your man from the other relationships in your life. If you are not having sex with him, he might as well just be a friend. Sex is the heart and blood of a passionate relationship. Fortunately, simply committing yourself to continuously expanding your sex-life is often enough to keep it vital.

7. *Keep Giving Him Wins and Making Him Feel Like a Provider*

By now this should be old news, but we'll repeat it again so you'll be even more likely to remember it: Your key to success with men at *any* stage in a relationship is to make him feel like a winner and like a provider.

To this we must add a few words about complaining. Everybody likes to complain, but when you complain to your man, it makes him feel bad. It makes him feel like he's failing to provide for you—if he wasn't failing, you wouldn't be complaining. Consequently, he takes your complaining as a personal affront to his skills and abilities as a man. It creates stress and fighting.

Do your complaining away from him, and your relationship will be much happier.

∞ *Continuing to Upgrade the Commitment Deal*

Nothing in the universe is static. It's a sad fact of life. Things are either being actively created, or they are actively falling apart. There's no way around it. Because the nature of the universe is to change, anything that stops immediately starts falling behind. You have to keep improving and changing just to stay where you are.

This is especially true in relationships. You'll need to keep doing the things that bring both you and your man joy and delight. You need to keep growing closer together. And, at some point, you are going to need to upgrade your commitment deal.

We suggest that you review the commitment conversation chapters (chapters 14 and 15) before entering into any new discussion of your relationship. Use the same structure we described there. Acknowledge what he has provided for you. Let him know that you appreciate the sacrifices he makes to give you what you want in the relationship. Review the high points of the relationship so far, then ask him for advice about the relationship. Let him know what you'd like, and the sacrifices you are willing to make so it will be easier for him to give you what you want. Ask him to look with you, back from the future at an ideal relationship. Review how some of those things are coming true. Open up a give-and-take conversation as you did before. If you're able to show him that your relationship has been moving in the direction of his dreams, it's likely he will be responsive. Together you'll then create the next step in your relationship.

Love Him for Who He Is and for Who He Is Not

Knowing how to maintain a relationship is crucial, but above all, tips and strategies notwithstanding, you must stay aware of why you love him. You must stay aware of the qualities he possesses which you adore. You must stay aware of your shared experiences, your connection to each other, and the magic you have experienced.

The other half of the picture is to love him for who he is not. When you love a man for who he is not, you find ways to make peace with the qualities he *doesn't* have. You find ways to make peace with his quirks, the ways he drives you crazy, the ways in which he is irritating and irrational. You make peace with anything about him which is less than idyllic. When you can accept a man for being imperfect, your relationship will deepen, and so will the level of intimacy and love.

When you stop loving your man conditionally, and stop hoping he will change, you will experience a new freedom in your relationship. When you accept him exactly as he is, without a hidden agenda of changing him, you will have the relationship of your dreams. When you unconditionally love him, he will amaze you. Your relationship will be more satisfying, less work, and more fulfilling than you ever dreamed possible.

∞ The Six Stumbling Blocks to Happy, Healthy, and Hot Long-Term Relationships

Just as there are things you must do to keep a long-term relationship happy, there are things you must avoid doing as well. You must keep your eyes open for the Stumbling Blocks that will prevent intimacy and love. When you become tripped up by the Stumbling Blocks, your relationship will degrade. While it is natural for you to be drawn off course by a Stumbling Block, you can avoid them if you are aware of them and the potential damage they can cause. If you are not vigilant, you will probably slip into any or all of them. When you stay aware of the Stumbling Blocks, you *can* prevent them from interfering with your long-term relationship.

1. Treating Him Like a Girlfriend

If you get nothing else from this chapter, get this: The best way to degrade your relationship with a man is to treat him like one of your girlfriends. Don't expect a man to be interested in fashion, gossip, clothing, make-up, soap operas, "chick flicks," women's issues, or the other topics you discuss with your girlfriends. This is a *man*, and your relationship with him is quite different from relationships with your girlfriends, family members, or with anyone else. The problem starts when you expect him to treat you like your girlfriends do, be interested in the same topics as your girlfriends, and to *act* like your girlfriends.

Collette made the mistake of treating her boyfriend Harold like one of her girlfriends. Over dinner, Collette began telling Harold how dumb men are for loving sports and other "useless" things. Collette mentioned that women were interested in more important things than men, like children, family values, and education. By criticizing men around Harold, Collette placed him in a bad position. Harold did not know how to respond to this criticism. Instead of talking about men and their problems to a girlfriend, or someone who could be supportive, Collette told Harold about her issues with men and placed him in a losing position.

If you insult or tease your boyfriend even one time per week, you are unnecessarily insulting him more than fifty times a year. Don't think he doesn't notice, because he does. And don't think he won't get you back for it, because he will do that, too.

Here's another way to think about this: It's like you have a bank account in a romantic relationship. The more "little things" you do, the more you have sex, and the more wins you give a man, the more you have in that account. The greater your balance in the account, the more he'll want to do things to make you happy.

On the other hand, the more you hurt his feelings and give him losses, the more you take out of this account. Making jokes at his expense that tease him for being a man takes more out of this account than you think. When the account gets negative, he'll start extracting revenge, and will find ways to hurt you back. This isn't because he's a bad person; he's just trying to balance the books.

As a woman, it is your job to make sure that the balance in this account is always positive, and greater than it's ever been in any relationship he's ever been in before. You want to constantly overwhelm him with the abundance of admiration, appreciation, and love you feel toward him. If you do this, he'll be forgiving and loving. If you don't, you can turn the nicest man into a raging bull.

Save your teasing for your buddies. Don't do it with the man you love.

2. Belittling Him

This is truly one of the worst things women do, and *lots* of women do it. When you belittle the man you are in a relationship with, you drive the love out of the relationship. Don't do it. Nothing will undermine your relationship like belittling him.

Belittling him often takes the form of teasing and questioning his intelligence. Some women nickname their boyfriends or husbands "fool," "moron," or "stupid." The tragedy is, women tell us that once they get used to belittling the man they are with, it starts to seem natural. They just get into the habit of remarking caustically upon their boyfriend's or husband's lack of intelligence. They find that saying "Geez, how can you be so dumb?!" just seems to fall out of their mouths.

We shouldn't have to tell you by now that the cost of doing this will be your happiness. Obviously, if you ever catch yourself belittling the man you are in a relationship with, you should apologize at once, and commit yourself to *never* doing it again. The man will be deeply resentful, deeply hurt, or deeply angry. In any case, you will damage your chances of having a great relationship.

3. Fighting

Want to kill a relationship? If you do, fighting is one sure-fire way to do it. Angry fighting tends to feed upon itself and, worse, feeds upon the relationship.

To understand why this is, first remember when we discussed the importance of having a man associate you with good feelings, so that when he sees you or even thinks about you, he feels good. You do this by always providing good feelings and wins while he is with you. In time, seeing you and feeling good become linked.

When you fight with a man this same dynamic works against you. If you have many angry, unpleasant fights with a man, you teach him to associate your presence with angry, bad feelings. You teach him to avoid you, to think of you as a nag, a bitch, or any other unpleasant association. When he sees you, or even thinks about you, he'll feel defeated and upset, and then angry, bad, and resentful.

To make matters worse, you will also feel upset and defeated. After a number of fights, you will associate him with fighting, anger, and bad feelings. Seeing him, or even just thinking about him, will make you angry.

For this reason, it's important that you don't get into out-of-control fights. People often think that they have the right to treat the people who are close to them poorly—remember the saying, "You always hurt the one you love"? If you find yourself starting to fight, make an effort to stay civil. Of course you will have disagreements, and of course you will get angry. Just moderate it. If you think that you are going to get out of control, get away from him, and deal with the problem when you are feeling calmer.

Another way women tend to fight in a relationship is to use a man as their emotional punching bag. They will irrationally torment him for how he dresses, how he acts, his jokes, or any other behavior they deem "stupid." The problem with treating a man in a degrading manner, is that it will cause trouble. He may react with anger, silence, or simply end the relationship. When you use a man as an emotional punching bag, you create an atmosphere where neither one of you can win, and you both begin to associate each other with painful and unpleasant feelings.

If you have a real problem with anger—and many women do—it may make sense for you to get professional help. A good therapist can help you let go of anger and be more successful in relationships. If you don't want to be in therapy, talk out your problems and issues with a girl-friend. Let *her* hear you at your worst, not your mate. Give yourself the opportunity to vent your most hostile feelings in an environment that won't hurt your relationship. If you do not handle your anger and con-stantly fight with your man, your relationship will eventually die, and you will end up enemies rather than partners.

4. Lying to Him

Some lying is "white lying," or is on the order of "not sharing every-thing." This is okay; it's actually a form of being polite. If he asks you how you like his new floor mats, for instance, and you couldn't care less about them, you certainly do want to say "I think they are very nice." If he asks you what you are thinking, he really wants to know the good things you've been thinking about him lately. Don't tell him that you are thinking about how hot Ricky Martin looked in a video you saw the previous night, and how great you think it would be to date him. Tell your boyfriend something truthful about how special he is to you. If you are doing the things we are teaching you in this chapter, you'll always be aware of something special about him, anyway.

Destructive lying is different. Destructive lying to your boyfriend or husband starts you down a slippery slope that will eventually destroy your relationship. Lying often starts after you decide, on some subcon-scious level, to wreck your relationship. It starts at that moment when you decide that doing the "little things" for this man is too much work, and that you aren't getting enough back to make it worth your while. It starts when you decide that he isn't worth the effort anymore. You start looking for someone else, and then you start to lie.

A man who is close to you may "just know" when you are lying to him.

He will feel you pulling away from him, and notice that you seem more distant than usual. Psychologists often say that eighty percent of communication is nonverbal. If you don't think he'll pick up on your duplicity, you are mistaken. When you try to hide the truth your face will change, your way of moving will change, and your vocal tone will change. He'll know something is wrong, and you will eventually pay the price.

Here's a true story about how this happened to Joy, a student of ours. She was dating Ronnie, who, a year into their relationship, moved to another city in order to go to school. They got together about once every two months, talked on the phone regularly, and sent e-mail to keep the relationship alive.

One day Joy met Ian and was overwhelmed by their mutual attraction. In short order she went to bed with Ian, even though cheating on Ronnie was something she had sworn she'd never do. The next morning, Ronnie called her up. A few moments into their conversation he asked Joy, "Did you have sex with another man last night?" Joy made her lie even worse by not telling Ronnie about her fling with Ian. Within two months after lying to Ronnie, they had a horrible breakup. Ian was disturbed by the fact that Joy lied to Ronnie, and broke up with her as well. She was left lonely and in pain, largely because of her lying.

Though it would have been more painful initially, honesty would have been the best policy for Joy. Her first lie was promising Ronnie she wouldn't cheat on him. Joy didn't know it was a lie, but it was. If she'd kept her word not to cheat on Ronnie, she wouldn't have had to tell him other lies as well.

When Ronnie asked her the next day if she'd slept with another man, it would have been better if she'd told the truth and faced the music right then. Ronnie would have been upset, but it would have given both Joy and Ronnie the option to break up or get the relationship back on track. It would have given him an opportunity to really acknowledge the problems the long-distance relationship was causing, and to take definite actions to solve them.

Instead, Joy lied, pretended everything was fine, and created a situation in which she had to continue to lie to keep up the facade. Ronnie ultimately found out the truth, and it lead to their breakup. There was no way he could trust Joy after she had repeatedly lied to him about having sex with another man.

While not all men are as psychically attuned as Ronnie was, many will be. The undercurrents of duplicity that lying puts into your relationship will inevitably wash away anything good about it. In almost any situation, you will find that the long-term consequences of telling the truth are easier to bear than the long-term consequences of lying. Don't lie to him. It's the bottom line.

5. Blaming Him for Your Problems

By this time, the theme of this book should be clear: You are responsible for the quality of your life and the quality of your relationships. Life will always work better for you if you operate from this philosophy.

Sadly, many women like to blame the men in their lives for their problems. Blaming men for your problems is childish and immature. In our experience, women who blame men for their problems do so because they don't want to take personal responsibility. For instance, Becky blamed her boyfriend James, for not being good in bed. "He wants sex, but is totally self-centered. He doesn't care about my feelings or what I want. I am tired of two-minute sexual encounters and then watching him roll over and sleep," she says. "Sex with him is horrible. He wasn't like this at the beginning." Upon investigation, however, we found that Becky never did the little things for him anymore. Instead of wearing sexy outfits in the bedroom and cuddling with James, she ignored him. Instead of enjoying sex and enjoying his body, Becky was completely passive in bed and stopped asking for what she wanted. As their sex life died, James stopped doing the little romantic things for her.

We showed Becky how to stop complaining and change her behavior. She found that her sex life with James became wonderful again. She never could have solved her problem while she was stuck blaming James. Before she could change, she had to first realize that she was blaming him, and then make a decision to stop.

Nine times out of ten, you are more of the cause of your problems than you are willing to admit. The tenth time, you are better off acting as though you are the cause of the problem, anyway. If you blame the man in your life for your problems, you will just reinforce those problems, and make everything worse.

6. Being Unwilling to Forgive Him

In any relationship there will be times when you have to be forgiving. As we've said many times before, he will do things that upset you, just as you will do things that upset him. If you aren't forgiving of him, your behavior will be corrosive to the relationship.

Many people don't know the simple basics of forgiveness. They know how to say "I forgive you," but they don't know how to make the forgiveness last. Many people don't understand how to forgive so that the past stays in the past and doesn't interfere with the present. Many women say they forgive, then bring up their partner's transgression again and again as a way of torturing the man they are with.

After Gary and Shelia had been dating for almost a year, they went to a party together where Gary got very drunk. He then disappeared with another woman. Shelia caught them in a back hallway, making out. Gary drunkenly explained that he didn't know what he was doing, and Shelia took him home.

The next day they talked about what happened, and whether or not their relationship had a future. Shelia was understandably angry, and thought about breaking the relationship off. She told Gary, "I've passed up other men because I was committed to this relationship! I expect you to do the same, or I want to break up with you." Gary apologized, and admitted that he had a problem with alcohol that made him impulsive when he drank too much. They talked about whether there was a deeper problem in the relationship, and decided there wasn't. He just got really drunk, and acted really stupid. He apologized sincerely, and promised to not drink that much again.

Gary kept his promise: From then on, he drank little or nothing at the parties they went to. He remained an attentive lover, did the little romantic things, and was a good boyfriend. But this wasn't enough for Shelia. She kept bringing up his transgression. Anytime she felt angry, she would say something like, "I guess I'm not as good as that girl at the party, eh?" or, "If you don't like me, I bet that party girl would take you. You seemed pretty into her." For Shelia, all conversational roads led back to reminding Gary of his mistake. Eventually, Gary started defending himself from her attacks, and they fought. Finally they broke up, because of Shelia's inability to forgive. "I apologized and apologized," Gary said later. "But Shelia was never able to let it go."

If you want to be truly forgiving, you must be able to let go of what happened. This means *not talking about it again*. If Shelia had really forgiven Gary, she would have never brought up his transgression again after their initial conversation. If she felt like bringing it up again, a truly forgiving woman would have restrained herself. She would have let bygones be bygones, and let the past stay in the past.

This isn't to say that she was wrong for being angry about it initially. Shelia was absolutely right to make sure he knew that his actions had created a big problem. And it was important that Gary feel uncomfortable about it, and that he apologize. But after Shelia accepted his apology, she shouldn't have brought the incident up again, unless he started drinking too much, or flirting too wildly with other women. As long as Gary kept his promise, she should have let it go.

When you are in a relationship, you will get justifiably angry from time to time. Your boyfriend will do things which you will have to forgive him for. To keep the relationship alive and happy, you must understand that when you forgive, you give up the right to torment him with what he did. You give up that right *forever*. This may be a sacrifice for you. Left to your own devices, you might bring it up again to "keep him in his place." Don't do it. Allow his transgressions to be over with your forgiveness, and don't drag them into the future. You both will be much happier and have a much greater success rate if you learn to really forgive.

∞ *Intimacy in the Bedroom*

Sexuality will sustain your relationship for the long-term more effectively than any other maintenance tool. When a couple has a healthy sex life, the relationship tends to flourish. When they have a bad sex life, the relationship usually becomes strained. Most vital long-term relationships have a good sex life. They have sex frequently and make it a priority. Hot sex is a good way to let a man win in the relationship. Sex will allow intimacy and passion to continue to nurture your relationship, and keep him away from other women.

The Triangle Offense: The Three Keys to Improving Any Woman's Sex Life

Many women have sex lives that are boring, bland, and unsatisfying because they haven't mastered three critical skills in the bedroom: Communication, technique, and attitude. As you increase your degree of mastery, your sex life will also inevitably improve. Better yet, each of these three solutions support the others. So, for instance, if you improve your technique, your attitude will improve. When your attitude improves, so does your technique. Besides, spending time perfecting these arenas can be a lot of fun.

We know you have a busy life and you don't need another set of things to do. There are hundreds of books that describe sexual etiquette and men's hottest fantasies. By routinely spending time increasing your knowledge and skill level in each of these three areas, you will become a master in the bedroom. When you are a master in the bedroom, your long-term relationship will continue to improve and your joy, intimacy, and romance will continue to deepen.

COMMUNICATION

Any problem can be resolved through communication. Any concern, fear, mood, or thought can be transformed by simply opening your mouth and talking. We are always communicating. Body language, listening skills, vocal tone, word choice, and volume all play a part in communication. In the bedroom, communication skills are particularly essential if you want to be a hot and memorable lover. They can make or break the mood. If a man feels nervous during sex, a good communicator can quickly boost his confidence and comfort him.

A chronic complaint among women is that men do not communicate and talk enough, especially in the bedroom. The best way to open up communication? Talk. If a man is shy and doesn't communicate, you must draw it out of him and give him openings to talk. Given that men's and women's bodies are so different, you will have to ask questions and communicate during sex.

It's not the sexual amateur, but the sexual master who asks questions. The master knows that talking will intensify things, not interrupt them. Penny was in bed with Craig. She licked his neck and Craig moaned. Penny continued, and began touching the other side of his neck with her hand. Craig moaned even more. This continued on for several minutes. Penny took a short break, and asked how hard Craig liked to be touched. "I love being touched roughly," he said. When Penny touched him again, she used more force. Craig moaned even louder. By asking a simple question and making a slight variation in touch, Craig was turned on even more.

TECHNIQUE

By technique we are referring to a woman's knowledge of male anatomy, and her familiarity with sexual interactions. To be specific: positions, sex toys, male sexual dysfunction, fantasies, products, birth control, foreplay, kissing, and much more.

This section is not going to tell you all the secret sex positions in one easy lesson. We recommend that you go into a bookstore and pick up books on male sexual fantasies, a massage book, a detailed sex position book, and one that turns you on and gives you material to fantasize about. Your best bet is to purchase a copy of Ron Louis' book titled, *Sexpectations: Women Talk Candidly about Sex and Dating*. His book will expose you to many sexual fantasies that you have most likely been too timid to try, or even discuss. His book will be a great resource for you to improve your sexual technique. When you feel comfortable with your skill level, you will have an easier time relaxing and the sex will be even hotter.

ATTITUDE

Attitude is everything! If you have a good attitude in the bedroom, sex will be fun, easy, and ecstatic. A bad attitude will leave the man thinking you are hard-headed, nasty, scared, and to be avoided.

We recommend that you adopt a fun, outrageous, confident, playful, and easygoing attitude in the bedroom. If you want to be a memorable lover, you will have to leave him feeling special, full of passion, and fun. You must let him feel like a winner!

To improve your attitude, study women who interact with men in ways you find sexy and you respect. Find a female movie star who you think is a wonderful lover. What do they do to drive men crazy? Study their moves, their attitudes, and it will rub off on you. Before you get into bed with a man, decide what attitude you want to convey. Use the exercises to psych yourself up, and then create the ultimate experience for the man you are with.

∞ Conclusion

Long-term relationships require maintenance. You have to keep grow-ing, keep resolving conflicts, and keep having fun. If you are commited to having a long and healthy relationship you *will* do the little things along the way to keep both of you happy and content.

While it may seem like hard work when you first take the steps to maintain your relationship, after a while it will get easier, energizing, and you will see the results of your actions.

Sometimes relationships are not fair. Throughout this entire book we have focused on *you* as the central character in your life. If your previous relationships did not work, *you* most certainly had something to do with it. While the guy may have been a jerk and the relationship doomed from the start, all you can change is *you*. If you want a dream relation-ship, you will have to do the things to keep it alive and healthy. Guess what? If you don't do the maintenance on a relationship, it will die quickly. You will drive each other crazy, stop communicating, stop going on fun dates, and revert to children throwing simultaneous fits because neither one of you got *their* way.

The solution? Use the Seven Keys to Keeping a Long-Term Relation-ship Happy, Exciting, and Hot. These keys are: keep doing the little things, support him fully, listen to him, maintain your sanity (that is, have female friends, don't share everything with him, and keep building a life you love), don't try to change his maleness, keep your sex life hap-pening, and keep giving him wins and making him feel like a provider.

Ready for more? While the seven keys are useful and brilliant, there is more. Continue to upgrade the commitment deal. This will keep the relationship alive and vital.

Just as we have provided a list of how to solve the problems, and gave you the keys to having a successful relationship, we also warned you of the potential blocks to a happy relationship. Let's review the blocks again so that you can avoid them in *your* relationship: treating him like a girlfriend, belittling him, fighting, lying to him, blaming him for your problems, and being unwilling to fogive him.

The key is to be more commited to loving him and having a wonderful relationship than you are to revenge, or to being "right" when you fight or disagree with him.

One of the most important keys to a long term relationship is a healthy sex life. This includes sexual fantasies, cuddling, foreplay, afterplay, and maybe even role playing. The best way to explore your own sexuality and your sex life with your mate is to study the Triangle Offense: the Three Keys to Improving Any Woman's Sex Life. These three skills, communication, technique, and attitude, hold the secrets of mind-blowing sex. If you master these areas you find ecstacy, intimacy, romance, passion, and the most happy man in the world.

Copeland and Louis want you to have the relationship you have always wanted. We want your relationship to include total intimacy, great sex, juicy communication, mutual support, and much more. We also want you to be more fulfilled than you ever thought was possible. When you follow the keys for a wonderful long-term relationship that we have given you, you *can* make all your dreams come true.

CHAPTER 17

Conclusion

Wᴇ ʟɪᴠᴇ ɪɴ ᴀ ᴡᴏʀʟᴅ ᴡʜᴇʀᴇ ᴛʜᴇʀᴇ ᴀʀᴇ ɴᴏ ʟᴏɴɢᴇʀ ᴡᴇʟʟ-ᴋɴᴏᴡɴ dating procedures. The discrete steps that made up the dating dance have been lost over the last few decades. The sexual revolution left us in a world where neither men nor women knew the steps to take to find a mate. We've all been floundering ever since, trying to find our way.

Fortunately, while the dating rituals themselves have been lost, the psychological bedrock upon which they were originally founded has remained consistent. Women are still women. Men are still men. We still want basically the same things we have always wanted, and we still respond to the same stimuli we always have. Men still want to feel like winners and providers. Women still want to feel cherished and swept away in the good feelings of romance. If you know the steps to take, you can still dance the dating dance and enjoy every step of it. Teaching you to do this has been the purpose of this book.

You now know the steps of the dating dance, the rules of the dating game. From this moment forward you never have to feel like you are "stuck" in your dating life again.

At any time, during any interaction with a man, you can refer to your ten-step Master Plan and know exactly where you are in your romantic interaction, where you've been, and what your next step should be. Any time you feel stuck in any aspect of your dating life, you can look at this book and find the step you are stuck on. Are you having a hard time meeting men? That's chapters 4 and 5. You can review those chapters and learn how to put structures in place to meet more men. Or perhaps the problem is that you are not clear about what you want. In that case, you can return to chapter 2 and reassess the key qualities you are looking for in your ideal long-term relationship. Or perhaps the problem is in your flirting—you may find that you are having trouble being approachable, or keeping a conversation with a man alive once he does approach you. You can always return to chapter 6 and brush up on your flirting skills, if that is your problem.

Or perhaps you are having difficulty testing men, and you keep finding yourself in relationships with men who don't want the same things you want. Review chapter 7, and deepen your understanding of testing men. Or perhaps you are in a relationship, but have problems? Refer to chapter 13 to study up on how to handle problems in a relationship.

You may find that you are in a relationship, and need to have a relationship conversation about your level of commitment to one another. Refer to chapters 14 and 15 to hone your relationship conversation skills. Or you may find that your long-term relationship is less exciting than it was. Re-reading chapter 16 may help. While no single book will solve all dating problems for every woman, this book should keep you on track and keep your quest moving forward. Use it!

We know that most women will read this book all the way through before going back to implement the program step-by-step. That's fine. We don't expect you to read the first few chapters, then to wait until you've accomplished those steps before reading any more. We don't expect you to wait until you have a qualifying date set up before you read the chapters on it, or to wait until you need to conduct a commitment conversation before you read what we have to say about one. We expect that you probably have read the book straight through, and now are thinking about going back and implementing the steps in your life.

We encourage you to do this. If you didn't take the time to create your lists about the ideal man and the ideal relationship, for instance, we suggest you take the time to do so soon. If you didn't take the time to create your plan for meeting men, then we suggest you do so, as well.

We also encourage you to use this book as a reference during your dating and relationship progress. You'll read the chapters on flirting a lot more attentively when you are finding yourself in a lot of flirting interactions in your life. You'll pay a lot more attention to all the information about qualifying dates when you are about to go out on one. You'll read the chapters on middle dates more thoroughly when you start having middle dates. And you'll read the chapters on the commitment conversation much more closely when you are getting ready to have a relationship conversation with the man you are dating.

It is our hope that this book will be a reference for you, to which you will return again and again. Remember: You don't need to get "stuck" in your dating ever again. Most of the problems you will encounter will be somewhere in the ten-step Master Plan. Return to the plan, figure out what step you are on, learn how to conduct that step, get clear on what the next step is, then get back to building your relationship.

Let's review the Master Plan one last time:

Step One: Figure Out Exactly What You Want in a Man and in a Relationship

You did this in chapter 2. You looked at what you wanted in a long-term relationship, and discovered the key qualities in a man that could allow a relationship to last forever.

⌒ *Step Two: Make Yourself Worth Winning*

You learned how to do this in chapter 3. You learned that *personal style* is a key trait of women who are worth winning. You learned that such style goes far beyond merely keeping up with the current fashions. A woman who has personal style is in charge of the message that she sends to herself, to men, and to the world with how she dresses. Such a woman also has confidence in herself. She's confident about the inevitable outcome of her thorough and methodical search for the right man. She's the kind of woman who creates a life she loves whether there is a man in it or not.

⌒ *Step Three: Interview a Lot of Applicants*

In step three you learned that dating is a numbers game, and that the harsh reality is that you must have a lot of men moving through your dating system if you are to meet the one you'll want to keep. In chapters 4 and 5 you learned where men are, and how to create structures in your life that keep you meeting men on a regular basis. You also learned the importance of taking many separate actions to meet men, rather than doing one thing occasionally and wondering where all the men are.

⌒ *Step Four: Test the Applicants*

In chapters 6 and 7 you learned about flirting with men, and about the essential tests of the flirting interactions. You learned specific things you can do to be more approachable by men. You learned opening lines and opening gambits you can use to start flirting conversations with men. You learned how to make a man into a flirting winner, and how to figure out which of his flirting mistakes are fatal, and which are just examples of his inexperience with women. You learned the "dirty dozen" flirting mistakes he'll make, and how you can put things back on track. You learned to test men for their attraction to you, their safety, patience, values, and a host of other qualities. You learned to do this quickly and efficiently, so you wouldn't have to spend a lot of time dating men who were basically incompatible with your relationship goals.

Step Five: Give Men Emotional Wins and Losses

You began doing this in the flirting and testing interactions (chapters 6 and 7). You learned that a man wants to feel like a winner with you, and that if you can make him feel like one, he will be attracted to you. You learned about giving men losses, and the critical importance of following a loss with an immediate win, so that you don't lose the man forever. You learned the importance of being "winnable." You began the process of allowing men to win your heart.

Step Six: Spend Time with a Man

You began sorting through your available men on your qualifying dates (chapters 8 and 9). You learned that qualifying dates are fact-finding missions that usually take under an hour and take place in a coffee shop or other casual venue. After qualifying enough men, you found one or two to move on to middle dates (chapters 10 through 12), finally settling on one man as a possible long-term relationship partner. You started spending time with him on middle dates. You learned how to speak seductively and sensually to a man, and how to speed up or slow down the seduction. You learned how to maintain a man once you start on your middle dates: How to send a love note, buy a gift for a man, talk to him via e-mail, and so on. You began to get more relaxed and informal with him as the relationship developed.

∞ Step Seven: Handle Problems

No relationship goes completely smoothly at all times. You have to be able to handle problems as they arise if you want a relationship to last. In chapter 13 we taught you about the different kinds of problem men, and the different ways men fight. We gave you some guidance about handling problem men, and putting your relationship back on track when you encounter difficulties.

∞ Step Eight: Present Him with a "Commitment Deal"

In chapter 14 you learned how and when to present a man with a commitment deal. You learned the key mistakes women make in initiating relationship conversations, and the things you must do to be the kind of woman a man wants to have a committed relationship with. You made yourself compassionate about what a man gives up in order to commit to you. You learned how to tell when a man is ready for a commitment conversation, and you figured out what you'd be willing to sacrifice in order to make the relationship work. You constructed your commitment conversation step-by-step.

∞ Step Nine: Close the Commitment Deal

In chapter 15 you learned how to construct a successful commitment deal conversation. You learned how to present a commitment deal to a man so it seems to him like a productive joining of forces, rather than a bending to your ultimatums and threats. You learned how to have an interactive conversation about your future together, and learned from him what is important to him in a long-term relationship.

∞ Step Ten: Keep the Commitment Deal Closed

Because nothing in the universe is static, you must do what it takes to keep your commitment deal closed, or it will fall apart. In chapter 16 you learned the key things you must keep doing to keep a long-term relationship alive. You learned how to love a man for who he is *and* who he is not. You learned about the Stumbling Blocks to a good long-term relationship, and how to avoid them. And you learned the importance of reviewing your relationship occasionally and upgrading your commitment deal with your man.

∞ In Conclusion

Ultimately, the conclusion of this book is written by you. It's written by you in how you live your life and how you use this material. If you look at this as an interesting book which you got a few tips out of, that's fine. But it will be all the more powerful if you review the program, and set it to work. You write the conclusion by how you use this book in your life.

Even though we don't know you personally, we do care what happens to you and your relationships. We want this book to speak directly to you, and we hope it will make a real and positive difference in your life. We hope to meet you someday, at a seminar, through our coaching program, or anywhere in the world where we may have the good fortune to connect. We sincerely thank you for reading this book, and putting up with our obnoxiousness and our jokes. We acknowledge you for getting through the sections you might have disagreed with, or the sections which seemed difficult or too harsh. In all sincerity, we commend you for taking the steps you need to take to develop the kind of relationship your heart desires. Feel free to contact us and let us know how it goes. You can e-mail us at succeed@pobox.com, at www.howtosucceedwithmen.com, or by U. S. mail at P. O. Box 55094, Madison, WI 53705. Good luck and great relationships!

Index